POSTCARDS FROM

Frommer's

Bermuda

Horseshoe Bay Beach in Southampton Parish is one of Bermuda's finest places to enjoy sun and sand. See chapter 6. © *Robert Holmes Photography.*

Since visitors can't rent cars, your transportation options include mopeds and old-fashioned carriages. See chapter 3. *Image above © Bob Krist Photography; image below © J. Barry O'Rourke/The Stock Market.*

Jobson's Cove, one of the island's many secluded beaches. See chapter 6. © Bob Krist Photography.

Bermuda Cathedral, the mother church of the Anglican diocese in Bermuda. See chapter 7.
© M. Timothy O'Keefe Photography.

Bermuda is a great destination for sailing and boating. See chapter 6. Above, boats moored off Sandys Parish. © Bob Krist Photography.

In the Crystal Caves, you can take a guided tour through a network of subterranean lakes, caves, and caverns with dramatic formations of stalagmites and stalactites. See chapter 7. © Bob Krist Photography.

Bermuda is one of the world's top golf destinations. See chapter 6 for reviews of the top courses, plus details on the island's best tennis facilities. *Image above © Jay Thomas / International Stock; image below © Carl & Ann Purcell / Words and Pictures.*

One of Bermuda's top attractions is the Botanical Gardens in Paget Parish. See chapter 7.
© Bob Krist Photography.

In St. George's Parish, you'll find Fort St. Catherine, first built in the 17th century. © *Bob Krist Photography.*

The island is full of colorful local characters... © *Bob Krist Photography.*

...and buttoned-up businessmen, who often don Bermuda shorts in warm weather.
© *Catherine Karnow Photography.*

Above: A guest room at Horizons and Cottages, one of the most upscale places to stay on the island. Below: At Marley Beach Cottages, you can rent your own ocean-view cottage, complete with kitchen. See chapter 4 for complete reviews of both.

Both images © Bob Krist Photography.

The sands at Warwick Long Bay. See chapter 6. © William Roy / The Stock Market.

You can learn more about the island's underwater world at the Bermuda Aquarium. See chapter 7. © Bob Krist Photography.

An aerial view of Hamilton Parish. © *Bob Krist Photography.*

Front Street in the city of Hamilton, Bermuda's capital, is a great place for shopping and dining. © *Michael Ventura Photography.*

If it's too crowded at lovely Horseshoe Bay Beach, take one of the trails that wind through the park nearby; they'll lead you to more secluded cove beaches. See chapter 6. © Kindra Clineff Photography.

St. George's Parish is full of lovely, secluded places to soak up the sun. See chapter 6.
© Michael Ventura / International Stock.

An amazing view from atop Gibbs Hill Lighthouse. See chapter 7.
© M. Timothy O'Keefe Photography.

A touch of pink. © *Bob Krist Photography.*

The pool, golf course, and ocean views from the Southampton Princess. See chapter 4 for a complete review. © Howard Millard/The Viesti Collection.

A New Star-Rating System & Other Exciting News from Frommer's!

In our continuing effort to publish the savviest, most up-to-date, and most appealing travel guides available, we've added some great new features.

Frommer's guides now include a new **star-rating system.** Every hotel, restaurant, and attraction is rated from 0 to 3 stars to help you set priorities and organize your time.

We've also added **seven brand-new features** that point you to the great deals, in-the-know advice, and unique experiences that separate travelers from tourists. Throughout the guide look for:

Finds	Special finds—those places only insiders know about
Fun Fact	Fun facts—details that make travelers more informed and their trips more fun
Kids	Best bets for kids—advice for the whole family
Moments	Special moments—those experiences that memories are made of
Overrated	Places or experiences not worth your time or money
Tips	Insider tips—some great ways to save time and money
Value	Great values—where to get the best deals

We've also added a **"What's New"** section in every guide—a timely crash course in what's hot and what's not in every destination we cover.

Bermuda

2002

by Darwin Porter & Danforth Prince

Here's what the critics say about Frommer's:

"Amazingly easy to use. Very portable, very complete."

—Booklist

"The only mainstream guide to list specific prices. The Walter Cronkite of guidebooks—with all that implies."

—Travel & Leisure

"Complete, concise, and filled with useful information."

—New York Daily News

"Hotel information is close to encyclopedic."

—Des Moines Sunday Register

Hungry Minds™

Best-Selling Books • Digital Downloads • e-Books • Answer Networks •
e-Newsletters • Branded Web Sites • e-Learning

New York, NY • Cleveland, OH • Indianapolis, IN

About the Authors

A native of North Carolina, **Darwin Porter** was a bureau chief for the *Miami Herald* when he was 21, and later worked in television advertising. A veteran writer, he's the author of numerous best-selling Frommer's travel guides, notably to England, France, Germany, Italy, and the Caribbean. Working with Darwin is **Danforth Prince,** formerly of the Paris bureau of the *New York Times.* Both of these journalists discovered Bermuda during their various spring break College Weeks and have been frequent visitors ever since.

Published by:

Hungry Minds, Inc.

909 Third Ave.
New York, NY 10022

ISBN 0-7645-6439-0
ISSN 1069-3572

Editor: Christine Ryan
Production Editor: Heather Gregory
Photo Editor: Richard Fox
Production by Hungry Minds Indianapolis Production Services

Front cover photo: Chaplin Bay, South Shore.

Special Sales

For general information on Hungry Minds' products and services please contact our Customer Care department; within the U.S. at 800-762-2974, outside the U.S. at 317-572-3993 or fax 317-572-4002. For sales inquiries and reseller information, including discounts, bulk sales, customized editions, and premium sales, please contact our Customer Care department at 800-434-3422.

Contents

List of Maps

An Invitation to the Reader

In researching this book, we discovered many wonderful places—hotels, restaurants, shops, and more. We're sure you'll find others. Please tell us about them, so we can share the information with your fellow travelers in upcoming editions. If you were disappointed with a recommendation, we'd love to know that, too. Please write to:

Frommer's Bermuda 2002
Hungry Minds, Inc. • 909 Third Avenue • New York, NY 10022

An Additional Note

Please be advised that travel information is subject to change at any time—and this is especially true of prices. We therefore suggest that you write or call ahead for confirmation when making your travel plans. The authors, editors, and publisher cannot be held responsible for the experiences of readers while traveling. Your safety is important to us, however, so we encourage you to stay alert and be aware of your surroundings. Keep a close eye on cameras, purses, and wallets, all favorite targets of thieves and pickpockets.

New! Frommer's Star Ratings & Icons

Every hotel, restaurant and attraction listing in this guide has been ranked for quality, value, service, amenities, and special features using a star-rating scale. In country, state, and regional guides, we also rate towns and regions to help you narrow down your choices and budget your time accordingly. Hotels and restaurants in the Very Expensive and Expensive categories are rated on a scale of one (highly recommended) to three stars (exceptional). Those in the Moderate and Inexpensive categories rate from zero (recommended) to two stars (very highly recommended). Attractions, towns, and regions are rated according to the following scale: zero stars (recommended), one star (highly recommended), two stars (very highly recommended), and three stars (must-see).

In addition to the rating system, we also use seven icons to highlight insider information, useful tips, special bargains, hidden gems, memorable experiences, kid-friendly venues, places to avoid, and other useful information:

(Finds (Fun Fact (Kids (Moments (Overrated (Tips (Value

The following abbreviations are used for credit cards:

AE	American Express	DISC	Discover	V	Visa
DC	Diners Club	MC	MasterCard		

FROMMERS.COM

Now that you have the guidebook to a great trip, visit our website at **www.frommers.com** for travel information on nearly 2,000 destinations. With features updated regularly, we give you instant access to the most current trip-planning information available. At Frommers.com, you'll also find the best prices on air fares, accommodations, and car rentals—and you can even book travel online through our travel booking partners. At Frommers.com you'll also find the following:

- Daily Newsletter highlighting the best travel deals
- Hot Spot of the Month/Vacation Sweepstakes & Travel Photo Contest
- More than 200 Travel Message Boards
- Outspoken Newsletters and Feature Articles on travel bargains, vacation ideas, tips & resources, and more!

What's New in Bermuda

Even some diehard fans compare Bermuda to certain beauty queens—beautiful but dull. We prefer to think of it as "tranquil." If you're looking for exotic local color or sizzling rum- and reggae-filled nights, look farther south to the Caribbean.

But if you need to escape the stress and strain of daily life, look to Bermuda. This quiet island is one of the best places in the world for a honeymoon or a celebration of any romantic occasion. The joint may not be jumping, but it's the most relaxing—and safest—of the foreign islands off the American coast. Bermuda offers a relatively hassle-free environment where you can concentrate on your tan, minus the annoyance of aggressive vendors and worries about crime. If you're into sunning and swimming, it doesn't get much better than Bermuda between May and September. Pink sand and turquoise seas—it sounds like a corny travel poster, but it's for real. As Mark Twain often said, "Sometimes a dose of Bermuda is just what the doctor ordered."

Frankly, Bermuda is predictable, and its regular visitors wouldn't have it any other way. The tiny island chain has attracted vacationers for decades, and there aren't many secrets left to uncover. But those pink sandy beaches are just as inviting as ever, no matter how many times you return.

Even to friends of Bermuda who make an annual pilgrimage to the island, the Bermudians can be a bit smug. They know their island is more attractive than Chicago, New York, Los Angeles, or Miami, and they're not above reminding you. Bit of an imperial attitude, isn't it? Exactly.

Some critics claim that Bermuda has become Americanized. Look again. That's true of islands much farther south, such as The Bahamas, but Bermuda remains stoically Bermuda. The island and its population steadfastly adhere to British customs, even if at times that slavish devotion borders on caricature. (The afternoon tea ritual is pleasant enough, but the lawyers' and judges' powdered wigs are a bit much—those things must get hot in a semitropical climate!) Some visitors find all the British decorum rather silly on a remote island that's closer to Atlanta than to London. But many others find the stalwart commitment to British tradition colorful and quaint, enhancing the unique charm of the lovely, wonderful place that is Bermuda.

If you're looking for some of the best golf in the world, Bermuda is your Mecca. It has the scenery, the state-of-the-art courses, and the British tradition of golfing excellence. Even the most demanding player is generally satisfied with the island's offerings.

If you're a sailor, you'll find the waters of Bermuda reason enough for a visit. Better yet, reason enough to be alive. The farther you go from shore, of course, the greater the visibility. Discovering a hidden cove, away from the cruise-ship crowds, can make your day.

If you hate driving on the left side of the road, that's fine with Bermudians. You *can't* drive—they won't rent you a car. Bike around, or hop on a scooter and zip from one end of the island to the other.

We could go on and on with reasons for you to come to Bermuda, from exploring natural wonderlands to playing on choice tennis courts with gentle sea breezes and warm sunshine. But we'll end here with a couple of warnings: Demanding foodies will find better dining on other islands, such as Martinique—although Bermuda has made much culinary progress of late. And if you want nightlife, glittering casinos, and all that jazz, head for San Juan. There is some nightlife in Bermuda, if you enjoy nursing a pint in a pub. It's always wise to bring along some good company (or a good book) to ensure a blissful night here.

Locals will always tell you, "If you want change, go to The Bahamas. We stay the same in Bermuda." Defying local wisdom, we've come up with some developments.

PLANNING YOUR TRIP For the summer of 2002, expect more bookings aboard the *Norwegian Majesty* (✆ **800/327-7030**), which is better than ever since it was taken back to the shipyards and "stretched," with a whole new midsection added. That's not all. The 20,000-ton *Crown Dynasty* (✆ **800/832-1122**) now services those getaway voyages from Philadelphia and Baltimore to Bermuda. The *Dynasty* is the only ship to dock at the Royal naval Dockyard. For more details, refer to chapter 2, "Planning Your Trip to Bermuda."

ACCOMMODATIONS When **Daniel's Head Village,** Daniel's Head Rd. (✆ **415/693-0808**) opened on August 1, 2000, it became the first new accommodation on the island in 27 years. The environmentally sensitive village is set on a tranquil peninsula. Guests are lodged in "eco-tents" that bring them close to nature but still provide comfortable amenities. The $8-million resort is on the west side of the island at Daniel's head, just a 5-minute ride from the little village of Somerset.

More and more snug little retreats are receiving guests in Bermuda. These are not advertised and often depend on word of mouth for their promotion. Typical of these is **Robin's Nest,** 10 Vale Close, along the North Shore (✆ **800/637-4116**), a family-managed compound of little apartments, ideal for families. Out in Sandys Parish is another lovely choice—**Garden House,** 4 Middle Rd. (✆ **441/234-1435**) with a private dock for deep-water swimming. The place evokes a British country house aura. For complete details on each, see chapter 4, "Accommodations."

DINING Michael Douglas, whose family has long owned the **Ariel Sands,** 34 South Shore Rd. in Devonshire (✆ **441/236-1010**), has put the once-dull hotel restaurant, **Caliban's,** back on the dining map of Bermuda in recent months. Featuring both Bermudian and international cuisine, Caliban's serves memorable dishes, many evocative of California, such as tuna carpaccio and oriental duck strudel or steamed salmon with a pineapple and mango chutney accompanied by an orange couscous. Lunch is served both indoors and at the poolside terrace.

Other than Caliban's, there has been no major culinary breakthrough, but **Spring Garden,** on Washington Lane (✆ **441/295-7416**), has recently brought Bajan flavors to Bermuda. Named after a district in Barbados, Spring Garden features that southern Caribbean island's most famous dish, "flying fish." The chef serves a number of Bermudian staples as well, notably fish chowder and fish cakes. There's an alfresco bar, and you can also dine in the courtyard, shaded by palm trees. Not all of the culinary invasions are from islands to the south. Ireland has firmly landed in the form of **Flanagan's Irish Pub & Restaurant,** in the Emporium Building in Hamilton, 69 Front St. (✆ **441/295-8299**). A "taste of Ireland" is offered at both lunch and dinner from your balcony table overlooking Front Street and Hamilton Harbour. This is really a pub, sports bar, and restaurant combined; specialties are steaks and pub grub.

Out on the island in Smiths Parish, **North Rock Brewing Co.,** 10 South Rd. (✆ **441/236-6633**), has emerged as the great watering hole for the moped and bike crowd heading for the East End. A varied selection of fresh ales, brewed right on the premises, includes Whale of a Wheat, Old Colony Bitter, and North Rock Porter. The restaurant also serves British-inspired fare such as a classic steak-and-ale pie or beef and mushrooms simmered in ale. For complete details on each, see chapter 5 "Dining."

FUN IN THE SURF & SUN   *Skin Diver* magazine has recently hailed Bermuda as the world's top wreck-diving destination. Divers can explore firsthand the legacy of the Bermuda Triangle and the greatest number of diveable shipwrecks in the Western Hemisphere. Aquatic adventurers can immerse themselves in summer water temperatures averaging 83°F along the world's northernmost coral reefs. For a list of the best scuba outfitters, see chapter 6, "Fun in the Surf & Sun." Also refer to The Best Dive Sites in chapter 1, "The Best of Bermuda."

At Robinson's marina in Southampton, the island's oldest and largest full-service scuba-diving operation, **Blue Waters,** has added something new—underwater scooters. Called DPVs or "diver propulsion vehicles," this exciting new vehicle takes adventurers through underwater caves and canyons, and sometimes even shipwrecks. For more information, call ✆ **441/234-1034.**

The **Ocean Discovery Centre** at the new Bermuda Underwater Exploration Institute on East Broadway (✆ **441/292-7219**) has opened to give visitors an underwater adventure. The highlight of a visit is a simulated dive 12,000 feet to the bottom of the Atlantic. Author Peter Benchley's videotaped commentary adds to the fun of the underwater exploration in and around Bermuda's reefs. You'll learn about newly discovered ocean animals that live in the murky depths during what is called "an in-depth investigation of earth's final frontier." For complete details on each of these, refer to chapter 6, "Fun in the Surf & Sun."

SEEING THE SIGHTS   In overcrowded Bermuda, the search for solace and tranquility grows harder and harder. But we recently stumbled upon the 43-acre **Heydon Trust** (✆ **441/234-1831**), on Somerset Road in Smiths Parish, open daily from dawn to dusk. This setting, which is also a sanctuary for migratory birds, is Bermuda the way it used to be. The grounds are filled with flower gardens, citrus orchards, walkways, and even a tiny chapel dating from 1620, where services are held in Gregorian chant at 7am and 3pm Monday through Saturday. Throughout the preserve are park benches where you can sit and contemplate nature or your navel. For complete details, refer to chapter 7, "Seeing the Sights."

SHOPPING   The international airport in Bermuda has recently launched duty-free shops for those last-minute purchases. One shop is found in the international departures lounge, and the other lies near the U.S. departures lounge. U.S. citizens clear customs before flying back to the States. For that specialty purchase, you should still shop around the island.

The major shopping pattern that has recently changed on Bermuda is the emergence of the historic port of St. George's as a big-time competitor to Hamilton, which has held the monopoly on island shopping for decades. Because it's easier to walk around St. George's, and more architecturally intriguing, many shoppers now prefer to hunt for merchandise here. The best place to begin is at the new **Somers Wharf & Branch Stores** along Water Street, a coterie of shops that include all the big names from Hamilton's such as a A. S. Coopers, Trimingham's, and the Crown Colony Shop. Of course, the parent stores in Hamilton are better stocked, but the Somers Wharf "name" shops are clustered together, making it easier for comparison shopping. For a preview of the best shops at the port, see chapter 9, "Shopping."

AFTER DARK Thanks to the efforts of actor Michael Douglas, whose family owns the Ariel Sands resort in Devonshire, 34 Shore Rd. (✆ 441/236-1010), **Caliban's Bar** has emerged as a hot address for drinks and for live Bermudian entertainment nightly. While downing a rum swizzle, you can also peruse some of Michael's personal photographs. Dinner theater has come to Bermuda and is performed by the **Jabulani Repertory Company** (✆ 441/295-3000). Plays are presented in the Gazebo Lounge of the Hamilton Princess, Wednesday through Saturday at 9:15pm, with tickets costing $25. For complete details, see chapter 10, "Bermuda After Dark."

The Best of Bermuda

If you've decided that Bermuda sounds like the perfect place to relax, spend your vacation in peace and let us do the work. Below you'll find our carefully compiled lists of the best that Bermuda has to offer, from beaches and dive sites to resorts, restaurants, and sightseeing—and nearly everything else you'll want to see and do.

1 The Best Beaches

Your first priority on your Bermuda vacation probably will be to kick back at the beach. But which beach? Hotels often have private stretches of sand, which we've described in each accommodation review (see chapter 4, "Accommodations"). There are many fine public beaches as well. Here's our top 10 list, arranged clockwise around the island, beginning with the south-shore beaches closest to the City of Hamilton. See chapter 6, "Fun in the Surf & Sun," for details and a map.

- **Elbow Beach** (Paget Parish): Pale-pink sand stretches for almost a mile at Elbow Beach, one of the most popular beaches in Bermuda. At least three hotels sit on its perimeter. Because protective coral reefs surround it, Elbow Beach is one of the safest on the island for swimming. Around Easter, it tends to be packed with college students who invade Bermuda for College Weeks.

- **Astwood Cove** (Warwick Parish): At the bottom of a steep, winding road that intersects with South Shore Road, this beach is so remote that it's rarely over-crowded. Come here when you want to be alone. The trees and shrubbery of Astwood Park provide a verdant backdrop.

- **Warwick Long Bay** (Warwick Parish): This popular beach, on the south side of South Shore Park, features a half-mile stretch of sand against a backdrop of scrubland and low grasses. Despite frequent winds, an offshore reef keeps the waves surprisingly small. Less than 200 feet offshore, a jagged coral island appears to be floating above the water.

- **Chaplin Bay** (Warwick and Southampton parishes): At the southern extremity of South Shore Park, straddling the boundary of two parishes, this small but secluded beach almost completely disappears during storms and particularly high tides. An open-air coral barrier partially separates one half of the beach from the other.

- **Horseshoe Bay** (Southampton Parish): This is Bermuda's most famous beach, and it's one of the best for families. Unlike most island beaches, Horseshoe Bay has a lifeguard on duty from May to

Bermuda

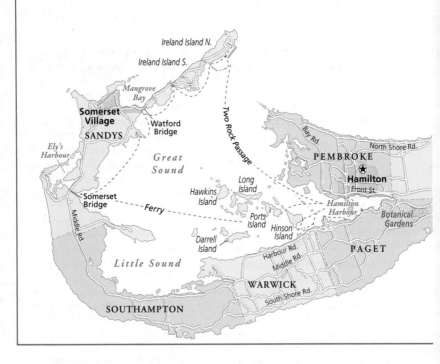

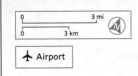

September. The **Horseshoe Bay Beach House** (© 441/238-2651) offers complete facilities, including equipment rental.

- **Church Bay** (Southampton Parish): If you like to snorkel, this southwestern beach is for you. The relatively calm waters, sheltered by offshore reefs, harbor a variety of marine life. Sunbathers love the unusually deep, pink sands of this beach.
- **Somerset Long Bay** (Sandys Parish): The waters off this beach are often unsafe for swimming, but its isolation will appeal to anyone who wants to escape the crowds. With about a quarter-mile of sand, the crescent-shaped beach is ideal for strolling. The

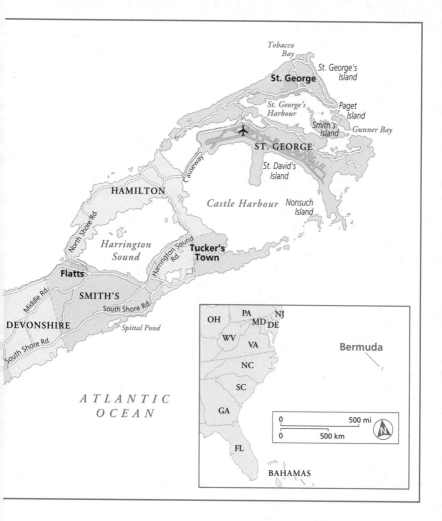

undeveloped parkland of Sandys Parish shelters it from the rest of the island.

- **Shelly Bay** (Hamilton Parish): On the north shore, you'll discover calm waters and soft, pink sand—and you'll want for nothing else.
- **Tobacco Bay** (St. George Parish): A popular stretch of pale-pink sand, this is the most frequented beach on St. George's Island. It offers lots of facilities, including equipment rentals and a snack bar.
- **John Smith's Bay** (Smith's Parish): The only public beach in Smith's Parish is long and flat. It boasts the pale-pink sand for which the south shore is famous. There's usually a lifeguard on duty from May to September—a plus for families. There are toilet and changing facilities on site.

2 The Best Outdoor Pursuits

See chapter 6, "Fun in the Surf & Sun," for details on arranging any of these activities.

- **Golf:** Known for its outstanding courses, Bermuda attracts the world's leading golfers (and those who'd like to be). Over the years, such luminaries as President Eisenhower, President Truman, and the Duke of Windsor have hit the island's links. Rolling, hummocky fairways characterize the courses. Many avid golfers come to Bermuda to "collect courses," or play them all. Some holes, such as Port Royal's notorious 16th, are from hell, as golfers say: Both the tee and the hole are high on cliff edges, with the rich, blue sea a dizzying 100 feet below. See "The Best Golf Courses," below, for our top picks.

- **Boating and Sailing:** Yachters around the world agree: Bermuda is one of the world's top destinations. Many people forget that Bermuda isn't one island, but an archipelago, waiting to be discovered. With the fresh wind of the Atlantic blowing in your hair, you can launch your own voyage of discovery. Explore Great Sound and its islets, including Long Island and Hawkins Island. Tiny, secluded beaches beckon frequently. Are you a novice? Try Mangrove Bay; it's protected and safer than some more turbulent seas.

- **Diving:** If you're happiest under the sea, Bermuda has what you're looking for. That includes the wrecks of countless ships, underwater caves, rich reefs, and, during most of the year, warm, gin-clear waters. All around you'll find a kaleidoscope of coral and marine life that's the most varied in this part of the world. Many scuba experts consider Bermuda one of the safest and best places to learn the sport. Depths begin at 25 feet or less, but can exceed 80 feet. Some wrecks are in about 30 feet of water, which puts them within the range of snorkelers. See "The Best Dive Sites," below.

- **Biking:** You can't rent a car on Bermuda, so you might as well hit the road on two wheels. Most of the island isn't great cycling terrain, because the roads are narrow and the traffic heavy. We suggest that you head for the Railway Trail, the island's premier bike path. The paved trail, which follows the former route of Bermuda's railway line, runs almost the entire length of the island.

- **Horseback Riding:** Guiding a horse through the dune grass and oleander of the island, especially at South Shore Park, is an experience you won't want to miss. Because this sport is so restricted on Bermuda, it can be all the more memorable. Horseback-riding centers guide you on trail rides through not only the best of the countryside, but also beautiful hidden spots along the north coast.

3 The Best Dive Sites

The following are some of the most exciting shipwreck and coral-reef dives. See chapter 6, "Fun in the Surf & Sun," for more information about dive outfitters.

- **The *Constellation:*** This 200-foot, four-masted schooner, which was en route to Venezuela in 1943, lies in 30 feet of water off the northwest side of the island, about 8 miles west of the Royal Naval Dockyard. The true story of this ship inspired Peter Benchley to write *The Deep.*

- **The *Cristóbal Colón:*** The largest known shipwreck in Bermuda's waters is this 480-foot Spanish luxury liner; it ran aground in 1936 on a northern reef between North Rock and North Breaker. It lies in 30 to 55 feet of water.

- **The *Hermes:*** This 165-foot steamer ship rests in some 80 feet of water about a mile off Warwick Long Bay on the south shore. It foundered in 1985. The *Hermes,* the *Rita Zovetta,* and the *Tauton* (see below) are Bermuda favorites because of the incredible multicolored variety of fish that populate the waters around the ships. You might see grouper, brittle starfish, spiny lobster, crabs, banded coral shrimp, queen angels, tube sponge, and more.

- ***L'Hermanie:*** A first-class, 60-gun French frigate, *L'Hermanie* was 17 days out of its Cuban port en route to France when it sank in 1838. The ship lies in 20 to 30 feet of water off the west side of the island, with 25 cannons still visible.

- **The *Marie Celeste:*** This paddle wheeler sank in 1964. Its 15-foot-diameter paddle wheel, off the southern portion of the island, is overgrown with coral standing about 55 feet off the ocean floor.

- **The *North Carolina:*** One of Bermuda's most colorful wrecks, this English sailing barkentine foundered in 1879 and today, lies in about 40 feet of water off the western portion of the island.

- **The *Rita Zovetta:*** A 360-foot Italian cargo ship, lying in 20 to 70 feet of water off the south side of the island, the *Rita Zovetta* ran aground off St. David's Island in 1924. This one's a favorite with underwater photographers because of the kaleidoscope of fish that inhabit the area.

- **South West Breaker:** This coral-reef dive off the south shore, about 1½ miles off Church Bay, has hard and soft coral decorating sheet walls at depths of 20 to 30 feet.

- **Tarpon Hole:** Near Elbow Beach off the south shore, this dive's proximity to the Elbow Beach Hotel makes it extremely popular. The honeycombed reef—one of the most beautiful off the coast of Bermuda—is known for its varieties of coral: yellow pencil, elkhorn, fire, and star.

- **The *Tauton:*** This popular dive site is a British Royal Mail steamer that sank in 1914. It lies in 10 to 40 feet of water off the north end of the island and is home to scores of varieties of colorful marine life.

4 The Best Golf Courses

All four of these courses are 18 holes. See chapter 6, "Fun in the Surf & Sun," for more details.

- **Belmont Golf & Country Club** (Warwick Parish): Scotsman Emmett Devereux designed this par-70, 5,777-yard course in 1923. It has been challenging golfers ever since, especially on its par-5 11th hole, a severe dogleg left with a blind tee shot. Trade winds play havoc with the listed lengths. Critics complain that the layout is "maddening," yet they continue to return for new challenges. The grass is dense thanks to a modern irrigation system.

- **Fairmont Southampton Princess Golf Club** (Hamilton Parish): This is a par-54, 2,684-yard

The Baffling Bermuda Triangle

The area known as the Bermuda Triangle encompasses a 1.5-million-square-mile expanse of open sea between Bermuda, Puerto Rico, and the southeastern shoreline of the U.S. This bit of the Atlantic is the source of the most famous, and certainly the most baffling, legend associated with Bermuda.

Tales of the mysterious Bermuda Triangle persist, despite attempts by skeptics to dismiss them as fanciful. Below are three of the most popular. Can they be true? See what you think:

- In 1881, a British-registered ship, the *Ellen Austin,* encountered an unnamed vessel in good condition sailing aimlessly without a crew. The captain ordered a handful of his best seamen to board the mysterious vessel and sail it to Newfoundland. A few days later, the ships encountered each other again on the high seas. But to everyone's alarm, the crewmen who had transferred from the *Ellen Austin* were nowhere to be found—it was completely unmanned!

- Another tale concerns the disappearance of a merchant ship, the *Marine Sulphur Queen,* in February 1963. It vanished suddenly and without warning, and no one could say why. The weather was calm when the ship set sail from Bermuda, and everything onboard was fine—the crew never sent a distress signal. In looking for explanations, some have theorized that the ship's weakened hull gave way, causing it to descend quickly to the bottom. Others attribute the loss to more mysterious forces.

- The most famous of all the legends concerns an incident in 1945. On December 5, five U.S. Navy bombers departed from Fort Lauderdale,

course, with elevated tees, strategically placed bunkers, and an array of water hazards to challenge even the most experienced golfer. One golfer said of this course, "You not only need to be a great player, but have a certain mountaineering agility as well."

- **Port Royal Golf Course** (Southampton Parish): This public course ranks among the best on the island, public or private; in fact, it's one of the greatest public courses in the world. Jack Nicklaus apparently agrees—he likes to play here. Robert Trent Jones designed the par-71, 6,565-yard course along the ocean. The 16th hole is the most famous in Bermuda; photos of it have appeared in countless golf magazines. Greens fees are relatively reasonable, too.

- **St. George's Golf Club** (St. George Parish): One of the island's newest courses—and one of its best—this par-62, 4,043-yard course was designed by Robert Trent Jones. Within walking distance of historic St. George, it lies on a windy headland at the northeastern tip of Bermuda. Although you'll enjoy panoramic vistas, your game is likely to be affected by Atlantic winds. The greens are the smallest on the island, at no larger than 24 feet across.

Florida, on a routine mission. The weather was fine; no storm of any kind threatened. A short time into the flight, the leader of the squadron radioed that they were lost, and then the radio went silent. All efforts to establish further communication proved fruitless. A rescue plane was dispatched to search for the squadron—but it, too, disappeared. The navy ordered a search that lasted 5 days, but there was no evidence of any wreckage. To this day, the disappearance of the squadron and the rescue plane remains a mystery as deep as the waters of the region.

How do those who believe in the Bermuda Triangle legend explain these phenomena? Some contend that the area is a time warp to another universe; others think the waters off Bermuda is the site of the lost kingdom of Atlantis, whose power sources still function deep beneath the surface. Still others believe laser rays from outer space are perpetually focused on the region, or that underwater signaling devices are guiding invaders from other planets, who have chosen the site for the systematic collection of human beings for scientific observation and experimentation. (Smacks of *The X-Files*, doesn't it?) Some, drawing upon the Book of Revelation, are fully persuaded that the Bermuda Triangle is really one of the gates to Hell (in this version, the other gate lies midway between Japan and the Philippines, in the Devil's Sea).

No matter what your views on these mysteries, you're bound to provoke an excited response by asking residents what they think about it. On Bermuda, almost everyone has an opinion about the island's biggest and most fascinating legend.

5 The Best Tennis Facilities

For more details, see chapter 6, "Fun in the Surf & Sun."

- **The Fairmont Southampton Princess** (Southampton Parish): This is Bermuda's premier destination for avid players. Its tennis court layout is not only the largest on the island, but also is maintained in state-of-the-art condition. The deluxe hotel, one of the finest on Bermuda, offers 11 Plexipave courts. The courts are somewhat protected from the north winds, but swirling breezes may affect your final score.

- **Government Tennis Stadium** (Pembroke Parish): Although Bermuda has been known as the tennis capital of the Atlantic since 1873, players often complain that the trade winds around the island affect their game, especially near the water. That's why many prefer inland courts, such as those at this government-owned stadium. It offers three clay and five Plexicushion courts (three illuminated for night play). The facility, which is north of Hamilton, requires players to wear proper tennis attire. On site you'll find a pro shop, a ball machine, and a pro offering private lessons.

- **Port Royal Club** (Southampton Parish): Serious tennis coexists with serious golf here, and the well-maintained courts are among the island's best. There are four Plexipave courts, two illuminated for night games. You can borrow racquets and balls if you didn't come prepared. Even golfing luminaries such as Jack Nicklaus have been spotted on these courts. They overlook the pink sands and blue waters of Whale Bay, one of the island's leading areas for fishing and boating.

6 The Best Day Hikes

For more details, see chapter 6, "Fun in the Surf & Sun," and chapter 8, "Island Strolls."

- **The Bermuda Railway Trail** (Sandys Parish): Stretching for about 21 miles, this unique trail was created along the course of the old Bermuda Railway. It served the island from 1931 to 1948 (cars weren't allowed on the island until the late 1940s). Armed with a copy of the *Bermuda Railway Trail Guide,* available at visitor centers, you can follow the route of the train known as "Rattle and Shake." Most of the trail still winds along a car-free route, and you can travel as much (or as little) of it as your stamina allows.
- **From the Royal Naval Dockyard to Somerset** (Sandys Parish): A 4-mile walk leads from the dockyard, the former center of the British navy on Bermuda, to Somerset Island. From the dockyard's southern entrance, follow Pender Road for about half a mile, crossing Cut Bridge to Ireland Island South. After crossing Grey's Bridge, the route continues west along Watford Island. It crosses Watford Bridge, which eventually leads to Somerset Village in Sandys Parish. Sandy beaches along the route are perfect for pausing from your hike to stretch out on the sand.
- **Spittal Pond Nature Reserve Tour** (Smith's Parish): This 60-acre sanctuary is the island's largest nature reserve, home to both resident and migratory waterfowl. You can spot some 25 species of waterfowl from November to May. Scenic trails and footpaths cut through the property. You can explore on your own or take a guided hike offered by the Department of Agriculture.

7 The Best Sailing Outfitters

Bermuda is one of the Atlantic's major sailing capitals. Many sail-yourself boats are available for rent to qualified sailors. See chapter 6, "Fun in the Surf & Sun," for more information. The best outfitters include the following:

- **Blue Hole Water Sports** (Grotto Bay Beach Hotel, Hamilton Parish; © **441/293-2915**): Here you'll find a large selection of watercraft, including a Sunfish, Boardsailer, kayak, Paddle Cat, and Sun Cat. Rentals are available for up to 8 hours.
- **Pompano Beach Club Watersports Centre** (Southampton Parish; © **441/234-0222**): This is the best outfitter in this tourist-laden parish. Open from May to late October, it offers a variety of equipment, including the O'Brien Windsurfer, which is suitable for one person (novice or experienced). Its fleet also includes vessels that hold one or two people and can be rented for up to 4 hours: Dolphin paddleboats, Buddy Boards, Aqua-Eye viewing boards, Aqua Finn sailboats, and kayaks.

- **Somerset Bridge Watersports** (Somerset Parish; © **441/ 234-0914**): This is the best place to rent a Boston whaler, which can hold three or four passengers. It's an ideal craft for exploring the archipelago's uninhabited islands. This outfitter rents 13-foot whalers and a 30-hp, 15-foot Open Bowrider, which accommodates four.

8 The Best Views

Bermuda is incredibly scenic, with lovely panoramas and vistas unfolding at nearly every turn. But not all views are created equal. Below are some of our personal favorites. See chapter 7, "Seeing the Sights," for additional suggestions.

- **Fort Scaur:** From Somerset Bridge in Sandys Parish, head for this fort atop the parish's highest hill. Walk the fort's ramparts, enjoying the vistas across Great Sound to Spanish Point. You can also gaze north to the dockyard and take in the fine view of Somerset Island. On a clear day, a look through the telescope reveals St. David's Lighthouse, 14 miles away on the northeastern tip of the island. After enjoying the fantastic view from the fort, you can stroll through the 22 acres of beautiful gardens.
- **Gibbs Hill Lighthouse:** For an even better view than the one enjoyed by Queen Elizabeth II (see below), climb the 185 spiral steps of the lighthouse. Built in 1846, it's the oldest cast-iron lighthouse in the world. From the top, you can relish what islanders consider the single finest view in all of Bermuda. You can, that is, if the wind doesn't blow you away—be sure to hang on to the railing. In heavy winds, the tower actually sways.
- **The Queen's View:** At Gibbs Hill Lighthouse in Southampton Parish, a plaque designates the spot where Queen Elizabeth II paused in November 1953 to take in the view of Little Sound. You can admire that same view, which includes Riddells Bay golf course and Perot's Island. (Although Ross Perot has a home in Bermuda, the island is not named for him, but for the father of William Bennett Perot, Bermuda's first postmaster.)
- **Warwick Long Bay:** This stretch of pristine pink sand is a dream beach of the picture-postcard variety. It backs up to towering cliffs and hills studded with Spanish bayonet and oleander. A 20-foot coral outcrop, rising some 200 feet offshore and resembling a sculpted boulder, adds variety to the stunning beachscape.

9 The Best Historic Sights

See chapter 7, "Seeing the Sights," for more details. Also see "The Best Places to Experience Old Bermuda," below, for a description of the Royal Naval Dockyard.

- **Fort St. Catherine** (St. George Parish): This fort—with its tunnels, cannons, and ramparts—towers over the beach where the shipwrecked crew of the *Sea Venture* first came ashore in 1609. The fort was completed in 1614, and extensive rebuilding and remodeling continued until the 19th century. The audiovisual presentation on St. George's defense system helps you better understand what you're seeing.

- **Fort Scaur** (Sandys Parish): Fort Scaur and Fort St. Catherine were part of a ring of fortifications that surrounded Bermuda. Built by the British navy, the fort was supposed to protect the Royal Naval Dockyard from an attack that never materialized. During World War II, U.S. Marines were billeted nearby. Overlooking Great Sound, the fort offers some of the island's most dramatic scenery.

- **St. Peter's Church** (St. George Parish): This is the oldest Anglican house of worship in the Western Hemisphere. At one time virtually everybody was buried here, from governors to criminals; to the west of the church lies the graveyard of slaves. This is the site of the original church, which colonists built in 1612. A hurricane destroyed the church in 1712, but some parts of the interior survived. It was rebuilt on the same site in 1713.

- **Verdmont** (Smith's Parish): This 1770s mansion is on property once owned by William Sayle, founder and first governor of South Carolina. Filled with portraits, antiques, and china, the house offers a rare glimpse into a long-faded life of style and grace. Resembling a small English manor house, it's the finest historic home in Bermuda.

10 The Best Places to Experience Old Bermuda

Although much of Bermuda is modern, the first settlers arrived in 1609. The following places provide insights into the old, largely vanished Bermudian way of life. See chapter 7, "Seeing the Sights," for more details.

- **The Back Streets of St. George** (St. George Parish): Almost every visitor to the island has photographed the 17th-century stocks on King's Square in historic St. George. In the narrow back alleys and cobblestone lanes such as Shinbone Alley, you'll really discover the town's old spirit. Arm yourself with a good map and wander at leisure through such places as Silk Alley (also called Petticoat Lane), Barber's Lane Alley (named for a former slave from South Carolina), Printer's Alley (where Bermuda's first newspaper was published), and Nea's Alley (former stamping ground of the Irish poet Tom Moore). Finally, walk through Somers Garden and head up the steps to Blockade Alley. On the hill is the aptly named Unfinished Cathedral.

- **The Royal Naval Dockyard** (Sandys Parish): Nothing recaptures the maritime spirit of this little island colony more than this sprawling complex of attractions (with a multimillion-dollar cruise-ship dock) on Ireland Island. Britain began building this dockyard in 1809, perhaps fearing attacks on its fleet by Napoleon or greedy pirates. Convicts and slaves provided much of the construction labor, and the Royal Navy occupied the shipyard for almost 150 years. It closed in 1951, and the navy has little presence here today. The Maritime Museum—the most important on the island—and other exhibits on Bermuda's nautical heritage give you a good feel for a largely vanished era.

- **St. David's Island** (St. George Parish): Though most of Bermuda looks pristine and proper, you'll still find some vestiges of rustic maritime life on St. David's. Some St. David's islanders never even bother to visit neighboring St. George; to some locals, a trip to the West End of Bermuda would be like a trip to the moon. St. David's Lighthouse has been a local landmark since 1879. To see how people used to cook and eat, drop by Dennis's Hideaway (see below).

11 Bermuda's Best-Kept Secrets

- **Dining at Dennis's Hideaway** (St. George Parish; © 441/297-0044): At his small home on remote St. David's Island, Dennis Lamb is an unforgettable host. He personifies the eccentricity of his fellow islanders. Not only will Dennis feed you shark hash, mussel pie, and other seafood dishes, but he'll also give you some insight into how life was on Bermuda long ago. When he's not tending his pots, cleaning fish, or throwing food to one of his yapping dogs, he might also share his philosophy of life with you. No ties allowed. Call ahead for a reservation. See chapter 5, "Dining," for details.
- **Escaping to a Remote Natural Setting** (Smith's Parish; © 441/234-1831). Bermuda still has some oases that aren't overrun with visitors. Such a place is the **Heydon Trust** along Somerset Road, a sanctuary for migratory birds. It's like a walk through nature with flowering bushes and citrus orchards. See chapter 7, "Seeing the Sights."
- **Spelunking in Crystal Caves** (Hamilton Parish): A spelunker's paradise, Bermuda has the highest concentration of limestone caves in the world. They form one of the island's major natural wonderlands. Their surreal formations took millions of years to create, and the great stalactites and stalagmites have a Gothic grandeur. The best caves are Crystal Caves at Bailey's Bay. Discovered in 1907, the caves include crystal-clear Cahow Lake. For details, see chapter 7, "Seeing the Sights."

12 The Best Resorts for Honeymooners (& Other Lovers)

Bermuda has long been one of the world's favorite destinations for newlyweds. Its hotels, from deluxe resorts to guesthouses, attract lovers of all kinds looking for a little peace, solitude, and seclusion.

Although some couples seek out small housekeeping cottages and guesthouses, most prefer a package offered by one of the splashy resort hotels. The following resorts feature not only romance, but also some of the best deals.

Note: It's a good idea to consult a travel agent for help in getting the best bargain. Before you call any of these hotels directly, see our "Package Deals" section in chapter 2, "Planning Your Trip to Bermuda." For full hotel reviews, see chapter 4, "Accommodations."

- **Elbow Beach Hotel** (Paget Parish; © 800/223-7434 in the U.S., or 441/236-3535): This hotel promises "marriages made in heaven." Its Romance Packages include daily breakfast plus a candlelit dinner for two in your room on the first night. Upon departure, newlyweds receive a copy of the *Elbow Beach Cookbook*.
- **The Fairmont Southampton Princess** (Southampton Parish; © 800/223-1414 in the U.S., 800/268-7176 in Canada, or 441/238-8000): The island's most luxurious hotel does everything it can to attract honeymooners seeking lots of activities from water sports to nighttime diversions (other than those in the honeymoon suite). Its honeymoon

packages, which start at 4 days and 3 nights, include breakfast and dinner on a MAP "dine-around plan," a bottle of champagne, a basket of fruit, admission to the exercise club, and even a special-occasion cake, plus a souvenir photo and watercolor print by a local artist.

- **Grotto Bay Beach Hotel** (Hamilton Parish; ✆ **800/582-3190** in the U.S., 800/463-0851 in Canada, or 441/293-8333): This resort, which actively caters to honeymooners, features everything from midnight swims at a private beach to cozy lovers' nests with private balconies overlooking the ocean. The honeymoon packages include romantic dinners and arrangements for cruises and walking tours as well as optional champagne, fruit, and flowers.
- **Harmony Club** (Paget Parish; ✆ **888/427-6664**): If you shun the big splashy resorts which attract a lot of families with children, head to this small, couples-only all-inclusive resort. Guests are

housed in romantic Queen Anne–style buildings in a setting of formal gardens and gazebos. Dinners are by candlelight on fine china and crystal. Honeymoon packages are available. See chapter 4, "Accommodations," for more details.

- **Sonesta Beach Resort** (Southampton Parish; ✆ **800/766-3782** in the U.S., or 441/238-8122): You'll find champagne chilling in your room when you arrive—and it just gets better from there. To set the mood, the staff will arrange an introductory horse-and-buggy ride in the old Bermuda tradition. The following day, they'll give you a motor scooter for getting around. The sports director will also offer one free tennis or scuba lesson. The hotel is right on the beach; it's also a fully equipped, professionally staffed health spa. Honeymooners can dance to live music at the Boat Bay Club and Lounge, with its views of moonlit Boat Bay.

13 The Best Places to Stay with the Kids

Bermuda is more kid-friendly than any other place we know in the Caribbean or the Bahamas. It's a safe, clean environment in a politically stable country. Nearly all Bermuda hotels go the extra mile to welcome families with children, but these are our top choices. Turn to chapter 4, "Accommodations," for full reviews.

- **The Fairmont Southampton Princess** (Southampton Parish; ✆ **800/223-1414** in the U.S., 800/268-7176 in Canada, or 441/238-8000): From June through Labor Day, this hotel features the best children's program in Bermuda. Children under 17 stay free; and if the parents choose the

MAP, kids also get free meals. With its many sports facilities, including two freshwater pools and 11 tennis courts, this Princess is definitely for families who enjoy the sporting life. The former Touch Club has been redesigned as Lenny's Loft, the social center for children's activities, and from there, kids are taken on excursions around the island.

- **Grotto Bay Beach Hotel** (Hamilton Parish; ✆ **800/582-3190** in the U.S., 800/463-0851 in Canada, or 441/293-8333): With its excellent summer children's program, this hotel attracts many families. It sits on 21 tropically landscaped acres, so guests usually don't mind its relative isolation across from the airport. The swimming pool has been blasted out of natural rock, and there are subterranean caves to explore. Beachside barbecues and other activities make this a lively place.

- **Paraquet Guest Apartments** (Paget Parish; ✆ **441/236-5842**): Although somewhat sterile and motel-like in character, these apartments are a good bet for bargain-hunting families. Nine of the units have kitchenettes, and families often prepare their own meals, which cuts down on Bermuda's high dining costs. There's an inexpensive restaurant on the premises.
- **Elbow Beach Hotel** (Hamilton Parish; ✆ **800/223-7434,** or 441/236-3535): This longtime family favorite on one of the best beaches in Bermuda allows children under 13 to stay free when sharing a room with their parents. It also offers a "Family Value Package"—call the hotel or ask a travel agent for details.
- **Sonesta Beach Resort** (Southampton Parish; ✆ **800/766-3782** in the U.S., or 441/238-8122): This luxurious resort offers one of the best family packages on the island. A maximum of four people, including two children, is accepted for the 4-day, 3-night packages; children eat free, and a second guest room is provided at 25% off the regular rate. A "Just Us Kids" activities program for ages 5 to 12 is held daily in summer, with pizza parties, unlimited free ice cream, and children's games, among other diversions. The "Just Us Little Kids" program entertains the 2- to 4-year-olds with a wading pool, playroom, ice-cream parties, and other activities.

14 The Best Hotel Bargains

See chapter 4, "Accommodations," for full reviews.

- **Astwood Cove** (Warwick Parish; ✆ **800/637-4116** in the U.S., or 441/236-0984): This place is definitely a good buy in pricey Bermuda. For families seeking a self-contained studio or suite apartment with a fully equipped kitchenette and a private porch or patio, this is a great choice. You prepare your own meals and use the hotel's English bone china and wine glasses. Studio apartments have sofa beds that can accommodate a third person.
- **Loughlands** (Paget Parish; ✆ **441/236-1253**): Set on 7 acres of landscaped grounds, this guesthouse offers privacy, old-fashioned elegance, and plenty of Bermuda charm. Staying here is like living at a country house with attractively appointed bedrooms. There's a swimming pool, and arrangements can be made to participate in many other activities nearby, including golf, tennis, deep-sea fishing, and water-skiing.
- **Rosemont** (City of Hamilton, Pembroke Parish; ✆ **800/367-0040** in the U.S., 800/267-0040 in Canada, or 441/292-1055): A collection of housekeeping cottages near the Hamilton Princess, Rosemont has long been a family favorite, offering a central location at a good price. The site offers panoramic views of Hamilton Harbour and the Great Sound. Guests often prepare their own meals.
- **Sky-Top Cottages** (Paget Parish; ✆ **441/236-7984**): This cottage

cluster stands close to Elbow Beach, on a hilltop overlooking the southern shoreline. The cottages have a certain charm and character, and the property is well maintained. Each unit is named for a flower that grows in the garden, such as "Morning Glory," and each has a kitchenette.

15 The Best Restaurants

Admittedly, you don't come to Bermuda for grand cuisine. That said, there are quite a few places to enjoy a memorable meal. See chapter 5, "Dining," for full reviews of the restaurants listed below.

- **The Norwood Room** (Hamilton Parish; ℂ 441/236-5416): The students may be the chefs, but the cuisine served here is among the finest in Bermuda, each dish is prepared with care. Of course, a master chef of the Caribbean oversees the action, and the service from the in-training staff is the island's finest.
- **Black Horse Tavern** (St. George Parish; ℂ 441/297-1991): When you crave good, hearty food served in a casual atmosphere, this is the place to come. Islanders fill most of the tables at night, ordering shark hash or curried conch.
- **Fourways Inn Restaurant** (Paget Parish; ℂ 441/236-6517): In this 1700s Georgian house of cedar and coral stone, you'll dine as they did in plantation days, with traditional crystal, silver, and china. As the best piano music on the island plays in the background, introduce yourself to a bowl of Bermudian fish chowder, followed by French or Bermudian dishes.
- **La Coquille** (Pembroke Parish; ℂ 441/292-6122): One of the island's most sophisticated French restaurants enjoys a faithful following. Right in the heart of Bermuda, the international staff serves delectable French-inspired Mediterranean cuisine.
- **Lobster Pot & Boat House Bar** (City of Hamilton, Pembroke Parish; ℂ 441/292-6898): If you don't find the local foodies at the restaurants we discuss above, they'll surely be at this local favorite, enjoying some of the island's best regional dishes. Black rum and sherry peppers are the secret ingredients in the fish chowder, and baked fish and lobster are sure to tempt you.
- **Newport Room** (at The Fairmont Southampton Princess, Southampton Parish; ℂ 441/238-8000): Part of the resort complex, this nautically decorated restaurant attracts an upscale crowd, especially yachters. The glistening teak decor makes it the most expensively furnished restaurant in Bermuda, and its French cuisine is worthy of the decor. The rack of lamb with mixed-nut crust is the stuff of which memories are made.
- **Tamarisk Dining Room** (at Cambridge Beaches, Sandys Parish; ℂ 441/234-0331): This is an elegant enclave at the western tip of Bermuda. Housed in one of the island's premier accommodations, it offers excellent service and a frequently changing menu of impeccably prepared international cuisine. For your main course, you can't do better than juicy tenderloin of beef with grain mustard and blanched garlic sauce. The wine cellar is worthy of the menu.
- **Tom Moore's Tavern** (Hamilton Parish; ℂ 441/293-8020): The

Irish poet Tom Moore reportedly was a frequent visitor to this restaurant, which dates from 1652 and overlooks Walsingham Bay. The menu, however, is no relic—it's quite innovative. Duck is a specialty, as is Bermuda lobster; but who can forget the quail in puff pastry stuffed with foie gras?

- **Waterlot Inn** (at The Fairmont Southampton Princess, Southampton Parish; © **441/238-8000**): In a historic inn and warehouse, this restaurant serves the island's most famous Sunday brunch, but it's also an ideal choice for dinner. Everybody from Eleanor Roosevelt to Mark Twain has praised the Mediterranean cuisine.

2

Planning Your Trip to Bermuda

In this chapter, you'll find everything you need to plan your trip, from when to go to how to land the best package deals. Getting to Bermuda is easier than ever, thanks to more frequent flights from such gateway cities as New York, Boston, and Washington. We've also included information on several cruise lines that sail to the island from spring until late autumn.

1 Visitor Information

Your best sources may be relatives, friends, or colleagues who have been to Bermuda, so ask around. For information sources once you're in Bermuda, see "Orienting Yourself: The Lay of the Land," in chapter 3, "Getting to Know Bermuda."

THE BERMUDA DEPARTMENT OF TOURISM

IN THE UNITED STATES To receive a visitor information packet about Bermuda before you go, call *©* **800/237-6832.**

To speak to a travel representative, contact the **Bermuda Department of Tourism** office at 205 E. 42nd St., New York, NY 10017 (*©* **212/818-9800,** Ext. 213); 44 School St., Suite 1010, Boston, MA 02108 (*©* **617/742-0405**); or 245 Peachtree Center Ave. NE, Suite 803, Atlanta, GA 30303 (*©* **404/524-1541**).

IN CANADA Contact the **Bermuda Department of Tourism** at 1200 Bay St., Suite 1004, Toronto, ON, Canada M5R 2A5 (*©* **416/923-9600**).

IN THE UNITED KINGDOM Contact the **Bermuda Department of Tourism** at 1 Battersea Church Rd.,

London SW11 3LY (*©* **020/7771-7001**).

TRAVEL AGENTS

Travel agents can save you plenty of time and money by hunting down the best package deal or airfare. For the time being, most travel agents charge you nothing for their services—they're paid through commissions from the airlines and other agencies. However, most airlines have cut commissions, and increasingly agents are finding they have to charge customers fees. Some unscrupulous agents might offer you only the travel options that bag them the juiciest commissions. Shop around and ask hard questions. The best way to use a travel agent is to make preliminary decisions using this guide, and go into your meeting as a smart and informed consumer.

If you decide to use a travel agent, make sure the agent is a member of the **American Society of Travel Agents** (ASTA), 1101 King St., Alexandria, VA 22314 (*©* **703/739-8739;** www.astanet.com). To receive a copy of the free booklet *Avoiding Travel Problems,* send ASTA a self-addressed, stamped envelope.

⌜Tips   **Your Own Personal "Weblet"**

The Bermudian government remains committed to attracting more and more visitors. Its latest offering is to arrange a personalized Bermuda mini-guidebook for potential visitors. Within minutes of hanging up the phone, Internet-connected **800/BERMUDA** callers received a personalized "weblet" that gives specific and detailed information on hotels and activities or interests based on information supplied by the caller. For dining and hotels, weblet search engines allow guests to supply personal criteria and receive a selection of hotels and eating spots designed to appeal to their tastes and pocketbooks. Special-interest buttons can be pressed for data on golf, honeymoon packages, nightlife, and sports facilities.

2 Entry Requirements & Customs

ENTRY REQUIREMENTS

U.S. and **Canadian** citizens do not officially need a passport to enter Bermuda, but we strongly recommend that you carry one whenever you travel to a foreign country.

Bermuda Immigration authorities require U.S. citizens to have in their possession one of the following items: a birth certificate (or a certified copy of it accompanied by a photo ID), a U.S. naturalization certificate, a valid passport, a U.S. Alien Registration card, or a U.S. reentry permit. Go with the passport.

Canadian citizens must have either a birth certificate (or a certified copy), a Canadian certificate of citizenship, or a valid passport plus proof of Landed Immigrant status.

Bermuda Immigration authorities require visitors from the **United Kingdom** and **Europe** to show a valid passport. All visitors must have a return or onward ticket in addition to their valid passport or original birth certificate.

Any traveler staying in Bermuda longer than 3 weeks must apply to the **Chief Immigration Officer,** Government Administration Building, 30 Parliament St., Hamilton HM 12, Bermuda (✆ **441/295-5151**), for an extended stay.

Passport applications are downloadable from the Internet sites listed below:

- **For Residents of the United States:** If you're applying for a first-time passport, you need to do so in person at one of 13 passport offices throughout the U.S.; a federal, state, or probate court; or a major post office. Not all post offices accept applications; call the number below to find the ones that do. You need to present a certified birth certificate as proof of citizenship, and it's wise to bring along your driver's license, state or military ID, and Social Security card as well. You also need two identical passport-sized photos (2 in. × 2 in.), taken at a photo shop (not a strip of photos from a vending machine).

For people over 15, a passport is valid for 10 years and costs $60 ($45 plus a $15 handling fee); for those 15 and under, it's valid for 5 years and costs $40. If you're over 15 and have a valid passport that was issued within the past 12 years, you can renew it by mail and bypass the $15 handling fee. Allow plenty of time before your trip to apply; processing normally takes 3 weeks but can take longer

---

Tips Planning Pointer

Before leaving home, make copies of your most valuable documents, including the inside page of your passport that has your photograph. Also copy your driver's license, airline ticket, hotel vouchers, and any other pertinent documents. You should also make copies of the prescriptions for any medications you take. Leave one copy at home, place one copy in your luggage, and carry the original with you. The information on these documents is extremely valuable if your possessions are lost or stolen.

---

during busy periods (especially spring). For general information, call the **National Passport Agency** (℃ 202/647-0518). To find your regional passport office, call the **National Passport Information Center** (℃ **900/225-5674;** 35¢ per minute) or visit its website (http://travel.state.gov).

- **For Residents of Canada:** You can pick up a passport application at one of 28 regional passport offices or most travel agencies. The passport is valid for 5 years and costs Can$60. Children under 16 may be included on a parent's passport but need their own to travel unaccompanied by the parent. Applications, which must be accompanied by two identical passport-sized photographs and proof of Canadian citizenship, are available at travel agencies throughout Canada or from the central **Passport Office, Department of Foreign Affairs and International Trade,** Ottawa, ON K1A 0G3 (℃ **800/567-6868;** www.dfait-maeci.gc.ca/passport). Processing takes 5 to 10 days if you apply in person, or about 3 weeks by mail.
- **For Residents of the United Kingdom:** To pick up an application for a regular 10-year passport (the Visitor's Passport has been abolished), visit your nearest passport office, major post office, or travel agency. You can also contact the **London Passport Office**

(℃ **0870-521-0410;** www.open.gov.uk/ukpass/ukpass.htm). Passports are £28 for adults, £11 for children under 16.

- **For Residents of Ireland:** A 10 year passport costs IR£45. Apply at the Passport Office, Setanta Centre, Molesworth Street, Dublin 2 (℃ **01/671-1633;** www.irlgov.ie/iveagh/foreignaffairs/services). Those under age 18 and over 65 must apply for a 3-year passport, which costs IR£10. You can also apply at 1A South Mall, Cork (℃ **214/272-525**), or over the counter at most main post offices.
- **For Residents of Australia:** Apply at your local post office or passport office or search the government website at www.dfat.gov.au/passports/. Passports for adults are A$126; for those under 18, A$63.
- **For Residents of New Zealand:** You can pick up a passport application at any travel agency or Link Centre. For more info, contact the Passport Office, P.O. Box 805, Wellington (℃ **0800/225-050**). Passports for adults are NZ$80; for those under 16, NZ$40.

CUSTOMS

Visitors may bring into Bermuda duty-free apparel and articles for their personal use, including sports equipment, cameras, 200 cigarettes, 1 quart of liquor, 1 quart of wine, and approximately 20 pounds of meat. Other foodstuffs may be subject to duties.

All imports may be inspected on arrival. Visitors entering Bermuda may also claim a duty-free gift allowance.

When you're ready to return home, U.S. Customs pre-clearance is available for all scheduled flights. Passengers leaving for the United States must fill out written declaration forms before clearing U.S. Customs in Bermuda. The forms are available at Bermuda hotels, travel agencies, and airlines.

Collect receipts for all your purchases. If a merchant suggests giving you a false receipt that misstates the value of your goods, beware: The merchant may be a Customs informer. You must also declare all gifts received during your stay abroad.

Compile a list of your more expensive carry-on items, and ask a U.S. Customs agent to stamp your list at the airport before your departure; this way, upon your return, Customs won't think you've purchased the items overseas.

Returning **U.S. citizens** who have been away for 48 hours or more are allowed to bring back, once every 30 days, $400 worth of merchandise duty-free. You'll be charged a flat rate of 10% duty on the next $1,000 worth of purchases. Be sure to have your receipts handy. On gifts, the duty-free limit is $100. You cannot bring fresh foodstuffs into the United States; tinned foods, however, are allowed. For more information, contact the **U.S. Customs Service,** 1301 Constitution Ave., P.O. Box 7407, Washington, DC 20044 (✆ **202/ 927-6724;** www.customs.ustreas.gov/ travel/kbygo.htm), and request the free pamphlet *Know Before You Go.*

U.K. citizens returning from a non-EC country such as Bermuda (its colony status does not affect these limits) have a customs allowance of: 200 cigarettes; 50 cigars; 250g of smoking tobacco; 2 liters of still table wine; 1 liter of spirits or strong liqueurs (over 22% volume); 2 liters of fortified wine, sparkling wine or other liqueurs; 60cc (ml) perfume; 250cc (ml) of toilet water; and £145 worth of all other goods, including gifts and souvenirs. People under 17 cannot have the tobacco or alcohol allowance. For more information, contact HM Customs & Excise, Passenger Enquiry Point, 2nd Floor Wayfarer House, Great South West Road, Feltham, Middlesex, TW14 8NP (✆ **020/ 8910-3744;** from outside the U.K., 44/181-910-3744; www.open.gov.uk).

For a clear summary of **Canadian** rules, request the booklet *I Declare* from **Revenue Canada,** 2265 St. Laurent Blvd., Ottawa, ON K1G 4KE (✆ **613/636-5064**). Canada allows its citizens a $750 exemption, and you're allowed to bring back duty-free 200 cigarettes, 2.2 pounds of tobacco, 40 imperial ounces of liquor, and 50 cigars. In addition, you may mail up to Can$60 worth of gifts per day to Canada from abroad, provided they're unsolicited and don't contain alcohol or tobacco (write on the package "Unsolicited gift, under $60 value"). All valuables should be declared on the Y-38 form before departure from Canada, including serial numbers of valuables you already own, such as expensive foreign cameras. *Note:* The $750 exemption can be used only once a year and only after an absence of 7 days.

The duty-free allowance in **Australia** is A$400 or, for those under 18, A$200. Personal property mailed back from Bermuda should be marked "Australian goods returned" to avoid payment of duty. Upon returning to Australia, citizens can bring in 250 cigarettes or 250 grams of loose tobacco, and 1,125ml of alcohol. If you're returning with valuable goods you already own, such as foreign-made cameras, you should file form B263. A helpful brochure, available from Australian consulates or Customs offices, is *Know Before You Go.* For more information, contact **Australian Customs Services,** GPO Box 8, Sydney NSW 2001 (© **02/9213-2000**).

The duty-free allowance for **New Zealand** is NZ$700. Citizens over 17 can bring in 200 cigarettes, 50 cigars, or 250 grams of tobacco (or a mixture of all three if their combined weight doesn't exceed 250g); plus 4.5 liters of wine and beer, or 1.125 liters of liquor. New Zealand currency does not carry import or export restrictions. Fill out a certificate of export, listing the valuables you are taking out of the country; that way, you can bring them back without paying duty. A free pamphlet available at New Zealand consulates and Customs offices, *New Zealand Customs Guide for Travellers, Notice no. 4,* answers most questions. For more information, contact New Zealand Customs, 50 Anzac Ave., P.O. Box 29, Auckland (© **09/359-6655**).

3 Money

WHAT YOUR TRIP WILL COST

Time is money, and because Bermuda is less than 2 hours from most cities on the U.S. East Coast, the savings begin even before you land on the island. A 4-day, 3-night vacation in Bermuda can actually include 4 days of vacation for the price of 3 nights' accommodations. An 8:30am flight from New York gets you to Bermuda in time for lunch, with the whole afternoon to play.

The variety of accommodations—there are luxury resort hotels, small hotels, intimate guesthouses, and cottage colonies—allows visitors to indulge their preferences and tastes regardless of budget.

Hotel costs also depend on what time of year you travel. If you're seeking major discounts—sometimes as much as 60% off high-season rates—try visiting during the off-season. (For more information, see "When to Go," below.) Off-season rates, which we've listed in this guide, are a bonanza for cost-conscious travelers—though you're not guaranteed that it'll be warm enough to truly enjoy the beach.

Travel agents sometimes offer special packages, which can represent a substantial savings over regular hotel rates for families, golfers, tennis players, honeymooners, and others; for more information, see "Package Deals," below.

Dining out is an expensive undertaking. In the top places, you can end up spending as much as $80 per person for a meal, excluding wine. Even moderate to expensive restaurants charge $25 to $50 per person. Any dinner under $25 per person is considered inexpensive. You might want to investigate the package plans that most of the large resorts offer, which include meals. For details on meal plans, see "Rates & Reservation Policies" in chapter 4, "Accommodations." Other ways to reduce dining costs are to pack a picnic lunch, or to have your main meal in the middle of the day, at a pub. To cut costs even more, families and others planning to stay for a week or more might opt for a housekeeping unit (efficiencies and apartments are available), a cottage with a kitchenette, or even a condominium (some are rented like time-share units).

In figuring your budget, be sure to consider transportation costs. Getting around the island isn't always easy, and because rental cars are not available, you'll have to rely on local transportation. With the exception of taxis, which are very expensive, public transportation is efficient and inexpensive. Options include the simple and comprehensive bus system, ferries, and bicycle or moped rentals; see "Getting Around," in chapter 3, "Getting to

What Things Cost in Bermuda	BD $/US $
15-minute taxi ride	14.00
Ferry from Hamilton to Ireland Island	3.75
Local telephone call	0.25
Double room at Elbow Beach Hotel (expensive)	435.00
Double room at Rosemont (moderate)	160.00
Double room at Salt Kettle House (inexpensive)	104.00
Lunch for one at Fourways Inn (expensive)	18.00
Lunch for one at Wickets Brasserie & Cricket Club (inexpensive)	15.00
Dinner for one at Ascots (expensive)	50.00
Dinner for one at La Trattoria (moderate)	27.50
Dinner for one at Chopsticks Restaurant (inexpensive)	18.00
Bottle of beer in a bar	5.00
Coca-Cola in a cafe	3.00
Cup of coffee in a cafe	2.00
Glass of planter's punch in a restaurant	6.00
Roll of ASA 100 color film, 36 exposures	8.85
Admission to Bermuda Maritime Museum	9.00

Know Bermuda," for complete details. Once you reach a particular parish, many attractions are accessible on foot.

In general, athletic and cultural activities—such as tennis, riding, guided tours, museums, and attractions—are good values. Golfers will find that greens fees are comparable to or less than fees at other destinations.

If you find the idea of unknown or extra costs intimidating, you might consider a package tour, where everything will be arranged for you. That way, you'll know the cost of your vacation before leaving home. For more information, see "Package Deals," below.

CURRENCY

Legal tender is the Bermuda dollar (BD$), which is divided into 100 cents. It's pegged through gold to the U.S. dollar on an equal basis—BD$1 equals US$1.

U.S. currency is generally accepted in shops, restaurants, and hotels. Currency from the United Kingdom and other foreign countries is usually not accepted, but can be easily exchanged for Bermuda dollars at banks and hotels.

ATMS

ATMs are linked to a national network that most likely includes your bank at home. **Cirrus** (©800/424-7787; www.mastercard.com) and **Plus** (© 800/843-7587; www.visa.com) are the two most popular networks; check the back of your ATM card to see which network your bank belongs to. Use the 800 numbers to locate ATMs in Bermuda.

Before you leave, ask your bank for a list of overseas ATMs. Be sure to check the daily withdrawal limit before you depart, and ask whether you need a new personal ID number.

The Bermuda Dollar, the U.S. Dollar & the British Pound

The Bermuda Dollar is tied at a constant rate to the U.S. dollar, and is valued on an equal basis: BD$1=US$1. At the time of this writing, the British pound trades at an average of US$1.50 = £1. The chart below gives a rough approximation of conversion rates you're likely to find at the time of your trip. Rates fluctuate, so be sure to confirm the rate before you make any serious transactions.

U.S.$	UK £	U.S.$	UK £
0.25	0.17	15.00	9.99
0.50	0.33	20.00	13.32
0.75	0.50	25.00	16.65
1.00	0.67	50.00	33.30
2.00	1.33	75.00	49.95
3.00	2.00	100.00	66.60
4.00	2.66	150.00	99.90
5.00	3.33	200.00	133.20
6.00	4.00	250.00	166.50
7.00	4.66	300.00	199.80
8.00	5.33	350.00	233.10
9.00	5.99	400.00	266.40
10.00	6.66	500.00	333.00

CREDIT CARDS

Credit cards are invaluable when traveling. They are a safe way to carry money and provide a convenient record of all your expenses. You can also make cash advances against your credit cards at any bank (though you'll start paying hefty interest on the advance the moment you receive the cash, and you won't receive frequent-flyer miles on an airline credit card). At most banks, you don't even need to go to a teller; you can get a cash advance at the ATM if you know your personal identification number, or PIN. (If you've forgotten your PIN or didn't even know you had one, call the phone number on the back of your credit card well before you leave home and ask the bank to send it to you. It usually takes 5–7 business days, though some banks will provide the number over the phone if you tell them your mother's maiden name or pass some other security clearance.)

Almost every credit card company has an emergency toll-free number that you can call if your wallet or purse is stolen. The company may be able to wire you a cash advance against your credit card immediately; and in many places, companies can deliver an emergency credit card in a day or two. The issuing bank's emergency number is usually on the back of the credit card—though of course that doesn't help you much if the card was stolen. The toll-free information directory (© 800/555-1212) can provide the number. Citicorp Visa's U.S. emergency number is © 800/336-8472. American Express cardholders and traveler's check holders should call © 800/221-7282 for all money emergencies. MasterCard holders should call © 800/307-7309. The good news? There's not much theft on Bermuda.

Odds are that if your wallet is gone, the police won't be able to recover it for you. However, after you realize that it's gone and you cancel your credit cards, it is still worth informing them. Your credit card company or insurer may require a police report number.

TRAVELER'S CHECKS

Traveler's checks are something of an anachronism from the days before the ATM made cash accessible at any time. The only sound alternative to traveling with dangerously large amounts of cash, traveler's checks were as reliably accepted as currency, unlike personal checks, but could be replaced if lost or stolen, unlike cash.

These days, traveler's checks seem less necessary since ATMs abroad make it easy to access your bank account just as you would at home. But some travelers still prefer the security offered by traveler's checks.

You can get traveler's checks at almost any bank. **American Express** offers denominations of $10, $20, $50, $100, $500, and $1,000. You'll pay a service charge ranging from 1 to 4% of your total purchase. You can also get American Express traveler's checks over the phone by calling ℂ **800/221-7282;** by using this number, Amex gold and platinum cardholders are exempt from the 1% fee. AAA members can obtain checks without a fee at most AAA offices. **Visa** offers traveler's checks at Citibank locations nationwide, as well as several other banks. The service charge is 1.5 to 2%; checks come in denominations of $20, $50, $100, $500, and $1,000. **MasterCard** also offers traveler's checks. Call ℂ **800/223-9920** for a location near you. If you opt to carry traveler's checks, be sure to keep a record of their serial numbers—separate from the checks—so that you're ensured a refund in the event of an emergency.

4 When to Go

THE WEATHER

A semitropical island, Bermuda enjoys a mild climate; the term "Bermuda high" has come to mean sunny days and clear skies. The Gulf Stream, which flows between the island and North America, keeps the climate temperate. There's no rainy season and no typical month of excess rain. Showers may be heavy at times, but the skies clear quickly.

Being farther north in the Atlantic than the Bahamas, Bermuda is much cooler in winter. Springlike temperatures prevail from mid-December to late March, with the average temperature ranging from the low 60s to 70°F. Unless it rains, winter is fine for golf and tennis but not for swimming; it can be downright cool, and you may even need a sweater or a jacket. Water temperatures in winter are somewhat like the air temperature, ranging from

about 66°F in January to 75°F until spring. Scuba divers and snorkelers will find the Caribbean waters appreciably warmer in winter. From mid-November to mid-December and from late March to April, be prepared for spring or summer weather.

In summer, the temperature rarely rises above 85°F. There's nearly always a cool breeze in the evening, but some hotels have air-conditioning. And local water temperatures can be as high as 86°F—warmer than many inshore and offshore Caribbean waters.

As a result, Bermuda's off-season is the exact opposite of that in the Caribbean. It begins in December and lasts until about March 1. In general, hotels offer low-season rates—with discounts ranging from 20% to 60%—in winter. This is the time to go if you're traveling on a tight budget.

During autumn and winter, many hotels also offer discounted package deals, and some hotels even close for a couple of weeks or months.

A look at the official chart on temperature and rainfall will give you a general idea of what to expect during your visit.

Bermuda's Average Daytime Temperatures & Rainfall

	Jan	Feb	Mar	Apr	May	June	July	Aug	Sept	Oct	Nov	Dec
Temp. (°F)	65	64	64	65	70	75	79	80	79	75	69	65
Temp. (°C)	19	18	18	19	21	24	30	27	30	24	21	19
Rainfall (inches)	4	5	4.6	3	3.9	5.2	4	5.3	5.3	6	4.5	3.9

THE HURRICANE SEASON

This curse of the Caribbean, the Bahamas, and Bermuda lasts officially from June to November, but don't panic—more tropical storms pound the U.S. mainland than Bermuda. It's also less frequently hit than islands in the Caribbean. Satellite forecasts are generally able to give adequate warning of any really dangerous weather.

If you're concerned, you can call the nearest branch of the National Weather Service (it's listed under the U.S. Department of Commerce in the phone book). Radio and TV weather reports from the National Hurricane Center in Coral Gables, Florida, will also keep you posted.

To receive automated information about climate conditions in Bermuda, you can also contact the information service associated with the Weather Channel. It costs 95¢ per query and works like this: Dial ℂ **800/ WEATHER** and listen to the recorded announcement. When you're prompted, enter the account number of a valid Visa or MasterCard. After the card is approved, punch in the name of any of 1,000 cities worldwide whose weather is monitored by the Weather Channel—in this case, Hamilton.

HOLIDAYS

Bermuda observes the following public holidays: New Year's Day (Jan 1), Good Friday, Easter, Bermuda Day (May 24), the Queen's Birthday (first or second Mon in June), Cup Match Days (cricket; Thurs and Fri preceding first Mon in Aug), Labor Day (first Mon in Sept), Christmas Day (Dec 25), and Boxing Day (Dec 26). Public holidays that fall on a Saturday or Sunday are usually celebrated the following Monday.

BERMUDA CALENDAR OF EVENTS

January & February

Bermuda Festival. Throughout January and February, island-wide events abound. They include golf and tennis invitationals, an international marathon, a dog show, open house and garden tours, and the Bermuda Festival, the 6-week International Festival of the Performing Arts, held in Hamilton. It features drama, dance, jazz, classical, and popular music as well as other entertainment by the best international artists. Some tickets for the festival are reserved until 48 hours before curtain time for visitors. For details and a schedule for the 2001 festival, contact the **Bermuda Festival,** P.O. Box HM 297, Hamilton HM AX, Bermuda (ℂ **441/295-1291;** www.bermudafestival.com).

The Bermuda International Marathon, with international and local runners, takes place the third weekend in January. For further information and entry forms,

(Fun Fact The Devil's Triangle: Real or Hoax

In response to a flood of concern from travelers about the possibility of getting sucked into the so-called Bermuda Triangle and disappearing forever, the U.S. Board of Geographic Names has recently issued an official statement: "We do not recognize the Bermuda Triangle as an official name and do not maintain an official file on the area. The 'Bermuda or Devil's Triangle' is an imaginary area located off the southeastern Atlantic coast of the United States, which is noted for a high incidence of unexplained losses of ships, small boats, and aircraft. The apexes of the triangle are generally accepted to be Bermuda, Miami, and San Juan. In the past, extensive but futile Coast Guard searches prompted by search and rescue cases such as the disappearances of an entire squadron of TBM Avengers shortly after take-off from Fort Lauderdale, or the traceless sinking of Marine Sulphur Queen in the Florida Straits, have lent credence to the popular belief in the mystery and the supernatural qualities of the Bermuda Triangle."

---

contact the **International Race Weekend Committee,** Bermuda Track and Field Association, P.O. Box DV 397, Devonshire DV BX, Bermuda (© **441/236-6086;** www.bermudatrackfield.com).

March

Bermuda College Weeks. At least 10,000 students flock here every year—so it may not be the best time for the rest of you to come. These weeks began as Rugby Weeks in 1933, when teams from Ivy League schools came to compete against British or Bermudian teams. "Where the boys are," to borrow the popular song title, led to "where the girls are," and a tradition was born.

The Department of Tourism issues a College Week Courtesy Card to those who have a valid college ID card. This becomes a passport to a week of free island-wide beach parties, lunches, boat cruises, dances, and entertainment, courtesy of the Bermudian government. Dates coincide with U.S. college vacations. Contact a Bermuda Department of Tourism office (see "Visitor Information," above) to obtain a list of events.

Home and Garden Tours. Each spring the Garden Club of Bermuda lays out the welcome mat at a number of private homes and gardens. A different set of houses, all conveniently located in the same parish, is open every Wednesday during this event. The program usually includes a total of 20 homes, many of them dating from the 17th and 18th centuries. The tourist office provides a complete listing of homes and viewing schedules. End of March to mid-May.

April

Beating Retreat Ceremony. The Bermuda Regiment and massed pipes and drums create an event that combines a marching band concert and a parade. The ceremony's roots are in the 17th century, when British soldiers were stationed on the island and a roll of drums called them back to their garrisons at nightfall. It's presented once or twice per month, rotating among Hamilton, St. George, and the Royal Naval Dockyard. The tourist office supplies exact times and schedules.

Peppercorn Ceremony. His Excellency the governor collects the annual rent of one peppercorn for use of the island's Old State House in St. George. Mid- to late April. For information and the exact date, call ✆ **800/223-6106.**

Agriculture Exhibit. Held over 3 days in late April at the Botanical Gardens in Paget, this event is a celebration of Bermuda's agrarian and horticultural bounty. In addition to prize-winning produce, the Agriculture Exhibit provides a showcase for local arts and crafts. For more information, contact the **Department of Agriculture and Fisheries,** P.O. Box HM 834, Hamilton HM BX, Bermuda (✆ **441/236-4201**), or the **Bermuda Department of Tourism** (✆ **800/223-6106**).

International Race Week. Every year during late April and early May, this yachting event pits equivalent vessels from seven classes of sailing craft against one another. Yachting enthusiasts around the world follow the knockout, elimination-style event with avid interest. The Marion to Bermuda race (see below) takes place in June.

Other sailing contests are scheduled for alternate years. The world's most famous wind-driven contest, the Newport-to-Bermuda Race, falls next in June 2002. The record to date: a 56-hour transit. The event is supplemented by October's Match Racing, when pairs of identical sailing vessels, staffed by a rotating roster of teams from throughout the world, compete in elimination-style contests.

Unfortunately for spectators, the finish lines for the island's sailing races usually lie several miles offshore. Afterward, boats often are moored in Hamilton Harbour; any vantage point on the harbor is good for watching the boats come in.

Even better: Head for any of Hamilton's harbor-front pubs, where racing crowds celebrate their wins (or justify their losses) over pints of ale.

For information on all sailing events held off the coast of Bermuda, contact the **Sailing Secretary,** Royal Bermuda Yacht Club, P.O. Box HM 894, Hamilton HM DX, Bermuda (✆ **441/295-2214**), or (for races originating off the U.S. coast) the **New York Yacht Club,** 37 W. 44th St., New York, NY 10036 (✆ **212/382-1000**).

May

Bermuda Heritage Month. Culminates on **Bermuda Day,** May 24, a public holiday that's Bermuda's equivalent of Independence Day. Bermuda Day is punctuated with parades through downtown Hamilton, dinghy and cycling races, and the Bermuda Half-Day Marathon (open only to island residents). In addition to the Office of Tourism, any hotel in town can fill you in on the events planned for the year's biggest political celebration.

June

Queen's Birthday (first or second Mon in June). Celebrated by a parade down Front Street in Hamilton.

Marion to Bermuda Race. See the entry for "International Race Week," under April, above. For more information, call ✆ **441/236-2250.**

Marine Science Day. Lectures, hands-on demonstrations, and displays for adults and children, by the **Bermuda Biological Station.** The date varies, but is usually mid-month; call ✆ **441/297-1880** for the schedule and more information.

August

Cup Match and Somers Days. Also known as the Cup Match Cricket Festival, this annual event celebrates the year's bounty with Bermuda's most illustrious cricket match. It's often compared to American Thanksgiving. Cricketers from the East End (St. George's Cricket Club) play off against those from the West End (Somerset Cricket Club), with lots of attendant British-derived protocol and hoopla. Tickets cost about $10; they're available at the gate on match day. The event is held on Thursday and Friday before the first Monday in August. For more information, call ℰ **800/223-6106.**

September

Labor Day. This public holiday features a host of activities; it's also the ideal time for a picnic. The high point is a parade from Union Square in Hamilton Bernard Park. First Monday in September.

October

Match Racing. For details on this international sailing event, see the entry for "International Race Week," under April, above.

November

The Opening of Parliament. Traditional ceremony and military guard of honor connected with the opening of Parliament by His Excellency the governor as the Queen's personal representative. In anticipation of the entry of MPs into Parliament at 11am, crowds begin gathering outside the Cabinet Building around 9:30 or 10am. Spectators traditionally include lots of schoolchildren being trained in civic protocol, as well as nostalgia buffs out for a whiff of British-style pomp. November 6.

World Rugby Classic. Former international rugby players compete with Bermudians at the Bermuda National Sports Club(ℰ **441/236-6994**). Mid-November.

Guy Fawkes Day. Small annual celebration with a mini-fair. It starts with the traditional burning of the Guy Fawkes effigy at the Keepyard of the Bermuda Maritime Museum, Royal Naval Dockyard, at 4:30pm. November 7.

Remembrance Day. Bermudian police, British and U.S. military units, Bermudians, and veterans' organizations participate in a small parade. November 11.

Invitation Tennis Weeks. More than 100 visiting players vie with Bermudians during 2 weeks of matches. Unlike at Wimbledon—this event's role model—virtually everyone buys tickets at the gate. For information, contact the **Bermuda Lawn Tennis Association,** P.O. Box HM 341, Hamilton HM BX, Bermuda (ℰ **441/296-0834**).

December

Bermuda Goodwill Tournament. Pro-amateur foursomes from international golf clubs play more than 72 holes on four of Bermuda's eight courses. Anyone who wants to compete must pass the sponsors' stringent requirements and may appear only by invitation. Spectators are welcome to watch from the sidelines free. For more information, contact the **Bermuda Goodwill Golf Tournament,** P.O. Box WK 127, Warwick WK BX, Bermuda (ℰ **441/238-3118**). Early December.

5 Planning an Island Wedding or Honeymoon

GETTING MARRIED ON BERMUDA

Couples who would like to get married on Bermuda must file a "Notice of Intended Marriage" with the Registry General, accompanied by a fee of $205 (in the form of a bank draft or money order, not a personal check). Make out the draft to "The Accountant General" and mail or deliver it in person to the **Registry General,** Government Administration Building, 30 Parliament St., Hamilton HM 12, Bermuda (© **441/297-7709**). Bermuda Department of Tourism offices in Atlanta, Boston, Chicago, and New York (see "Visitor Information," above) distribute "Notice of Intended Marriage" forms. If either of the prospective marriage partners has been married before, that person must attach a photocopy of the final divorce decree to the "Notice of Intended Marriage."

Once the "Notice of Intended Marriage" is received, it will be published, including names and addresses, in any two of the island's newspapers. Assuming that there is no formal objection, the registry will issue the license 15 days after receiving the notice. Airmailing your completed notice to Bermuda takes 6 to 10 days, so plan accordingly. The marriage license will be valid for 3 months.

HIRING A WEDDING CONSULTANT

Many hotels can help make wedding arrangements—reserving the church and clergy, hiring a horse and buggy, ordering the wedding cake, and securing a photographer. Bermuda weddings range from simple ceremonies on the beach to large-scale extravaganzas at the Botanical Gardens. Other sites include churches and yachts.

Wedding consultants can discuss your options with you and arrange all the details. **The Wedding Salon,** 51 Reid St., P.O. Box HM 2085, Hamilton HM HX, Bermuda (© **441/295-6771;** fax 441/292-2955; e-mail: barbara.whitecross@gte.net), operates its planning office in North Carolina. After a contractual agreement is made, the office puts customers in contact with the Bermuda consultant. **The Bridal Suite,** Parkside Building, 3 Park Rd., Suite 7, Hamilton HM 09, Bermuda (© **888/253-5585,** or 441/292-2025; fax 441/296-2070; e-mail: wedding@ibl.bm), arranges packages that cost from $1,000 to as much as $15,000.

Some hotels—including the Belmont Hotel Golf & Country Club, the Elbow Beach Hotel, the Sonesta Beach Resort, and both of the Fairmont Princess hotels—will arrange weddings; see chapter 4, "Accommodations," for contact information. If you're staying at a small hotel, it's better to go through a wedding consultant.

HONEYMOONING ON BERMUDA

There are good reasons Bermuda attracts more than 23,000 honeymooners and second honeymooners each year: It offers an ideal environment for couples, whether they prefer an active schedule or a relaxing one. Many of Bermuda's hotels, from luxurious resorts to intimate cottage colonies, offer honeymoon packages. Typically, these include airfare, accommodations, meal plans, champagne upon arrival, flowers in your room, and discounts at local attractions and

---

(Fun Fact **Cut the Cake**

Custom dictates that Bermudians have two wedding cakes: a plain pound cake covered with gold leaf for the groom, and a tiered fruit cake covered with silver leaf and topped with a miniature cedar tree for the bride. The tiny tree is planted on the day of the wedding to symbolize the hope that the marriage will grow and mature like the tree. The rest of the first tier of the bride's cake is frozen until the christening of the first child.

restaurants. See "The Best Resorts for Honeymooners (& Other Lovers)," in chapter 1, "The Best of Bermuda," for the best packages. For other options, consult your travel agent or call the hotels listed in chapter 4 directly and inquire about packages.

6 Health & Insurance

STAYING HEALTHY

If you need medical attention while on Bermuda, finding a doctor or getting a prescription filled is no real problem. See "Drugstores" under "Fast Facts: Bermuda," in chapter 3, "Getting to Know Bermuda," for addresses of pharmacies. In an emergency, call **King Edward VII Hospital,** 7 Point Finger Rd., Paget Parish (© 441/236-2345), and ask for the emergency department. For less serious medical problems, ask someone at your hotel for a recommendation.

Limit your exposure to the sun, especially between the hours of 11am to 2pm and during the first few days of your trip. Use a sunscreen with a high protection factor and apply it liberally. Remember that children need more protection than adults do.

If you worry about getting sick away from home, you may want to consider **medical travel insurance** (see the section on travel insurance under "Insurance," below). In most cases, however, your existing health plan will provide all the coverage you need. Be sure to carry your identification card in your wallet.

If you suffer from a chronic illness, consult your doctor before your departure. For conditions like epilepsy, diabetes, or heart problems, wear a **Medic Alert Identification Tag** (© 800/825-3785; www.medicalert.org), which alerts doctors to your condition and gives them access to your records through Medic Alert's 24-hour hot line. Membership is $35, plus a $15 annual fee.

Pack prescription medications in your carry-on luggage in their original labeled vials. Carry written prescriptions in generic, not brand-name, form Also bring along copies of your prescriptions in case you lose your pills or run out.

If you wear contact lenses, pack an extra pair in case you lose one.

The **International Association for Medical Assistance to Travelers** (© **716/754-4883** or 519/836-0102; www.sentex.net/~iamat) offers tips on travel and health concerns abroad.

INSURANCE

There are three kinds of travel insurance: trip-cancellation, medical, and lost luggage coverage. **Trip-cancellation insurance** is a good idea if you have paid a large portion of your vacation expenses up front—say, by paying for a package or cruise. Some trip-cancellation insurance covers you if, for example, the tour operator you booked through goes out of business. Other policies cover you if you can't go on a trip due to a serious illness or death in your family. Make sure you read the fine print and know what you're getting. The other two types of insurance don't make sense for most travelers. Rule number one: Check your existing policies before you buy any additional coverage.

Your existing health insurance should cover you if you get sick while on vacation. If you belong to an HMO, you should check to see whether you are fully covered when away from home. If you need hospital treatment, most health insurance plans and HMOs will cover out-of-country hospital visits and procedures, at least to some extent. However, most make you pay the bills up front at the time of care, and issue a refund after you've returned and filed all the paperwork. Members of **Blue Cross/Blue**

Shield can now use their cards at select hospitals in most major cities worldwide; call © **800/810-BLUE** or check www.bluecares.com for a list of hospitals. For independent travel health-insurance providers, see below. Your homeowner's insurance should cover stolen luggage. The airlines are responsible for $9.07 per pound on international flights if they lose your luggage, with a maximum of $634.90 per bag; for an additional $2 you can purchase another $100 per bag up to a maximum of $5,000. If you plan to carry anything more valuable than that, keep it in your carry-on bag.

The differences between travel assistance and insurance are often blurred, but in general the former offers on-the-spot assistance and 24-hour hot lines (mostly oriented toward medical problems), while the latter reimburses you for travel problems (medical, travel, or otherwise) after you have filed the paperwork. The coverage you should consider depends on how much protection your existing health insurance or other policies already includes. Some credit- and charge-card companies may insure you against travel accidents if you buy plane, train, or bus tickets with their cards. Before purchasing additional insurance, read your policies and agreements carefully. Call your insurers or credit- or charge-card companies if you have questions.

Some credit cards (American Express and certain gold and platinum Visa and MasterCards, for example) offer automatic flight insurance against death or dismemberment in case of an airplane crash.

If you do require additional insurance, try one of the companies listed below. But don't pay for more than you need. For example, if you need only trip-cancellation insurance, don't buy coverage for lost or stolen property. Trip-cancellation insurance costs approximately 6% to 8% of the total value of your vacation. Among the reputable issuers of travel insurance are: **Access America,** 6600 W. Broad St., Richmond, VA 23230 (© **800/284-8300); Healthcare Abroad (MEDEX),** c/o Wallach & Co., P.O. Box 480 (107 W. Federal St.), Middleburg, VA 20118-0480 (© **800/237-6615** or 540/687-3166; www.wallach.com); **Travelex,** 11717 Burt St., Suite 202, Omaha, NE 68175 (© **800/228-9792;** www.travelex-insurance.com); **Travel Guard International,** 1145 Clark St., Stevens Point, WI 54481 (© **800/826-1300** or 715/345-0505; www.noelgroup.com), and **Travel Insured International, Inc.,** P.O. Box 280568, East Hartford, CT 06128-0568 (© **800/243-3174** in the U.S. or 860/528-7663 outside the U.S., between 7:45am and 7pm EST); www.travelinsured.com).

Medicare only covers U.S. citizens traveling in Mexico and Canada. For Blue Cross/Blue Shield coverage abroad, see "Health Insurance," above. Companies specializing in accident and medical care include: **Travel Assistance International** by Worldwide Assistance Services, Inc., 9200 Keystone Crossing, Suite 300, Indianapolis, IN 46240 (© **800/335-0611** in the U.S.,

---

Tips Daily Life in Bermuda

Savvy locals will give you some tips for survival. First, know that ATMs only dispense Bermuda dollars, and that buses only accept coins. Also, don't get caught in Hamilton's rush-hour traffic, which is Monday to Friday 8:30 to 9am and 5 to 6pm.

or 317/575-2652; www.specialtyrisk.com). It offers on-the-spot medical payment coverage up to $15,000, or $60,000 for emergency care practically anywhere in the world as well as unlimited medical evacuation/repatriation coverage back to the United States if necessary. For an additional fee you can be covered for trip cancellation/ disruption, lost/delayed luggage, and accidental death and dismemberment. Fees are based on the length of your trip and the coverage you select. Prices begin at $65 per person ($95 per family) for a 1- to 8-day trip. The **Divers Alert Network** (© **800/446-2671** or 919/684-2948) insures scuba divers.

7 Tips for Travelers with Special Needs

FOR TRAVELERS WITH DISABILITIES

Bermuda is not a great place for persons with disabilities not planning to stay on site at a resort. Getting around is a bit difficult even for the agile, who must rely on motorbikes. It is difficult to walk with a cane outside the town of St. George and City of Hamilton, because most roads don't have sidewalks or adequate curbs. When two vehicles pass, you are crowded off the road.

Taking taxis to everything you want to see can be a very expensive undertaking. The public buses are not geared for passengers in wheelchairs. However, you can ask your hotel to check on the availability of volunteer buses operated by the Bermuda Physically Handicapped Association (no phone). It occasionally runs buses with hydraulic lifts. You can also call the tourist office and request a schedule for such transportation; make arrangements as far in advance as possible.

Before you go, you can seek information from the Bermuda chapter of the Society for the Advancement of Travel for the Handicapped (see below). Visitors planning to bring a guide dog must obtain a permit in advance from any Bermuda Department of Tourism office.

The most accessible hotels in Bermuda are Elbow Beach Hotel, the Sonesta Beach Resort, the Fairmont Hamilton Princess, and The Fairmont Southampton Princess.

A World of Options, a 658-page book of resources for travelers with disabilities, covers everything from biking trips to scuba outfitters. It costs $45 ($30 for members) and is available from **Mobility International USA,** P.O. Box 10767, Eugene, OR 97440 (© **541/343-1284,** voice and TDD; www.miusa.org). Annual membership is $35, which includes the quarterly newsletter *Over the Rainbow.* **Twin Peaks Press,** P.O. Box 129, Vancouver, WA 98666 (© **360/694-2462**), publishes travel-related books for people with disabilities.

The **Moss Rehab Hospital** (© **215/456-9600**) has provided friendly, helpful phone advice and referrals to travelers with disabilities for years through its **Travel Information Service** (© **215/456-9603;** www.mossresourcenet.org).

You can join The **Society for the Advancement of Travel for the Handicapped (SATH)**, 347 Fifth Ave. Suite 610, New York, NY 10016 (© **212/447-7284;** fax 212/725-8253; www.sath.org), for $45 annually, $30 for seniors and students. Membership includes access to the society's vast network of connections in the travel industry. SATH provides information sheets on travel destinations, and referrals to tour operators that specialize in traveling with disabilities. The quarterly magazine *Open World for Disability and Mature Travel,* is full of good information and resources. A year's subscription is $13 ($21 outside the U.S.).

Travelers with disabilities may also want to consider joining a tour that caters specifically to them. One of the best operators is **Flying Wheels Travel,** 143 W. Bridge (P.O. Box 382), Owatonna, MN 55060 (✆ **800/535-6790**). It offers escorted tours and cruises, with an emphasis on sports, as well as private tours in minivans with lifts.

You can obtain a copy of *Air Transportation of Handicapped Persons* by writing to Free Advisory Circular No. AC12032, Distribution Unit, U.S. Department of Transportation, Publications Division, M-4332, Washington, DC 20590.

Vision-impaired travelers should contact the **American Foundation for the Blind,** 11 Penn Plaza, Suite 300, New York, NY 10001 (✆ **800/232-5463**), for information on traveling with seeing-eye dogs.

IN THE UNITED KINGDOM

The Royal Association for Disability and Rehabilitation (RADAR), Unit 12, City Forum, 250 City Rd., London EC1V 8AF (✆ **02/7250-3222;** fax 0171/250-0212; www.radar.org. uk), publishes holiday "fact packs" that sell for £2 each or £5 for a set of all three. The first provides general information, including planning and booking a holiday, insurance, finances, and useful organization and holiday providers. The second outlines transport and equipment, transportation available when going abroad, and equipment for rent. The third deals with specialized accommodations.

FOR GAY & LESBIAN TRAVELERS

Think twice before planning a holiday on Bermuda. Although many gays live in and visit Bermuda, the colony has rather repressive antihomosexual laws. Relations between homosexuals, even between consenting adults, are subject to criminal sanctions and a maximum sentence of 10 years in prison. Even attempted contacts among homosexuals, at least according to the law, can be punished with up to 5 years in prison.

If you want really happening gay beaches, bars, or clubs, consider heading to South Miami Beach, Key West, Puerto Rico, or the U.S. Virgin Islands.

FOR SENIORS

Don't be shy about asking for discounts, but always carry identification, such as a driver's license, that shows your date of birth. Also, mention the fact that you're a senior citizen when you first make your travel reservations. For example, many hotels offer discounts. Bermuda's buses do not offer discounted fares to seniors.

The **American Association of Retired Persons (AARP),** 601 E St., NW, Washington, DC 20049 (✆ **800/424-3410** or 202/434AARP; www.aarp.org) is the best U.S. organization for seniors. It offers discounts on car rentals and hotels.

The nonprofit **National Council of Senior Citizens,** 8403 Colesville Rd., Suite 1200, Silver Spring, MD 20910 (✆ **301/578-8800**), offers a bimonthly newsletter (partly devoted to travel tips) and discounts on hotel and auto rentals. Annual dues are $13 per person or couple.

Mature Outlook, P.O. Box 9390, Des Moines, IA 50306 (✆ **800/336-6330**), began as a travel organization for people over 50, though it now caters to those of all ages. Members receive a bimonthly magazine. Annual membership is $39.95, which entitles members to discounts and, often, free coupons for discounted merchandise from Sears.

Another helpful publication is *101 Tips for the Mature Traveler,* available from Grand Circle Travel, 347 Congress St., Suite 3A, Boston, MA 02210 (✆ **800/221-2610** or 617/350-7500; fax 617/346-6700).

Grand Circle Travel is also one of the hundreds of travel agencies specializing in vacations for seniors. Many of these packages, however, are of the tour-bus variety, with free trips thrown in for those who organize groups of 10 or more. Seniors seeking more independent travel should probably consult a regular travel agent. **SAGA International Holidays,** 222 Berkeley St., Boston, MA 02116 (© **800/343-0273**), offers inclusive tours and cruises for those 50 and older. SAGA also sponsors the more substantial "Road Scholar Tours" (© **800/621-2151**), which are fun but with an educational bent.

Although the **specialty books** on the market focus on the U.S., three do provide good general advice and contacts for the savvy senior traveler. Thumb through *The 50+ Traveler's Guidebook* (St. Martin's Press), *The Seasoned Traveler* (Country Roads Press), or *Unbelievably Good Deals and Great Adventures That You Absolutely Can't Get Unless You're Over 50* (Contemporary Books). Also check your newsstand for the quarterly magazine *Travel 50 & Beyond.*

FOR FAMILIES

Bermuda is one of the best vacation destinations for the entire family. Toddlers can spend blissful hours in shallow seawater or pools constructed for them, and older children can enjoy boat rides, horseback riding, hiking, and snorkeling. Most resort hotels offer advice (including help with finding a baby-sitter), and many have play directors and supervised activities for various age groups.

Outside the town of St. George and City of Hamilton, walking with a baby stroller is difficult—most roads don't have sidewalks or adequate curbs.

Several books offer tips. Most concentrate on the U.S., but two— *Family Travel* (Lanier Publishing International) and *How to Take Great Trips with Your Kids* (The Harvard Common Press)—are full of good general advice that can apply to travel anywhere. Another reliable tome, with a worldwide focus, is *Adventuring with Children* (Foghorn Press).

Family Travel Times newsletter costs $40 (online only—www.family traveltimes.com), and it's updated every 2 weeks. Subscribers also can call in with travel questions but only on Wednesday from 10am to 1pm Eastern Standard Time. Contact Family Travel Times, 40 5th Ave., New York, NY 10011 (© **888/822-4322,** or 212/477-5524).

FOR STUDENTS

The Bermuda Department of Tourism offers Spring Break Programs for sports teams from the mainland, as well as Spring Break Arts Programs. Inquire with the tourism office for details.

8 Package Deals

Before you start your search for the lowest airfare, you may want to consider booking your flight as part of a package that includes accommodations. It's often possible to save serious money by going this route.

Package tours are not the same as escorted tours. They are simply a way to buy airfare and accommodations at the same time. For popular destinations like Bermuda, they are a smart way to go, because they save you a lot of money. In many cases, a package that includes airfare, hotel, and transportation to and from the airport costs less than the hotel alone would have, if you book it yourself. That's because tour operators buy packages in bulk and resell them to the public at a cost that drastically undercuts standard rates.

Packages vary widely. Some offer a better class of hotels than others. Some offer the same hotels for lower

A Timesaving Tip

Shopping around for the right package can be time-consuming. To speed up the process, contact **TourScan Inc.,** P.O. Box 2367, Darien, CT 06820 (© **800/962-2080** or 203/655-8091; fax 203/655-6689; www.tourscan.com). Its computerized list provides hotel and air package deals to Bermuda, The Bahamas, and the Caribbean. This organization usually has a range of offerings. Its twice-yearly *Island Vacation Catalog* contains complete details; the price ($4) is refunded if you book a tour. If you decide to take a tour, you can book it through TourScan or use any travel agent.

prices. Some offer flights on scheduled airlines, while others book charters. In some packages, your choice of accommodations and travel days may be limited. Some packages let you choose between escorted vacations and independent vacations; others allow you to add on a few excursions or escorted day trips (also at lower prices than you could locate on your own) without booking an entirely escorted tour. Each destination usually has one or two packages that are cheaper than the rest because they buy in even greater bulk. If you spend the time to shop around, you can save in the long run. Use the reviews in this guide to choose your hotel wisely.

The best place to start your search is the travel section of your local Sunday newspaper. Also check the ads in the back of national travel magazines like *Arthur Frommer's Budget Travel, Travel & Leisure, National Geographic Traveler,* and *Condé Nast Traveler.*

Liberty Travel (© **888/271-1584;** www.libertytravel.com) has many local branches nationwide. One of the

biggest packagers in the Northeast, Liberty usually has a full-page ad in Sunday papers. You won't get much in the way of service, but you will get a good deal. **American Express Vacations** (©**800/241-1700;** www.leisureweb.com) is another option. Check out its **Last Minute Travel Bargains** site, offered in conjunction with **Continental Airlines**(www.americanexpress.com/travel/lastminutetravel/default.asp), with deeply discounted vacation packages and reduced airfares that differ from the E-savers bargains that Continental e-mails weekly to subscribers.

Another good resource is the airlines themselves, which often package their flights with accommodations. Your options include **American Airlines FlyAway Vacations** (© **800/321-2121**), **Delta Dream Vacations** (© **800/872-7786**), and **US Airways Vacations** (© **800/455-0123**).

The biggest hotel chains and resorts also offer package deals. If you already know where you want to stay, call the resort and ask if it offers land-air packages.

9 Flying to Bermuda

From North America's East Coast, you can be in Bermuda in approximately 2 hours. From London, England, the trip takes about 7 hours.

American Airlines (© **800/433-7300;** www.aa.com) flies nonstop twice a day from New York's JFK Airport. Departures coincide with dozens

of connecting flights from elsewhere throughout North America.

Delta (© **800/241-4141;** www.delta.com) offers daily nonstop service from Boston and Atlanta. The Boston flight departs in the morning (around 9am). The Atlanta flight leaves around noon—late enough to allow connections from most of the other cities in Delta's vast network.

Continental Airlines (© 800/525-0280; www.flycontinental.com) offers daily nonstop service from New Jersey's Newark Airport.

US Airways (© 800/428-4322; www.usairways.com) offers nonstop flights from Philadelphia and Baltimore year-round, plus nonstop flights from New York (La Guardia) from November 6 to May 6. There's also a flight from Charlotte with a stopover in Philadelphia (but no change of plane).

Air Canada (© 800/776-3000 in the U.S., or 888/247-2262 in Canada; www.aircanada.ca) offers daily nonstop flights from Toronto, with frequent connections into Toronto from virtually every other city in Canada. The flight departs around 9am, permitting convenient connections from Montreal and Quebec City. The airline also offers a nonstop flight from Halifax on Saturday at noon.

The airline of choice from the United Kingdom is **British Airways** (© 0845/773-3377; www.britishairways.com). It flies from London's Gatwick Airport about three times a week year-round. No other airline flies nonstop between Britain and Bermuda.

Most airlines offer the best deals on tickets booked at least 14 days in advance, with a stopover in Bermuda of at least 3 days. You might need to stay over on a Saturday night to keep fares down. Airfares fluctuate according to the season but tend to remain competitive among the companies vying for a piece of the lucrative Bermuda run.

Peak season (summer) is the most expensive time to go; low season (usually mid-Sept or early Nov until mid-Mar) offers less expensive fares. The airlines that fly to Bermuda seldom observe a shoulder (intermediate) season. Because most aircraft flying from North America to Bermuda are medium-size, there's space for only two classes of service: first class and economy.

To give you some idea of the fares, we checked with American when researching this book. It offered round-trip flights from New York starting at $464 Monday to Thursday in low season and at $524 in high season. Fares for travel in both directions between Friday and Sunday entail a surcharge of around $50 to $100. Round-trip first-class fare was the same regardless of the season, beginning at $1,160.

FLYING FOR LESS: TIPS FOR GETTING THE BEST AIRFARES

Package deals are the number one way to save, but most accommodations featured in packages are the bigger resort hotels. Especially if you prefer to rent a cottage or stay in a more intimate place, you may wind up booking your airfare separately.

Consolidators, also known as bucket shops, are a good place to find low fares. Consolidators buy seats in bulk from the airlines and sell them to the public at prices below even the airlines' discounted rates. Their small, boxed ads usually run in the Sunday travel section at the bottom of the page. Before you pay a consolidator, however, ask for a record locator number and confirm your seat with the airline. Be prepared to book your ticket with a different consolidator—there are many to choose from—if the airline can't confirm your reservation. Also be aware that bucket-shop tickets are usually nonrefundable or carry stiff cancellation penalties, often as high as 50% to 75% of the ticket price.

Council Travel (© 888/COUNCIL; www.counciltravel.com) and **STA Travel** (© 800/781-4040; www.sta.travel.com) cater especially to young travelers, but their bargain-basement prices are available to people of all ages. Council Travel offices are at

---

Packing Tip

Bermuda is more formal than most resort destinations, so men planning to dine at upscale restaurants should be sure to pack a jacket and tie.

---

844 E. Lancaster Ave., Bryn Mawr, PA 19010 (℃ **610/527-6272**); 565 Melville, University City, MO 63130 (℃ **314/721-7779**); and Franklin House Suite 102, 480 E. Broad St., Athens, GA (℃ **706/543-9600**). **Travel Bargains** (℃ **800/AIR-FARE;** www.800airfare.com) was formerly owned by TWA but now offers the deepest discounts on many other airlines, with a 4-day advance purchase. Other reliable consolidators include **1-800-FLY-CHEAP** (www.800fly cheap.com). You might also try **Travac,** 989 6th Ave., New York, NY 10018 (℃ **800/TRAV-800** or 212/ 563-3303; www.travelsite.com) or 2601 E. Jefferson St., Orlando, FL 32803 (℃ **407/896-0014**); **TFI Tours International,** 34 W. 32nd St., 12th Floor, New York, NY 10001 (℃ **800/745-8000,** or 212/736-1140 in New York State), or **Travel Avenue,** 10 S. Riverside Plaza, Suite 1404, Chicago, IL 60606 (℃ **800/333-3335;** www.travelavenue.com).

TIPS FOR FLYING IN COMFORT

You'll find the most legroom in a bulkhead seat, in the front row of each cabin. Consider, however, that you will have to store your luggage in the overhead bin, and you won't have the best seat in the house for the in-flight movie. Also, parents traveling with infants are often placed in the bulkhead rows.

When you check in, ask for one of the emergency-exit-row seats, which also have extra legroom. They are assigned at the airport, usually on a first-come, first-served basis. In the unlikely event of an emergency, however, you'll be expected to open the emergency-exit door and help direct traffic.

Ask for a seat toward the front of the plane. You'll be one of the first to disembark after the gangway is in place.

When you make your reservation, order a special meal if you have dietary restrictions. Most airlines offer a variety of special meals, including vegetarian, macrobiotic, kosher, and meals for the lactose intolerant.

Wear comfortable clothes and dress in layers. The climate in airplane cabins is unpredictable. You'll be glad to have a sweater or jacket to put on or take off as the temperature on board dictates.

Pack some toiletries for long flights. Airplane cabins are notoriously dry places, so it may be a good idea to carry a travel-size bottle of moisturizer or lotion with you. If you wear contact lenses, bring eye drops.

If you're flying with a cold or chronic sinus problem, use a decongestant 10 minutes before ascent and descent, to minimize pressure buildup in the inner ear.

If you're flying with kids, don't forget a deck of cards, toys, extra bottles, pacifiers, diapers, and chewing gum to help them relieve ear pressure buildup during ascent and descent.

10 Cruising to Bermuda

Cruise ships tie up at three harbors in Bermuda: St. George in the East End, the Royal Naval Dockyard in the West End, and Hamilton Harbour at the City of Hamilton. While the cruise experience isn't for everyone, it's very appealing to some people, and is certainly a carefree, all-inclusive vacation. Ships from the East Coast of the United States reach Bermuda in a little over a day. You'll spend a few full days (usually three) moored at the island, exploring during the day and returning to the ship at night. It's convenient and comfortable—like having a luxury hotel and restaurant that travels with you.

Of course, that's also its major disadvantage. Most cruisers don't get to know the real Bermuda as well as those who stay in hotels ashore. Cruise-ship passengers generally eat all their meals aboard the ship, for instance—mainly because they've already paid for the meals as part of their cruise price—and so miss out on sampling Bermuda's cuisine. They also rarely get to meet and interact with Bermudians the way land-based visitors do.

Seven-day cruises out of New York usually spend 4 days at sea, with 3 days in port. Most cruise ships arrive in the traditional port of Hamilton, the capital of Bermuda and its chief commercial and shopping center. If shopping is more important to you than sightseeing, be sure that your cruise ship docks here. Once you're ashore, head to Front Street for shopping, or get your bearings by taking the walking tour that we describe in Chapter 8, "Island Strolls."

If you're more interested in historic Bermuda, make sure that your ship is scheduled to anchor at St. George, at the eastern tip of the island. With its narrow lanes and old buildings and streets, St. George has been called the island's equivalent of Colonial Williamsburg. Your ship will probably offer a guided tour of the town as a shore excursion; we've provided a self-guided tour in Chapter 8 if you'd rather explore on your own. St. George has become more of a shopping destination than it used to be, but this still isn't the primary place to come for shopping. Depending on the cruise line, its schedules, and the current tides, some cruise ships dock at both St. George and Hamilton while in Bermuda. Ships often plan to dock at St. George, but find that they cannot do so because of the tides.

It's not too likely that you'll disembark at Somerset, which is at the western end of the island and farthest from Bermuda's major attractions. The West End has its own charm and sightseeing appeal; it is home of the Royal Naval Dockyard, one of the island's major attractions. In a shopping mall at the dockyard, craft stores and museums exist side by side.

WHICH CRUISE LINE IS FOR YOU?

If you decide that a Bermuda cruise is right for you, you'll need to choose your cruise line. Some lines want their passengers to have a total vacation—one filled with activities from sunup to sundown. Others see time at sea as a period of tranquillity and relaxation, with less emphasis on organized activities. The cruise lines listed here offer regularly scheduled Bermuda sailings. See the section that follows for tips on getting a good deal on the price.

- **Celebrity Cruises** (✆ **800/437-3111** or 305/539-6000) Noted for modern, state-of-the-art, large but not mammoth cruise ships and for its exceptional cuisine and service, Celebrity is unpretentious but classy. It's several notches above mass market but still competitively priced. Cabins are roomy and well equipped, and the decor in general is elegantly modern, eschewing the glitz of some of competitors. Celebrity attracts a broad range of passengers, including families drawn by the line's children's programs. Its *Zenith* and *Horizon* both sail 7-night Bermuda itineraries from New

York between April and October. They spend 2 nights in St. George and 2 nights in Hamilton. Runs from other East Coast cities are interspersed throughout the .season.

- **Crown Cruise Line** (© 877/ 276-9621 or 954/967-2100) An attractive alternative to the megaships, the one and only ship in the recently revived Crown Cruise Line is an immaculate, well-designed, midsize vessel and a bargain way to see Bermuda. The 800-passenger *Crown Dynasty* offers a quality low-key experience that is a far cry from the "party hearty" atmosphere of many other mainstream ships. Most passengers enjoy mellow pastimes like playing cards and relaxing, snoozing, or reading a book from the comfort of a deck chair. Crown attracts primarily mature professional couples; though you can find younger couples in their thirties and forties and a few honeymooners onboard, very few singles or families with children choose this line. You'll find good, though not excellent, food on board, but unlike all the other Bermuda-bound ships, there's only one dining room open for dinner. In the summer of 2000, the *Dynasty* became the sixth ship permitted to visit Bermuda on a regular seasonal basis, offering Wednesday departures from Philadelphia and Baltimore from May through October. (The *Dynasty* is the only ship that docks in Bermuda over the weekend.) Passengers can also opt to fly one-way and cruise the other, with a 3- or 4-day hotel stay in between.

- **Norwegian Cruise Line** (© 800/ 327-7030) NCL offers affordable (sometimes downright cheap) down-to-earth cruises. The *Norwegian Majesty* makes Bermuda

runs from Boston between April and October, allowing 4 days of "shore leave" in St. George. The *Norwegian Majesty* was "stretched" a whole new midsection length, gaining more than 110 feet in size with an additional 220 new cabins added. There's a lot more deck space and a new casino and swimming pool, too. NCL's ships offer a great roster of activities and sports, both of the active and spectator variety. The ship has sports bars with links to ESPN, so you won't miss the big game. NCL's latest innovation is what they call "Freestyle Cruising." As part of this new concept, passengers are no longer assigned a dining time; passengers can eat at a different time, in whichever dining room they choose, with whomever they choose every night. Dinner dress code is "resort casual," with occasional dress-up nights that are completely optional. Not surprisingly, NCL tends to attract a somewhat younger, more laid-back crowd. Most passengers are couples aged 25 to 60, with a fair number of honeymooners and families with kids during holidays.

- **Princess Cruises** (© 800/421-0522) Princess operates the small, 1970-vintage liner *Pacific Princess* on Bermuda itineraries. One of the ships used in the original *Love Boat* TV series, the vessel is old and small, but beloved. About a quarter of the size of the newer ships in Princess's fleet, and carrying about a third as many passengers, it looks more like a ship than the huge floating resorts of today, and offers a more intimate experience. Something important for fans of the TV series to note: The cabin sets used in the show were *massive* compared to the real accommodations (and, for that matter, compared to the accommodations on *any* ship). This is a good choice for a calm, intimate, relaxing cruise, but not the best option for party animals.

- **Royal Caribbean Cruises, Ltd.** (© 800/327-6700) Royal Caribbean sails its 1,600-passenger *Nordic Empress* on Bermuda runs from New York between May and October. The ship, built in 1990, has compact but well-designed cabins and a wide variety of entertainment, including a casino, a health spa, a children's program, and much more. Its onboard atmosphere is a little more high-energy than Celebrity and Princess, and roughly comparable to NCL. Stopovers include 2 days in St. George and 2½ days in Hamilton Harbour. You can find all walks of life on a Royal Caribbean cruise. The common denominator: passengers looking for fun and action in an attractive setting. Most passengers are couples, but there also tend to be plenty of families and singles on board as well. Overall, passengers are active, social, and looking for a good time, no matter what their age.

HOW TO GET THE BEST DEAL ON YOUR CRUISE

Cruise lines operate like airlines, setting rates for their cruises and then selling them in a rapid-fire series of discounts, offering almost whatever it takes to fill their ships. Because of this, great deals come and go in the blink of an eye, and most are available only through travel agents.

If you have a travel agent you trust, leave the details to him or her. If not, try contacting a travel agent who specializes in booking cruises. Some of the most likely contenders include the following: **Cruises, Inc.,** 5000 Campuswood Dr. E., Syracuse, NY 13057 (© 800/854-0500 or 315/463-9695); **Cruise Masters,** Century Plaza Towers, 2029 Century Park E., Suite 950, Los Angeles, CA 90067 (© **800/456-4FUN** or 310/556-2925); **The Cruise Company,** 10760 Q St., Omaha, NE 68127 (© **800/289-5505** or 402/339-6800); **Kelly Cruises,** 1315 W. 22nd St., Suite 105, Oak Brook, IL 60523 (© **800/837-7447** or 630/990-1111); **Hartford Holidays Travel,** 129 Hillside Ave., Williston Park, NY 11596 (© **800/828-4813** or 516/746-6670); and **Mann Travel** and **Cruises American Express,** 6010 Fairview Rd., Suite 104, Charlotte, NC 28210 (© **800/849-2301** or 704/556-8311).

A FEW MONEY-SAVING TIPS

- **Book early:** You can often receive considerable savings on a 7-day cruise by booking early. Ask a travel agent or call the cruise line directly.
- **Book an inside cabin:** If you're trying to keep costs down, ask for an inside cabin (one without a

---

Tips **Ahoy, Philadelphia/Baltimore Cruisers**

The 20,000-ton *Crown Dynasty* (© 800/832-1122; 400 Hollywood Blvd., Hollywood, FL 33021) has begun voyages from Philadelphia and Baltimore to Bermuda. Bedecked in a Bermudian décor, it is the only ship to dock at the western Royal Naval Dockyard (the others dock at the harbor of Hamilton and St. George's). Through a partnership with Apple Vacations and island hotels, a percentage of berths are dedicated to an innovative "Cruise-Stay-Fly Program" that incorporates a midweek departure and a weekend stay.

window). They're often the same size and offer the same amenities as the more expensive outside cabins. If you're planning on using the space only to sleep, who needs natural light during the day?

- **Take advantage of senior discounts:** The cruise industry offers some discounts to seniors (usually defined as anyone 55 or older), so don't keep your age a secret. Membership in AARP, for example, can net you substantial discounts; always ask your travel agent about these types of discounts when you're booking.

- **Don't sail alone:** Cruise lines base their rates on double occupancy, so solo passengers usually pay between 150% and 200% of the per-person rate. If you're traveling alone, most lines have a program that allows two solo passengers to share a cabin.

11 Planning Your Trip Online

With a mouse, a modem, and a certain do-it-yourself determination, Internet users can tap into the same travel-planning databases that were once accessible only to travel agents. Sites such as **Travelocity, Expedia,** and **Orbitz** allow consumers to comparison shop for airfares, book flights, learn of last-minute bargains, and reserve hotel rooms and rental cars.

But don't fire your travel agent just yet. Although online booking sites offer tips and hard data to help you bargain shop, they cannot endow you with the hard-earned experience that makes a seasoned, reliable travel agent an invaluable resource, even in the Internet age. And for consumers with a complex itinerary, a trusty travel agent is still the best way to arrange the most direct flights to and from the best airports.

Still, there's no denying the Internet's emergence as a powerful tool in researching and plotting travel time. The benefits of researching your trip online can be well worth the effort:

- **Last-minute specials,** known as "E-savers," such as weekend deals or Internet-only fares, are offered by airlines to fill empty seats. Most of these are announced on Tuesday or Wednesday and must be purchased online. Most are only valid for travel that weekend, but some can be booked weeks or months in advance. Sign up for weekly e-mail alerts at airline websites or check mega-sites that compile comprehensive lists of E-savers, such as Smarter Living (smarterliving.com) or WebFlyer (www.webflyer.com).

- Some sites will send you **e-mail notification** when a cheap fare becomes available to your favorite destination. Some will also tell you when fares to a particular destination are lowest.

- The best of the travel planning sites are now **highly personalized;** they track your frequent-flier miles, and store your seating and meal preferences, tentative itineraries, and credit-card information, letting you plan trips or check agendas quickly.

- All major airlines offer **incentives**—bonus frequent-flier miles, Internet-only discounts, sometimes even free cellphone rentals—when you purchase online or buy an e-ticket.

- Advances in mobile technology provide business travelers and other frequent travelers with **the ability to check flight status, change plans, or get specific directions** from handheld computing devices, mobile phones, and pagers. Some sites will e-mail or page a passenger if a flight is delayed.

Complete Travel Resource

For an excellent travel planning resource, we highly recommend **Arthur Frommer's Budget Travel Online** (www.frommers.com). We're a little biased, of course, but we guarantee you'll find the travel tips, reviews, monthly vacation giveaways, and online-booking capabilities thoroughly indispensable. Among the special features are: **"Ask the Expert"** bulletin boards, where Frommer's authors answer your questions via online postings; **Arthur Frommer's Daily Newsletter,** for the latest travel bargains and inside travel secrets; and Frommer's **Destinations archive,** where you'll get expert travel tips, hotel and dining recommendations, and advice on the sights to see for more than 200 destinations around the globe Once your research is done, the **Online Reservation System** (www.frommers.com/booktravelnow) takes you to Frommer's favorite sites for booking your vacation at affordable prices.

TRAVEL PLANNING & BOOKING SITES

The best travel planning and booking sites cast a wide net, offering domestic and international flights, hotel and rental-car bookings, plus news, destination information, and deals on cruises and vacation packages. Keep in mind that free (one-time) registration is often required for booking. Because several airlines are no longer willing to pay commissions on tickets sold by online travel agencies, be aware that these online agencies will either charge a $10 surcharge if you book a ticket on that carrier or neglect to offer those air carriers' offerings.

The sites in this section are not intended to be a comprehensive list, but rather a discriminating selection to get you started. Recognition is given to sites based on their content value and ease of use and is not paid for—unlike some website rankings, which are based on payment. Remember: This is a press-time snapshot of leading websites—some undoubtedly will have evolved or moved by the time you read this.

- **Travelocity** (www.travelocity.com or www.frommers.travelocity.com)

and **Expedia** (www.expedia.com) are the most longstanding and reputable sites, each offering excellent selections and searches for complete vacation packages. Travelers search by destination and dates coupled with how much they are willing to spend.

- The latest buzz in the online travel world is about **Orbitz** (www.orbitz.com), a site launched by United, Delta, Northwest, American, and Continental airlines. It shows all possible fares for your desired trip, offering fares lower than those available through travel agents. (Stay tuned: At press time, travel-agency associations were waging an antitrust battle against this site.)
- **Qixo** (www.qixo.com) is another powerful search engine that allows you to search for flights and hotel rooms on 20 other travel-planning sites (such as Travelocity) at once. Qixo sorts results by price, after which you can book your travel directly through the site.

SMART E-SHOPPING

The savvy traveler is one armed with good information. Here are a few tips to help you navigate the Internet successfully and safely.

- **Know when sales start.** Last-minute deals may vanish in minutes. If you have a favorite booking site or airline, find out when last-minute deals are released to the public. (For example, Southwest's specials are posted every Tuesday at 12:01am central time.)
- **Shop around.** Compare results from different sites and airlines—and against a travel agent's best fare, if you can. If possible, try a range of times and alternate airports before you make a purchase.
- **Follow the rules of the trade.** Book in advance, and choose an off-peak time and date if possible. Some sites will tell you when fares to a particular destination tend to be cheapest.
- **Stay secure.** Book only through secure sites (some airline sites are not secure). Look for a key icon (Netscape) or a padlock (Internet Explorer) at the bottom of your web browser before you enter credit card information or other personal data.
- **Avoid online auctions.** Sites that auction airline tickets and frequent-flier miles are the number-one perpetrators of Internet fraud, according to the National Consumers League.
- **Maintain a paper trail.** If you book an e-ticket, print out a confirmation, or write down your confirmation number, and keep it safe and accessible—or your trip could be a virtual one!

ONLINE TRAVELER'S TOOLBOX

Veteran travelers usually carry some essential items to make their trips easier. Following is a selection of online tools to bookmark and use.

- **Visa ATM Locator** (www.visa.com/pd/atm) or **MasterCard ATM Locator** (www.mastercard.com/atm). Find ATMs in hundreds of cities in the U.S. and around the world.
- **Foreign Languages for Travelers** (www.travlang.com). Learn basic terms in more than 70 languages and click on any underlined phrase to hear what it sounds like. *Note:* Free audio software and speakers are required.
- **Intellicast** (www.intellicast.com). Weather forecasts for all 50 states and cities around the world. *Note:* temperatures are in Celsius for many international destinations.
- **Mapquest** (www.mapquest.com). This best of the mapping sites lets

---

 Bermuda's Best Websites

Here are some of the best sites to help you start planning your Bermuda itinerary online.

- The **Bermuda Department of Tourism** site (www.bermudatourism.com) has an extensive calendar of events.
- The **Bermuda Online** site (www.bermuda-online.org) includes dining advice, transportation tips, and local TV and radio information.
- The handy **Map Guide** (www.bermudamapguide.com) site offers maps of the islands with separate overlays showing the location of hotels and attractions as well as bus and ferry routes.

you choose a specific address or destination, and in seconds, it will return a map and detailed directions.

- **Cybercafes.com** (www.cyber cafes.com) or **Net Café Guide** (www.netcafeguide.com/map index.htm). Locate Internet cafes at hundreds of locations around the globe. Catch up on your e-mail and log onto the Web for a few dollars per hour.

- **Universal Currency Converter** (www.xe.net/currency). See what your dollar or pound is worth in more than 100 other countries.

- **U.S. State Department Travel Warnings** (www.travel.state.gov/ travel_warnings.html). Reports on places where health concerns or unrest might threaten U.S. travelers. It also lists the locations of U.S. embassies around the world.

3

Getting to Know Bermuda

Settling into Bermuda is relatively easy. First-timers soon learn that Bermuda isn't one island, as is commonly thought, but a string of islands linked by causeways and bridges—at least the 20 or so that are inhabited. The other islands can be reached by boat.

Unlike many islands in the Caribbean (including the Dominican Republic) that are dotted with poverty-stricken slums, Bermuda is a prosperous island characterized by neat, trim houses that are a source of great pride to their owners. There won't be a casino at your megaresort— Bermuda has no casinos—and you'd better have your fill of Big Macs before you leave home. There are some fast-food joints, but nothing like those on the U.S. mainland, or even in the Bahamas. There's a sense of order in Bermuda, and everything seems to work efficiently, even when the weather's hot.

1 Arriving

BY PLANE

Planes arrive at the **Bermuda International Airport,** Kindley Field Road, St. George (© 441/293-2470), 9 miles east of Hamilton and about 17 miles east of Somerset at the far western end of Bermuda.

The flight from most East Coast destinations, including New York, Raleigh/ Durham, Baltimore, and Boston, takes about 2 hours. Flights from Atlanta take $2\frac{1}{2}$ hours; from Toronto it's less than 3 hours.

After clearing Customs (see "Entry Requirements & Customs," in chapter 2, "Planning Your Trip to Bermuda," for details), you can pick up tourist information at the airport before heading to your hotel. Because you aren't allowed to rent a car in Bermuda, and buses don't allow passengers to board with luggage, you must rely on a taxi or minivan to reach your hotel.

LEAVING THE AIRPORT BY TAXI OR MINIVAN

More than 600 taxis are available on Bermuda, and cabbies meet all arriving flights. Taxis are allowed to carry a maximum of four passengers. If you and your traveling companion have a lot of luggage, you will need the taxi to yourselves.

Including a tip of 10% to 15%, it costs about $20 to $28 to reach a destination in Hamilton. The fare to St. George is about $20; to Tucker's Town, $16. To the south-shore hotels, the charge is likely to be $26 to $30. To the West End, the charge is more than $45. Fares go up 25% between 10pm and 6am, as well as all day on Sundays and holidays. Luggage carries a surcharge of 25¢ per piece. A meter determines the fare. Expect to pay about $4 for the first mile and $1.40 for each additional mile.

There are several authorized taxi companies on the island, including **C.O.O.P.** (© 441/292-4476), **B.T.S.L.** (© 441/295-4141), and **Sandys** (© 441/234-2344).

Did You Know?

- More than 23,000 couples honeymoon on Bermuda each year.
- Bermudians imported the idea of moon gates—large rings of stone used as garden ornaments—from Asia centuries ago. Walking through a moon gate is supposed to bring good luck.
- William Shakespeare's 1610 play, *The Tempest,* was inspired by this mysterious island.
- Somerset Bridge is the world's smallest drawbridge. Only 22 inches wide, the opening is just large enough for a ship's mast to pass through.
- Bermuda has more golf courses per square mile than any other place in the world; there are eight of them on the island's approximate 21 square miles.
- Sir Brownlow Gray, the island's chief justice, played the first game of tennis in the Western Hemisphere on Bermuda in 1873.
- With the arrival of spring comes the blossoming of Bermuda's Easter lilies, first brought to the island from Japan in the 18th century.
- Bermuda has no billboards: There is a ban on outdoor advertising and neon signs.

It's cheaper for a party of four to call a minivan and split the cost. Arrange one before you arrive by contacting **Bermuda Hosts,** 2 Kindley Field Rd., St. George CR 04 (℡ **441/293-1334**). This outfit can arrange to have a bus waiting for your flight. If you're part of a party of two people (rather than four), you can ask a waiting bus at the airport if it has room to take on two extra passengers. Trips cost about $20 per person to the farthest hotel. Bermuda Hosts can provide transportation for golfers and can arrange sightseeing tours.

BY CRUISE SHIP

This is the easiest way to arrive in Bermuda. The staff presents you with a list of tour options long before you arrive in port; almost everything is done for you, unless you opt to make your own arrangements. (An independent taxi tour is far more expensive than an organized tour.) Most passengers book shore excursions at the same time they reserve their cruise.

Depending on your ship, you will probably arrive either in Hamilton (best for shopaholics) or St. George (best for architecture and history buffs). A few ships also dock at the Royal Naval Dockyard on Bermuda's West End. Whatever port you dock at, you can avail yourself of the waiting taxis near your ship, or rent a moped or bicycle (see "Getting Around," below) and do some touring and shopping on your own. For more information about cruising to Bermuda, see p. 40.

2 Orienting Yourself: The Lay of the Land

For administrative purposes, the islands of Bermuda are divided into **parishes,** all named for shareholders of the original 1610 Bermuda Company. From west to east, they are:

SANDYS PARISH

In the far western part of the archipelago, Sandys (pronounced *Sands*) Parish encompasses the islands of **Ireland, Boaz,** and **Somerset.** This parish (named for

Bermuda's Parishes

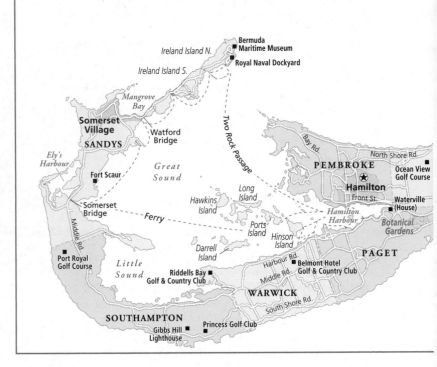

Sir Edwin Sandys, a major shareholder of the 1610 Bermuda Company) centers on Somerset Village. Somerset Island, site of Somerset Village, pays tribute to Sir George Somers of Sea Venture fame; Sandys Parish is often called Somerset.

Some visitors to Bermuda head directly for Sandys Parish and spend their entire time here; they feel that the far western tip, with its rolling hills, lush countryside, and tranquil bays, is something special. (This area has always stood apart from the rest of Bermuda: During the U.S. Civil War, when most Bermudians sympathized with the Confederates, Sandys Parish supported the Union.) Sandys Parish has areas of great natural beauty, including **Somerset Long Bay,** the biggest and best public beach in the West End (which the Bermuda Audubon Society is developing into a nature preserve), and **Mangrove Bay,** a protected beach in the heart of **Somerset Village.** Try to walk around the old village; it's filled with typically Bermudian houses and shops. On Somerset Road is the **Scaur Lodge Property;** the waterfront hillside is open daily at no charge.

If you want to be near the shops, restaurants, and pubs of Hamilton, you may want to stay in a more central location and visit Sandys Parish on a day trip. However, the parish's isolation is part of its charm for those who prefer tranquillity and unspoiled nature to shopping for cashmeres or lingering over an extra pint in a pub. This is the perfect parish for couples seeking privacy and romance.

An advantage of staying here is that the parish has several embarkation points for various types of sea excursions. Sandys also has some of the most elegant places to stay in Bermuda. You can commute to Hamilton by ferry, although it's a bit time-consuming, especially if your days on Bermuda are limited.

SOUTHAMPTON PARISH

Southampton Parish (named for the third earl of Southampton) is a narrow strip of land opening at its northern edge onto Little Sound and on its southern shore onto the Atlantic Ocean. It stretches from Riddells Bay to Tucker's Island, and is split by Middle Road.

Tips **Visitor Information on the Island**

You can get answers to most of your questions at the Visitors Service Bureau locations at the **Ferry Terminal**, Hamilton (© **441/295-1480**); **King's Square**, St. George (© **441/297-1642**); and the **Royal Naval Dockyard** (© **441/234-3824**). During the summer, the offices are open Monday to Saturday 9am to 4pm; off-season they're open Monday to Saturday 9am to 2pm.

If dining at waterfront restaurants and staying at big resort hotels is part of your Bermuda dream, then Southampton is your parish; it's the site of such famed resorts as The Fairmont Southampton Princess and the Sonesta Beach Resort. Southampton is also the best place to stay if you plan to spend a great deal of time on the island's fabled pink, sandy beaches. Among its jewels is **Horseshoe Bay,** one of Bermuda's most attractive public beaches, with changing rooms, a snack bar, and space for parking.

Southampton lacks the intimacy and romance of Sandys, but it has a lot of razzle-dazzle going for it. It's great for a golfing holiday. If you like to sightsee, you can easily occupy 2 days just exploring the parish's many attractions. It also has more nightlife than Sandys—but not as much as in Hamilton.

WARWICK PARISH

Named in honor of the second earl of Warwick, this parish lies in the heart of Great Bermuda Island. Like Southampton, it is known for its long stretches of pink sands. Along the south shore is **Warwick Long Bay,** one of Bermuda's best public beaches. Warwick also boasts parklands bordering the sea, winding country roads, two golf courses, and a number of natural attractions. This area is the best on the island for horseback riding, which is the best way to see pastoral Bermuda up close.

Warwick is the choice of visitors who seek cottage or apartment rentals (where they can do some of their own cooking to cut down on the outrageous expense of food). The parish is not strong on restaurants; one of its disadvantages is that you have to travel a bit if you like to dine out. Nightlife is also spotty—just about the only action you can find after dark is in hotel lounges. This parish is for tranquillity-seekers, but because of its more central location, it doesn't offer quite the seclusion Sandys does.

PAGET PARISH

Paget Parish lies directly south of the capital city of Hamilton, separated from it by Hamilton Harbour. Named after the fourth Lord Paget, it has many residences and historic homes; it's also the site of the 36-acre **Botanical Gardens.** But the south-shore beaches—the best in the chain of islands—are what draw visitors here in droves. In spring, the Elbow Beach Hotel is the center of most College Weeks activities. Paget Parish is also the site of **Chelston,** on Grape Bay Drive, the official residence of the U.S. consul general. Situated on 14½ acres of landscaped grounds, it's open only during the Garden Club's Home and Garden Tours in the spring (see "Calendar of Events," in chapter 2, "Planning Your Trip to Bermuda," for details).

This is one of the best parishes to stay in—it has many excellent accommodations, including Elbow Beach Hotel. It's close enough to the City of Hamilton for an easy commute, but far enough away to escape the hordes. Because public transportation is all-important (you can't rent a car), Paget is a good place to situate yourself; it has some of the best and most convenient ferry connections and bus schedules. There are docks at Salt Kettle, Hodson's, and Lower Ferry; you can even "commute" by ferry to Warwick Parish or Sandys Parish to the west. If you'd like to bike, Paget's relatively flat terrain is ideal for that, and the parish abounds with rural lanes and streets lined with old mansions. Hikers will find many small trails bordering the sea.

If you don't like big resort hotels, you can find many rental cottages and several little guesthouses here. Unlike Warwick, Paget has a number of dining choices. Elbow Beach offers the most, but other fine options include Fourways Inn and Paraquet Guest Apartments. Most of the parish's nightlife centers on Elbow Beach.

There are no major disadvantages to staying in Paget. You will find overcrowded beaches during spring break, though, and congestion in Hamilton in the summer, when many cruise ships arrive.

PEMBROKE PARISH

This parish (named after the third earl of Pembroke) is home to one-quarter of Bermuda's population. It is home to the **City of Hamilton,** Bermuda's capital and only full-fledged city. The parish opens at its northern rim onto the vast Atlantic Ocean and on its southern side onto Hamilton Harbour; its western border is on Great Sound. Hamilton is the first place passengers arriving aboard most cruise ships will see.

This parish is not ideal for those seeking a tranquil holiday. Pembroke, with the island's greatest population density, also attracts the most visitors. The little city is especially crowded when cruise ships are in the harbor and travelers pour into the stores and restaurants. Yet for those who like to pub-crawl English style, enjoy shopping until they drop, and prefer to be near the largest concentration of dining choices, Pembroke—the City of Hamilton in particular—is without equal.

Whether or not you stay in Pembroke, try to fit a shopping (or window-shopping) stroll along Front Street into your itinerary. The area also boasts a number of sightseeing attractions, most of which are easily accessible on foot

Tips Finding an Address

The island chain of Bermuda doesn't follow a rigid system of street addresses. Most hotels, even in official government listings, don't bother to include an address, although they do include post-office boxes and zip codes. Bermudians just assume that everybody knows where everything is, which is fine if you've lived on Bermuda all your life. But if you're a first-time visitor, get a good map before setting out—and don't be shy about asking directions. Most people are very helpful.

Most of the establishments you'll be seeking are on some street plan. However, some places use numbers in their street addresses, and others—perhaps their neighbors—don't. The actual building number is not always important, because a building such as a resort hotel is likely to be set back so far from the main road that you couldn't see its number anyway. Look for signs with the name of the hotel rather than the street number. Cross streets will also aid you in finding an address.

(a plus because you don't have to depend on taxis, bikes, or scooters—which can get to be a bit of a bore after a while). Nightlife, such as it is, is the finest on the island. Don't expect splashy Las Vegas–type revues, however; instead, think restaurants, pubs, and small clubs.

DEVONSHIRE PARISH

Lying east of Paget and Pembroke parishes, near the geographic center of the archipelago, Devonshire Parish (named for the first earl of Devonshire) is green and hilly. It has some housekeeping apartments, a cottage colony, and one of Bermuda's oldest churches, the **Old Devonshire Parish Church,** which dates from 1716. Three of Bermuda's major roads traverse the parish: the aptly named South Shore Road, Middle Road, and North Shore Road. As you wander its narrow lanes, you can, with some imagination, picture yourself in the namesake county of Devon, England.

Golfers flock to Devonshire to play at the **Ocean View Golf Course.** Along North Shore Road, near the border of Pembroke Parish, is **Devonshire Dock,** long a seafarer's haven. During the War of 1812, British soldiers came to Devonshire Dock to be entertained by local women. Today, fishers still bring in grouper and rockfish, so you can shop for dinner if you're staying at a nearby cottage with a kitchen.

Devonshire has a number of unspoiled nature areas. The **arboretum** on Montpelier Road is one of the most tranquil oases on Bermuda. This open space, created by the Department of Agriculture, Fisheries, and Parks, is home to a wide range of Bermudian plant and tree life, especially conifers, palms, and other subtropical trees. Along South Shore Road, west of the junction with Collector's Hill, is the **Edmund Gibbons Nature Reserve.** This portion of marshland, owned by the National Trust, provides living space for a number of birds and rare species of Bermuda flora.

Devonshire is one of the sleepy residential parishes, known for its hilly interior, beautiful landscape, and fabulous estates bordering the sea. There's little sightseeing here; all those stunning private estates aren't open to the public, so unless you get a personal invite, you're out of luck. But the parish is right in Bermuda's geographic center, so it's an ideal place to base yourself if you'd like to explore both the West End and the East End. However, there are two major drawbacks: With a few notable exceptions, the parish has very few places to stay and almost no dining choices.

SMITH'S PARISH

Named for Sir Thomas Smith, this parish faces the open sea to the north and south. To the east is Harrington Sound; to the west, bucolic Devonshire Parish.

The parish encompasses **Flatts Village,** one of the island's most charming parish towns (take bus no. 10 or 11 from Hamilton). It was a smugglers' port for about 200 years and served as the center of power for a coterie of successful "planter politicians" and landowners. Their government ranked in importance second only to that of St. George, then the capital. People gathered at the rickety Flatts Bridge to "enjoy" such public entertainment as hangings; if the offense was serious enough, victims were drawn and quartered here. From Flatts Village, you have panoramic views of both the inlet and Harrington Sound. At the top of McGall's Hill is St. Mark's Church, based on the same designs used for the Old Devonshire Parish Church.

Most visitors view Smith's Parish as a day trip or a half-day trip, although the parish does have places to stay, such as the Pink Beach Club and Cottages.

Dining choices are extremely limited, however, unless you stick to the hotels. Again, if you're seeking lots of nighttime diversion, you'll have to go to another parish. Because the Spittal Pond Nature Reserve is here, many nature lovers prefer Smith's over the more populated parishes. Basically, Smith's Parish is for the connoisseur who wants serenity and tranquillity but not at the celestial prices charged at the "cottages" of Sandys.

HAMILTON PARISH

Not to be confused with the City of Hamilton (which is in Pembroke Parish), Hamilton Parish lies directly north of Harrington Sound, opening onto the Atlantic. It's bordered on the east by St. George and on the southwest by Smith's Parish. Named for the second marquis of Hamilton, the parish surrounds Harrington Sound, a saltwater lake stretching some 6 miles. On its eastern periphery, it opens onto Castle Harbour.

The big attractions here are the **Bermuda Aquarium,** the **Crystal Caves,** and **Leamington Caves.** Scuba diving and other water sports are very popular in the area.

Around **Harrington Sound,** the sights differ greatly from those of nearby St. George (see below). There's more action and less history. Some experts believe that Harrington Sound was a prehistoric cave that fell in. Its gateway to the ocean is an inlet at Flatts Village (see "Smith's Parish," above). However, evidence suggests that there are underwater passages as well—several deep-sea fish have been caught in the sound.

For the best panoramic view of the north shore, head for **Crawl Hill,** the highest place in Hamilton Parish, just before you come to Bailey's Bay. Crawl is a corruption of the word *kraal,* which is where turtles were kept before slaughter. **Shelly Bay,** named for one of the passengers of the *Sea Venture,* is the longest beach along the north shore. The **Hamilton Parish Church,** reached by going down Trinity Church Road, stands on Church Bay; built as a one-room structure in 1623, it has been much altered.

(Tips Finding Your Way

We've included bulleted maps throughout this book to help you locate Bermuda's accommodations, restaurants, beaches, and sights. There's also a handy full-color foldout map in the back of the book.

The Bermuda Department of Tourism publishes a free *Bermuda Handy Reference Map.* The tiny pocket map, distributed by the tourist office and available at most hotels, includes an overview and orientation map of Bermuda, highlighting its major attractions, golf courses, public beaches, and hotels. (It does not, however, pinpoint individual restaurants unless they are attached to hotels.) On the other side is a detailed street plan of the City of Hamilton, indicating all its major landmarks and service facilities, such as the ferry terminal and the post office. There's also a detailed map of the Royal Naval Dockyard, the West End, and the East End, plus tips on transportation—ferries, taxis, buses—and other helpful hints, such as a depiction of various traffic signs. For exact locations of Visitors Service Bureau locations where you can pick up a copy of the *Bermuda Handy Reference Map,* see the "Visitor Information on the Island" box, above.

At Bailey's Bay, **Tom Moore's Jungle** consists of wild woods. The poet Tom Moore is said to have spent many hours writing poetry here under a calabash tree (which is still standing). The jungle is now held in private trust, so you must obtain permission to enter it. It's much easier to pay your respects to the Romantic poet by going to Tom Moore's Tavern (see "Hamilton Parish" in chapter 5, "Dining").

Although the parish has some major resorts, such as Grotto Bay Beach Hotel, most visitors come here for sightseeing. We have to agree: In our judgment, Hamilton is a good place to go exploring for a day or half day, but you're better off staying elsewhere. If you stay here, you'll spend a great deal of your holiday time commuting into Hamilton or St. George. Bus no. 1 or 3 from Hamilton gets you here in about an hour.

ST. GEORGE PARISH

At Bermuda's extreme eastern end, this historic parish encompasses several islands. The parish borders Castle Harbour on its western and southern edges; St. George's Harbour divides it into two major parts, **St. George's Island** and **St. David's Island.** A causeway links St. David's Island to the rest of Bermuda. Many parish residents are longtime sailors and fishers. St. George Parish also includes **Tucker's Town** (founded in 1616 by Gov. Daniel Tucker), on the opposite shore of Castle Harbour.

Settled in 1612, the **town of St. George** was once the capital of Bermuda; Hamilton succeeded it in 1815. The town was settled 3 years after Sir George Somers and his shipwrecked party of English sailors came ashore in 1609. (After Admiral Somers died in Bermuda in 1610, his heart was buried in the St. George area, while the rest of his body was taken home to England for burial.) Founded by Richard Moore, of the newly created Bermuda Company, and a band of 60 colonists, St. George was the second English settlement in the New World, after Jamestown, Virginia. Its coat of arms depicts St. George (England's patron saint) and the dragon.

Almost 4 centuries of history come alive here, and generations upon generations of sailors have set forth from its sheltered harbor. St. George even played a role in the American Revolution: Bermuda depended on the American colonies for food, and when war came, supplies grew dangerously low. Although Bermuda was a British colony, the loyalties of its people were divided, because many Bermudians had relatives living on the American mainland. A delegation headed by Col. Henry Tucker went to Philadelphia to petition the Continental Congress to trade food and supplies for salt. George Washington had a different idea. He needed gunpowder, and a number of kegs of it were stored at St. George. Without the approval of the British Bermudian governor, the parties struck a deal. The gunpowder was trundled aboard American warships waiting in the harbor of Tobacco Bay under cover of darkness. In return, the grateful colonies supplied Bermuda with food.

Although St. George still evokes a feeling of the past, it's actively inhabited. When cruise ships are in port, it's likely to be overrun with visitors. Many people prefer to visit St. George at night, when they can walk around and enjoy it in relative peace and quiet. You won't be able to enter any of the sightseeing attractions, but they're of minor importance. After dark, a mood of enchantment settles over the place: It's like a storybook village.

Would you want to live here for a week? Probably not. Several chains, including Club Med, have tried and failed to make a go of it here. Accommodations are extremely limited, although there are a number of restaurants (many of which, frankly, are mediocre). For history buffs, no place in Bermuda tops St. George. But as a parish to base yourself in, you might do better in the more centrally located and activity-filled Pembroke or Southampton parishes. Once you've seen the glories of the town of St. George—which you can do in a day—you're really isolated at the easternmost end of Bermuda for the rest of your stay. As for nightlife, you can always go to a pub on King's Square.

BERMUDA IN A NUTSHELL: SUGGESTED SIGHTSEEING ITINERARIES FOR 1 TO 5 DAYS

You may be eager to start exploring right away, especially if your time is short. Below is a suggested itinerary for the first 5 days. A week's visit will let you break up your sightseeing trips with time on the beach, boating, or engaging in some of the island's other outdoor pursuits, such as golf, scuba diving, or boating. Hitting the beach is the first priority for most visitors—but you don't need us to tell you how to schedule your time in the sun!

If You Have 1 Day

If you have only 1 day for sightseeing, we suggest you spend it in the historic former capital of **St. George,** a maze of narrow streets with quaint names: Featherbed Alley, Duke of York Street, Petticoat Lane, Old Maid's Lane, Duke of Kent Street. You can spend a day exploring British-style pubs, seafood restaurants, shops (several major Hamilton stores have branches here), old forts, museums, and churches. You can even see stocks, a ducking stool, and a pillory, all used generations ago to humiliate wrongdoers.

And what would a day in Bermuda be without time spent on the beach? **Elbow Beach** and **Warwick Long Bay** are among the most appealing spots. The no. 7 bus will take you there from St. George.

If You Have 2 Days

Spend **Day 1** as indicated above. Devote **Day 2** to sightseeing and shopping in the City of Hamilton. You'll likely be staying in Paget or Warwick, and a ferry from either parish will take you right into the city. For many visitors, Hamilton's shops are its most compelling attraction. Try to time your visit to avoid the arrival of cruise ships; on those days, the stores and restaurants in Hamilton can really get crowded.

If you took our advice and went to the beach yesterday, try a different one today. After all, Bermuda isn't just about sightseeing and shopping—it's about those marvelous pink sands, too.

If You Have 3 Days

Spend **Days 1 and 2** as outlined above. On **Day 3,** take the ferry from Hamilton across Great Sound to Somerset. Carry your cycle on the boat—you'll need it later (see "Getting Around," below, for details on rentals). You'll disembark at the western end of Somerset Island in Sandys Parish, where you'll find the smallest drawbridge in the world. It's easy to spend an hour walking around Somerset Village. Then head west until you reach Somerset Long Bay beach, along the northern rim of the island.

Sandys Parish has several places for lunch (see chapter 5, "Dining"). The **Somerset Country Squire Tavern,** a typical village inn near the Watford Bridge ferry stop at the western end of the island, is one of the best.

After lunch, cross Watford Bridge to **Ireland Island,** home of the **Royal Naval Dockyard** and the **Maritime Museum.** On your way back to Somerset Bridge and the ferry back to Hamilton, you might take the turnoff to Fort Scaur; from **Scaur Hill,** you'll have a commanding view of Ely's Harbour and Great Sound. If you don't want to go through Somerset again, the ferry at Watford Bridge will take you back to Hamilton.

If You Have 4 or 5 Days

Spend **Days 1 through 3** as outlined above. Make **Day 4** a beach day. Head for **Horseshoe Bay beach** in the morning. Spend most of your time there, exploring hidden coves in all directions. You can have lunch right on the beach at a concession stand. In the afternoon, visit **Gibbs Hill Lighthouse.** After

a rest at your hotel, sample some Bermudian nightlife.

On **Day 5,** conclude your stay with an excursion to **Flatts Village,** which lies in the eastern sector of Smith's Parish. Explore the Bermuda Aquarium, **Natural History Museum & Zoo;** consider an undersea walk (see the "Walking Underwater" box in chapter 6, "Fun in the Surf & Sun").

Have lunch at the **Inlet Restaurant,** in the Palmetto Hotel, then visit **Elbow Beach.** After relaxing over afternoon tea at one of the hotels, arrange to see a show—perhaps gombey dancing, if it's scheduled—in the evening.

3 Getting Around

Driving is on the left, and the national speed limit is 20 mph in the countryside, 15 mph in busier areas. Cars are limited to one per resident family—and visitors are not allowed to rent cars at all. You'll rely on taxis, bikes, motorized bicycles called "putt-putts," and maybe even a romantic, colorful fringe-topped surrey.

BY TAXI

Dozens of taxis roam the island, and virtually every hotel, restaurant, and shop is happy to call one for you. The hourly charge is $30 for one to four passengers. A luxury tour van accommodating up to six passengers costs $42 an hour. If you want to use one for a sightseeing tour, the minimum is 3 hours.

BY CYCLE & SCOOTER

Bermuda is the only Atlantic island that restricts car ownership to local residents. Part of the reason for this is the notoriously narrow roads, which have small or nonexistent shoulders and hundreds of blind curves. Add frequent rainfall and the British custom of driving on the left, and there would probably be traffic chaos if every newcomer were allowed to take to the roads in a rented car.

The resulting dependence on cabs and rented motor scooters, mopeds, and bicycles is simply a fact of Bermudian life that newcomers quickly accept as part of the island's charm. Although not having a car at your disposal is inconvenient, the island's tourist brochures make it seem just wonderful: A happy couple

---

(*Tips* Taxi Touring Tip

When a taxi has a blue flag on its hood (locals call the hood the "bonnet"), the driver is qualified to serve as a **tour guide.** The government checks out and tests these drivers, so you should use them if you plan to tour Bermuda by taxi. "Blue-bonnet" drivers charge no more than regular taxi drivers.

For a radio-dispatched cab, call **C.O.O.P.** (© **441/292-4476**).

bicycling or mopeding around Bermuda on a sunny day, slowly putt-putting across the island.

What the brochures don't tell you is that the roads are too narrow, and Bermudians—who are likely to own cars, and pay dearly for the privilege—feel that the road is theirs. Sometimes it starts raining almost without warning, but the skies usually clear rapidly, and the roads dry quickly. During inclement weather, scooter riders are likely to be edged close—sometimes disturbingly close—to the shoulder; in the aftermath of rainstorms, they'll almost certainly be splattered with water or mud. Many accidents occur on slippery roads after a rain, especially involving those not accustomed to using a motor scooter.

Who should rent a moped or scooter, and who should avoid them altogether? Frankly, the answer depends on your physical fitness and the time of day. Even the most stiffly starched might find a wind-whipped morning ride from the hotel to the beach or tennis courts invigorating and fun. Dressed to the nines for a candlelit dinner, you'd find the experience horrifying. And although the putt-putters can be a lot of fun on a sunny day, the machines can be dangerous and capricious after dark—and, of course, when you've had too many daiquiris. Not everyone is fit enough. Visitors on mopeds have a high accident rate, with at least some of the problems related to driving on the left.

Considering the hazards, we usually recommend that reasonably adept sports enthusiasts rent a moped for a day or two. For evening outings, we firmly believe that a taxi is the way to go.

What are the requirements for renting a motorbike? You must be 16 or older. Some vehicles are big enough for two cozy adults. Helmets are required, and rental companies must provide them. Know in advance that on a hot day, they're uncomfortable. But, what the hell—you'll be at the beach soon enough.

What's the difference between a moped and a motor scooter? Frankly, many visitors rent one or the other and never really understand the difference. They're basically alike, with equivalent maximum speeds and horsepower. Mopeds have larger wheels than scooters, and subject riders to fewer shocks as they traverse bumps in the road. Most (but not all) mopeds are designed for one rider; scooters accommodate either a single passenger or two passengers riding in tandem.

There are quite a few gas stations (called "petrol stations"). Once you "tank up" your motorbike, chances are you'll have plenty to get you to your destination; for example, one tank of gas in a motorbike will take you from Somerset in the west to St. George in the east.

Among the rental companies listed below, there's a tendency toward price-fixing. Rental fees across the island tend to be roughly equivalent, and shopping around for a better deal is usually a waste of time. Mopeds for one rider rent for $53 for the first day, $77 for 2 days, $112 for 3 days, and $154 for 7 days. Scooters for two riders cost $57 to $62 for 1 day. You must pay with a major credit card; it serves as a deposit in case of damage or theft. You must also purchase a one-time insurance policy for $15. The insurance is valid for the length of the rental.

You can rent mopeds and 50cc scooters at **Wheels** (✆ **441/292-2245**), which has two locations on Front Street in Hamilton; one at Flatts Village; and at the following resorts: the Fairmont Hamilton Princess, the Sonesta Beach Resort, Coral Beach Cottages, the Stonington Beach Resort, White Sands Hotel and Cottages, and Horizons and Cottages. You'll find comparable prices at **Concord Cycle Shop,** at The Fairmont Southampton Princess (✆ **441/238-3336**).

Oleander Cycles Ltd., Valley Road, P.O. Box 114, Paget Parish (✆ **441/236-5235**), rents scooters and mopeds at prices comparable to Wheels' and

Concord Cycle Shop's. There is another location on Gorham Road in Hamilton (© **441/295-0919**), and at Middle Road in Southampton (© **441/234-0629**). All locations are open daily from 8:30am to 5:30pm. Rentals require a $20 deposit.

Eve's Cycle Livery, 114 Middle Rd., Paget Parish (© **441/236-6247**), offers one of the best rental deals on the island. Named after the legendary matriarch who founded the company more than 40 years ago, Eve's rents men's and women's pedal bicycles (usually 10- to 12-speed mountain bikes, well suited to the island's hilly terrain). They go for $20 for the first day, $15 for the second day, and $10 for the third day. A $20 deposit is required. The shop is within a 10-minute taxi ride (or a leisurely 20-min. cycle) west of Hamilton. The company also rents a variety of scooters; they cost $42 to $60 for the first day, and $181 to $250 for 7 days, depending on the model, with successively lower prices for each additional day.

Island-Hopping on Your Own

Most first-time visitors think of Bermuda as one island, but in fact it's a small archipelago. Many of the islands that make up the chain are uninhabited. If you're a bit of a skipper, you can explore them on your own. With a little guidance and the proper maps, you can discover small islands, out-of-the-way coral reefs, and hidden coves that seem straight from the old Brooke Shields B-movie, *The Blue Lagoon.*

For this boating adventure, rent a Boston whaler with an outboard engine. The name of these small but sturdy boats reveals their origins: They were once used by New Englanders in their pursuit of Moby Dick. It's important to exercise caution, remembering that the English found Bermuda in 1612 only after the *Sea Venture,* en route to the Jamestown Colony, was wrecked off the Bermuda coast.

In the East End, you can explore Castle Harbour, which is almost completely surrounded by islands, forming a protected lake. If you stop to do some fishing, snapper is your likely catch. (Visitors who rent condos or apartments often take their quarry back to their kitchenette to prepare it for dinner.) To avoid the often-powerful swells, drop anchor on the west side of Castle Harbour, near Castle Harbour Golf Club and Tucker's Town. Then head across Tucker's Town Bay to Castle Island and Castle Island Nature Reserve. In earlier days, Castle Island was fortified to protect Castle Harbour from enemy attack. In 1612, Governor Moore ordered the construction of a fort, the ruins of which you can see today.

In the West End, begin your exploration by going under Somerset Bridge into well-protected Ely's Harbour. To the north, you can visit Cathedral Rocks before making a half-circle to Somerset Village; from here, you can explore the uninhabited islands off Mangrove Bay.

You can rent a 13- to 15-foot Boston whaler—and pick up some local guidance—at **Blue Hole Water Sports,** Grotto Bay Beach Hotel, Hamilton Parish (© **441/293-2915**). Prices begin at $65 for 2 hours, $110 for 4 hours, and $165 for 8 hours. Rates do not include gas.

BY BICYCLE

Looking for a more natural means of locomotion than a putt-putt? You can rent bikes at most cycle liveries (see "By Cycle & Scooter," above), but for cyclists who don't work out 6 hours a day, pedaling a bike up Bermuda's steep hills can be a bit of a challenge. Prices range from $10 to $15 a day, depending on your steed's brand name and degree of stylishness. See "Biking," in chapter 6, "Fun in the Surf & Sun," for more details.

BY BUS

You can't rent a car. Taxis are expensive. Horse-drawn carriages aren't really a viable option. You may not want to ride a bicycle or a motorbike. What's left for getting around Bermuda? Buses, of course.

The bus network covers all major routes, and nearly all hotels, guesthouses, and restaurants have bus stops close by. There's even a do-it-yourself sightseeing tour by bus and ferry. Regularly scheduled buses go to most of the destinations that interest visitors in Bermuda, but be prepared to wait. Some buses don't run on Sundays and holidays, so be sure you know the schedule for the trip you want to make.

Bermuda is divided into 14 zones of about 2 miles each. The regular cash fare for up to three zones is $2.50; using tokens, it's $2.25. For more than three zones, it's $4, or $3.75 using tokens. Children 5 to 16 pay $1 for all zones; children under 5 ride free. *Note:* You must have the exact change or tokens ready to deposit in the fare box as you board the bus. Drivers do not make change or accept bills. On the run from Hamilton to the Royal Naval Dockyard (no. 7 or 8), the fare is $3.75 for adults, $1 for children.

You can purchase tokens at subpost offices or at the **Central Bus Terminal** on Washington Street in Hamilton, where all routes, except route 6, begin and end. The terminal is just off Church Street, a few steps east of City Hall. You can get there from Front Street or Reid Street by going up Queen Street or through Walker Arcade and Washington Mall.

If you plan to travel a lot, you might want to purchase a booklet of 15 tickets. A booklet of 14-zone tickets costs $25.50; of 3-zone tickets, $16. For children, 15 tickets cost $6, regardless of the number of zones. You can buy the booklets at post offices or the central bus terminal. You can also purchase passes that allow travel for 1 day to 1 month. A 1-day pass costs $11, a 1-week pass is $36, and a 1-month pass is $40.

For more information on bus service, call © **441/292-3854.**

In the east, **St. George's Mini-Bus Service** (© **441/297-8199**) operates a minibus service around St. George Parish and St. David's Island. The basic one-way fare is $2. Buses depart from King's Square in the center of St. George, and can be flagged down along the road. Service is year-round daily from 7:30am to 10pm. The service also offers 1-hour historical tours of St. George; the cost is $20 per person.

Trolley-like **buses** that seat 60 serve the capital of Hamilton and the Royal Naval Dockyard. Passengers can get on and off throughout the day for the single fare of $10. The Hamilton trolley stops at the major points of interest, including the Botanical Gardens; the dockyard bus calls at the crafts market. Tickets are for sale at most hotels, the Hamilton train station, and the Oleander cycle shop.

BY FERRY

One of the most interesting means of getting around is the government-operated ferry service. Ferries crisscross Great Sound between Hamilton and

Somerset; the one-way fare is $4. They also take the harbor route, from Hamilton to the hotel-intensive parishes of Paget and Warwick. The ride from Hamilton to Paget costs $2.50. Children 5 to 16 pay $1; children under 5 ride free. Motorbikes are allowed on the Hamilton to Somerset run for $4. Bicycles can be carried on free.

For ferry service information, call © **441/295-4506** in Hamilton. Ferry schedules are posted at each landing and are available at the Ferry Terminal, the Central Bus Terminal in Hamilton, and most hotels.

BY HORSE-DRAWN CARRIAGE

Once upon a time, this was the only way a tourist had to get around Bermuda. Before 1946 (when automobiles first came to the island), horses were the principal means of transportation. But the allure and appeal of the horse-drawn carriage has waned so much that there are only about a dozen left. The drivers often seem a little bored. They don't take you to any unusual places, but along routes both the driver and horses know only too well. You can book one of the four-wheeled rigs for a chauffeured tour of the island's midriff.

Drivers congregate on Front Street in Hamilton, adjacent to the no. 1 passenger terminal near the cruise-ship docks. A single carriage (accommodating one to four passengers) drawn by one horse costs $30 for 30 minutes. An additional 30 minutes costs another $30. If the carriage picks you up, the cost is $40 for the first 30 minutes. For rides lasting more than 3 hours, the fee is negotiable. Unless you make special arrangements for a night ride, you aren't likely to find any carriages after 4:30pm. Contact **Terceira's Stables** at © **441/236-3014.**

 FAST FACTS: **Bermuda**

American Express The representative in Hamilton, **Meyer Agencies,** 35 Church St. (P.O. Box 510), Hamilton HM 12 (© **441/295-4176**), provides complete travel service, traveler's checks, and emergency check cashing.

Banks The main offices of Bermuda's three banks are in Hamilton. All banks and their branches are open Monday to Thursday 9:30am to 3pm, Friday 9:30am to 4:30pm. Banks are closed Saturday, Sunday, and public holidays. Many big hotels will cash traveler's checks, and there are ATMs all around the island.

The **Bank of Bermuda Ltd.,** 6 Front St., Hamilton (© **441/295-4000**), has branches on Church Street, Hamilton; Par-la-Ville Road, Hamilton; King's Square, St. George; and in Somerset.

The **Bank of N.T. Butterfield & Son, Ltd.,** 65 Front St., Hamilton (© **441/ 295-1111**), has several branches, including St. George and Somerset.

The **Bermuda Commercial Bank Ltd.** is at 44 Church St., Hamilton (© **441/295-5678**).

Bookstores **Bermuda Book Store (Baxters) Ltd.,** Queen Street, Hamilton (© **441/295-3698**), stocks everything that's in print about Bermuda, including titles on gardening, flowers, local characters, and poets, and other topics; some are available only through this store. There are also many English publications not easily obtainable in the United States, as well as a fine selection of children's books. You can also buy maps, prints, and that beach novel you forgot to bring. Open Monday to Saturday 9am to 5pm.

Business Hours Most businesses are open Monday to Friday 9am to 5pm. Stores are generally open Monday to Saturday 9am to 5pm; several shops open at 9:15am. A few shops are also open in the evening, but usually only when big cruise ships are in port.

Car Rentals There are no car-rental agencies in Bermuda. For transportation information, see "Getting Around," earlier in this chapter.

Climate See "When to Go," in chapter 2, "Planning Your Trip to Bermuda."

Crime See "Safety," below.

Currency Exchange Because the U.S. dollar and the Bermudian dollar are on par, both currencies can be used. It's not necessary to convert U.S. dollars into Bermudian dollars. Canadian dollars and British pounds must be converted into local currency. For more information, see "Money," in chapter 2, "Planning Your Trip to Bermuda."

Customs For details on what you can bring into Bermuda and what you can carry home, see "Entry Requirements & Customs," in chapter 2, "Planning Your Trip to Bermuda."

Dentists For dental emergencies, call **King Edward VII Hospital,** 7 Point Finger Rd., Paget Parish (© **441/236-2345**), and ask for the emergency department. The hospital maintains lists of dentists on emergency call.

Doctors In an emergency, call **King Edward VII Hospital,** 7 Point Finger Rd., Paget Parish (© **441/236-2345**), and ask for the emergency department. For non-emergencies, ask the concierge at your hotel for a recommendation.

Documents Required See "Entry Requirements & Customs," in chapter 2, "Planning Your Trip to Bermuda."

Drinking Age See "Liquor Laws," below.

Driving Rules Visitors cannot rent cars. To operate a motor-assisted cycle, you must be age 16 or over. All cycle drivers and passengers must wear securely fastened safety helmets. Driving is on the left side of the road, and the speed limit is 20 mph in the countryside, 15 mph in busy areas.

Drug Laws Importation of, possession of, or dealing in unlawful drugs (including marijuana) is illegal in Bermuda; there are heavy penalties for infractions. Customs officers, at their discretion, may conduct body searches for drugs or other contraband goods.

Drugstores Try the **Phoenix Drugstore,** 3 Reid St. (© **441/295-3838**), open Monday to Saturday 8am to 6pm, Sunday noon to 6:30pm.

In Paget Parish, **Paget Pharmacy,** 130 South Shore Rd. (© **441/236-7275**), is open Monday to Saturday 8am to 8pm, Sunday 10am to 6pm. The **Somerset Pharmacy,** 49 Mangrove Bay, Somerset Village (© **441/234-2484**), is open Monday to Saturday 8am to 6pm, Sunday 11am to 4pm.

Electricity Electricity is 110 volts AC (60 cycles). American appliances are compatible without converters or adapters. Visitors from the United Kingdom or other parts of Europe need to bring a converter.

Embassies & Consulates The **American Consulate General** is at Crown Hill, 16 Middle Rd., Devonshire (© **441/295-1342**). It does not keep general business hours, but has hours for specific services. Call before you go to find out whether the service you need is available. The **Canadian**

Consulate General (Commission to Bermuda) is at 1251 Avenue of the Americas, New York, NY 10020 (*©* **212/596-1600**). Britain doesn't have an embassy or consulate in Bermuda.

Emergencies To call the police, report a fire, or summon an ambulance, dial *©* **911.** The non-emergency police number is *©* **441/295-0011.** For Air-Sea Rescue, dial *©* **441/297-1010.**

Etiquette Well-tailored Bermuda shorts are acceptable on almost any occasion, and many men wear them with jackets and ties. On formal occasions, they must be accompanied by knee socks. Aside from that, Bermudians are rather conservative in their attitude toward dress—bikinis, for example, are banned more than 25 feet from the water. Men are usually required to wear a jacket to dinner.

Eyeglass Repair **Argus Optical Company** (Henry Simmons, O.D.), Melbourne House, Parliament Street, Hamilton (*©* **441/292-5452**), works with prescription glasses and contact lenses. Hours are Monday to Friday 9am to noon and 1 to 4:45pm.

Gasoline Mopeds take a mixture of oil and gas, and always have a separate pump at gasoline (petrol) stations. Honda scooters require regular unleaded gasoline. The typical touring biker needs about one refill per week. Both Honda scooters and mopeds are rented with full tanks. Gasoline stations are conveniently situated around the island, and gas for cycles costs $3 to $4 per liter.

Holidays See "When to Go," in chapter 2, "Planning Your Trip to Bermuda."

Hospitals **King Edward VII Memorial Hospital,** 7 Point Finger Rd., Paget Parish (*©* **441/236-2345**), has a highly qualified staff and Canadian accreditation.

Hot Lines Call *©* **441/236-0224,** ext. 226 or 227, for a consultation on psychiatric problems, but only Monday to Friday from 8:45am to 5pm. After 5pm, call *©* **441/236-3770;** you'll be connected to the Bermuda Psychiatric Hospital's outpatient clinic or (in the evening) St. Brendan's Hospital. Either can help with life-threatening problems, personal crises, or referral to a medical specialist.

Information For information before you go, see "Visitor Information," in chapter 2, "Planning Your Trip to Bermuda"; once you're on the island, see "Orienting Yourself: The Lay of the Land," earlier in this chapter. For telephone directory assistance, call *©* **411.**

Legal Aid The U.S. consulate will inform you of your limited rights and offer a list of attorneys. However, the consulate's office cannot interfere with Bermuda's law-enforcement officers. The **Citizens' Emergency Center** of the Office of Special Consular Services in Washington, D.C. (*©* **202/647-5225**), operates a hot line that's useful in an emergency for U.S. citizens arrested abroad. The staff can also tell you how to send money to U.S. citizens arrested abroad.

Liquor Laws Bermuda sternly regulates the sale of alcoholic beverages. The legal drinking age is 18, and most bars close at 1am. Some nightclubs and hotel bars can serve liquor until 3am. Many bars are closed on Sunday.

Hard liquor is sold in specialty stores selling liquor, beer, and wine. Although it's legal for grocery stores to sell hard liquor, most limit their inventories to beer and wine. Alcohol can't be sold on Sunday. You can bring beer or other alcohol to the beach legally, as long as your party doesn't get too rowdy and you generally stay in one spot. The moment you actually *walk* on the beach or the streets with an open container of liquor, it's illegal. (The thinking behind this law is apparently that roaming gangs of loud, obnoxious drunks are more dangerous and disruptive than sedentary gangs of loud, obnoxious drunks.)

Mail Deposit regular mail in the red pillar boxes on the streets. You'll recognize them by the monogram of Queen Elizabeth II. The postage rates for airmail letters up to 10 grams and for postcards is 65¢ to the United States and Canada, 80¢ to the United Kingdom. Airmail letters and postcards to the North American mainland can take 5 to 7 days, to Britain possibly a little longer. Often visitors return home before their postcards arrive.

Newspapers/Magazines Bermuda has one daily newspaper, the *Royal Gazette*. Three weekly papers—the *Bermuda Sun,* the *Bermuda Times,* and the *Mid-Ocean News*—are issued on Friday. Major U.S. newspapers, including the *New York Times* and *USA Today,* and magazines such as *Time* and *Newsweek* are delivered to Bermuda on the day of their publication on the mainland. *This Week in Bermuda* is a weekly guide for tourists.

Passports See "Entry Requirements & Customs," in chapter 2, "Planning Your Trip to Bermuda."

Pets If you want to take your pet with you to Bermuda, you'll need a special permit issued by the director of the **Department of Agriculture, Fisheries, and Parks,** P.O. Box HM 834, Hamilton HM CX, Bermuda (*(C)* **441/ 236-4201**). The island has no quarantine facilities, so animals arriving without proper documents will be refused entry and will be returned to the point of origin. Some guesthouses and hotels allow you to bring in small animals, but others will not, so be sure to inquire in advance. Always check to see what the latest regulations are before attempting to bring a dog or other pet—including Seeing-Eye dogs—to Bermuda.

Pharmacies See Drugstores.

Photographic Needs If you want to buy a camera or film, or develop Kodak or Fuji film, try Hamilton's leading camera store, **Stuart's,** 5 Reid St., near the corner of Queen Street (*(C)* **441/295-5496**). Film can be developed in-house in about 3 hours (sometimes within 1 hr., for a surcharge). Open Monday to Saturday 9am to 5pm.

Police In an emergency, call *(C)* **911;** otherwise, call *(C)* **441/295-0011.**

Post Offices The **General Post Office,** 56 Church St., Hamilton (*(C)* **441/ 295-5151**), is open Monday to Friday 8am to 5pm, Saturday 8am to noon. Post office branches and the Perot Post Office, Queen Street, Hamilton, are open Monday to Friday 9am to 5pm. Some post offices close for lunch from 11:30am to 1pm. Daily airmail service for the United States and Canada closes at 9:30am in Hamilton. See also "Mail," above.

Radio & TV News is broadcast on the hour and half hour over AM stations 1340 (ZBM), 1230 (ZFB), and 1450 (VSB). The FM stations are 89 (ZBM) and 95 (ZFB). Tourist-oriented programming, island music, and information on activities and special events air over AM station 1160 (VSB) daily from 7am to noon.

The television channel, 10 (ZBM), is affiliated with America's Columbia Broadcasting System (CBS).

Restrooms Hamilton and St. George provide public facilities, but only during business hours. In Hamilton, toilets are at City Hall, in Par-la-Ville Gardens, and at Albouy's Point. In St. George, facilities are available at Town Hall, Somers Gardens, and Market Wharf. Outside of these towns, you'll find restrooms at the public beaches, the Botanical Gardens, in several of the forts, at the airport, and at service stations. Often you'll have to use the facilities in hotels, restaurants, and wherever else you can find them.

Safety Bermudians are generally peaceful people, not given to violence. To be sure, the island has experienced racial tensions in the past, but right now relations between white and black residents seem to be harmonious, as blacks assume a greater role in Bermuda's affairs.

Crimes, violent or otherwise, against tourists are rare, but don't be lulled into a false sense of security. Crime does exist in Bermuda, as it does in any society. Take care to protect your valuables, especially when you're at the beach. Lock your moped each time you leave it. If you bring very valuable items with you (this is not advisable), place them in your hotel safe and never leave them carelessly in your room.

Smoking Tobacconists and other stores carry a wide array of tobacco products, generally from either the United States or England. Prices vary but tend to be high. At most tobacconists you can buy classic cigars from Havana, but Americans must enjoy them on the island—they can't be taken back to the United States. Smoking in public places (such as restaurants) is generally permitted, but check before lighting up. Movie theaters set aside a section for nonsmokers.

Taxes Bermuda charges visitors a Passenger Tax before they depart from the island. For those who leave by air, the tax, collected at the airport, is $20 for adults or children (children under 2 are exempt). For those who leave by ship, the tax, collected in advance by the cruise-ship company, is $60 (children under 2 are exempt).

All room rates, regardless of the category of accommodation or the plan under which you stay, are subject to a government tax of 6% (for simple guesthouses) to 7.5% (for the large majority of Bermuda's conventional hotels).

Taxis See "Getting Around," earlier in this chapter.

Telephone/Telegrams/Telexes/Faxes Worldwide direct-dial phone, fax, and cable service is available at the **Cable & Wireless Office,** 20 Church St., Hamilton, opposite City Hall (© **441/297-7022**). Prepaid phone cards may be purchased and used island-wide, and calling cards may be used from selected call boxes. Hours are Monday to Saturday 9am to 5pm.

Cable & Wireless, in conjunction with the Bermuda Telephone Co., provides international direct dialing (IDD) to more than 150 countries. Country codes and calling charges may be found in the Bermuda telephone directory. Telephone booths are available at the Cable & Wireless office, and customers can either prepay or buy cash cards in $10, $20, and $50 denominations. Cash-card phone booths are available at numerous locations around the island. Making international calls with cash cards can be a lot cheaper than using the phone at your hotel, which might impose stiff surcharges. To make a local call, deposit 20¢ (Bermudian or U.S.). Hotels often charge 20¢ to $1 for local calls.

Special phones at passenger piers in Hamilton, St. George, and the dockyard will connect you directly with an AT&T, Sprint, or MCI operator in the United States, permitting you to make collect or calling-card calls.

Telephone Directory All Bermuda telephone numbers appear in one phone book, revised annually. The Yellow Pages list all the goods and services you are likely to need in the back.

Time Bermuda is 1 hour ahead of eastern time. Daylight saving time is in effect from the first Sunday in April until the last Sunday in October, as it is in the United States.

Tipping In most cases, a service charge is added to hotel and restaurant bills. In hotels, the charge is in lieu of tipping various individuals, such as bellhops, maids, and restaurant staffers (for meals included in a package or in the daily rate). Check for this carefully to avoid double tipping. Otherwise, a 15% tip for service is customary. Taxis drivers usually get 10% to 15%.

Tourist Offices See "Visitor Information," in chapter 2, "Planning Your Trip to Bermuda," and the "Visitor Information on the Island" box, earlier in this chapter.

Transit Information For information about ferry service, call ✆ **441/295-4506.** For bus information, call ✆ **441/292-3854.**

Useful Telephone Numbers For time and temperature, call ✆ **977-1.** To learn "What's On in Bermuda," dial ✆ **974.** For medical emergencies or the police, dial ✆ **911.** If in doubt during any other emergency, dial ✆ **0** (zero), which will connect you with your hotel's switchboard or the Bermuda telephone operator.

Water Tap water is generally safe to drink.

Weather Call ✆ **977** at any time for a forecast covering the next 24-hour period.

4

Accommodations

Bermuda offers a wide choice of lodgings, from small, casual guesthouses to large, luxurious resorts. Facilities vary greatly in size and amenities within each category.

CHOOSING THE PLACE THAT'S RIGHT FOR YOU

Accommodations in Bermuda basically fall into five categories:

- **Resort Hotels:** These generally large properties are Bermuda's best, offering many facilities, services, and luxuries—but also charging the highest prices, especially in summer. The lowest rates, usually discounted about 20%, are in effect from mid-November to March. The large resorts usually have their own beaches or beach clubs, along with swimming pools; some have their own golf courses. It's cheaper to choose Modified American Plan (MAP) rates, which include breakfast and dinner, than to order all your meals a la carte. However, if you go the MAP route, you'll be confined to the same dining room every night and miss the opportunity to sample different restaurants.
- **Cottage Colonies:** This uniquely Bermudian option typically consists of a series of bungalows constructed around a clubhouse, which is the center of social life, drinking, and dining. The cottages, usually scenically arranged on landscaped grounds, are designed to provide maximum privacy and are typically equipped with kitchenettes for preparing light meals. In many of the cottage colonies, breakfast isn't available; you can go out, or buy supplies the night before and prepare your own meal. Most colonies have their own beaches or swimming pools.
- **Small Hotels:** This option might be right for those who absolutely hate megaresorts. Bermuda's small hotels offer the intimacy of upscale bed-and-breakfasts, but with considerably more facilities. At a small hotel, you might feel more connected to the island and its people. Another plus? They're often cheaper than the big resorts.
- **Housekeeping Units:** These cottage or apartment-style accommodations (often called efficiencies in the U.S.) usually occupy landscaped estates surrounding a main clubhouse. All of them offer kitchen facilities—perhaps a full, well-equipped kitchen, but at least a kitchenette where you can whip up snacks and breakfast. Most offer minimal daily maid service. Generally housekeeping units are simpler and less expensive than cottage colonies.
- **Guesthouses:** These are Bermuda's least expensive accommodations. The larger guesthouses are old Bermuda homes in garden settings. Generally, they've been modernized and have comfortable guest rooms. Some have their own swimming pools. A number of guesthouses are small, modest places, offering breakfast only; you may share a bathroom with other guests. If you stay in a guesthouse, you may have to "commute" to the beach.

Another option is renting a **villa** or vacation home. Villa rentals are like renting someone's home. At some, you're entirely on your own; others provide maid service. Most are on or near a beach. This is generally an expensive option.

Private **apartments** offer fewer frills than villas or condos; the building housing the apartment may not have a swimming pool, or even a front desk. Apartments are available with or without maid service.

Cottages, or cabanas, offer the most independent lifestyle in this category of vacation accommodations—they're entirely self-catering. Some open onto a beach, and others surround a communal swimming pool. Most of them are fairly basic, consisting of a simple bedroom plus a small kitchen and bathroom. For the peak summer season, make cabana reservations at least 5 or 6 months in advance.

Several U.S. and Canadian agents can arrange these types of rentals. **Villanet,** 12600 SE 38 St., Suite 202, Bellevue, WA 98006 (✆ **206/417-3444;** www. rentavilla.com), specializes in condos and villas. It can arrange bookings for a week or longer.

RATES & RESERVATION POLICIES

The rates that we've listed throughout this chapter are "rack rates"—the rates you'd be quoted if you walked in off the street. These are helpful largely for purposes of comparison. Especially at the big resorts, almost no one ever pays the rack rate. By booking a package deal that includes airfare, or just by asking for packages and discounts at the hotel when you make your reservation, you can usually do much better. At small hotels and guesthouses, the rates quoted here are much more likely to be accurate. Before you book anything, read the "Package Deals" section in chapter 2, "Planning Your Trip to Bermuda."

All room rates, regardless of meal plan, are subject to a 7.5% tax, which will be tacked onto your bill. A service charge (10%–15%) is also added to your room rate in lieu of tips; remember that service charges do not cover bar tabs. Third-person rates (for those occupying a room with two other people) are lower, and children's rates vary according to their age. The rack rates we've listed in this chapter include tax and service charge unless otherwise noted. However, we strongly encourage you to confirm what the rates include when you reserve, to avoid any misunderstanding. Hotels usually quote you the full rate you'll pay upon checkout; they don't want misunderstandings, either.

Bermuda's high season is spring and summer—the opposite of the Bahamian and Caribbean high season. Most of Bermuda's hotels charge high-season rates from March (Easter is the peak period) through mid-November. A few hotels have year-round rates, and others charge in-between, or "shoulder," prices in spring and autumn. If business is slow, many smaller places shut down in winter.

You may see some unfamiliar terms and abbreviations used to describe rate plans. **AP** (American Plan), sometimes called full board, includes three meals a day. **MAP** (Modified American Plan), sometimes called half-board, includes breakfast and dinner. **BP** (Bermuda Plan) includes full American or English

---

Tips **Planning Pointer**

The rack rates in this chapter include tax and service charge unless we note otherwise. To avoid any possible misunderstanding, be sure you understand what is included in the rates at your hotel when you make reservations.

Bermuda's Hotels at a Glance

	Access for disabled	Directly beside the beach	On-site swimming pool	Restaurant on premises	Cable TV in bedroom	Fitness facilities	Access to golf nearby	On-site tennis courts	Convention facilities	Welcomes children	Childcare facilities	On-site spa facilities	Access to water sports	Accepts credit cards	Air-conditioned bedrooms	Live on-site entertainment	Wharf or marina facilities
Angel's Grotto	✓			✓		✓		✓				✓	✓	✓			
Ariel Sands Beach Club		✓	✓	✓		✓	✓		✓	✓		✓	✓	✓	✓		
Astwood Cove			✓						✓					✓			
Aunt Nea's Inn at Hillcrest												✓	✓				
Barnsdale Guest Apartments			✓		✓				✓				✓	✓			
Cambridge Beaches		✓	✓	✓		✓	✓	✓	✓			✓	✓		✓	✓	✓
Clear View Suites & Villas	✓	✓	✓	✓	✓		✓	✓	✓	✓	✓		✓	✓			
Daniel's Head Village		✓		✓					✓			✓	✓				
Dawkin's Manor			✓	✓					✓				✓	✓			
Edgehill Manor			✓		✓				✓					✓			
Elbow Beach Hotel	✓	✓	✓	✓	✓	✓	✓	✓	✓	✓	✓	✓	✓	✓	✓	✓	
Fairmont Hamilton Princess	✓		✓	✓	✓	✓	✓	✓	✓	✓	✓	✓	✓	✓	✓	✓	✓
Fairmont Southampton Princess	✓	✓	✓	✓	✓	✓	✓	✓	✓	✓	✓	✓	✓	✓	✓	✓	✓
Fordham Hall				✓									✓	✓			
Fourways Inn			✓	✓	✓		✓		✓				✓	✓			
Garden House			✓		✓									✓			
Grape Bay Cottages					✓			✓	✓				✓	✓			
Greenbank Guest House									✓			✓	✓	✓		✓	
Greene's Guest House			✓		✓		✓		✓					✓			
Grotto Bay Beach Hotel	✓	✓	✓	✓	✓	✓	✓	✓	✓	✓		✓	✓	✓	✓	✓	✓
Hamiltonian Hotel & Island Club			✓		✓		✓		✓			✓	✓				
Harmony Club		✓	✓	✓		✓	✓					✓	✓	✓			
Horizons and Cottages			✓	✓			✓	✓		✓	✓				✓	✓	
Little Pomander Guest House	✓				✓		✓		✓			✓	✓	✓			
Loughlands			✓				✓	✓	✓						✓		
Marley Beach Cottages		✓	✓		✓		✓		✓			✓	✓	✓			

Bermuda's Hotels (cont.)

	Access for disabled	Directly beside the beach	On-site swimming pool	Restaurant on premises	Cable TV in bedroom	Fitness facilities	Access to golf nearby	On-site tennis courts	Convention facilities	Welcomes children	Childcare facilities	On-site spa facilities	Access to water sports	Accepts credit cards	Air-conditioned bedrooms	Live on-site entertainment	Wharf or marina facilities
Harbour Resort	✓		✓	✓	✓	✓		✓	✓	✓	✓		✓	✓	✓	✓	
Mermaid Beach Club		✓	✓	✓					✓			✓	✓				
Munro Beach Cottages					✓		✓		✓	✓			✓	✓			
Newstead Hotel			✓	✓			✓	✓	✓	✓		✓	✓	✓	✓	✓	✓
The Oxford House				✓					✓				✓	✓			
Palmetto Hotel & Cottages			✓	✓			✓		✓	✓		✓	✓	✓	✓	✓	✓
Paraquet Guest Apartments			✓	✓		✓			✓				✓				
Pink Beach Club & Cottages		✓	✓	✓			✓	✓	✓	✓	✓	✓	✓	✓	✓	✓	
Pompano Beach Club		✓	✓	✓		✓	✓	✓	✓	✓	✓	✓	✓	✓	✓	✓	
The Reefs		✓	✓	✓	✓		✓	✓	✓	✓	✓	✓	✓	✓	✓	✓	✓
Robin's Nest			✓		✓									✓			
Rosedon			✓		✓				✓				✓				
Rosemont			✓		✓				✓	✓			✓	✓			
Royal Heights Guest House			✓		✓				✓				✓	✓			
Royal Palms Hotel			✓	✓	✓				✓			✓	✓				
St. George's Club	✓	✓	✓	✓	✓	✓		✓	✓	✓	✓	✓	✓	✓	✓		
Salt Kettle House					✓				✓			✓	✓				✓
Sandpiper Apartments			✓		✓				✓				✓	✓			
Sky-Top Cottages					✓				✓				✓	✓			
Sonesta Beach Resort	✓	✓	✓	✓	✓	✓	✓	✓	✓	✓	✓	✓	✓	✓	✓	✓	
Stonington Beach Hotel		✓	✓	✓			✓	✓	✓	✓	✓		✓	✓	✓	✓	
Surf Side Beach Club		✓	✓	✓	✓		✓		✓	✓			✓	✓	✓		
Valley Cottages & Apartments			✓		✓		✓		✓				✓	✓			
Vienna Guest Apartments			✓		✓	✓							✓	✓			
Waterloo House			✓	✓				✓	✓			✓	✓	✓	✓		
Whale Bay Inn	✓			✓	✓										✓		
White Sands Hotel & Cottages		✓	✓	✓	✓		✓		✓	✓			✓	✓	✓		

Bermuda Accommodations

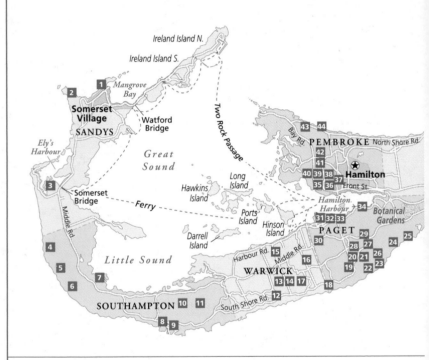

ATLANTIC OCEAN

Ireland Island N.
Ireland Island S.
Mangrove Bay
Somerset Village
SANDYS
Watford Bridge
Ely's Harbour
Great Sound
Two Rock Passage
Bay Rd.
PEMBROKE North Shore Rd.
Hamilton
Front St.
Somerset Bridge
Ferry
Hawkins Island
Long Island
Middle Rd.
Little Sound
Ports Island
Hinson Island
Darrell Island
Hamilton Harbour
Botanical Gardens
PAGET
Harbour Rd.
Middle Rd.
WARWICK
South Shore Rd.
SOUTHAMPTON

Airport ✈

0   3 mi
0   3 km

Newstead Hotel **33**
The Oxford House **37**
Paraquet Guest Apartments **21**
Pink Beach Club & Cottages **50**
Pompano Beach Club **4**
The Reefs **8**
Robin's Nest **43**
Rosedon **38**
Rosemont **39**
Royal Heights Guest House **10**
Royal Palms Hotel **42**
Salt Kettle House **32**
Sandpiper Apartments **17**
Sky-Top Cottages **28**

Sonesta Beach Resort **9**
St. George's Club **47**
Stonington Beach Hotel **23**
Surf Side Beach Club **18**
Valley Cottages & Apartments **16**
Vienna Guest Apartments **15**
Waterloo House **36**
Whale Bay Inn **6**
White Sands Hotel & Cottages **24**

See also "Accommodations in the City of Hamilton" map

(Tips **Dining at Your Hotel**

Chances are, you'll take more meals at your hotel in Bermuda than you would in other sunny destinations, such as Florida. Although you're generally out and about for lunch, many dinner guests don't like to hire an expensive taxi or else take a bike or motorbike along Bermuda's narrow roads. The first is expensive and the latter a bit hazardous. Since you can't rent a car, you are often stuck for meals at your hotel, and therefore you might want to consider food options when deciding where to stay.

In many destinations hotel restaurants aren't a big factor in selecting an accommodation. But because of transportation difficulties in Bermuda, especially at night, consider the cuisine served at a hotel before checking in. To help you out, we've added more details about hotel dining than you can find in most other guidebooks.

---

breakfast. **CP** (Continental Plan) includes only continental breakfast (basically bread, jam, and coffee). **EP** (European Plan) is always cheapest—it includes only the room, no meals.

Note that prices aren't uniform in several of the larger, older resorts, which offer a wide range of rooms. For instance, one guest at the Elbow Beach Hotel might be paying a price that can be categorized as "moderate," whereas another might be booked at a "very expensive" rate—it all depends on your room assignment. So even if you can't pay $200 a night, it might be worth a call to see if a cheaper room is available.

Members of the Bermuda Hotel Association require 2 nights' deposit within 14 days of confirming a reservation; full payment 30 days before arrival; and notice of cancellation 15 days before scheduled arrival, or you'll forfeit your deposit Some smaller hotels and other accommodations levy an energy surcharge; inquire about this when you make your reservations.

TIPS FOR SAVING ON YOUR HOTEL ROOM

- **Don't be afraid to bargain.** Get in the habit of asking for a lower price than the first one quoted. Most rack rates include commissions of 10% to 25% or more for travel agents, which many hotels will cut if you make your own reservations and haggle a bit. Always ask politely whether a less-expensive room is available, or whether any special rates apply to you. You may qualify for corporate, student, military, senior citizen, or other discounts. Be sure to mention membership in AAA, AARP, frequent flyer programs, or trade unions, which may entitle you to special deals as well.
- **Rely on a qualified professional.** Certain hotels give travel agents discounts in exchange for steering business their way, so if you're shy about bargaining, an agent may be better equipped to negotiate discounts.
- **Dial direct.** When booking a room in a chain hotel, call the hotel's local line, as well as the toll-free number, and see where you get the best deal. A hotel makes nothing on a room that stays empty. The clerk who runs the place is more likely to know about vacancies and will often grant deep discounts in order to fill rooms.
- **Consider a suite.** If you are traveling with your family or another couple, you can pack more people into a suite (which usually comes with a sofa bed) and

thereby reduce your per-person rate. Remember that some places charge for extra guests and some don't.

- **Book an efficiency.** A room with a kitchenette allows you to grocery shop and eat some meals in. Especially during long stays with families, you're bound to save money on food this way.

LANDING THE BEST ROOM

Somebody has to get the best room in the house, and it might as well be you.

Always ask for a corner room. They're usually larger, quieter, and closer to the elevator. They often have more windows and light than standard rooms, and they don't always cost more.

When you make your reservation, ask if the hotel is renovating; if it is, request a room away from the renovation work. Many hotels now offer no-smoking rooms; if smoke bothers you, by all means ask for one. Inquire, too, about the location of the restaurants, bars, and discos, which could all be a source of irritating noise. If you aren't happy with your room when you arrive, talk to the front desk. If the hotel has another room, the staff should be happy to accommodate you, within reason.

1 Resort Hotels

With their wealth of amenities, the big resort hotels can keep you so occupied that you may not feel the need to leave the premises (but make sure you resist the urge and venture out!). The large hotels typically have their own beaches or beach clubs and swimming pools; some have their own golf courses. Most of these hotels also boast such luxury services and facilities as porters, room service, planned activities, sports facilities (such as tennis courts), shops (including bike shops), beauty salons, bars, nightclubs, entertainment, and taxi stands.

VERY EXPENSIVE
SOUTHAMPTON PARISH

The Fairmont Southampton Princess ✦✦✦ (Kids)   This Princess, even more than the Hamilton Princess, deserves to be called royal, especially after its recent $2.5 million renovation. Sitting atop Bermuda's highest point, it's the largest and most luxurious property on the island. It overlooks the ocean, the bay, and its own good beach, in front of the hotel. The hotel's beach is sheltered in a jagged cove, flanked by cliffs and studded with rocky outcroppings lashed by the tides. It more than justifies its membership in "The Leading Hotels of the World." (The only complaint we've ever heard is from someone who stayed next door to a couple who "appeared to be in training for the Sex Olympics," and truly regretted not having more soundproofing!) Often compared to its sibling, the Hamilton Princess, this is more a resort hotel on the beach, whereas the Princess in Hamilton is not on the beach but is close to shops and attractions. Still, we don't think it's the place for those who want an intimate, romantic hideaway; in fact, its biggest drawback is that it's a favorite with conventions and tour groups. Nonetheless, it and Elbow Beach are the finest choices for the well-heeled family who wants to stay at a place where's there's virtually everything on site—from sports to beaches to a wide selection of dining.

The hotel is decorated in 18th-century English style, with well-upholstered furnishings. Baronial staircases connect the public rooms, situated on three floors. The plush guest rooms are arranged in wings that radiate more or less symmetrically from a central core. This design gives each luxurious room a private veranda with a sweeping view of the water. Rooms are generally spacious, with one king or two double beds. Bathrooms tend to be modest. For those who can afford it, the choice spot here is the Entrée Gold floor, a hotel-within-a-hotel, pampering its guests in ultimate luxury on the top floor, offering an array of services from shoeshines to private check-ins. The club offers complimentary continental breakfast, newspapers, and the use of a fax and VCR.

The cuisine is among the island's finest—we recommend several of the resort's restaurants even if you're not staying here (see chapter 5, "Dining"). In an organization this large that does so much catering, it's hard to keep an eye on quality, but the Southampton Princess does admirably well. This is a mammoth operation, but the hotel has wisely split its dining into smaller enclaves. The dining rooms include Windows on the Sound, a three-tiered palace reminiscent of Mayfair in the 1930s and New York's late, great Rainbow Room; through 20-foot-high arched windows, you can see the islands of Great Sound. Other choices include Wickets Brasserie & Cricket Club, Newport Room, Rib Room Steak House, the Whaler Inn, and the Waterlot Inn. Nightlife is more staid here than at the Sonesta, and not every restaurant has a bar that's open to non-diners (the Waterlot Inn and the Whaler Inn do). The Lobby Lounge has live music, usually a jazz combo, beginning at 8pm. The Neptune Club functions after 9:30pm as a bar with live music or a disco with recorded music.

Guests who never want to leave enjoy a self-contained village of bars, restaurants, shops, and athletic facilities that are among the island's finest. Everyone's favorite pool is a re-creation of a Polynesian waterfall, with streams of heated water spilling from an artificial limestone cliff. You can swim here even during cold weather, thanks to the greenhouse above. A shuttle bus transports guests to and from various hotel facilities, and hotel ferries make runs along Little Sound into Hamilton.

101 South Shore Rd. (P.O. Box HM 1379), Hamilton HM FX, Bermuda. © 800/223-1414 in the U.S., 800/268-7176 in Canada, or 441/238-8000. Fax 441/239-6916. www.fairmont.com. 626 units. Apr 9–May 1 and Sept 7–Nov 14 $279–$369 double; Nov 15–Apr 8 $179–$229 double; May 2–Sept 6 $359–$499 double. Suite from $939 in summer, from $438 off-season. AE, DC, MC, V. $4 private ferry from The Fairmont Hamilton

---

The Spa Treatment

Sonesta Beach Resort, Southampton (© 800/766-3782 in the U.S., or 441/238-8122; www.sonesta.com), has the island's most comprehensive spa facilities. Designed in the European style, it offers health and fitness programs you'd find in an American spa, including Ionithermie, the inch-reducing treatment from Europe; deluxe facial care from Paris; and ancient forms of therapeutic and relaxing massage such as aromatherapy, reflexology, and Swedish massage. Some people check into the hotel on 4-, 5-, or 7-day programs that incorporate calorie-controlled menus. The staff usually keeps guests busy every day from 8:30am to 7pm with aerobics, skin and body care, supervised indoor and outdoor stretching exercises, massages, facials, beauty regimens, and the like.

The facilities are also available to hotel guests and nonguests who want selected treatments (priced separately) rather than the full spa experience. The up-to-date accouterments include Universal gym equipment, saunas, steam baths, and massage rooms. The staff conducts daily exercise classes. Half- and full-day packages are available to nonguests. For after-workout pick-me-ups, there's a beauty salon adjacent to the health spa.

⌒Moments Hanging Out with the Dolphins

The Fairmont Southampton Princess runs a well-publicized **Dolphin Quest Interactive Program** that offers in-the-water encounters with Atlantic bottlenose dolphins. In a 2-acre holding pen that's 4 to 12 feet deep and separated from the open sea with underwater netting, the hotel keeps seven dolphins. Four "Dolphin Experiences" are scheduled each day (year-round, weather permitting, at 9 and 11am, and 2 and 4pm). Up to 10 swimmers (wearing bathing suits in summer, wet suits in winter) cavort in the water with the dolphins for just under 30 minutes. The price for adults is $95; for children under 16, $85. In winter, it's easy to get a slot, but in summer, there's so much demand that the hotel has a lottery. Is all this cruel to the dolphins? The staff is rigorous about protecting and caring for them; the overall atmosphere is playful and lighthearted; and the dolphins have a fairly large area to swim in. But we can't help worrying that the continued contact with hordes of people and their separation from their natural habitat must have something of a traumatizing effect on these beautiful animals. You decide.

Princess. **Amenities:** 6 restaurants; 4 bars; private beach club; outdoor pool; indoor pool; par-3, 18-hole golf course; tennis; fitness center with spa facilities; dive shop; moped rental; children's program in summer; concierge; business services; salon; room service; massages; baby-sitting; laundry. *In room:* A/C, TV, dataport, minibar, coffeemaker, hairdryer, iron, safe.

Sonesta Beach Resort ⊀ (Kids) This is the only major luxury resort on Bermuda with access to three beaches, including Church Bay, 5 minutes away by bike. Among full-service hotels, only Elbow Beach and the Southampton Princess outclass it. Built in the shape of a crescent, the resort sits on 25 acres of prime seafront property, curving along the spine of a rocky peninsula whose jagged edges provide ocean views. It boasts ample lengths of oceanside walkways. Those who seek Bermudian charm and character would probably prefer Cambridge Beaches, but spa goers, honeymooners, and water-sports and beach buffs like this resort a lot. The Sonesta also caters to families, who gravitate to its wide selection of activities, including beaches, spacious rooms with private terraces, a large swimming pool, and even first-rate baby-sitters.

The circular bay in front, flanked by limestone cliffs and sandy beaches, was used long ago by gunpowder smugglers, and later by rumrunners, who loved its well-camouflaged entrance. Circled with palm-shaded cabanas and bars, the bay has a soft, sandy bottom and looks like a small corner of Polynesia transported to the Atlantic.

The resort was last renovated in 1996. Rooms have private terraces, thick carpeting, high-quality light woods, louvered closets, and electronic locks. Baths are generous in size, with tiled tub areas. Some units open onto garden views, whereas the more expensive units boast ocean or beach views. Some accommodations are set aside for nonsmokers and those with disabilities.

The hotel has three restaurants, including the elegant Lillian's, which serves northern Italian cuisine. There's also the bistro-style Boat Bay Club, and the Sea Grape, which offers alfresco dining overlooking Boat Bay. Lillian's and the Sea Grape are worthy choices even if you're not staying at the hotel. Overall, the food here is perfectly good, if not truly gourmet or as excellent as that at the Southampton Princess. You'll never go thirsty at the Sonesta—each restaurant has a bar. The one at the Boat Bay Club is particularly fun, with live entertainment—calypso, jazz, merengue, or at least a deejay—almost every night. There's also a jukebox and a row of big-screen TVs in Splits, the hotel's sports bar.

South Shore Rd., Southampton Parish (P.O. Box HM 1070), Hamilton HM EX, Bermuda. ℂ 800/766-3782 in the U.S., or 441/238-8122. Fax 441/238-8463. www.sonesta.com. 400 units. May–Aug $290–$410 double, from $450 suite; Sept–Nov 15 and Apr $260–$370 double, from $410 suite; Nov 16–Mar $135–$190 double, from $230 suite. MAP (breakfast and dinner) $61 per person. Discount honeymoon and family packages available. AE, DC, MC, V. Bus: 7. **Amenities:** 3 restaurants; 2 bars; outdoor swimming pool, indoor swimming pool; 6 tennis courts (2 illuminated for night play); full-time tennis pro; health club & spa; diving center for snorkelers and scuba divers; children's program (May 1–Labor Day); business services; salon; room service; baby-sitting; laundry. *In room:* A/C, TV, minibar, coffeemaker, iron, hairdryer, safe.

PAGET PARISH
Elbow Beach Hotel ⊛⊛⊛ (Kids)   Elegant and commanding, this is the best full-service resort on the island, though it lacks the intimacy and local charm you'd find at a smaller place like The Reefs. The hotel complex opens onto Elbow Beach, where a prime strand of sand is reserved for hotel guests. Following a $42 million sprucing up—and that is one massive renovation—Elbow Beach reopened in 1999. The renovations added a decidedly upscale colonial English gloss to the hotel, with miles of expensive chintzes and piles of reproduction antiques. Elbow Beach appeals to vacationers, especially families, who like everything under one roof (or at least on site). Another advantage is the proximity to Hamilton, which is 10 minutes away by taxi. The resort sits on 50 acres of gardens with its own quarter-mile pink-sand beach on the south shore. Long gone are the days when rowdy college students descended at Easter.

You can choose from a wide array of accommodations, from rooms with balconies overlooking the water to duplex cottages; some lanai rooms overlook the pool and the Atlantic, and others are surfside. Many guest room walls are draped in silk. Bathrooms are Italian marble, with up-to-date plumbing, plus touches of luxury like robes. The most spacious units are in low-rise buildings on terraces leading to the sands; the least desirable rooms open onto a heavily trafficked corridor on the lobby floor.

The cuisine here has never been better; the culinary "dream team" includes chefs who have worked at some of the grandest dining rooms of the world, from Atlanta's Ritz-Carlton to Wolfgang Puck's California restaurants. All guests, including those on MAP, may choose dinner at either of the hotel's two ocean-view restaurants or at a nightly outdoor theme party. The main dining room, the Seahorse Grill, is the most formal of the restaurants. At the beachfront Cafe Lido, the kitchen focuses on seafood with a Mediterranean accent. The resort also participates in a "dine around" program with several Hamilton restaurants; hotel guests can eat at a participating restaurant and charge their meals to the resort.

60 South Shore Rd. (P.O. Box HM 455), Hamilton HM BX, Bermuda. ℂ 800/223-7434 in the U.S., or 441/236-3535. Fax 441/236-5882. 244 units. Apr 10–Oct $435–$615 double, from $615 suite; off-season $235–$385 double, from $385 suite. Packages available. Children under 18 free in adults' room. AE, DC, MC, V. Bus: 1, 2, or 7. **Amenities:** 4 restaurants; 3 bars; large swimming pool; 5 all-weather tennis courts (2 lit for night play); health club with exercise room and whirlpool; water sports (including deep-sea fishing and windsurfing); moped rental; summer children's program (the best on island); salon; room service; baby-sitting; laundry. *In room:* A/C, TV, hairdryer.

PEMBROKE PARISH (CITY OF HAMILTON)
The Fairmont Hamilton Princess ⊛   This landmark luxury hotel launched Bermuda's tourist industry and is still going strong. Its sibling, the Southampton

> ## ⌒Tips Package Deals
>
> Refer to the "Package Deals" section of chapter 2, "Planning Your Trip to Bermuda" before you call these resorts yourself. Buying a package is the way to go; you can save hundreds of dollars over what you would pay by booking your hotel and airfare separately.

Princess, has better dining, grander facilities, and the advantage of being on a beach, but it is somewhat remote; the Hamilton Princess earns fans and devotees because it is more conveniently positioned for shopping and sightseeing. This hotel, which evokes a wedding cake, is near downtown Hamilton, on the edge of Hamilton Harbour. Elbow Beach (the closest beach), is a 20-minute taxi ride or 45-minute bicycle ride from the hotel. The easily accessible ferry delivers guests to the Southampton Princess, and sun lovers can get their fill at the sandy stretch there. The lack of a beach here doesn't keep the glitterati away: This is the hotel of choice for Hollywood and European movie stars as well as the yachting set. Past visitors have included everyone from Mark Twain to Michael Jackson (quite a stretch!).

Opened in 1884 and named for Princess Louise (Queen Victoria's daughter), this Princess is far more staid than its cousin in Southampton (see above). It doesn't even attempt to offer the roster of activities available at Elbow Beach, so the young and the restless might want to book elsewhere. This is the flagship of the Princess Hotel chain, and it's certainly the one with the most history: British intelligence officers stationed here during World War II worked to crack secret Nazi codes.

Modern wings, pierced with row upon row of balconied loggias, surround the hotel's colonial core. The property was designed around a concrete pier that extends into the harbor, near a Japanese-style floating garden. The botanical theme carries over to the lobby. In 1996, management renovated the well-decorated guest rooms and public salons, making a good property even better. Many of the spacious rooms have private balconies; they were designed "to create the feeling that you'd choose the same kind of bedroom if you owned a home here." Most of the tiled bathrooms are generous in size. Some 40% of the guests are repeat visitors.

The hotel has a wide array of bars and restaurants. For reviews of Harley's and The Colony Pub, see chapter 5, "Dining."

76 Pitts Bay Rd. (P.O. Box HM 837), Hamilton HM CX, Bermuda. ℭ **800/441-1414** in the U.S., or 441/295-3000. Fax 441/296-7171. www.fairmont.com. 413 units. Apr 11–Nov $269–$359 double, from $430 suite; off-season $189–$249 double, from $329 suite. AE, DC, MC, V. Bus: 7 or 8. **Amenities:** 3 restaurants; 2 bars; heated freshwater swimming pool; unheated saltwater swimming pool; access to tennis, sailing, white-sand beaches, and golf at the Southampton Princess; fitness center featuring an exercise room with extensive exercise equipment, massage area, saunas, and showers; water-aerobics classes; dive shop (an independent concessionaire); moped rental; concierge; business center; salon; room service; baby-sitting; laundry; frequent ferry service to and from the Southampton Princess, weather permitting. *In room:* A/C, TV, minibar, hairdryer, iron, safe.

EXPENSIVE

HAMILTON PARISH

Grotto Bay Beach Hotel ⋒ ⒦ⁱᵈˢ   The resort (named after its subterranean caves) is lushly planted with tropical fruit trees. A sandy but mediocre beach nearby offers a view of an unused series of railroad pylons, leading onto forested

Coney Island across the bay. The nearby coastline is enchanting, with many natural caves and intimate coves. From the seaside, the airy public areas look like a modern version of a mogul's palace, with big windows, thick white walls, and three peaked roofs with curved eaves.

This recently restored resort appeals to young couples and families who don't expect all the activities of a resort like Elbow Beach. Although it's unattractively located across from the airport, noise from planes is not a problem. The sprawling, 21-acre property contains 11 three-story buildings with balconies and sea views (but no elevators). If your room is far from the main building, you may think you've been sentenced to Siberia (though there are secluded units that appeal to honeymooners). All accommodations are well furnished; the bathrooms are medium in size but well-maintained. The children's programs and playground make this a good bet for families. There are also a lot of activities offered, including nature walks, twice-weekly "cave crawls," daily cave swims, organized activities for teenagers, scavenger hunts, communal croquet near the bar, fish feeding, and bridge competitions. The best rooms are directly on the beach, but they're at the bottom of a serpentine flight of about 30 masonry steps. That's no big deal for guests of average fitness, but those with limited mobility might opt for oceanview, but not oceanfront, rooms.

The on-site restaurants serve fair if unremarkable continental cuisine, enlivened by fresh seafood. A multi-million dollar renovation has perked up the physical plant of all food and beverage outlets, including the Bayside Bar & Grill, the Rumhouse Bar, the Greenhouse Restaurant, an the Hibiscus dining room, the latter of which now offers an outside patio letting guests dine alfresco. The lounge books live entertainment nightly, and there are a handful of other bars on the property. Afternoon tea is served every day, and there's a daily happy hour. Blasted out of natural rock, the swimming pool has a swim-up bar.

11 Blue Hole Hill, Hamilton CR 04, Bermuda. 𝒞 **800/582-3190** in the U.S., 800/463-0851 in Canada, or 441/293-8333. Fax 441/293-2306. www.netlinkbermuda.com/grottobay. 201 units. Apr–Oct $220–$240 double, Nov–Mar $99–$110 double; suites from $350 year-round. MAP (breakfast and dinner) $48 per person. AE, MC, V. Bus: 1, 3, 10, or 11. **Amenities:** Restaurant; 2 bars; outdoor fresh water pool; nearby golf course; 4 tennis courts (2 lit for night play); frequent tennis clinics; small health club; Jacuzzi; daily Jazzercise in the Rum House Lounge before breakfast; excursion boat; water sports center and dive shop; baby-sitting; laundry. *In room:* A/C, TV, mini-fridge, coffeemaker, hairdryer, iron, safe.

2 Small Hotels

In contrast to the sprawling resorts are Bermuda's more intimate, informal small hotels. Many have their own dining rooms and bars, and some even have their own beaches or beach clubs; all offer pools and patios.

VERY EXPENSIVE
SOUTHAMPTON PARISH
Pompano Beach Club ℱ　Next to the Port Royal Golf Course, this seaside hotel is perched above a lovely cove beach fringed with rocky outcroppings. From the terraced beach above the hotel's clubhouse, waist-deep water covers the clean, sandy bottom for the length of 2½ football fields before the deep water begins. This place appeals to those seeking a personal, friendly welcome— something impossible to come by at a megaresort. It attracts couples of all ages who want privacy and tranquillity; golfers especially like this place. The Pompano Beach Club is one of best-known smaller hotels on the island, owned and operated by the Lamb family. The setting is on the side of a limestone hill, virtually surrounded by the Port Royal Golf Club.

Accommodations in the City of Hamilton

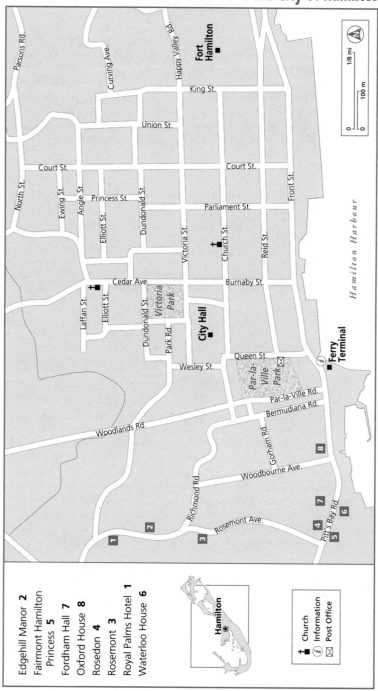

Edgehill Manor **2**
Fairmont Hamilton Princess **5**
Fordham Hall **7**
Oxford House **8**
Rosedon **4**
Rosemont **3**
Royal Palms Hotel **1**
Waterloo House **6**

Hamilton

🕇■ Church
ⓘ Information
⊠ Post Office

The hillside villas scattered over the landscaped property have a balcony or terrace to take advantage of the ocean view. Frankly, your liking or disliking of this place depends on your room assignment. Some rooms are renovated and are fresh in appearance; others have drawn dragon fire from readers. If you can afford it, request the deluxe rooms at the top of the price scale (see below), as these accommodations often have wet bars and oversized tubs. Other units look old and in need of rejuvenation. Some bathrooms are large; others are like tiny hall closets. If the hotel isn't booked, try to look at the room before checking in. If you're a devotee of this special type of small Bermudian inn, you might find The Reefs or Newstead more to your liking, as their rooms are more consistently good and their cuisine better.

The club maintains a dine-around plan with four other small Bermuda hotels. We suggest you avail yourself of this privilege as much as possible until a major shake-up occurs in the Pompano kitchen. Serious attention needs to be paid to the food served here before this hotel can return to its previous high ratings.

36 Pompano Beach Rd., Southampton SB 03, Bermuda. ℂ **800/343-4155** in the U.S. and Canada, or 441/234-0222. Fax 441/234-1694. www.pompano.bm. 56 units. May 1–Nov 14 $410–$420 double, from $420 suite; Apr $330–$340 double, $360 suite; off-season $250–$270 double, from $280 suite. Packages available. Rates include MAP (breakfast and dinner). AE, MC, V. Hamilton ferry to Somerset. Bus: 7 or 8. **Amenities:** Restaurant; bar; freshwater heated swimming pool; easy access to the government-owned Port Royal Golf Course; 4 all-weather tennis courts (2 lit); fitness center; ocean and poolside Jacuzzi; Sunfish and Windsurfer rentals; on-site moped rental; baby-sitting with 24-hour notice; laundry. *In room:* A/C, TV, mini-fridge, hairdryer, iron, safe.

The Reefs 𝒜𝒜 Not as refined, but also not as stuffy as Horizons or Cambridge Beaches, this is one of the island's state-of-the-art inns, opening onto a private beach of pink-flecked sand surrounded by palm trees and jutting rocks, and it was extensively renovated and vastly improved in late 2000 and early 2001. It boasts top-notch maintenance, first-class personal service, and unmatched ocean views. This "lanai colony" of salmon-pink cottages on Christian Bay spreads along a low coral ridge. The lanais are cheerfully decorated in rattan and bright island colors. All have private sundecks and ocean views. The mid-size accommodations have tasteful furnishings and small bathrooms with separate dressing areas and dual basins. In 2000, the hotel introduced eight new "Cottage Suites by the Reefs," and these are the most desirable; a series of one-, two-, or three-bedroom cottages built along the cliffs and hillside of the resort and featuring the privacy of home with the amenities and services of a resort. If you're looking for action, head over to the nearby Sonesta Beach, or even consider checking into Elbow Beach or the Southampton Princess. But if you want a smaller place and more tranquility, consider one of the pink lanais here.

(Tips) Hotel Forecast at Castle Harbour

Marriott's Castle Harbour, one of the three most famous hotels in Bermuda, is in the middle of a reconstruction and restoration. The rejuvenated golf course, it is anticipated, will open first, perhaps as early as 2001, followed by the complete resort some time in 2002. It is hoped that this newly restored five-star property will rival similar resort hotels around the world. The new Marriott is expected to have slightly fewer rooms than the old one, which had 400.

The attentive staff of the plant-filled Terrace Dining Room, the more formal option, serves Continental and North American cuisine. The chefs concentrate on bringing out the food's natural flavors; they don't overpower your taste buds with extra sauces and gimmicks. If you want to let your hair down a bit, opt for Coconuts; there's no finer or more romantic spot in Bermuda for an alfresco sunset dinner than this beach terrace. The chefs draw inspiration from around the world—Thailand to the U.S. The main clubhouse, with its beamed-ceiling lounge, offers nightly entertainment in summer, ranging from calypso to pub-style sing-along favorites. The kidney-shaped swimming pool sits on a ledge with an ocean view.

56 South Shore Rd., Southampton SN 02, Bermuda. © **800/742-2008** in the U.S. and Canada, or 441 /238-0222. Fax 441/238-8372. www.thereefs.com. 75 units. Apr 15–Nov 5 $298–$476 double, $494–$1,294 suite; off-season $248–$390 double, $408–$968 suite. Rates include MAP (breakfast and dinner). AE, MC, V. Bus: 7. **Amenities:** 3 restaurants; 2 bars; pool; 3 golf courses nearby; 2 all-weather tennis courts; fitness center; complimentary kayaks and snorkeling equipment; moped and mountain-bike rental; baby-sitting; laundry. *In room:* A/C, TV, dataport, fridge, hairdryer, iron, safe.

PAGET PARISH

Harmony Club ⚡   This is Bermuda's only all-inclusive hotel—you'll know exactly what your vacation will cost in advance. It's for couples only; however, the couple can be any combination of gender or age (over 18). Elbow Beach, the closest beachfront, is a 15-minute walk or a 5-minute scooter ride away. Named after the circa-1830 home of a 19th-century merchant that stood on the site, this hotel retains only a few vestiges of its original historic core, but tries to keep the friendly informality of a private home. It was renovated in 1997.

The accommodations, furnished in Queen Anne style, occupy a series of rambling pink-sided wings that encircle formal gardens with gazebos. Those near the road tend to be somewhat noisy. Units are generous in size, with sitting areas, double or king beds, oversized closets, and well-maintained private bathrooms.

If you stay here, you'll eat all your meals here, because you're paying for an all-inclusive plan. The chefs are competent if not dazzling. However, there's such a wealth and variety of food that you're almost certain to find something you like. Evening meals are served by candlelight on fine china and crystal in the Casuarina. A full English tea is served every afternoon; there are also weekly cocktail parties and entertainment 6 nights a week.

109 South Shore Rd., Paget PG BX, Bermuda. © **888/427-6664** or 441/236-3500. Fax 441/236-2624. www. harmonyclub.com. 68 units. Dec 21–Apr 15 $350 double; Apr 16–Oct $440 double. Rates include all meals and drinks, activities. AE, DC, MC, V. Closed Nov–Dec 20. Bus: 7 or 8. No children under 18 accepted. **Amenities:** Restaurant; bar; freshwater swimming pool; 2 tennis courts; putting green; whirlpool; Jacuzzis; sauna; moped rental; unlimited use of double-seat motor scooter (1 per couple) during a week's stay; laundry. *In room:* A/C, TV, dataport, coffeemaker, hairdryer, safe.

Newstead Hotel ⚡   Long known as a favorite of older and more staid clients, in 2000, this hotel poured $5 million into renovating its physical plant and in bringing its image up to date. The hotel originated in 1923 around the substantial-looking Edwardian home of Sir Richard and Lady Fairey. Shortly thereafter, it expanded to include another half-dozen buildings, each of which are clustered within a flowering garden at the edge of the harbor. Don't expect a sandy beachfront—swimming is conducted either within a heated swimming pool or from a pair of piers jutting out into the sheltered harbor. Evoking a country house that's supervised by a well-bred hostess, the ambience of this small hotel is dignified and refined—definitely not the place for hell-raisers. The property contains drawing rooms, a library, and lounges that are furnished in part with English antiques. Traditionalists prefer the old-fashioned bedrooms of the main house, but you can also opt for up-to-date comforts in the more contemporary modern buildings. Each accommodation has a traditional decor, including gleaming brass and lots of polished hardwoods. Most rooms have twin beds and tiled bathrooms, complete with dressing area; newer units contain double sinks. The least desirable rooms in the main house (those opening onto the road in front of the house) have older-looking bathrooms and might be exposed to street noise. The most luxurious options are the modern poolside units, with furnished terraces, comfortable sitting rooms, and king-size beds.

The Rockfish Grill serves breakfast, lunch, and dinner in an a la carte setting that was newly configured. Less formal lunches and dinners (but not breakfasts) are served at Noah's, a casual dining spot overlooking Hamilton Harbour.

27 Harbour Rd. (P.O. Box PG 196), Paget PGBX, Bermuda. (C) **800/468-4111** in the U.S. and Canada, or 441/236-6060. www.Newsteadhotel.com. 43 units. May–Oct $295–$340 double, $395–$435 suite; off-season $215 double, $250–$435 suite. AE, MC, V. Ferry from Hamilton. **Amenities:** 2 restaurants; bar; heated swimming pool; swimming in the harbor from a pair of private docks; 2 Har-Tru tennis courts; a somewhat out-of-shape putting green; mini-gym; spa; sauna; salon; room service (only during mealtimes); baby-sitting; laundry. *In room:* A/C, TV, dataport, mini-fridge.

Stonington Beach Hotel ⊛

The Hospitality and Culinary Institute of Bermuda operates this offbeat place near Elbow Beach, one of the island's best beaches. Training ground or not, this is a good choice, with a gracious atmosphere and welcoming service, which is far better than the better-known Harmony Club. Stonington is smart, neat, modern, and almost corporate looking. It lacks softness and a sense of tradition, which some visitors will like more than others. Some employees are students, under the supervision of a professional international staff. The students are likely to be more helpful than many battle-trained, jaded veterans of the hotel field, but if you're looking for mistakes you'll no doubt find them.

A lamp-lit drive leads up to the buff-colored facade, where you'll follow a stucco passageway to an inner octagonal courtyard. The accommodations are in four outlying buildings; a complete renovation was done in 1994. The rooms are comfortably spacious, equipped with a wide balcony or a patio offering ocean views. Each has a ceiling fan, a small refrigerator, and a love seat that can serve as an extra folding bed. The large baths have shower and tub combinations. Steps cut through foliage and limestone lead to the hotel's sandy beach.

The library, with its glowing fireplace, is most inviting, as is the restaurant and bar, The Norwood Room (see chapter 5, "Dining," for a full review). In the unlikely event that you don't like the food here, the hotel has a dinner-exchange program with four surrounding properties—so you won't be trapped in the same dining room every night if it doesn't suit you.

South Shore Rd. (P.O. Box HM 523), Hamilton HM CX, Bermuda. (C) **800/447-7462** in the U.S. and Canada, or 441/236-5416. Fax 441/236-0371. www.stoningtonbeach.com. 64 units. May–Oct $375–$475 double; Nov–Apr 15 $250–$325 double; Apr 16–30 $375–$475 double. Rates include MAP (breakfast and dinner). AE, MC, V. Bus: 7. **Amenities:** Restaurant; bar; freshwater swimming pool; 2 tennis courts; access to a nearby fitness center; business center; room service; baby-sitting; laundry. *In room:* A/C, TV, hairdryer.

White Sands Hotel & Cottages ⊛

Honeymooners and families seek out this rather British hotel lying just a walk uphill from a wide beach with exceptionally fine sand at Grape Bay. It evokes the period when it was built (the 1950s), although it's constantly being upgraded and improved. The compound of salmon-colored buildings sits amid terraced gardens.

Rooms have wall-to-wall carpeting and large closets. Each is spacious, airy, and bright, and generally decorated with modern furniture. Especially noteworthy is tower room 222, whose five oversized windows provide an eagle's-nest view of the surrounding shoreline. In addition to the rooms in the main building, there are several two- and three-bedroom cottages. Bathrooms with shower units are well maintained with adequate shelf space.

Much of the food here is what you'd expect at an upscale British hotel: solid, reliable fare, not daring at all, but consistently prepared with decent ingredients. The convivial atmosphere in the eating and drinking facilities seems to give the sometimes-bland fare more zest. The Captain's Table, the formal but relaxed dining room, is outfitted in a colonial English motif. The Terrace Club poolside restaurant serves lunch. There's also an English-inspired pub, the Sandbar.

55 White Sands Rd., Paget Parish PG BX, Bermuda. (©) **800/548-0547** in the U.S., 800/228-3196 in Canada, or 441/236-2023. Fax 441/236-2486. www.white-sands-bermuda.com. 40 units. Mid-Apr to Sept $339–$399 double; off-season $229–$369 double. Cottages mid-Apr to Sept $725–$999; off-season $650–$900. Rates include MAP (breakfast and dinner). AE, MC, V. Bus: 7 or 8. **Amenities:** 2 restaurants; pub; heated freshwater swimming pool; easy access to tennis, golf, and water-sports facilities at nearby south-shore hotels; moped rentals; room service (8–8:45am and 7–8:30pm); baby-sitting (with advance notice). *In room:* A/C, TV, fridge, coffeemaker, hairdryer.

PEMBROKE PARISH (CITY OF HAMILTON)

Waterloo House (♠)   This is the favorite of business people in Hamilton who want the convenience of its location—on the harbor, not on a beach. It is more intimate and tranquil than its main competitor, the Hamilton Princess, but the Waterloo isn't as well maintained. Nonetheless, Waterloo still has its devotees. Even if parts of it are in need of better maintenance and housekeeping, it is a long-standing favorite. Two recent guests told us they stay here every year, and wouldn't think of checking into another hotel. There is a lot of charm to the place if you can overlook some flaws such as fabrics in need of renewal.

On the edge of Hamilton Harbour (on the outskirts of town), this enlarged and remodeled private home was built around 1910. Terraced gardens descend to the water in the Italian Riviera style; behind salmon-colored walls, the gardens contain palms, magnolias, poinsettias, urns overflowing with ivy, a splashing fountain, and white wrought-iron garden furniture shaded with fringed parasols. There are nooks for drinks and sunbathing around the property, and shade trees surround the swimming pool.

Inside, the drawing room has English antique furnishings and decorative tile floors. Rooms vary in size and decoration; each evokes the feeling of a country-house guest room. Most guest rooms and public areas were upgraded in 1997. A newer wing offers small studios and twin-bedded units, though accommodations in the main unit have more character. The highest prices are for the five cottages, which have living and dining areas and refrigerators (though no kitchens). The tiled bathrooms in the newer wing are larger and better maintained, even though we still prefer the older unit for its quaint charm.

The main dining room (reviewed in chapter 5, "Dining") overlooks the terrace and harbor. On the lower terrace level is a bar lounge with Moorish arches, English armchairs, and hand-woven pillow covers. You can enjoy afternoon tea on the lawn at the water's edge.

Pitts Bay Rd. (P.O. Box HM 333), Hamilton HM BX, Bermuda. (©) **800/468-4100** in the U.S. and Canada, or 441/295-4480. Fax 441/295-2585. www.waterloohouse.com. 30 units. Apr–Nov $260–$420 double, $410–$700 suite; Dec–Mar $190–$330 double, $340–$560 suite. Rates include full breakfast; MAP (breakfast and dinner) $40 per person. AE, MC, V. Bus: 1, 2, 10, or 11. **Amenities:** Restaurant; bar; freshwater outdoor swimming pool; private dock; privileges at the members-only Coral Beach and Tennis Club, 4 miles from Hamilton, where the pink sands and protected waters create some of the best swimming conditions on the island; waterside barbecue area. *In room:* A/C, TV, hairdryer.

EXPENSIVE
PEMBROKE PARISH (CITY OF HAMILTON)

Rosedon ☞   If you'd like a small local hotel of charm and character, in Hamilton, this is for you. Those who want a megahotel with lots of facilities can check into the Hamilton Princess across the street. Otherwise, head for this stately 1906 mansion that has been successfully converted into an inn. The staff is helpful, polite, and personable. Although its rates are rather high for what it is— basically, an overblown guesthouse—it has its fans. Business travelers often stay here because of its proximity to Hamilton.

Rosedon resembles a colonial-era plantation great house, with a pristine white exterior and royal blue shutters. Extensive gardens and lawns encircle the house. Look for the loquat tree, a Bermuda trademark; other shrubs include hibiscus, banana plants, and bird of paradise. Once occupied by an English family, this was the first house in Bermuda with gaslights. The building has a formal entry hall and two antique-filled lounges. A flagstone terrace with parasol-shaded tables surrounds the large, temperature-controlled pool.

The individually decorated, mid-size bedrooms have balconies or patios, along with small but neat bathrooms. Preferred are the modern veranda accommodations in the rear. Called lanai suites, they open onto the pool. The colonial-style bedrooms in the main house, however, have more island flavor and character.

The honor system prevails at the self-service bar. The full breakfast included in the rates is good and plentiful, with plenty of variety even if you stay a week. It can also be delivered to your room. There's afternoon tea, but no restaurant.

Pitts Bay Rd. (P.O. Box HM 290), Hamilton HM AX, Bermuda. ✆ 800/742-5008 in the U.S. and Canada, or 441/295-1640. Fax 441/295-5904. www.rosedonbermuda.com. 47 units. Apr–Nov $204–$284 double; off-season $204–$214 double. Extra person $35. Rates include full breakfast and afternoon tea. AE, MC, V. **Amenities:** Bar; swimming pool; access to tennis courts; business services; room service (7am–9pm); baby-sitting; same-day laundry service; free round-trip shuttle service to Stonington Beach, 10 minutes away. *In room:* A/C, TV, fridge, coffeemaker, hairdryer, iron, safe.

MODERATE
PEMBROKE PARISH (CITY OF HAMILTON)

Hamiltonian Hotel & Island Club   Set on a hill less than a mile northwest of Hamilton, this is a quiet, relatively simple hotel that markets its rooms as time-share units. Don't expect a particularly cozy reception—think of it as an anonymous getaway from the pressures of urban life, with no particular facilities for dining or partying. The one-bedroom accommodations are in four pink-sided, stone-roofed, apartment-style buildings. They're comfortable and well maintained, with average-size baths. Units don't have a full kitchen, but you can heat up food, make toast or coffee—in other words, prepare yourself a snack.

Langton Hill (P.O. Box HM 1738), Hamilton HM GX, Bermuda. ✆ 441/295-5608. Fax 441/295-7481. 32 units. Apr–Nov $156 double; off-season $88 double. AE, MC, V. **Amenities:** Swimming pool on a plateau about 15 steps uphill from the rest of the complex and 3 tennis courts (2 lit for night play). *In room:* A/C, TV, coffeemaker, fridge.

3 Cottage Colonies

These accommodations are uniquely Bermudian. Each colony has a main clubhouse with a dining room, lounge, and bar, plus its own beach or pool. The cottage units, spread throughout landscaped grounds, offer privacy and sometimes luxury. Most have kitchenettes suitable for beverages and light snacks, but not for full-time cooking.

If you were a travel agent working for Brooke Astor, Barbara Walters, and Goldie Hawn, you'd book them as follows: the aristocratic Astor into Cambridge Beaches; the media star Walters into Horizons; and the actress and producer Hawn into Ariel Sands.

VERY EXPENSIVE
SANDYS PARISH
Cambridge Beaches ✿✿✿ The recently restored Cambridge Beaches attracts rich honeymooners, old-money families, and *Vanity Fair* couples who seek privacy, pampering, and plenty of facilities. The ambience is even more refined than that at Horizons, and guests have access to five private palm-fringed beaches. If you're a first-time visitor, the clubby atmosphere may make you feel like an outsider. For snob appeal, Cambridge Beaches is numero uno in Bermuda (followed by Horizons). It's the natural choice for Saudi royalty. If your children are under 5, make sure they show up with a nanny—it's a house rule.

On a peninsula overlooking Mangrove Bay in Somerset, the colony's 25 acres of semitropical gardens and green lawns occupy the entire western tip of the island. Everything centers on an old sea captain's house. The main lounges are tastefully furnished with antiques; the dominant feeling here is that of a country estate. Scattered throughout the gardens are nicely furnished pink-and-white cottages, some of which are nearly 300 years old. They have distinct Bermudian architectural features, with an added British starchiness. All of the cottages (some of which were once private homes) are conservatively furnished, and come with sun-and-breakfast terraces, generally with unobstructed views of the bay and gardens. A cottage can comfortably house four. The least expensive units have land rather than ocean vistas. Clad in marble, the bathrooms contain dual basins and whirlpool tubs along with showers.

Dining is in the excellent and very pricey Tamarisk Dining Room (reviewed in chapter 5, "Dining"), or on the terrace, where barbecues are sometimes held. There's also an informal lounge, the Port O' Call Pub, with nightly entertainment during the high season.

30 Kings Point Rd., Sandys Parish MA 02, Bermuda. © **800/468-7300** in the U.S., 800/463-5990 in Canada, or 441/234-0331. Fax 441/234-3352. www.cambridgebeaches.com. 93 units. Apr 16–Oct $440–$665 double, $714 suite, $1,400 cottage for 4; off-season $305–$565 double, $600–$605 suite, $908–$1175 cottage for 4. Rates include MAP (breakfast and dinner). MC, V. Bus: 7 or 8. **Amenities:** 2 restaurants; 3 bars; 2 temperature-controlled pools; nearby Robert Trent Jones–designed golf course, Port Royal; putting green; 3 tennis courts. The full-service European-style spa features exercise equipment, whirlpool, massages, steam, sauna, and hair dressing, plus 50-odd types of skin, beauty, and relaxation treatments. Water sports include windsurfing with instruction, canoeing, kayaking, snorkeling, fishing (equipment is available), sailing, snorkeling trips, plus glass-bottom–boat excursions and fishing voyages and a full marina with Boston whalers and sailboats available for both self-piloted rentals and guided sailing excursions. Adjacent to the colony are 2 bone-fishing flats. Room service 7am–10pm, baby-sitting, dry cleaning, laundry. *In-room:* A/C, fridge, coffeemaker, hairdryer, safe. TV and iron upon request.

PAGET PARISH
Horizons and Cottages ✿✿✿ This deluxe cottage colony sits atop a hill overlooking Coral Beach, a 10-minute walk away. The lack of a beach might be a serious drawback for some visitors, especially at these prices. Otherwise, you'll be a pampered darling here. Both of Bermuda's top cottage colonies—Cambridge Beaches and Horizons—are popular with a well-heeled crowd. Subdued sophistication characterizes both, though Horizons is perhaps a touch less

snobbish. At Horizons, families with big bank accounts predominate in summer, and there's a mature repeat clientele in winter; trust-fund honeymooners show up year-round. Sometimes the atmosphere evokes a discreet house party, with fellow guests regularly being introduced. You might find more privacy, anonymity, and seclusion at Cambridge Beaches.

Horizons and Cottages have at their core a converted manor farm (ca. 1690), where the traditional ambience remains. A Relais & Châteaux member, Horizons is on a 25-acre estate with terraced gardens and lawns. The reception rooms of the manor house have old Bermudian architectural details, as well as antiques from England and the Continent; several drawing rooms have open fireplaces.

All guest units are handsomely furnished with Italian terra-cotta tile floors, scatter rugs, traditional tray ceilings, and ceiling fans. They have separate dressing areas and private terraces overlooking the ocean. Some units are split-level. Minibars and TVs are available on request. The good-size tiled bathrooms come with oversize mirrors and tub and shower combinations.

(Kids) Family-Friendly Accommodations

Elbow Beach Hotel (see p. 78)   Children stay free in their parents' room at this hotel, one of the best full-service resorts on the island. Your best bet is the "Family Value Package," which includes accommodations, transfers, daily breakfast buffet, and a host of activities and extras; inquire about it when you book.

Grotto Bay Beach Hotel (see p. 79)   A longtime family favorite, this hotel features a heavily discounted "Family Special" for two adults and two children under 16 spending at least 4 nights.

The Fairmont Southampton Princess (see p. 75)   This giant resort offers the best children's program on the island, including parties and reliable baby-sitting. Children under 17 stay free in a room with one or two adults, and receive complimentary breakfast and dinner daily.

Sandpiper Apartments (see p. 94)   Families looking for a moderately priced vacation might check in here. Some units have living/dining areas with two double pull-out sofa beds. Each unit has a kitchen where Mom and Dad can prepare simple meals to cut down on the high cost of dining out in Bermuda.

Rosemont (see p. 96)   Rosemont caters to families, and each of its units contains a kitchen. Some rooms can be joined together to accommodate larger broods. Baby-sitting can be arranged.

Royal Palms Hotel (see p. 98)   Although it can't compete with the big resorts in facilities, this longtime family favorite extends a cordial welcome. It's within walking distance of Hamilton, so families can save on transportation. There's a freshwater pool, but the beach is a 10-minute ride or 30-minute walk away.

Sonesta Beach Resort (see p. 77)   Try to book into this stellar resort on a family package plan (consult a travel agent). Most rooms accommodate two parents and two kids, and there are plenty of activities and diversions for children, including unlimited free ice cream and pizza parties.

The main dining room, the Middleton Room (reviewed in chapter 5, "Dining"), serves French *cuisine naturelle*, using all fresh products. The food, especially the tender steak and fresh seafood dishes, is exceptional for Bermuda, although the chefs at Cambridge Beaches seem to work more magic. Lunch is served on the terrace; in the evening, it's transformed into an entertainment area, with informal dancing and often calypso music. Guests can have lunch and dinner, by reservation, at Newstead and Waterloo House.

33 South Shore Rd., Paget PG04, Bermuda. © 800/468-0022 in the U.S. and Canada, or 441/236-0048. Fax 441/236-1981. www.horizonscottages.com. 48 units. Mar 15–Jan 4 $360–$730 double; off-season $270–$550 double. Rates include MAP (breakfast and dinner). AE, MC, V. Bus: 2 or 7. **Amenities:** Restaurant; bar; heated freshwater swimming pool; 9-hole golf course; 18-hole putting green; 3 tennis courts; access to nearby health club; bike and scooter rentals; room service (breakfast only); massage; baby-sitting; laundry. *In room:* A/C, hairdryer, safe; TV upon request.

DEVONSHIRE PARISH

Ariel Sands Beach Club *✿✿*   At the ocean's edge, with a sandy beach just a 2-minute walk away, secluded Ariel Sands is one of the best cottage colonies in Bermuda, though not quite in the platinum class of Cambridge Beaches and Horizons. This is a quiet place, popular with well-heeled families looking for a summer retreat. The grounds are well landscaped, with flowering trees and coconut palms; one of the most original sculptures on the island is Seward Johnson, Jr.'s stainless-steel statue of Ariel, who dances like a water sprite on the surf.

One part-owner is the mother of actor Michael Douglas (and ex-wife of film legend Kirk Douglas), and the movie star contributed $5 million to the resort's recent refurbishment. It looks fresh, bright, and new—better than it has in years. In chilly weather, a double-hearth fireplace warms a reception lounge and bar area. The smallish accommodations have private entrances. They're attractively decorated, with white walls, cool pastels, Bermudian flower paintings, straw matting on terra-cotta floors, and bentwood furniture; most have private porches. The art in many of the private and public rooms is based on themes from *The Tempest,* and guest rooms have names such as Miranda's Cabana, Sea Nymph, and Prospero. The midsize bathrooms are handsomely tiled and well maintained.

The first-class Nirvana Spa offers such services as beachside massages, aromatherapy, skin and hair treatments, and a full exercise facility. Complete health and fitness appraisals are available, including programs devoted to nutrition, cardiac risk, and lifestyle health issues.

Caliban's, one of the finest hotel dining rooms on the island, serves refined international and Bermudian cuisine (see chapter 5, "Dining"). Caliban's Bar is the parish's hot new bar.

34 South Shore Rd., Devonshire (P.O. Box HM 334), Hamilton HM BX, Bermuda. © 800/468-6610 in the U.S., or 441/236-1010; call collect from Canada. Fax 441/236-0087. www.arielsands.com. 47 units. May–Oct $430–$900 double; Nov $330–$700 double; Dec–Mar $290–$620 double; Apr $360–$760 double. Rates include breakfast; MAP (breakfast and dinner) $75 per person. AE, MC, V. Bus: 1. **Amenities:** Restaurant; bar; 1 freshwater and 2 saltwater pools; 3 tennis courts (2 lit for night games); health club & spa; snorkeling equipment rental; moped rental; room service (at mealtimes only); baby-sitting; laundry. *In room:* A/C, TV, dataport, fridge, coffeemaker, hairdryer, iron, safe.

SMITH'S PARISH

Pink Beach Club & Cottages *✿✿*   Two pretty south-shore pink beaches surrounded this complex of pink cottages, and bay grape trees and hibiscus bushes grace the 16-acre garden setting. This remote cottage colony, the largest on Bermuda, doesn't have the opulence or flair of Cambridge Beaches or Horizons, but it does attract an affluent international crowd. The staff, among the best on

the island, includes many people who have been with Pink Beach since it opened in 1947. The cottages range from studios—with a combination bed-room/sitting room, good-sized bathroom, and patio—to full units with a living room and terrace. Contemporary furnishings, fully equipped kitchens, and plush carpeting add to the allure. The bathrooms have combination tub and shower. If you can snare them, the very best accommodations and the most luxurious is a quartet of oceanfront suites added in 2000. These are ideal for honeymooners or other couples, or even families seeking spacious accommoda-tions. Also in 2000, the club opened Sea Rock Cottage with 17 new junior suites, offering much of the same luxury as the oceanfront suites. With the com-pletion of this new extension, half of the club's accommodations will have been either refurbished or totally rebuilt around the turn of this century.

The heart of the colony is the pink-painted limestone clubhouse, with a natural-wood dining room where "backyard" vegetables and fresh seafood go into the international cuisine. Every table provides a view of the ocean, and occasionally of a celebrity diner. The food is well prepared if not outstanding. The chefs strive for variety, but you might find dining here every night a bit monotonous. Breakfast here is a treat; request it the night before and a maid will serve you on your private terrace.

South Shore Rd. (P.O. Box HM 1017), Hamilton HM DX, Bermuda. ✆ 800/355-6161 in the U.S., or 441/293-1666. Fax 441/293-8935. www.pinkbeach.com. 112 units. Apr–Nov 15 $365–$550 double; off-season $300–$450 double. Rates include MAP (breakfast and dinner). AE, MC, V. Closed Dec 15–Mar 20. Bus: 1. **Amenities:** Restaurant; bar; large freshwater pool; sun terrace; 2 championship golf courses 2 minutes from the hotel; 2 tennis courts; fitness center; spa services; moped rental; baby-sitting; laundry. *In room:* A/C, TV, hairdryer, iron, safe.

ST. GEORGE PARISH

St. George's Club ✮ Far less stuffy than the cottage colonies listed above, this resort encompasses 18 acres atop Rose Hill (off York St.). It features clusters of traditionally designed Bermudian one- and two-bedroom cottages; all were completely renovated in 1996. A family or two or three couples traveling together can share a cottage and bring the price down to a reasonable level. A shuttle bus takes guests to the beach club at Achilles Bay, about a 2-minute ride away. The complex functions primarily as a time-share property; units are rented to the public when the owners are not using them. Cottages have private bal-conies or patios, comfortable living and dining areas, fully equipped kitchens, and bathrooms with sunken tubs (also showers) and marble vanities. Views are of the ocean, the pool, or the golf course.

The colony's elegant restaurant, Tillies, is open to the public; it's among the finest dining rooms in the East End. The Sir George Pub and the Blackbeard's Hideout restaurant are popular rendezvous spots.

Rose Hill (P.O. Box GE 92), St. George GE BX, Bermuda. ✆ 441/297-1200. Fax 441/297-8003. www.stgeorgeclub.com. 71 units. Apr–Nov $275 cottage for up to 4, $375 cottage for up to 6; Dec–Mar $185 cottage for up to 4, $225 cottage for up to 6. AE, MC, V. Bus: 6, 8, 10, or 11. **Amenities:** Restaurant; bar; 3 freshwater swimming pools (1 heated); 3 all-weather tennis courts (2 can be lit at night); adjacent Robert Trent Jones–designed 18-hole golf course (guests receive preferential tee times and reduced rates); water-sports equipment; moped rental; business center; baby-sitting; laundry. *In room:* A/C, TV, dataport, fully equipped kitchen, iron.

MODERATE
HAMILTON PARISH

Clear View Suites & Villas Adjacent to a grassy, rock-strewn patch of seafront, Clear View offers units that feature kitchenettes and a good deal of privacy. Midway between Hamilton and St. George, it's a cluster of one- and two-story pink concrete buildings erected during the 1970s. Each holds two to six units decorated with pastel upholstery, tiled surfaces, and big windows. Units with sea views are more expensive. Bathrooms are tiled and midsize.

The centerpiece of the resort is a white-sided farmhouse that holds the restaurant, Landfall, and a bar. You can swim in the ocean, but there's no beach—most guests head a mile west to the sands of Shelly Bay Beach. A small art gallery displays the works of local painters. Ruth Paynter (and her husband Gerald) arranges art classes that are popular among the island's community of retirees.

Sandy Lane, Hamilton Parish CR 02, Bermuda. ℭ 800/468-9600 in the U.S. or Canada, or 441/293-0484. Fax 441/293-0267. 45 units. $170–$214 double. MAP (breakfast and dinner) $40 per person. AE, DC, MC, V. Bus: 10 or 11. **Amenities:** Restaurant; bar; 2 pools; tennis court. In room: A/C, TV.

SANDY'S PARISH

Daniel's Head Village   The newest, and most controversial, resort in Bermuda lies near the island's extreme northeastern tip (Sandy's Parish), on 17 acres of rolling, scrub-covered landscape that functioned during World War II as a Canadian Air Force base. No other resort emphasizes the local ecosystems as rigorously as this one. It was built with the hopes that if a hurricane ever blasted the resort off the face of the island, no lasting damage would remain from human-imposed construction. Part of this derives from the design of the accommodations themselves. Each is compiled from a tough synthetic cloth that's stretched over a metal frame, all of it raised on a platform, and each with a front veranda that many guests quickly adopt as their favorite spot. These "eco-tents" are positioned either on piers above the water (the most expensive units), nearly adjacent to the water, or on a hillside overlooking the water. Inside, you'll find deliberately simple furniture that some visitors describe as "moderno and monastic," plus a prefabricated bathroom composed almost entirely of plastic. None contains a TV. Although cabins are spaced far apart from one another, walls are tissue-thin, and the evenings here are quiet. In the words of a particularly loyal and outspoken fan, "You'd better at least try to keep your lovemaking here as quiet as possible."

Even the hotel describes its main source of entertainment as "Mother Nature," warning clients in advance that this is a place to appreciate the Great Outdoors and to do a bit of star-watching after dark, since entertainment is nonexistent other than what you might create for yourself. Stanley Selengut, whose pioneering work on eco-sensitive resorts was most recently seen in the Virgin Islands, is your host. Fellow clients tend to be sensitive academics, and anyone interested in extremely low-key, extremely nature-oriented holidays. Recycling programs, composting, and efficient uses of energy are rigorously, even aggressively pursued at this unusual and emerging resort; there's even an on-site "conservation engineer" whose mission involves "saving the skinks" (a photogenic species of local lizard) and maintaining the integrity of the resort's self-appointed ecological mission. The use of mopeds is discouraged on the property.

The resort's social centerpiece is Daniels, a breezy, artfully offhanded restaurant where a Pacific Rim/Fusion cuisine is prepared by a Chinese chef who worked for years at an all-couples resort in Jamaica.

Daniel's Head Rd. (off Cambridge Rd.), Somerset Village, Sandys Parish, MA BX Bermuda. ℭ 800/225-4255 in the U.S., or 441/234-4272. Fax 441/234-4270. www.danielsheadvillage.com. 96 units. May–Oct $160–$295 double; Nov–Apr $115–$200 double. Rates include breakfast. AE, DC, MC, V. Bus: 7 or 8. **Amenities:** Restaurant; freshwater pool; 2 tennis courts; complimentary use of canoes, kayaks, sailboats, and scuba/snorkeling equipment; moped rentals. In room: Coffeemaker, fridge, safe.

4 Housekeeping Units

Housekeeping apartments, Bermuda's efficiency units, vary from modest to superior. Most have kitchens or kitchenettes and provide minimal daily maid service. Housekeeping cottages, which are air-conditioned and have fully equipped kitchens or kitchenettes, offer privacy and casual living on or close to a beach.

VERY EXPENSIVE
WARWICK PARISH
Mermaid Beach Club   Set beside a curvy shoreline that has both rocky cliffs and a sandy beachfront, this informal place avoids the stiff, snobby appeal of cottage colonies like Cambridge Villas and attracts couples of all ages who want to have a good time without having to dress up ... ever. The complex consists of two-story cement-sided buildings, the outgrowth of a beach club founded in the 1940s. All units have patios or balconies overlooking the sea. Guest rooms are simple and summery, decorated with pastels and rattan furniture. The kitchenettes are fine for whipping up salads and sandwiches, but too small for anything more ambitious.

There's a snack bar and a nautical-theme main bar. You'll need a cab or moped to pick up groceries—a mini-mart in a Shell gas station is 15 minutes on foot or 2 minutes by moped from the hotel; a more substantial market is about an 8-minute moped ride away.

South Shore Rd. (P.O. Box WK 250), Warwick WK BX, Bermuda. ℭ **800/441-7087** in the U.S. and Canada, or 441/236-5031. Fax 441/236-8325. 32 units, 22 with kitchenettes. Apr–Oct $253 double, $293–$430 apt with kitchenette; off-season $130 double, $150–$260 apt with kitchenette. AE, MC, V. Bus: 7. **Amenities:** Snack bar; bar; pool; bike rental shop; baby-sitting; laundromat. *In room:* A/C, coffeemaker, some units with kitchenette.

PAGET PARISH
Fourways Inn ℱ   This posh little place feels like a secret hideaway. Pink-sided, airy, and stylish, the Bermudian cottages occupy the well-maintained gardens of one of the best restaurants on the island, the Fourways Inn Restaurant (reviewed in chapter 5, "Dining"). The sands of Elbow Beach and Mermaid Beach lie within a 15-minute walk or 5-minute scooter ride. The main building is a former private home dating from 1727. Each two-bedroom cottage has a patio and a fully equipped kitchenette, plus a good-sized tile bathroom. They contain conservatively comfortable furniture. The kitchenettes are more useful than those at Mermaid Beach, but still, better suited to sandwiches and snacks than anything more ambitious. There's a medium-sized grocery store across the road.

1 Middle Rd. (P.O. Box PG 294), Paget PG BX, Bermuda. ℭ **800/962-7654** in the U.S. and Canada, or 441/236-6517. Fax 441/236-5528. fourways@ibl.bm. 5 units, 5 cottages. Apr–Oct $250 double, $350–$555 suite; off-season $150 double, $190–$340 suite. Extra person $40. Rates include continental breakfast; MAP (breakfast and dinner) $45 per person. AE, MC, V. Bus: 8. No children under 16 accepted. **Amenities:** Heated swimming pool. *In room:* A/C, TV, minibar, safe.

EXPENSIVE
WARWICK PARISH
Marley Beach Cottages ℱ ℭᵥₐₗᵤₑ   For two couples traveling together, this may be your best bargain. The pink-walled cottages sit on a steep, beautifully landscaped plot of land. Atop a low cliff on the south shore, near Astwood Park, it was used for scenes in *The Deep* and *Chapter Two*. More recently, part of another film, *Bermuda Grace*, was shot there. Three narrow beaches lie at the bottom of the slope that leads to the sea. It's not an ideal place for children, because there's

little for them to do other than swimming in the pool or at the beach. Parents who do bring the kids are warned to keep a close eye on them, because of the steep drop-off to the beaches below. We wouldn't recommend this place for anyone who might have a problem with the steps leading down the cliff to the ocean, but reasonably fit guests won't mind.

The spacious cottages have fully equipped kitchens, hibachis, and sea views from the patio. Each cottage has both a suite and a studio apartment, which you can rent as one unit or two. If you're cooking in, you can phone in an order to a local grocery that delivers, or give a list to the staff, who'll phone in your order. There's no delivery charge for orders over $20.

South Shore Rd. (P.O. Box PG 278), Warwick PG BX, Bermuda. (C) 800/637-4116 in the U.S., or 441/236-1143. Fax 441/236-1984. www.bermudahotels.com. 13 units. Apr 15–Oct $190–$270 double; Mar 15–Apr 14 and Nov–Jan 2 $150–$215 double; Jan 3–Mar 14 $115–$160 double. Extra person $35 in summer, $28 off-season. AE, M, V. Bus: 7. **Amenities:** Heated freshwater swimming pool; whirlpool. In room: A/C, TV, fridge, coffeemaker, iron.

Surf Side Beach Club /ʀ   With more style than the Mermaid Beach Club, the Surf Side Beach Club occupies a steeply sloping hillside that descends through gardens to a crescent-shaped sweep of private beachfront. (The steps down to the beach may be hard for mobility-impaired guests to manage.) A varied array of flowering trees and panoramic walkways dots the terraced property. From lookout points in the garden, visitors can see grouper and other fish swimming among the distant rocks of the shallow sea.

Accommodations consist of one-bedroom apartments near the terrace pool and other lodgings in hillside buildings. The self-contained units are simple and sunny, outfitted in bright colors with comfortable accessories. Each has a fully equipped kitchenette (including English china, wineglasses, and even salt and pepper shakers). The small tiled bathrooms are neatly kept and contain showers. A local grocery accepts phone orders and will deliver to your unit, with no delivery charge for orders over $20. The apartments also have private balconies or patios; some have sitting rooms as well.

A small cafe serves breakfast and lunch during the high season. The restaurant and bar, Palms, offers American and international cuisine; the menu changes daily.

South Shore Rd. (P.O. Box WK 101), Warwick WK BX, Bermuda. (C) 800/553-9990 in the U.S., or 441/236-7100. Fax 441/236-9765. www.surfside.bm. 37 units, 10 with shower only. Apr–Oct $250–$275 double, $325–$400 for up to 4; off-season $130–$165 double, $225–$350 for up to 4. Extra person $35–$40. Off-season extended-stay discounts available. AE, MC, V. Bus: 7. **Amenities:** Restaurant; bar; cafe; pool; tennis; mini-spa; 2 hot tubs; sauna; laundry, dry cleaning. In room: A/C, TV, fridge, coffeemaker, hairdryer, safe.

MODERATE
SOUTHAMPTON PARISH

Grape Bay Cottages   This organization consists of two well-maintained cottages, each directly beside the sea, and each of which is reserved sometimes six months in advance. Each is a cozy saltbox-style cottage, with comfortably unpretentious furniture and lots of reminders of Bermuda's maritime traditions. Each has a fully equipped kitchen, a wide front veranda, and the kind of ambience that's conducive to families taking holidays together and getting to know one another again. Maid service is provided for the bedrooms and living rooms (but not for the kitchens) every Monday to Saturday. The venue is about as *laissez-faire* as you're likely to find anywhere in Bermuda, but it's usually well suited to the many clients who prefer self-catered holidays in a simple cottage by the beach.

Grape Bay Dr. (off Middle Rd.), P.O. Box HM 1851, Hamilton, HM HX Bermuda. ℂ **800/637-4116** in the U.S., or 441/236-1194. 2 2-bedroom cottages, each with kitchen. Apr–Oct $315 1–4 persons; Nov–Mar $210 1–4 persons. Extra person $35 in summer, $20 off-season. AE, MC, V. Bus: 4. *In-room:* A/C, TV, iron.

Munro Beach Cottages   At a secluded seaside resort overlooking a private beach at Whitney Bay, this cottage complex borders the Port Royal Golf Course and its tennis courts. It sits at the western end of the south shore and opens onto Munro Beach, which boasts some of the best bone-fishing and snorkeling in Bermuda. Each spacious unit has a fully equipped kitchen, a combination dining, living, and bedroom area, and a separate tiled bathroom. No-smoking accommodations are available. All cottages provide homelike comforts, and there is daily maid service. If you don't feel like cooking, several first-class restaurants are within a 10- to 15-minute taxi ride. Snorkeling, sailing, and scuba diving are close at hand.

2 Port Royal Golf Course Rd., Southampton SN BX, Bermuda. ℂ **800/637-4116** in the U.S., or 441/234-1175. Fax 441/234-3528. www.munrobeach.com. 17 units. Apr 15–Nov 15 $210 double, $240 triple; $270 quad; off-season $115 double, $145 triple, $175 quad. MC, V. Bus: 7 or 8. *In-room:* A/C, TV.

WARWICK PARISH

Astwood Cove 🐾   Nigel (Nicky) and Gabrielle (Gaby) Lewin own this homestead, which was built in 1720 on a dairy farm. (Sisters Maude, Ada, and Mary Astwood stipulated in their will that the house should always carry their name.) The apartment complex occupies a peaceful setting, overlooking lightly wooded meadows and the south shore. The closest large beach, Long Bay, is a quarter-mile away; Astwood Beach and Mermaid Beach are only a 3-minute stroll from the complex.

Each self-contained apartment has a ceiling fan and a terrace or porch. Local phone calls are free. Some units have sitting rooms, and all have kitchens or kitchenettes equipped with English china. Most of the kitchens are generously proportioned units with stoves, microwaves, and enough basic accessories to prepare a real meal. A few smaller units have just microwaves and stovetop burners. Each unit comes with a small tiled bathroom, with a shower.

There's a mini-mart less than 2 miles away. A grocery store somewhat farther away delivers orders over $20. A building added in 1985 has a communal terrace, pavilion, and TV.

49 South Shore Rd., Warwick WK 07, Bermuda. ℂ **800/637-4116** in the U.S., or 441/236-0984. Fax 441/236-1164. www.astwoodcove.com. 20 units, all with shower only. Apr–Nov 15 $130–$175 double; Nov 16–Mar $95–$120 double. AE, MC, V. Bus: 7. **Amenities:** Pool; sauna; bike rentals; baby-sitting; laundromat; gas-fired barbecue grills. *In room:* A/C, TV, kitchenette, fridge, coffeemaker, hairdryer, iron; safe upon request.

Sandpiper Apartments *(Kids)*   Built in 1979 and frequently upgraded, this apartment complex is a bargain, attracting self-sufficient families who like the spacious accommodations and who often shop for groceries to prepare some of their own meals to cut down on the pricey restaurant bills in Bermuda. Nine units are studios for one or two people, with two double beds, a small tiled bathroom, and a fully equipped kitchenette that's sufficient for simple meals. Five units contain a bedroom (with king-size or twin beds), a kitchen, a bathroom, and a living/dining area with two double pull-out sofa beds. Every apartment has a radio and balcony. There's daily maid service. The Sandpiper is minutes away from restaurants and the supermarket. The closest beach is 500 yards away; the property has gardens for lounging.

South Shore Rd. (P.O. Box HM 685), Hamilton HM CX, Bermuda. ℂ **441/236-7093**. Fax 441/236-3898. www. bermudahotel.com. 14 units. Apr–Oct $130 double, $170–$200 suite for 3 or 4; off-season $100 double,

$115–$145 suite for 3 or 4. AE, DC, MC, V. Bus: 7. **Amenities:** Pool; outdoor whirlpool; baby-sitting; laundromat. *In room:* A/C, TV, kitchen, fridge, coffeemaker, hairdryer, iron, safe.

Vienna Guest Apartments   This apartment complex lies on attractively landscaped grounds, with panoramic views of Forest Hills, Gibbs Hill Lighthouse, and Great Sound. It opened in the early 1990s and underwent renovation in 1999. Informality is definitely the keynote—you're even welcomed with beer or wine. Five units can accommodate up to four guests, and one unit holds two comfortably. Each good-sized apartment has a double bedroom, a combined living and dining room with a ceiling fan, a clock radio, a fully equipped kitchen with a patio, and a small tiled bathroom with shower.

63 Cedar Hill (P.O. Box WK 761), Warwick WK BX, Bermuda. ✆ 441/236-3300. Fax 441/236-6100. www. Bermuda.com. 6 units. Apr–Oct $130 double, $35 third person, $20 child 4–12; off-season $65–$85 double, $20 third person, $20 child. AE, MC, V. Bus: 7. **Amenities:** Pool; golf courses and tennis courts nearby; sundeck; barbecue facilities; coin-operated laundry facilities. *In room:* A/C, TV.

PAGET PARISH
Barnsdale Guest Apartments   This small apartment complex—a concrete structure—may not be cozy, but it offers guests a fairly priced hideaway. It's a neutrally decorated, unremarkable, modern-looking building. If you like to feel anonymous and independent when you're on vacation, it'll suit you. It's 15 minutes from Elbow Beach by scooter or taxi, on a 1-acre site in a quiet residential neighborhood overlooking a banana grove. Furnishings are durable but unexciting, in the small but comfortable units containing cramped bathrooms with shower units. All units have attractive, well-accessorized kitchenettes where you can prepare a moderately ambitious meal.

2 Barnes Valley, Paget PG 03, Bermuda. ✆ 441/236-0164. Fax 441/236-4709. www.bermuda.com/ barnsdale. 8 units. Summer $140 double, $165 triple, $195 quad; off-season $90 double, $100 triple, $120 quad. AE, MC, V. Ferry to Hamilton. **Amenities:** Pool; barbecue pit; grocery store with a liquor counter within a 2-minute walk. *In room:* A/C, TV.

Paraquet Guest Apartments (Value)   If you're looking for a bargain and are happy with rather motel-like accommodations, this is the place for you. This buff-colored collection of Bermudian houses sits in a gentle knoll, a 5-minute walk from Elbow Beach and a 10-minute bus ride from Hamilton. Built in the mid-1970s, the complex is owned by the Portuguese-born Correia family. Nine units have kitchenettes that are attractive and compact but efficient, filled with the basic equipment you'd need to prepare a meal. All the small to mid-size units contain functional but comfortable modern furniture, plus a small tiled bathroom with shower. The apartment groupings also operate a decently priced restaurant, Paraquet (reviewed in chapter 5, "Dining").

South Shore Rd. (P.O. Box PG 173), Paget PG BX, Bermuda. ✆ 441/236-5842. Fax 441/236-1665. 12 units. Apr–Oct $144 double without kitchen, $182 double with kitchen; Nov–Mar $130 double without kitchen, $155 double with kitchen. No credit cards. Bus: 7. **Amenities:** Grocery store 50 yards from hotel. *In room:* A/C, TV.

Valley Cottages & Apartments   In a semitropical setting in the center of the island, this is a good choice for self-sufficient types, although we think you get a better deal at the Paraquet Guest Apartments. The complex of typical pink Bermuda buildings lies a short walk from Elbow Beach and a number of food markets and tennis courts; ferry and bus connections to the rest of Bermuda are good. The mid-size cottages and studios are in a garden, containing kitchens, living rooms, and private balconies, along with small tiled bathrooms with shower units. The decor is minimalist but comfortable, with good beds.

Valley Rd. (P.O. Box PG 214), Paget PG BX, Bermuda. ℂ **441/236-0628.** Fax 441/236-3895. 9 units. Summer $90–$115 studio double, $150–$190 cottage (up to 4). Off-season $90–$100 studio double, $150–$170 cottage (up to 4). Bus: 8. **Amenities:** Spa pool and sun terrace in a secluded area. *In room:* A/C, TV.

PEMBROKE PARISH (CITY OF HAMILTON)

Rosemont ⚡ *Kids*   Having more character and island charm than Valley Cottages or Barnsdale Guest Apartments, this is a cluster of gray-walled cottages, each with a large veranda, on a flowered hillside near the Hamilton Princess. Two of the cottages are former private homes, built in the 1940s; the rest are more modern structures constructed within the past 2 decades. The harbor is visible from the raised terrace. The business travelers, the more "subdued" families, and older couples that frequent Rosemont come for the peace and tranquillity. The policy here is to "keep it quiet," so the hotel usually doesn't accept college students or large groups.

Each well-furnished room has a kitchen; we find some units a little on the dark side. As many as three rooms can be joined together to accommodate families. The hotel also has three suites with private entrances and better furnishings. Each accommodation comes with a small but neatly kept private tiled bath.

There's no restaurant on the premises, but everybody cooks in. A grocery store is close by, downtown Hamilton is 10 minutes away, and Elbow Beach is a 15-minute scooter or taxi ride away.

41 Rosemont Ave. (P.O. Box HM 37), Hamilton HM AX, Bermuda. ℂ **800/367-0040** in the U.S., 800/267-0040 in Canada, or 441/292-1055. Fax 441/295-3913. www.rosemont.bm. 47 units. Apr–Nov $160–$270 double; Dec–Mar $126–$200 double. Rates do not include service and taxes. MC, V. **Amenities:** Scooter rentals arranged; baby-sitting; laundry. *In room:* A/C, TV.

SMITH'S PARISH

Angel's Grotto ⚡ *Value*   These housekeeping cottages, among the best in Bermuda, appeal particularly to couples. Following recent renovations, they're better than ever. Situated on 1½ acres of seafront property overlooking Harrington Sound, this complex consists of three white-sided structures, originally built as a private home in the 1940s. Later it functioned as a disco and nightclub. Daisy Hart has owned the property since 1981. Each unit contains a bedroom, living/dining area, a small tiled bath with shower, and a well-equipped kitchen. Units that overlook the water are slightly more expensive and are more desirable, of course. The coastline adjacent to the complex is too rocky for swimming, but the pink sands of John Smith's Bay on the south shore are a 5-minute walk away. There's a small convenience store within a 5-minute walk, and a supermarket 7 minutes away by moped or taxi.

Harrington Sound Rd. (P.O. Box HS 81), Harrington Sound HS BX, Bermuda. ℂ **441/293-1986.** Fax 441/293-4164. www.angelsgrotto.com. 7 units. Apr–Nov 15 $145–$240 (up to 4); off-season $125–$190 (up to 4). AE, MC, V. Bus: 3. *In-room:* A/C, TV.

INEXPENSIVE

PAGET PARISH

Sky-Top Cottages ⚡ *Value*   On a hilltop above Paget's southern shoreline, opposite the Elbow Beach Hotel, this collection of cottages offers a great deal. The comfortable, secluded accommodations are in four cozy cottages, all upgraded and refurbished by owners Andrea and John Flood. Each unit has a fully equipped kitchen and a small private terrace. On all sides of the property, shrubs and trees dot emerald-colored lawns; everywhere there are lovely views of the sea. There are few social activities here, except an occasional rainy-day party to cheer everybody up, but there's a warm sense of camaraderie. Breakfast is not served, and there is no on-site restaurant. It's just a 5-minute walk to Elbow Beach, and a 10-minute ride by cab, bus, or moped to Hamilton.

65 South Shore Rd. (P.O. Box PG 227), Paget PG BX, Bermuda. ✆ 441/236-7984. Fax 441/232-0446. www. bermuda.com/skytop. 11 units. Mar 16–Nov 15 $100–$170 double; winter $85–$130 double. Extra person $25 in summer, $15 off-season. Children under 12 $10. Off-season weekly and monthly discounts available. MC, V. Bus: 2 or 7. *In-room:* A/C, TV, fridge, coffeemaker, iron.

PEMBROKE PARISH

Robin's Nest Consider this choice if you'd like a snug little apartment in a family-managed compound in a residential neighborhood. It consists of three separate buildings, each painted terra cotta, and each scattered amid a small but well-maintained garden that's supervised by Milt and Renée Robinson. Units are spacious and have a summery-looking decor that includes lots of wicker. Each unit contains a fully equipped kitchen, and hibachis are available in case anyone wants to expand his or her cooking facilities into the Great Outdoors. Two coves, suitable for swimming, lie within a ten-minute walk of the compound.

10 Vale Close, North Shore, Pembroke HM 04 Bermuda. ✆ 800/637-4116 in the U.S., or 441/292-4347. Fax 441/292-4347. rob@bspl.bm. 4 units, each with kitchen. Year-round $95 double; $125 triple; $150 quad. Children under 12 $10 each per night. No credit cards. Bus: 4. **Amenities:** Large freshwater swimming pool. *In room:* A/C, TV, fridge, coffeemaker, hairdryer, iron, safe.

SANDYS PARISH

Garden House ⭐ *(Finds)* This lovely Bermuda home sits in three acres of landscaped gardens in a secluded location, extending down to Ely's Harbour where there is a private dock for deep-water swimming. You have a choice of three cottages: a studio, a one-bedroom cottage with a separate living room and kitchen, and, the most luxurious of all, a two-bedroom cottage with a 37-foot living room leading to a separate kitchen. Beds are single kings or two twins, although one cottage has a lovely Bermudian antique four-poster bed. Midsize bathrooms have a full tub and shower combo plus a spacious cupboard faced with a full-length mirror. The living rooms in the units evoke a British country house style with Bermudian touches of cedar. All cottages have private patios where you can barbecue on your hibachi.

4 Middle Rd., Somerset Bridge, Sandys Parish, SB 01 Bermuda. ✆ 441/234-1435. Fax 441/234-3006. 3 units. Summer $115 studio for 2, $130 double cottage for 2, $255 2-bedroom cottage for 4; off-season $105 studio for 2, $120 cottage for 2, $225 2-bedroom cottage for 4. No credit cards. Bus: 7 or 8. **Amenities:** Saltwater swimming pool. *In room:* A/C, TV, fridge, coffeemaker, iron.

SOUTHAMPTON PARISH

Whale Bay Inn ⭐ *(Finds)* Overlooking the Port Royal Golf Course, this apartment complex opens onto Whale Bay Beach, which takes its name from the whales spotted off the coast in summer, as they head for their summer feeding grounds. A 20-minute walk from the nearest grocery store, the complex consists of five apartments, each with a full shower and tub combination, mid-size bedrooms with one double and one single bed. The owners obviously like the color blue—it's everywhere, from the curtains to the cutlery. Wicker and pine furnishings create a light, airy effect. All units have private patios overlooking the South Shore. Hibachis are on hand for outdoor barbecues.

34 Whaling Hill, Whale Bay Rd., Southampton SN BX Bermuda. ✆ 441/238-0469. Fax 441/238-1224. whalebayinn@northrock.bm. 5 units. Summer $140 double; off-season $100 double. Extra person $40. Kids 12 and under free. No credit cards. Bus: 7 or 8. *In-room:* A/C, TV, fridge, coffeemaker.

5 Guesthouses

Bermuda's guesthouses are usually comfortable, old converted manor houses in garden settings. Some have pools and terraces. The smaller ones are much more casual. They offer fewer facilities and are often outfitted with simple, lived-in furniture. Most guesthouses serve breakfast only. Those accommodating fewer than 12 guests are usually private homes. Some have housekeeping units, and others offer shared kitchen facilities for guests to prepare snacks.

EXPENSIVE

PEMBROKE PARISH (CITY OF HAMILTON)

Royal Palms Hotel ⊛ (Kids) Just a 5-minute walk from Hamilton, the Royal Palms is one of the most sought-after small hotels on the island, thanks to the care and restoration work of brother-and-sister owners Richard Smith and Susan Weare. Built in 1903, it's a fine example of Bermudian architecture, with coral-colored walls, white shutters, a white roof, and a wraparound front porch with rocking chairs and armchairs. Local residents often walk by the garden to admire the marigolds and zinnias. The closest beach is Elbow Beach, a 10-minute taxi or scooter ride or a 30-minute walk away.

The guest rooms were once the living rooms, parlors, and bedrooms of the grand private house. All are spacious, sunny, and comfortably furnished, with rich fabrics throughout. Most units have high ceilings and tall windows, and each comes with a small, well-maintained private bathroom. In the mews next to the hotel are four additional but less desirable units. This is an excellent choice for budget-minded families traveling together. Family travelers generally request one of the units that come with kitchen facilities.

Cozy public areas include Ascots (reviewed in chapter 5, "Dining"), which serves European and Bermudian cuisine.

24 Rosemont Ave. (P.O. Box HM 499), Hamilton HM CX, Bermuda. © **800/678-0783** in the U.S., 800/799-0824 in Canada, or 441/292-1854. Fax 441/292-1946. www.royalpalms.bm. 25 units. Apr–Nov 15 $190–$265 double; off-season $150–$178 double. Extra person $40. Children under 16 $25, children under 3 free. Rates include continental breakfast. AE, MC, V. Bus: 1, 2, 10, or 11. **Amenities:** Restaurant, bar, pool. *In room:* A/C, TV, coffeemaker.

MODERATE

SOUTHAMPTON PARISH

Royal Heights Guest House At the top of a steep driveway near the summit of Lighthouse Hill, this guesthouse is convenient to the Southampton Princess, with its varied nightlife and dining options. It's a modern, turquoise-trimmed building with two wings that embrace the front entryway. Guests are welcome to gather in the living room of the owners, Russel and Jean Richardson, who are happy to suggest activities. Each tidy but small room has a balcony and comfortable furniture, plus a tiled bath with shower. Horseshoe Bay, the closest beach, is a 5-minute taxi or scooter ride or 15-minute walk away. You can watch ships passing by on the Great Sound as you float in the guesthouse's swimming pool.

Lighthouse Hill (P.O. Box SN 144), Southampton SN BX, Bermuda. © **441/238-0043.** Fax 441/238-8445. www.royalheights@ibl.bm. 7 units. Apr–Nov $145 double, $195 triple; off-season $125 double, $175 triple. Rates include continental breakfast. Children under 12 in parents' room $50. AE, MC, V. Closed Feb. Bus: 7 or 8. **Amenities:** Pool. *In room:* A/C, TV, fridge, coffeemaker.

PAGET PARISH

Dawkin's Manor In a quiet residential neighborhood a 5-minute walk from Elbow Beach, this inn offers simple, unpretentious accommodations. Originally built in the 1930s, it has expanded massively since Jamaica-born Celia Dawkins bought the place in the early 1990s. Off-island lecturers conducting short-term classes at nearby Bermuda College sometimes stay here. Even the simplest rooms contain microwaves and coffeemakers; more elaborate accommodations contain kitchens that are bigger than those in lots of other rental properties, suitable for bona-fide cooking. Each unit comes with a small but tidy tiled bathroom with shower.

29 St. Michael's Rd. (P.O. Box PG 34), Paget PG BX, Bermuda. (©) **441/236-7419.** Fax 441/236-7088. www. bermuda-charm.com. 8 units. Summer $120 double without kitchenette, $140 double with kitchenette, $160 suite for 2 with kitchenette; off-season $95 double without kitchenette, $95 double with kitchenette, $105 suite for 2 with kitchenette. No credit cards. Bus: 7. **Amenities:** Pool; bike rentals; room service (9:30am–2:30pm); baby-sitting; laundromat; grocery store (2-min. walk). *In room:* A/C, TV, kitchen, fridge, coffeemaker, hairdryer, iron, safe.

Loughlands *(★ (Value))*   Built in 1920, Loughlands is the stately former residence of the president of the Staten Island (New York) Savings Bank, who bestowed his name, Lough, on the estate. Stanley and Mary Pickles bought Loughlands in 1973, sold their large country house in Cornwall, England, and shipped many of their antiques to what is now the largest guesthouse in Bermuda. On 9 acres of landscaped grounds in the center of the island, it's chalk-white, with a large portrait of Queen Victoria in the entry hall. The rooms are handsomely decorated, and some contain high-post beds and antique chests. Accommodations have both shower and tub.

At breakfast, you'll enjoy such Bermudian treats as citrus fruit or bananas and homemade preserves. Elbow Beach, the closest beach, is an 8-minute walk or 3-minute bike ride away.

79 South Shore Rd., Paget PG 03, Bermuda. (©) **441/236-1253.** 19 units. Mar 15–Nov 14 $130 double; off-season $85 double. Rates include continental breakfast. No credit cards. Bus: 2 or 7. **Amenities:** Pool, tennis court. *In room:* A/C, coffeemaker; no phone.

PEMBROKE PARISH (CITY OF HAMILTON)

Edgehill Manor   Just outside the city limits and a 15-minute walk from the nearest beach, Edgehill Manor is in a quiet residential area that's convenient to Hamilton's restaurants and shopping. It was built around the time of the American Civil War and exudes an old-fashioned, homey quality, attracting a rather middle-aged clientele. British-born proprietor Bridget Marshall continues the tradition of serving English tea in the afternoon. Although each unit has its own style, all have small balconies or patios; three have kitchenettes, and all come with small tiled bathrooms with shower units. Ms. Marshall's continental breakfast, she is proud to say, is "all home baked."

Rosemont Ave. (P.O. Box HM 1048), Hamilton HM EX, Bermuda. (©) **441/295-7124.** Fax 441/295-3850. www. bermuda.com/edgehill. 9 units. Mar 16–Nov 15 $160 double; off-season $138 double. Rates include continental breakfast. Extra person $30. Children under 12 in parents' room $20. No credit cards. Bus: 7 or 8. **Amenities:** Pool; room service (8:00–9:30am); baby-sitting. *In-room:* A/C, TV, kitchen (some rooms), fridge, safe.

Fordham Hall   On a hillside just outside the City of Hamilton, this guesthouse opens onto a panoramic view of Pitts Bay and the harbor beyond. Fordham Hall lies within walking distance of the city's best shops and restaurants, with the ferry practically at its doorstep. Since a change in ownership in 1999, the complex has been vastly improved. The place has a real Bermudian atmosphere, with a breezy lounge. The accommodations are spacious and comfortable, with good mattresses and attractive furnishings, plus small tiled bathrooms with showers. You can eat breakfast with a view of the boating activity of Hamilton Harbour.

Arrangements can be made for water-skiing, skin-diving, tours, carriages, taxis, and motorbikes.

53 Pitts Bay Rd., Pembroke (P.O. Box HM 692), Hamilton HM CX, Bermuda. ℂ **800/537-4163** in the U.S., or 441/295-1551. Fax 441/295-3906. fordan@northrock.bm. 12 units. Summer $130 double, $170–$190 suite; off-season $110 double, $150–$170 suite. AE, MC, V. Rates include continental breakfast. AE, MC, V. Bus: 7 or 8. **Amenities:** Arrangements for water-skiing, skin-diving, tours, carriages, taxis, and motorbikes. *In room:* A/C, TV, microwave, fridge.

The Oxford House ⍟ The Oxford House is one of the best and most centrally located guesthouses in Hamilton, about a 10-minute scooter ride or a 30-minute walk from Elbow Beach. The only property in Bermuda constructed specifically as a guesthouse, it's on a side street that leads to Front Street, near the Bermudiana Hotel.

The guesthouse was built in 1938 by a doctor and his French wife, who requested that some of the architectural features follow French designs. Doric columns, corner mullions, and urn-shaped balustrades flank the white- and cream-colored entrance portico. Inside, a curved stairwell sweeps up to spacious, well-furnished guest rooms, each named after one of Bermuda's parishes. They have high ceilings and dressing areas. Two accommodations are equipped with full bathrooms, the rest contain shower units. There's also a sunny upstairs sitting room. Breakfast might include a fresh fruit salad made with oranges and grapefruit grown in the yard. The gracious host is Welsh-born Ann Smith.

Woodbourne Ave. (P.O. Box HM 374), Hamilton HM BX, Bermuda. ℂ **800/548-7758** in the U.S., 800/ 272-2306 in Canada, or 441/295-0503. Fax 441/295-0250. www.oxford.com. 12 units. Mar 16–Nov $163 double, $208 triple, $236 quad; off-season $152 double, $193 triple, $218 quad. Rates include full breakfast. AE, MC, V. Bus: 7 or 8. *In-room:* A/C, TV, coffeemaker.

ST. GEORGE PARISH

Aunt Nea's Inn at Hillcrest ⍟ ⍟ᵥₐₗᵤₑ The only true B&B inn in historic St. George, this inviting place is now better than ever following an upgrade and major improvement. The early 18th-century house stands on a hill off Old Maid's Lane. Three beaches with great water sports are within 10 minutes on foot. In 1804, the Irish poet Thomas Moore roomed here for several weeks. He developed a passion for Nea Tucker next door and wrote several romantic verses for her.

Each room is uniquely furnished, with four-poster beds constructed of tropical hardwoods or wrought iron, and complementary armoires and accent pieces. Four rooms have whirlpools, the others come with shower units. Owners Delaey Robinson and Andrea Dismont have given the rooms names such as "Green Turtle" and "Queen Conch," which represent many of the natural treasures of Bermuda. Smoking is not allowed.

1 Nea's Alley (P.O. Box GE 96), St. George GE BX, Bermuda. ℂ **441/297-1630.** Fax 441/297-1908. www. auntneas.com. 12 units. Apr–Oct $135–$300 double, $185–$200 suite. AE, MC, V. Closed Nov–Mar. Bus: 1, 3, 6, 10, or 11. *In-room:* A/C, fridge, coffeemaker, hairdryer, iron, safe.

INEXPENSIVE
SOUTHAMPTON PARISH

Greene's Guest House From the outside, this guesthouse overlooking Great Sound appears well-maintained and unpretentious. A look on the inside reveals pleasant, conservatively furnished rooms that are more impressive than you might have supposed. A pair of lions resting on stone columns flanks the entry. The tables in the dining room, which adjoins the kitchen, are set with full formal dinner service throughout the day. Owners Walter "Dickie" Greene and his wife, Jane, welcome guests to use the spacious, well-furnished living room and the sun-washed terraces in back. Bedrooms are small to medium in size, each comfortably furnished with a tidily kept and compact private bathroom with a shower unit.

There's a swimming pool in the back garden, and Whale Bay Beach lies 3 minutes away by bus or 10 minutes by foot. Dinner is available in the dining room if requested in advance. Facing the sea is a cozy bar where guests record their drinks on the honor system. The bus to and from Hamilton stops right in front of the room.

71 Middle Rd. (P.O. Box SN 395), Southampton SN BX, Bermuda. ✆ **441/238-0834.** Fax 441/238-8980. 8 units. $110 double. Rates include full breakfast. No credit cards. Bus: 7 or 8. **Amenities:** Pool. *In room:* A/C, TV, fridge, coffeemaker, iron.

PAGET PARISH

Greenbank Guest House   This guesthouse stands at the water's edge in Salt Kettle, just across the bay—a 10-minute ferry ride—from Hamilton. It's an old home, hidden under pine and palm trees, with shady lawns and flower gardens. The oldest section dates from the 1700s; the manager welcomes guests in an antique-filled drawing room. The atmosphere is relaxed, and the service, by the Ashton family, personal.

Greenbank offers accommodations with private entrances and kitchens in waterside and garden-view cottages. Rooms vary in size and shape, but most are small, with small bathrooms as well, each with a shower unit. The furnishings are rather plain but comfortable. The four units in the main house afford less privacy than the cottages. The guesthouse has a private dock for swimming; the charter operation on the property rents motorboats and sailboats. The nearest beach is Elbow Beach, a 15-minute taxi or moped ride away.

17 Salt Kettle Rd. (P.O. Box PG 201), Paget PG BX, Bermuda. ✆ **800/637-4116** in the U.S., or 441/236-3615. Fax 441/236-2427. www.bermudamall.com/greenbank. 11 units. Apr–Nov $130–$150 waterside cottage with kitchen for 2, $240 waterside apt with kitchen and 2 baths for 4, $110 garden apt with kitchen for 2; off-season $110–$120 waterside cottage with kitchen for 2, $220 waterside apt with kitchen and 2 baths for 4, $90 garden apt with kitchen for 2. Extra person $25 year-round. AE, MC, V. Ferry from Hamilton. Bus: 7 or 8. *In-room:* A/C, fridge, coffeemaker.

Little Pomander Guest House ⋆ 🄵ᵢₙ𝒹ₛ   This guesthouse is a pink-sided home that once served as the annex to what is now a privately operated tennis club across the street. Little Pomander can trace its history and foundations to the 1630s. The grassy lawn stretches a short distance down to the rocky shoreline, where you can see cruise ships anchored in Hamilton Harbour. The small rooms are tastefully outfitted with floral prints and alpine-style curtains designed by decorator Irene Trott, who owns the inn with her daughters. There are three apartments, each with a full kitchenette. All rooms come with a small bathroom with a combo tub and shower. The closest beach is Elbow Beach; it's a 5-minute scooter ride or 15-minute walk away.

16 Pomander Rd. (P.O. Box HM 384), Hamilton HM BX, Bermuda. ✆ **441/236-7635.** Fax 441/236-8332. 5 units. Apr–Oct $125 double; off-season $90 double. Rates include continental breakfast. AE, MC, V. Bus: 1, 7, or 8. *In-room:* A/C, TV, fridge, microwave, hairdryer.

Salt Kettle House ⋆ 🄵ᵢₙ𝒹ₛ   Informal and secluded, this little charmer sits on a narrow peninsula jutting into Hamilton Harbour, and you can swim in a cove and watch ships going in and out of the harbor. The core of this guesthouse is a 200-year-old cottage that has been enlarged over the years. In the late 1970s, another cottage was custom built on the lot's only remaining space. Today, the compound is a cheerful architectural hodgepodge that's popular with boaters. Rooms are generally small but comfortably furnished; they evoke the feel of staying in a traditional Bermuda compound, without the glitz of the resort hotels. Four waterside cottages have sitting rooms, shaded patios, and kitchens. The Starboard, the best cottage, can comfortably accommodate four guests. Guests in the main house also have use of a fully equipped kitchen, and the guest lounge has cable TV. The owner-manager is Mrs. Hazel Lowe.

10 Salt Kettle Rd., Paget PG 01, Bermuda. ℭ **441/236-0407.** Fax 441/236-8639. 6 units. Mar–Dec 1 $104 double, $120 cottage for 2; Dec 2–Feb $90 double, $100 cottage for 2. Rates include full breakfast. No credit cards. Hamilton ferry to Salt Kettle, 3-min. walk. *In-room:* A/C, kitchen (in cottages), hairdryer, iron (upon request), safe; no phone.

5

Dining

Wahoo steak, shark hash, mussel pie, fish chowder laced with rum and sherry peppers, Hoppin' John (black-eyed peas and rice), and the succulent spiny Bermuda lobster (called "guinea chick") await you in Bermuda. Of course, you won't find these dishes on all menus as many resorts and mainstream restaurants specialize in a more continental or international cuisine. But for a true taste of Bermuda, you might want to search the menu for local concoctions.

Bermudian food has improved in recent years, but dining out is not a major reason to visit the island. American and British dishes are common. Truly innovative gourmet fare often isn't—although the prices would make you think you're getting something special. Dining in Bermuda is generally more expensive than it is in the United States and Canada. Because virtually everything except fish must be imported, restaurant prices are closer to those in Europe.

In general, it's not a good idea to order meat very often; it's flown in, and you can't be sure how long it has been in storage. Whenever possible, stick to local food; for a main course, that usually means fish. The seafood, especially Bermuda rockfish, is generally excellent—that is, when local fishers have caught something that day. Sometimes the waters are too rough for fishing. A lot of fish is imported frozen from the U.S.; you may want to ask before you order. To find the dishes that are truly worthy, you'll have to pick and choose your way carefully through the menu—and that's where we come in.

Most restaurants, at least the better ones, prefer that men wear a jacket and tie after 6pm; women usually wear casual, chic clothing in the evening. Of course, as most of the world dresses more and more casually, Bermuda's dress codes have loosened up a bit—but this is still a more formal destination than many other islands. It's always wise to ask when you're reserving a table. During the day, no matter what the establishment, be sure to wear a cover-up—don't arrive for lunch sporting a bikini.

Because of the absence of inexpensive transportation, many travelers on a budget eat dinner at their hotels. If you like to dine around and you're concerned about cost, find a hotel that offers a variety of dining options, or stay in or near Hamilton.

BERMUDA'S BEST DINING BETS

You'll find Bermuda's best sushi at the **New Harbourfront Restaurant & Sushi Bar** in Hamilton; the best steaks at the **Colony Pub** at the Fairmont Hamilton Princess; the best Chinese and Thai at **Chopsticks Restaurant** in Hamilton; the best sandwiches at **Paradiso Cafe** in Hamilton; the best British pub grub at **Hog Penny** in Hamilton; the best Bermudian cuisine at **M. R. Onions** in Hamilton; the best French food at **Fourways Inn Restaurant** in Paget Parish; the best pasta at **Pasta Pasta** in St. George; the best ice cream at **Bailey's Ice Cream & Food D'Lites Restaurant** in Hamilton Parish; and the best pizza at **Portofino** in

Hamilton. Our favorite for brunch is the **Waterlot Inn** in Southampton Parish. For a wide sampling of Bermuda seafood, go to the **Whaler Inn,** in the Fairmont Southampton Princess. Here you can enjoy the best of the day's catch, preceded, of course, with a bowl of Bermuda fish chowder. For a romantic dinner, head for **Tom Moore's Tavern** in Hamilton Parish. In 1652, it was a private home. It once housed Thomas Moore, the Irish romantic poet, and the sense of romance still lingers in a refined setting with a classic French and Mediterranean menu.

1 From Rockfish to Island Rum: Dining, Bermuda Style

For years, Bermuda wasn't known for its cuisine; the food was too often bland and lacking in flavor. In recent years, however, there has been a notable change. Bermuda shares the revived interest in fine cuisine that has swept across America. Chefs seem better trained than ever, and many top-notch (albeit expensive) restaurants dot the archipelago. Italian food is in vogue; the Chinese have also landed. (On the other side of the coin, fast food, including KFC, has arrived, too.)

In recent years, some Bermudians have shown an increased interest in their heritage. They've revived many traditional dishes and published the recipes in books devoted to Bermudian cooking (not a bad idea for a souvenir).

Bermuda imports most of its food from the United States. As the population grows, less and less farmland is available on the island. But lots of people still tend their own gardens; at one home, we were amazed at the variety of vegetables grown on a small plot of land, including sorrel, oyster plants, and Jerusalem artichokes.

WHAT'S COOKING?

SEAFOOD   Any local fisherman will be happy to tell you that more species of shore and ocean fish—including grunt, angelfish, yellowtail, gray snapper, and the ubiquitous rockfish—are found off Bermuda's coastline than in any other place.

Rockfish, which is similar to Bahamian grouper, appears on nearly every menu. From the ocean, it weighs anywhere from 15 to 135 pounds (or even more). Steamed, broiled, baked, fried, or grilled, rockfish is a challenge to any chef. There's even a dish known as "rockfish maw," which we understand only the most old-fashioned cooks (there are still a handful on St. David's Island) know how to prepare. It's the maw, or stomach, of a rockfish, stuffed with a dressing of forcemeat and simmered slowly on the stove. If you view dining as an adventure, you may want to try it.

The most popular dish on the island is **Bermuda fish chowder.** Waiters usually pass around a bottle of sherry peppers and some black rum, which you add to your soup; it adds a distinctive Bermudian flavor.

Shark isn't as popular on Bermuda as it used to be. Many traditional dishes, including hash, are made from shark. Some people use shark-liver oil to forecast the weather; it's said to be more reliable than the nightly TV report. The oil is extracted, then poured into a small bottle and left in the sun. If the oil lies still, that foretells fair weather; if droplets form on the sides of the bottle, expect foul weather.

The great game fish in Bermuda is **wahoo.** If it's on the menu, go for a wahoo steak. Properly prepared, it's superb.

The **Bermuda lobster** (or "guinea chick," as it's known locally) has been called a first cousin of the Maine lobster. It's in season from September to March. Its high price tag has led to overfishing, forcing the government to issue periodic bans on its harvesting. In those instances, lobster is imported.

You can occasionally get good **conch stew** at a local restaurant. **Sea scallops,** though still available, have become increasingly rare. **Mussels** are cherished in Bermuda; one of the most popular traditional dishes is Bermuda-style mussel pie.

FRUITS & VEGETABLES   In restaurants and homes, **Portuguese red-bean soup**—the culinary contribution of the farmers who were brought to the island to till the land—precedes many a meal.

The **Bermuda onion** figures in many recipes, including onion pie. Bermuda-onion soup, an island favorite, is usually flavored with Outerbridge's Original Sherry Peppers.

Bermudians grow more **potatoes** than any other vegetable; the principal varieties are Pontiac red and Kennebec white. The traditional Sunday breakfast of codfish and banana cooked with potatoes is still served in some homes.

"Peas and plenty" is a Bermudian tradition. Black-eyed peas are cooked with onions, salt pork, and sometimes rice. Dumplings or boiled sweet potatoes may also be added at the last minute. Another peas-and-rice dish, **Hoppin' John,** is eaten as a main dish or as a side dish with meat or poultry.

Both Bermudians and Bahamians share the tradition of **Johnny Bread,** or **Johnnycake,** a simple pan-cooked cornmeal bread. Fishermen would make it at sea over a fire in a box filled with sand to keep the flames from spreading to the boat.

The **cassava,** once an important food on Bermuda, is now used chiefly as an ingredient in the traditional Christmas cassava pie. Another dish with a festive holiday connection is **sweet-potato pudding,** traditionally eaten on Guy Fawkes Day (in early Nov).

Bermuda grows many **fresh fruits,** including strawberries, Surinam cherries, guavas, avocados, and, of course, bananas. Guavas are made into jelly, which in turn often goes into making the famous Bermuda syllabub, traditionally accompanied by Johnnycake.

WHAT TO WASH IT ALL DOWN WITH

For some 300 years, **rum** has been the drink of Bermuda. Especially popular are Bacardi (the company's headquarters are in Bermuda) and Demerara rum (also known as black rum). The rum swizzle is the most famous cocktail in Bermuda.

For decades, the true Bermudian has preferred a drink called **"Dark and Stormy."** Prepared with black rum and ginger beer (pronounced *burr*), it's been called the national drink of the island; you might want to give it a try.

Fun Fact LOCAL DINING CUSTOMS

Bermuda's most delightful tradition is the English ritual of **afternoon tea,** which many local homes and hotels maintain.

In hotels, the typical afternoon tea is served daily from 3 to 5pm. Adding a contemporary touch, it's often served around a swimming pool, with guests partaking in their bathing suits—a tolerated lapse from the usual formal social code.

More formal tea is served at a table laid with silver, crisp white linens, and fine china, often imported from Britain. The usual accompaniments include finger sandwiches made with thinly sliced cucumber or watercress, and scones served with strawberry jam.

> ⌒ **Tips** **A Note on Reservations**
>
> Nearly all major restaurants prefer that you make a reservation; many popular places require that you do so as far in advance as possible. Weekends in summer can be especially crowded. Some repeat visitors make their reservations for the most popular spots before they leave home.

An interesting drink is **loquat liqueur.** It can be made with loquats (local fruit), rock candy, and gin, or more elaborately with brandy instead of gin and the addition of such spices as cinnamon, nutmeg, cloves, and allspice.

You'll find all the usual name-brand alcoholic beverages in Bermuda, but prices on mixed drinks can run high, depending on the brand.

Like the British, Bermudians enjoy a sociable **pub lunch.** There are several pubs in Hamilton, St. George, and elsewhere on the island. For the visitor, a pub lunch—say, fish and chips or shepherd's pie, a pint or two of ale, and animated discussion about politics, sports, or the most recent royal visit—is an experience to be cherished.

Another favorite meal of the typical Bermudian is **Sunday brunch.** Your hotel is likely to feature a big buffet.

2 Restaurants by Cuisine

AMERICAN
M. R. Onions (City of Hamilton; $$; p. 127)

ASIAN
L'Oriental (City of Hamilton; $; p. 132)

BAJAN
Spring Garden ⍟ (City of Hamilton; $; p. 134)

BERMUDIAN
The Beach (City of Hamilton; $; p. 130)
Black Horse Tavern ⍟ (St. George Parish; $$; p. 137)
Caliban's ⍟⍟ (Devonshire Parish; $$$; p. 134)
Dennis's Hideaway ⍟ (St. George Parish; $$; p. 137)
Fisherman's Reef (City of Hamilton; $$; p. 125)
Fourways Inn Restaurant ⍟⍟⍟ (Paget Parish; $$$$; p. 118)
Hog Penny (City of Hamilton; $; p. 132)
Landfall (Sandys Parish; $$; p. 109)

M. R. Onions (City of Hamilton; $$; p. 127)
Paraquet Restaurant (Paget Parish; $; p. 120)
Pawpaws Restaurant & Bar (Warwick Parish; $$; p. 118)
Spring Garden ⍟ (City of Hamilton; $; p. 134)
Swizzle Inn (Hamilton Parish; $; p. 136)
T Time (Southampton Parish; $; p. 118)
Waterloo House ⍟ (City of Hamilton; $$$$; p. 120)
White Horse Tavern (St. George Parish; $$; p. 139)

BRITISH
The Beach (City of Hamilton; $; p. 130)
Frog & Onion (Sandys Parish; $; p. 113)
Henry VIII (Southampton Parish; $$$; p. 116)
Hog Penny (City of Hamilton; $; p. 132)
Lighthouse Tea Room (Southampton Parish; $; p. 117)

Mrs. Tea's Victorian Tearoom ✶
(Southampton Parish; $; p. 117)

Somerset Country Squire Pub &
Restaurant (Sandys Parish; $$;
p. 112)

Swizzle Inn (Hamilton Parish; $;
p. 136)

CARIBBEAN

The Norwood Room ✶ (Paget
Parish; $$$; p. 119)

CHINESE

Chopsticks Restaurant ✶ (City of
Hamilton; $; p. 130)

CONTINENTAL

Henry VIII (Southampton Parish;
$$; p. 116)

Lighthouse Tea Room
(Southampton Parish; $; p. 117)

Little Venice (City of Hamilton;
$$; p. 126)

Monte Carlo ✶ (City of
Hamilton; $$$; p. 123)

The Norwood Room ✶ (Paget
Parish; $$$; p. 119)

Pawpaws Restaurant & Bar
(Warwick Parish; $$; p. 118)

Tom Moore's Tavern ✶ (Hamilton
Parish; $$$$; p. 136)

Waterloo House ✶ (City of
Hamilton; $$$$; p. 120)

DELI/LIGHT BITES

Bailey's Ice Cream & Food D'Lites
Restaurant (Hamilton Parish; $;
p. 136)

The Hickory Stick (City of
Hamilton; $; p. 131)

Paradiso Cafe (City of Hamilton;
$; p. 133)

FRENCH

Ascots ✶ (City of Hamilton; $$$;
p. 122)

Fourways Inn Restaurant ✶✶✶
(Paget Parish; $$$$; p. 118)

La Coquille ✶ (City of Hamilton;
$$$; p. 122)

Le Figaro Bistro & Bar (City of
Hamilton; $; p. 132)

Newport Room ✶✶✶ (Southamp-
ton Parish; $$$$; p. 113)

Red Carpet Bar & Restaurant
(City of Hamilton; $$; p. 129)

Tom Moore's Tavern ✶ (Hamilton
Parish; $$$$; p. 136)

INDIAN

The Bombay (City of Hamilton;
$; p. 130)

House of India ✶ (City of
Hamilton; $; p. 132)

INTERNATIONAL

Black Horse Tavern ✶ (St. George
Parish; $$; p. 137)

Botanic Garden (City of
Hamilton; $; p. 130)

Caliban's ✶✶ (Devonshire Parish;
$$$; p. 134)

Carriage House (St. George Parish;
$$; p. 137)

Coconut Rock (City of Hamilton;
$; p. 131)

Coconuts ✶ (Southampton Parish;
$$$; p. 114)

The Colony Pub (City of
Hamilton; $$; p. 124)

Flanagan's Irish Pub & Restaurant
(City of Hamilton; $$; p. 125)

Freddie's Pub on the Square (St.
George Parish; $$; p. 139)

Front Street Terrace (City of
Hamilton; $; p. 131)

Green Lantern (City of Hamilton;
$; p. 131)

The Middleton Room ✶ (Paget
Parish; $$$; p. 119)

Monty's (City of Hamilton; $;
p. 133)

North Rock Brewing Company ✶
(Smith's Parish; $$; p. 135)

The Pickled Onion ✶ (City of
Hamilton; $$$; p. 124)

Pirates Landing (Sandys Parish; $$;
p. 112)

The Porch (City of Hamilton; $$;
p. 128)

Red Carpet Bar & Restaurant
(City of Hamilton; $$; p. 129)

3 Sandys Parish

The following restaurants are all on Somerset Island.

EXPENSIVE

Tamarisk Dining Room ⊛ INTERNATIONAL   This elegant cottage colony is the top dining spot in the parish for classic but also innovative cuisine and impeccable service. A dress-up place, it makes local eateries such as Pirates Landing and the Frog & Onion look pub-like.

The formal dining room has limed wood, impressive columns, and beamed ceilings, evoking an upscale country club. In warm weather, sliding glass doors extend the dining area onto a rambling, east-facing terrace that overlooks the bay. Princess Margaret no longer dines here; instead you will find groups of lawyers and business leaders, especially at night.

At lunch you're likely to find platters of chicken-macadamia salad, a signature pita-bread sandwich (stuffed, California-style, with chicken salad, avocado slices, and bean sprouts), and some of the best cheeseburgers in the parish. The dinner menu changes frequently. It nearly always includes juicy tenderloin of beef with grain mustard and blanched garlic sauce; "cushions" of lamb served with Stilton mousse soufflé, red-wine sauce, and lentils; and a flavor-filled thyme-and-garlic–roasted monkfish floating on a bed of ratatouille.

At Cambridge Beaches, 30 Kings Point Rd. ℭ **441/234-0331.** Reservations required. Lunch main courses $15–$20; fixed-price 5-course dinner $60. MC, V. Daily 12:30–2:30pm and 7–9pm. Bus: 7.

MODERATE

Il Palio ITALIAN   Named after the famous horse race in Siena, Italy, this restaurant in the center of Somerset serves some of the best pizzas on the island. The classic Italian cuisine—everything from steak Diane to roast duckling with zesty green peppercorn sauce—is also quite good. But chances are you might dine as well on these dishes in your own backyard. The emphasis is on the tried and true, such as fettuccine Alfredo and tender slices of sautéed veal; among the best choices are pasta primavera and ground meat and spinach–filled cannelloni. We also recommend the fresh fish, especially the selection that's sautéed with bits of garlic and paired with pine nuts, capers, and well-seasoned tomato sauce. If you arrive early, you can enjoy a drink in the downstairs bar. One plate of food here makes a meal unto itself.

64 Main Rd. ℭ **441/234-1049.** Reservations required. Main courses $24–$30. AE, DC, MC, V. Tues–Sun 6–10pm. Bus: 8.

Landfall BERMUDIAN   One of the most solidly entrenched restaurants in the district around the airport has thrived here for almost as long as anyone can remember. It's set within a white-sided antique home that's at least 200 years old, with a view that some locals claim is the "best in Bermuda." Though far from the sea, it encompasses goodly stretches of seacoast as well as faraway St. David's Island. Menu items are staunchly conservative, and deeply committed to the maintenance of their Bermuda roots.

Typical examples of that include macaroni and cheese and pork chops with peas and rice, those island staples that many remember from their childhood. We opt, however, for the fresh grilled grouper served with a homemade tartar sauce so good it should be bottled. You can also order your grouper or other fresh fish sautéed as well. For dessert, the chef often prepares that nostalgic

Bermuda Dining

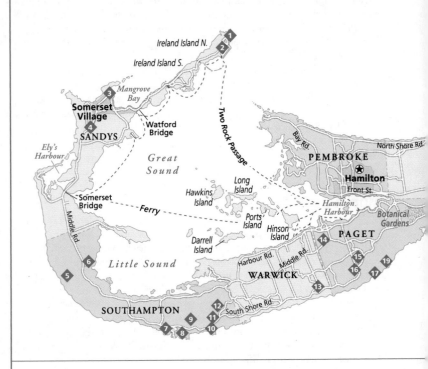

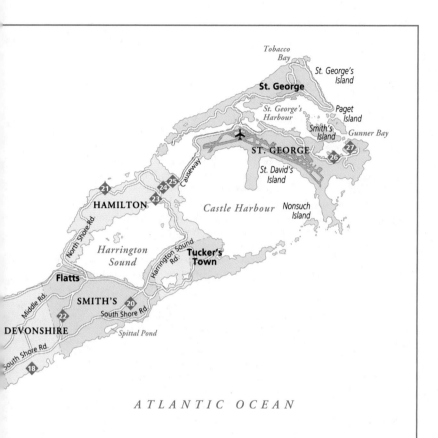

ATLANTIC OCEAN

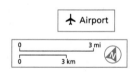

✈ Airport

Somerset Country Squire
Pub & Restaurant **4**
Specialty Inn **22**
Swizzle Inn **25**
T Time **5**
Tamarisk Dining Room **3**
Tio Pepe **11**
Tom Moore's Tavern **23**
Waterlot Inn **12**
Whaler Inn **12**
Wickets Brasserie & Cricket Club **12**

See also "Dining in the City of Hamilton"
and "Dining in St. George" maps

favorite still served to British school children—gingerbread with lemon sauce. Helpings are so generous that one plate of food is all you'll need to fill up, as main courses come with vegetables and the works.

At Clearview Suites and Villas, Sandy Lane, 🕿 **441/293-1322**. Reservations not necessary. Lunch main courses $10–$13; dinner main courses $20–$23. AE, DC, MC, BV. Daily 12:30–3pm; dinner seatings daily at 7, 8, and 8:30pm. Bus 10 or 11.

Pirates Landing INTERNATIONAL   Overlooking the Great Sound, this restaurant offers a diverse menu that pleases diners who aren't too demanding. If you want filling and satisfying food, it's a suitable choice, though not quite the fun spot that the Frog & Onion (reviewed later in this chapter) is. The seating, at pine tables and chairs, is comfortable, and the costumed serving staff is helpful. It's a little hokey, but everyone·seems to get into the spirit, especially after a rum punch or two. Most visitors who come for lunch sample the standard soups, burgers, pastas, and grilled specialties—nothing special here. The gyros on pita bread are spicy delights, especially the 6-inch gyro pizza made with fresh vegetables, pepperoni, and mozzarella.

At night the kitchen shines brighter, as the chefs search abroad for inspiration. Two of the finest dishes are beef tenderloin with porcini mushrooms and chicken cacciatore. Pastas, made fresh daily, are quite succulent. We are less devoted to the garlic shrimp and fresh fisherman's grill.

Royal Naval Dockyard. 🕿 **441/234-5151**. Lunch main courses $5.25–$18; dinner main courses $15.50–$24, early dinner special (6–7pm) $22. AE, MC, V. Daily 11:30am–4pm and 6–10pm. Closed Feb. Bus: 8. Ferry from Hamilton.

Somerset Country Squire Pub & Restaurant BRITISH/SEAFOOD   You pass through a moon-gate arch to reach the raised terrace of this waterside restaurant in the center of the village. Limestone blocks and hedges ring the terrace; inside, there's a dining room downstairs. Local Bermudian favorites, including curried mussel pie and fresh Bermuda tuna or wahoo, are your best choices here. Look for the specialties of the day, but count on charbroiled and barbecued meals. The bill of fare ranges from British pub grub to fresh local fish to traditional roast beef with Yorkshire pudding. Most of the food is fairly routine, but the chef is especially proud of his Bermuda fish chowder, a tomato-based soup that some locals consider the best in the West End. The restaurant often features outdoor barbecues.

10 Mangrove Bay Rd., Somerset Village. 🕿 **441/234-0105**. Reservations required for dinner. Lunch main courses $6.50–$14.50; dinner main courses $17–$29. AE, MC, V. Daily 11am–1am. Bus: 7 or 8.

INEXPENSIVE

Freeport Seafood Restaurant 🏃 (Value) STEAKS/SEAFOOD   Come here for the best of locally caught seafood. Somehow this old favorite manages to turn up a fresher catch than its Somerset competitors, as compared to the more "fish and chips" grub served at the other dockyard spots. There is no great presentation or dramatic flourish to the platters served, but the taste is often delectable, especially the fish platter or one of the broiled Bermuda rockfish dishes, our particular favorite. The menu is less formal—and somewhat less expensive—at lunch than at dinner. During the noon day, you get the regular chow you'd find almost anywhere, including burgers, salads, pizzas, and a steak on the grill. If you want something better, opt for the usually tasty fish sandwich. In the evening, your selection of fish might feature tuna or wahoo. For the man who wants a T-bone, there are those too. We've found the lobster a bit overpriced and overcooked.

At the Royal Naval Dockyard, 1 Freeport Rd. ℭ **441/234-1692.** Lunch main courses $10–$23; dinner main courses $13–$23. AE, MC, V. Daily 11am–11pm. Bus: 8.

Frog & Onion BRITISH   In the former 18th-century cooperage (barrel-making factory) of the Royal Naval Dockyard, this is the most traditional British pub in Bermuda. It's named for the owners, French-born Jean-Paul Magnin (the Frog) and Bermuda-born Carol West (the Onion). You can sit back with a pint of English lager in the shadows of the cooperage's enormous fireplace. Many folks stay to dine: At lunch there are the standard sandwiches, salads, lasagna, and some tasty bar pies. We especially like the mussel pie for a real taste of Bermuda, although you might opt for the lamb or vegetable and cheese pie. The dinner menu includes all of the lunchtime choices but some even more delicious European dishes. Your best bet for the evening might be the local fish plate featured. Food is not spectacular, but well prepared and rather hearty fare. Since portions are large, no one leaves hungry.

The Cooperage, at the Royal Naval Dockyard. ℭ **441/234-2900.** Lunch sandwiches, salads, and platters $8–$17; dinner main courses $12–$23. MC, V. Mon–Sat 11:30am–4pm and 6–9:30pm; Sun noon–4pm and 5:30–9pm. Bar daily noon–midnight. Closed Mon Dec–Feb. Bus: 8 or ferry from Hamilton.

4 Southampton Parish
VERY EXPENSIVE
Newport Room 🏵🏵🏵 FRENCH   The Newport Room is unequaled in its sumptuously understated decor and its French cuisine—it's among the best in Bermuda. The only establishment locally that can compete with it is the even more famous Waterlot Inn. But the cuisine at the Waterlot is Mediterranean and quite different from the Newport. The Newport is much more formal. The dining room, entirely paneled in teak and rosewood with nautical brass touches, evokes the interior of a yacht. A maître d' stationed beside a ship's compass greets diners at the entrance, and the service is attentive. In the center of the room are exact miniature replicas of two of the winning sailboats from the Newport-to-Bermuda Race.

Settle into a leather armchair and prepare yourself for what might be your most memorable meal in Bermuda. The regularly changing menu reads like a gourmet variation of *cuisine moderne;* it might include duck breast with cinnamon and fig sauce, or baby veal chops. The kitchen uses the freshest and best ingredients in its carefully prepared, artfully presented dishes. The wine list includes a wide array of international selections, all served in Irish crystal.

In The Fairmont Southampton Princess, 101 South Shore Rd. ✆ **441/238-8000.** Reservations required. Jacket and tie required. Main courses $29–$39. AE, DC, MC, V. Daily 6:30–9:30pm. Usually closed Dec to mid-Jan. Ferry from Hamilton.

Waterlot Inn ✵✵ MEDITERRANEAN   Less rigidly formal than the Newport, and with a more welcoming staff, this is one of our all-time favorites for a special night out in Bermuda. The service is impeccable, and the culinary repertoire is inventive—doubly impressive given the large number of diners every evening. The restaurant also serves a celebrated Sunday brunch (known here as "buffet breakfast").

About 300 years ago, merchant sailors unloaded their cargo directly into the basement of this historic inn and warehouse. Today, the best way to approach the inn is still by water, and that's precisely what many Bermudians do, mooring their sailing craft in its sheltered cove. Over the years the inn has attracted such guests as Mark Twain, James Thurber, Eleanor Roosevelt, and Eugene O'Neill.

You can enjoy a drink in an upstairs bar, where a classical pianist entertains. After descending a white-balustraded colonial staircase, you'll be seated in one of three conservatively nautical dining rooms. Each is filled with captain's or Windsor chairs, oil paintings of old clipper ships, and lots of exposed wood. The bouillabaisse is about as good as it gets on this side of the Riviera, and there are many other temptations, including Bermuda's best fish chowder. Veal chop served in sage-infused oil with young stuffed vegetables is an especially good choice. Occasionally we've settled happily for a plate of grilled Mediterranean vegetables, from artichokes to eggplant.

At The Fairmont Southampton Princess, Middle Rd. ✆ **441/238-8000.** Reservations required. Main courses $26.50–$38.50. AE, DC, MC, V. Daily 6:30–9:30pm. Closed Jan–Feb. Shuttle from hotel.

EXPENSIVE

Coconuts ✵ _Finds_ INTERNATIONAL   When on an island, many diners insist that the view be almost as good as the cuisine. It's that important to them. In that case, we recommend Coconuts, not only for its scenic vista, but also for its cuisine. It lies between high cliff rocks and a pink sandy beach on the south coast. Alfresco dining here is most romantic, although those breezy nights tend to cool your food before you've eaten it.

Cozy and personalized, this restaurant is at its best at dinnertime, when a four-course set-price menu is the only dining option for the dozens of diners who make detours to reach it. The setting is within an open-sided dining room, richly paneled with varnished cedar, that's set within a few steps of the beach. If you prefer that the staff set up a table directly on the sands, it can be done, although for a net fee of $85 per person. Many visitors don't find the added romance worth the extra money, and besides, sand invariably gets into your shoes. Lunch is nothing special—the usual, burgers, salads, sandwiches, and the like. But at night, chefs strut their stuff by offering a set menu of variety, flavor, taste, and scope, each daily changing selection offered with a certain flair. Freshly grown produce is presented with Caribbean zest, for a "taste of the islands." You're not sure what you're going to get on any given night here, but the scope is wide enough to appeal most diners unless you have very esoteric food tastes—in that case, you'd better call and check.

In the Reefs Hotel, 56 South Shore Rd. ✆ **441/238-0222.** Reservations recommended. Lunch main courses $12–$18; set-price 4-course dinner $52 per person. AE, MC, V. Apr–Nov daily noon–3pm; year-round daily 7–9:30pm. Bus 7.

Rib Room ✿✿ STEAKS/SEAFOOD This is the only restaurant on the island that compares favorably to one of London's finer chophouses, and its beef dishes are far superior to those served at the more highly touted Henry VIII.

Many of the Rib Room's juicy, tender beef dishes are broiled over charcoal. The broiled lamb chops are classic, or maybe you'll go all out for the roast prime rib of beef with Yorkshire pudding. For those who prefer fish, the chef will prepare the catch of the day, although the aptly named Rib Room is not the best choice for seafood. All dinners come with an extensive salad bar. The Rib Room sits atop the resort's golf pro shop, near the first tee. As you relax in upholstered armchairs, taking in the panoramic view, you might want to start your evening with a "Dark and Stormy," a black rum and ginger beer drink for the adventurous.

In The Fairmont Southampton Princess, 101 South Shore Rd. ✆ **441/238-8000.** Reservations recommended. Main courses $22.50–$43.50. AE, DC, MC, V. Daily 6:30–9:30pm. Ferry from Hamilton.

The Sea Grape ✿ PACIFIC RIM On an outdoor terrace by the sea, this restaurant prides itself on its Pacific Rim menu. We won't even pretend that the cuisine here is great, but we like to go here when the day is hot and we want to dine lightly with a view of the water. It generally includes calorie- and cholesterol-conscious foods with California-, Korean-, and Japanese-inspired sauces on the side. Zesty appetizers range from spiced poached pineapple with coconut yogurt and candied ginger to grilled shrimp with smoked-bacon guacamole. Main dishes are often grilled and served with fresh chutneys, salsas, and yakisoba (wheat) noodles. Our favorite main course is sesame-crusted pork tenderloin. There's also usually a daily catch, market priced.

In the Sonesta Beach Resort, South Shore Rd. ✆ **441/238-8122.** Reservations recommended. Main courses $23–$38; dinner buffet $36.50. AE, DC, MC, V. Daily noon–4pm and 6:30–9:30pm. Closed Oct–May. Bus: 7.

Whaler Inn ✿ SEAFOOD This oceanfront restaurant, perched atop a low cliff overlooking rocks and pink sands, is justifiably famous for its seafood. Clusters of sea grape, Norfolk Island pines, and padded iron armchairs dot its landscaped terraces; from here, you can watch the sun set over one of the island's

---

Moments **Where to Put Together the Perfect Picnic & Where to Enjoy It**

The kitchens of many major hotels will prepare a picnic lunch for you, but you need to request it at least a day in advance. On Front Street in Hamilton, you can order sandwiches at a cafe and pick up a bottle of wine or mineral water. If it's a weekday, the best place to buy picnic supplies is **The Hickory Stick** (see "City of Hamilton," later in this chapter).

If you enjoy picnicking and biking, you can do both in Sandys Parish. Start by crossing Somerset Bridge (heading in the direction of Somerset Village), and continue along Somerset Road to **Fort Scaur Park,** where you'll enjoy a panoramic view of Ely's Harbour.

Another ideal location is **Spanish Point Park** in Pembroke, where you will find a series of little coves and beaches. You don't need to go to the trouble of packing a picnic basket-in warm weather, a lunch wagon rolls around every day at noontime. We also love to picnic at one of the island's best beaches, **Warwick Long Bay,** which has restrooms at the western end.

most secluded beaches. The panoramic view through the huge windows is the airy restaurant's most prominent feature.

You might begin with baked oysters Rockefeller, Bermuda fish chowder, or something as exotic as roasted pumpkin potato gnocchi served with roasted sunflower seeds. The special main courses are well-seasoned portions of the daily catch—game fish such as yellowfin tuna, barracuda, shark, wahoo, or dolphin fish (mahimahi). All are excellently prepared, either broiled or sautéed in butter. We like to come here for a kettle of seafood prepared St. David's style—that is, flavored with sherry peppers and a glass of rum. The chef can also cook you a savory platter of mussels mariniére that beats out the deep-fried fisherman's platter any day. Locals like the pan-fried local fish but in our opinion, the almonds and bananas destroy the natural taste of the fresh food. Desserts are good. Two popular favorites—banana fritters with black rum sauce, or Armagnac ice with prunes—will make you want to come back for a second visit.

In The Fairmont Southampton Princess, 101 South Shore Rd. ℭ **441/238-8000.** Reservations recommended. Lunch main courses $11.95–$16.50; dinner main courses $19–$37.50. AE, DC, MC, V. May–Sept daily noon–2:30pm; Oct–Apr daily 6:30–9:30pm. Ferry from Hamilton.

MODERATE

Henry VIII *(Overrated)* BRITISH/CONTINENTAL This restaurant appears here mainly because hundreds of visitors to Southampton patronize it. Sad to report, it used to be good, but has fallen off in recent years. If you like a faux-Tudor place where the waitresses are still called "wenches,", it might be your cuppa.

There's nothing wrong about stopping in for a drink at this bustling spot lying below Gibbs Hill Lighthouse. But it's not worth a special trip to dine here. The restaurant is decorated with oak furnishing, brass railings, and period style lighting fixtures, a bit gimmicky and having no theme related to the island at all. The English draft beer in the split-level Oak Room is always refreshing, and in summer there is often entertainment.

As for the food, proceed carefully—simpler is better. And read the fine print: There's a $20 minimum. Appealing to a modern day Henry VIII, the menu attempts to entice with beef dishes but you'll fare better at another "chophouse," the Rib Room (reviewed earlier in this chapter).

South Shore Rd. (between The Fairmont Southampton Pricess and the Sonesta Beach Resort). ℭ **441/ 238-1977.** Reservations required for dinner. Lunch main courses $8.75–$22.50; dinner main courses $18.50–$32, early-bird dinner (6–7pm) $29.50, fixed-price dinner $35.50; Sun brunch $25.50 per person. AE, MC, V. Daily noon–2:30pm and 6–10pm. Bus: 7 or 8.

Tio Pepe ITALIAN/SPANISH Don't let the Spanish name fool you—the cuisine here is predominantly traditional Italian. The place is more or less in a category of its own, as other restaurants in the parish don't offer its cuisine. A few Spanish dishes do appear on the menu, including roast suckling pig. It's fairly straightforward fare: pizzas, pastas, and classic Italian cuisine in generous portions, all with a bit of Mediterranean pizzazz. The kitchen also prepares local fish, plus salmon and lobster, with subtle Italian flavors. Seating is on a wide garden-view terrace and in three indoor dining rooms. The restaurant is convenient to the Fairmont Southampton Princess and Horseshoe Bay Beach. In fact, if you're returning from a day at Horseshoe Beach, this place is most convenient. The friendly atmosphere, bountiful food, and prices are right on target.

117 South Shore Rd., Horseshoe Bay. ℭ **441/238-1897.** Reservations recommended. Lunch $7–$25; pizzas and pastas $13.50–$18.75; main courses $22–$29. AE, MC, V. May–Sept daily 11am–10:30pm; off-season daily noon–10pm. Bus 7.

INEXPENSIVE

Lighthouse Tea Room *(Finds)* CONTINENTAL/BRITISH   Step inside this lace-curtained room for the taste of an old-fashioned tearoom. It's a handy place if you're touring in the Southampton area on the south shore. After you've climbed the winding steps to the famous Gibbs Hill Lighthouse, you will have worked up an appetite. You can enjoy a full English breakfast while taking in a panoramic vista of Great Sound. Afternoon tea includes such delights as Devonshire cream, Bermuda honey, and homemade tea cakes and scones. If you're lunching, opt for a homemade soup of the day or a freshly-made quiche. Salads are also available, along with such English tearoom fare as Cornish-style minced-meat pies, English pork pie, and a ploughman's lunch of cheese and bread.

Gibbs Hill Lighthouse, 68 St. Anne's Rd. *(C)* **441/238-8679**. Breakfast $6–$9.50; lunch $8.45–$10.95. No credit cards. Daily 9am–5pm. Bus: 7 or 8.

Mrs. Tea's Victorian Tearoom *(Finds)* BRITISH   Opposite Port Royal Golf Course, this much-loved tearoom offers the island's most traditional English tea. The authentic Victorian decor is prissy enough that you could even invite the Queen of England here for a cuppa. The dainty china goes perfectly with the floral tablecloths. Locals come here for shepherd's pie at lunch—how British can you get? You can also enjoy stuffed sandwiches such as smoked turkey, or a selection of pastries and scones with your tea. The tearoom is in a Bermuda National Trust property off the Railway Trail.

25 Middle Rd. *(C)* **441/234-1374**. Lunch $10; afternoon tea with sandwiches and sweets $12.50. No credit cards. Tues–Sun noon–5pm. Bus: 7 or 8.

Wickets Brasserie & Cricket Club *(Kids)* INTERNATIONAL   Outfitted like a British cricket club, this brasserie and bistro features a health-conscious breakfast buffet with low-sodium and high-fiber offerings, as well as one of the most comprehensive lunch menus on the island. It's good food—nothing more. You'll probably be satisfied with it if your expectations don't run too high. Standard "family fare" includes deli-style sandwiches, soups, chowders, pastas, salads, and platters such as grilled steaks, pork chops, and veal. The most popular fish dish is grilled grouper with citrus-butter sauce, which has more flavor than the routine steaks and chops on the menu.

The restaurant, on the lower lobby level of the Southampton Princess, overlooks the swimming pool and the ocean beyond. Many Bermudians, with kids in town, come here for a late lunch or a light supper. The informal but traditional restaurant requests only that guests cover their bathing suits with a shirt. A children's menu is available.

In The Fairmont Southampton Princess, 101 South Shore Rd. *(C)* **441/238-8000**. Breakfast buffet $19.56–$21.85; lunch main courses $7.50–$18; dinner main courses $14–$20. AE, DC, MC, V. Daily 7–11am and noon–9:30pm. Ferry from Hamilton.

(Tips) **Dressing the Part**

Most of the upscale restaurants in Bermuda ask that men wear a jacket and tie for dinner; some restaurants require a jacket but not a tie. When making reservations, always ask what the dress code is. "Casual but elegant" dress is preferred at most Sunday buffets.

T Time BERMUDIAN   In the clubhouse of the Port Royal Golf Course, this restaurant has a friendly bar that's the perfect 19th hole. Outfitted with wicker furniture and big windows overlooking the 9th and 18th holes, it's unpretentious, and the well-prepared food tastes good after a day outdoors. It's reminiscent of the country-club fare you'd find at golf courses throughout North America. Options include chicken with maple-mustard sauce and generous sandwiches, including a steak sandwich. The most reliable dish is usually the catch of the day—perhaps mahimahi or wahoo, served with peas and brown rice. A specialty is the Bermuda fish cakes served on hot cross buns. For dessert, you can order everything from a slice of fresh pie to coconut custard. Bar snacks such as chicken fingers and hot dogs are served daily from 3 to 6pm. During tournaments, expect mobs of fellow drinkers and diners; otherwise, the place is laid-back, convivial, and relaxing.

Port Royal Golf Course, Port Royal. ✆ 441/234-5037. Breakfast $7.50–$8.25; lunch main courses $8–$12.95. AE, MC, V. Daily 8–11am and noon–3pm. Bus: 7 or 8.

5 Warwick Parish

MODERATE

Pawpaws Restaurant & Bar _Value_   CONTINENTAL/BERMUDIAN. This family favorite about 3 miles west of Hamilton offers a varied and unusual menu at reasonable prices. With the aura and ambience of a European bistro, Pawpaws attracts everybody from those seeking an upscale dinner to parents with kids in tow. On the walls are murals of papaw (papaya) trees and other scenes, along with trellis work and paintings by local artists.

The lunch menu features sandwiches, salads, and the restaurant's signature dish, Pawpaw Montespan (made from green papaw, ground beef, and herbs). In the evening, one of the most popular dishes (and deservedly so) is lobster ravioli in basil-cream sauce with strips of smoked salmon. Equally good is the seafood _vol-au-vent_. If you're yearning for island cuisine, sample the red snapper in banana sauce. You'll also find more classic but also more ordinary dishes, including tender pepper steak in cognac-cream sauce, and leg of lamb steak marinated in herbs.

87 South Shore Rd. ✆ 441/236-7459. Reservations recommended. Lunch main courses $6–$14.75; dinner main courses $18.50–$25.95. MC, V. Daily 11am–10pm. Bar open until 1am. Bus: 7.

6 Paget Parish

VERY EXPENSIVE

Fourways Inn Restaurant _✦✦✦_ FRENCH/BERMUDIAN   The Fourways Inn is the best restaurant in Bermuda. Housed in a coral, stone, and cedar 18th-century Georgian home with interior mahogany beams, it has traditional Bermudian character and a predominantly European staff that makes it a bit stuffy. You can dine inside or out, depending on the season. Most evenings there's a pianist playing. The old kitchen, which has a whitewashed fireplace, has been turned into the Peg Leg Bar.

The best seasonal ingredients go into the exquisite cuisine. Bermuda's most tempting selection of hot and cold hors d'oeuvres includes pan-roasted bay scallops and scampi with ratatouille and fresh basil purée. The nightly fish selection is limited but excellent. The lightly charcoal-grilled local tuna with braised scallions, sun-dried tomatoes, and sweet peppers is perfection itself. The chef's signature dish is thin slices of tender veal served with a zesty citrus sauce. Most

Jugglers, dancers and an assortment of acrobats fill the street.

She shoots you a wide-eyed look as a seven-foot cartoon character approaches.

What brought you here was wanting the kids

to see something magical while they still believed in magic.

America Online Keyword: Travel

With 700 airlines, 50,000 hotels and over 5,000 cruise and vaca-

tion getaways, you can now go places you've always dreamed of.

Travelocity.com
A Sabre Company
Go Virtually Anywhere.

WORLD'S LEADING TRAVEL WEB SITE, 5 YEARS IN A ROW." WORLD TRAVEL AWARDS

dishes are at the lower end of the price scale—chateaubriand is at the high end. A fine selection of fresh vegetables is served nightly. A non-vegetarian acquaintance of ours came here once, ordered only vegetables, and was extremely pleased. To complement its ambitious menu, the Fourways has the finest wine cellar on the island. At lunch, expect sandwiches, several hot dishes, and a catch of the day.

1 Middle Rd. ✆ 441/236-6517. Reservations required in summer (at least 1 day in advance). Jacket required, tie recommended. Lunch main courses $8–$18.50; dinner main courses $28–$39.75; Sun brunch $33.50. AE, MC, V. Daily noon–2:30pm and 6:30–9:30pm. Bus 8.

EXPENSIVE

Cafe Lido ✴ MEDITERRANEAN This well-recommended beachfront restaurant consists of an outdoor terrace and an indoor dining room with big windows that fill it with light. Come here for its location and convenience to Elbow Beach. If you're a serious foodie, you'll find the viands at Horizons and Cottages or at Stonington Beach Hotel more tasteworthy. Shades of Bermuda pink and salmon predominate, the chairs are comfortable enough to linger in, and the menu is one of the most diverse on the island. We strongly recommend trying one of the specialty pastas—some of the best are lobster ravioli, and spinach and potato gnocchi in a sauce of Taleggio cheese and spicy Italian sausage. The baby rack of lamb, sprinkled with sesame seeds, roasted garlic, and double port sauce, is tender and succulent. Grilled wahoo, rockfish, traditional veal in port wine, saffron-flavored casseroles whose specific ingredients depend on the whims of the chef, and tenderloin of beef are also staples.

In the Elbow Beach Hotel Sea Terrace, 60 South Shore Rd. ✆ 441/236-9884. Reservations recommended. Lunch main courses $12–$19.95; dinner main courses $20.75–$32.75. AE, MC, V. May–Nov daily noon–2:45pm and 6:30–10:30pm; Dec–Apr daily noon–2:30pm and 6:30–9:30pm. Bus: 1, 2, or 7.

The Middleton Room ✴ INTERNATIONAL On a hilltop overlooking 30 acres of carefully landscaped grounds and golf course, this well-recommended restaurant lies in a much-enlarged building that was originally constructed as a private home in the 17th century. It's a member of the prestigious Relais & Châteaux association of international hotels and restaurants, and it's associated with a clubby and very expensive cottage colony. The place is more formal and stuffier than the student-operated Norwood (see below). The food is better here but we still like to patronize the Norwood Room for the surprises (usually happy ones).

The eclectic cuisine often encompasses influences from France and the Far East. Menus, served only as fixed-price meals, change daily. They depend on the chef's whim and on whatever fish, produce, and meats were fresh and available that day. Artfully arranged sushi might serve as a foil for the European-style main courses. Examples from past (and memorable) meals include osso buco of ostrich, curried lamb in phyllo pastry, venison in port wine sauce, and fillets of marlin, snapper, or tuna. Midsummer diners usually appreciate the medley of chilled soups that is one of the restaurant's trademarks. The cellar has won the *Wine Spectator* international award 8 years in a row.

In Horizons and Cottages, South Shore. ✆ 441/236-0048. Reservations required. Jacket and tie required. Fixed-price menu $55. At press time, management told us they would soon be accepting credit cards: AE, DC, MC, V. Daily 12:30–3pm and 7–9:30pm. Bus: 7.

The Norwood Room ✴ Finds CONTINENTAL/CARRIBBEAN The students are the chefs, but don't be put off by that. They are strictly trained and supervised by Fred Ming, a local legend on the island who has some great insights about the art of Caribbean cookery. Born and raised in Bermuda, Ming learned how to cook as he sat on a stool in the kitchen watching how his grandmother, a culinary whiz, did it. The Norwood Room offers stately dining in a large, sun-filled room. From the wood-beamed room, a halo of arched windows looks out over the well-maintained lawn and the ocean. The restaurant is part of a state-run hotel training institute (see chapter 4, "Accommodations"). Although the young staff members are inexperienced, they're thoughtful, courteous, and hard-working. A pianist or harpist provides music in the evening.

The food is generally splendid, and each dish is prepared with care. We always choose the set menu, which is broadly continental or Caribbean. We once had tenderloin of pork stuffed with dried winter fruit in an exotic chile-plum dressing; another time it was pan-seared duck breast in tart orange sauce, flambéed with Gosling's Black Seal rum. Another memorable meal was grilled fillet of mahimahi with tiger shrimp, served over polenta and drizzled with gingered Malaysian sauce. The chef also prepares a pasta of the day.

In the Stonington Beach Hotel, South Shore Rd. © **441/236-5416.** Reservations required. Jacket and tie required in the evening. Lunch main courses $14–$23; fixed-price dinner $65. AE, DC, MC, V. Daily noon–2:30pm and 7–9pm. Bus: 7.

INEXPENSIVE

Paraquet Restaurant _(Value_ BERMUDIAN   This restaurant doesn't even pretend to offer a cuisine as fine as those restaurants already recommended in the parish, but it's the bargain of the area. In high priced Bermuda, it's a find. Near a major south-shore traffic junction, this unpretentious restaurant is at the center of an apartment cluster of the same name. From your table, you can see a circular formal flower garden created by the Portuguese owners. The coffeeshop setting—complete with lime-colored Formica—and the menu of substantial home-style Bermudian fare are straight out of the '50s. You'll find one of the island's largest sandwich menus (both hot and cold), as well as omelets, homemade soups (there's always a fish chowder of the day), and salads. You can order mixed platters with such ingredients as turkey breast and crabmeat, grilled dishes like T-bone steak, fried liver and onions, or roast half-chicken. A main course platter is a meal in itself, and you don't need to order extras unless you're ravenously hungry.

South Shore Rd. (near the Elbow Beach Hotel). © **441/236-9742.** Reservations not needed. Breakfast special (until 11am) $8.50; sandwiches $3.50–$11.20; main courses $15–$27. MC, V. Daily 9:30am–1:30am. Closed Feb. Bus: 2 or 7.

7 City of Hamilton (Pembroke Parish)

VERY EXPENSIVE

Waterloo House _&_ BERMUDIAN/CONTINENTAL   At the edge of Hamilton Harbour, this former private home—now the most famous inn on Bermuda—is a Relais & Châteaux property. Terraced gardens, which descend to the water, are often the setting for waterside buffets. Guests dine by candlelight on the harbor-front terrace or in the elegantly appointed, English-style dining room, where a fire roars in the fireplace on nippy evenings.

Some reports suggest that the food has declined in quality, but that's not what we found on recent visits. A discriminating reader from Virginia agreed, saying she found the food "absolutely fantastic—though somewhat expensive." Portions at lunch were so large that she skipped dinner. Although Waterloo has a

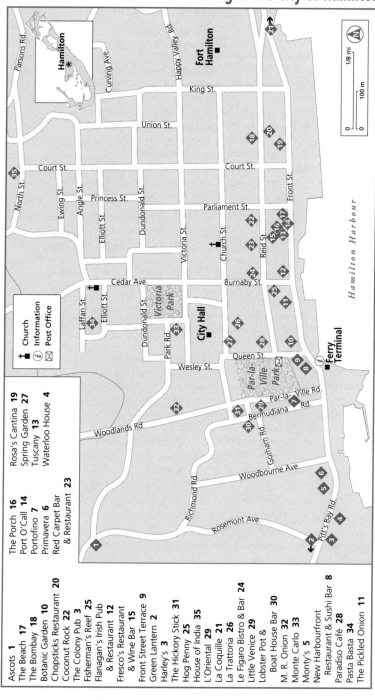

Dining in the City of Hamilton

Ascots **1**
The Beach **17**
The Bombay **18**
Botanic Garden **10**
Chopsticks Restaurant **20**
Coconut Rock **22**
The Colony Pub **3**
Fisherman's Reef **25**
Flanagan's Irish Pub
   & Restaurant **12**
Fresco's Restaurant
   & Wine Bar **15**
Front Street Terrace **9**
Green Lantern **2**
Harley's **3**
The Hickory Stick **31**
Hog Penny **25**
House of India **35**
L'Oriental **29**
La Coquille **21**
La Trattoria **26**
Le Figaro Bistro & Bar **24**
Little Venice **29**
Lobster Pot &
   Boat House Bar **30**
M. R. Onion **32**
Monte Carlo **33**
Monty's **5**
New Harbourfront
   Restaurant & Sushi Bar **8**
Paradiso Café **28**
Pasta Basta **34**
The Pickled Onion **11**

The Porch **16**
Port O'Call **14**
Portofino **7**
Primavera **6**
Red Carpet Bar
   & Restaurant **23**
Rosa's Cantina **19**
Spring Garden **27**
Tuscany **13**
Waterloo House **4**

dramatic and elegant setting, the French and Italian food at Monte Carlo has a more cutting edge.

You might begin with house-smoked rockfish on a bed of fennel or home-made lobster ravioli. The soups range from innovative (gazpacho with avocado compote) to classic (fish chowder with black rum). The best main dishes are seafood—perhaps steamed salmon with couscous, or seared jumbo scallops with red-onion salsa. Classic dishes such as roast lamb cutlets with wild mushroom–rosemary mousse share the menu with more unusual options—perhaps quail with honey, apple, and thyme sauce. Lunches include vegetarian specials, soups, salads, sandwiches, and several items from the grill, such as Bermuda codfish cakes with tomato-and-pineapple salsa.

Pitts Bay Rd. © 441/295-4480. Reservations required at dinner. Jacket required, tie optional. Lunch main courses $12–$18; dinner main courses $30–$34. Daily noon–2:30pm and 7–9:30pm. AE, MC, V.

EXPENSIVE

Ascots ⚓ ITALIAN/FRENCH This restaurant and its tempting continental menu are relatively undiscovered—but they deserve to be better known. Ascots is in a spacious house originally built in 1903, in a residential neighborhood at the end of a country lane at the edge of Hamilton. The antique porcelain, Queen Anne armchairs, and Welsh pine evoke a chintz-filled English country house. In the summer, diners sit at candlelit tables on the front porch, and some-times beneath a tent in the garden.

The menu relies on classic techniques and first-rate ingredients. It includes one of the best selections of hot and cold appetizers in Hamilton, ranging from Mediterranean chicken salad with goat cheese to fresh homemade ravioli filled with crabmeat and served in smoked-salmon-and-spinach cream sauce. Vegetar-ian dishes are available. Count on the chef's catch of the day, prepared as you like it, or try blackened mahimahi with tomato, pineapple, and lemon compote. If you prefer more traditional dishes, you might find the grilled sirloin steak with port glaze and roasted thyme polenta more to your taste. For dessert, the crêpe Garibaldi (warm crêpes filled with bananas and a chocolate-hazelnut sauce, served with fresh berries and crème chantilly) is a good choice. Even more exciting are seasonal berries with Frangelico and chocolate ice cream.

In the Royal Palms Hotel, 24 Rosemont Ave. © 441/295-9644. Reservations recommended. Lunch main courses $14–$20; dinner main courses $28–$32. AE, MC, V. Sun–Fri noon–2:30pm; daily 6:30–10pm. Bus: 1, 2, 10, or 11.

La Coquille ⚓ FRENCH/MEDITERRANEAN One of the most sophisti-cated French restaurants in Bermuda sits on the eastern extension of Front Street, within the Bermuda Underwater Exploration Institute. The decor is modern, with clean lines and tones of blue. The staff, among the most polished in Bermuda, hails from France, Germany, Austria, and Italy. The upscale, care-fully cultivated cuisine is vaguely Provençal—not typical of Bermuda. The menu is worthy of Paris or New York.

At lunchtime, expect a flavorful, relatively straightforward assortment of art-fully presented sandwiches, grilled fish, and steaks. Evening meals are more elab-orate. A worthy beginning is pan-fried foie gras with caramelized pears, served *en brioche* in a port wine reduction. Just-picked salad mingles the best of Bermuda with Provence—mesclun, pear tomatoes, local herbs, and kalamata olives. Two dinner dishes of which the chefs are particularly proud are gratin of scallops with saffron sauce, and aromatic grilled semi-boneless quail with wild boar sausages, served with porcini mushrooms, risotto pancakes, and roasted

---

Tips **A Note on Hotel Dining**

In high season (Apr–Nov), many resort hotels require guests to take the Modified American Plan (MAP), or half-board arrangement, of breakfast and dinner. To spare guests the routine of eating in the same dining room every night, some hotels offer a "dine around" program. It allows you to dine at other hotels on your plan or at somewhat reduced prices. Ask about dine-around arrangements when booking your room.

---

pearl onions. Especially succulent is rack of lamb in a sun-dried tomato crust, served with garlic-enriched whipped potatoes and sautéed baby artichokes. Monte Carlo still maintains a lead over this place, but few leave La Coquille disappointed.

Pembroke Hall, 40 Crow Lane. *©* **441/292-6122.** Reservations recommended. Lunch main courses $8–$21; dinner main courses $23.75–$32.00. AE, MC, V. Daily noon–2:30pm; Mon–Sat 6:30–10pm. Bus: 1, 2, 10, or 11.

Monte Carlo *©* CONTINENTAL/ITALIAN/MEDITERRANEAN   This cheery restaurant celebrates the cuisine of southern France and Italy. Booths and banquettes in the outer dining room sit beneath a local artist's impressions of the countryside around Monaco; seating in the main dining room centers on a brick-sided fireplace. The chefs prepare the best bouillabaisse in Hamilton; using Atlantic seafood, they achieve the savory style that's typical of Marseilles. One of the better dishes is fillet of tuna marinated in oil and herbs and grilled over charcoal. The rack of lamb is tender and well seasoned with Provençal herbs. Classic lamb chops appear with the flavoring of the Côte d'Azur, and veal scaloppine is sautéed and served with sun-dried tomatoes and peppers on angel-hair pasta.

9 Victoria St. (behind City Hall). *©* **441/295-5453.** Reservations recommended. Lunch main courses $10–$18; dinner main courses $18–$25. AE, DC, MC, V. Daily noon–2:30pm and 6–11pm. Bus: 1, 2, 10, or 11.

New Harbourfront Restaurant & Sushi Bar *©* ITALIAN/SEAFOOD/ SUSHI   Front Street was once known only for pubs and fish and chips, but this restaurant has challenged its neighbors. It offers innovative continental dishes and the town's best selection of sushi—no longer does fish have to be deep-fried in oil left over from last week! The cuisine fairly bursts with flavors and aromas. Even if some dishes aren't as successful as others, the kitchen should be applauded for trying to wake up Hamilton's sleepy taste buds. However, service remains sluggish and indifferent—one reader dismissed this place as a "classic tourist trap," but commended the food nevertheless.

For starters, the inevitable Bermudian fish chowder appears, but miso soup is also available. Of the pasta specialties, our pick is lobster and rockfish ravioli served open-faced with red-pepper sauce. Fresh fish appears in a variety of ways, including "fisherman style"—with shrimp, scallops, squid, mussels, and clams in a sun-dried tomato, mushroom, and wine sauce with angel-hair pasta. You might also try the shrimp and vegetable tower—vegetable ragout surrounded by grilled jumbo shrimp served in champagne-leek sauce. The restaurant also offers poultry and meat, including well-prepared sliced breast of duck served in orange Curaçao and cumin-scented sauce with glazed red cabbage. Pastries and cakes are prepared daily, and a wide variety of homemade Italian ice cream is always available.

The spacious restaurant is on the second floor of an old building across from the ferry terminal in the center of town. There's limited seating on the balcony, which juts out over the street and is quite popular in fair weather.

Front St. (between Queen St. and Par-la-Ville Rd.). ℂ **441/295-4207.** Reservations recommended. Lunch main courses $13.75–$21.75; dinner main courses $19–$29.75; Mon sushi buffet $23.75. AE, MC, V. Mon–Sat 11:30am–5:30pm and 6–10pm. Bus: 1, 2, 10, or 11.

The Pickled Onion ☆ INTERNATIONAL   In a onetime liquor warehouse overlooking Hamilton Harbour, this is a good, reasonably priced dining choice and an after-dark venue. The balcony opens onto Front Street. The menu is satisfying without being memorable. You might begin with Caribbean seafood salad, loaded with calamari, shrimp, fresh mussels, and other local fish, all in basil vinaigrette. Angus beef, cut and trimmed in-house, is the chef's signature dish; it's tender and cooked to your specifications, accompanied by steak-cut potatoes and zesty peppercorn sauce. Prime rib, sizzling pizza, and some of the island's best fish chowder are regularly featured, as is entertainment.

On Wednesday, the busiest night of the week, the street is closed off and the scene becomes a festive mini-celebration, with street performers and vendors setting the tone.

53 Front St. ℂ **441/295-2263.** Reservations recommended Wed, Fri–Sat. Main courses $11–$25. AE, MC, V. Daily 11am–1am. Bus: 1, 2, 10, or 11.

MODERATE

The Colony Pub INTERNATIONAL   Many locals drop in here for a drink and to soak up the atmosphere of old Bermuda, complete with nautical memorabilia and English overtones. Three of the six beers on tap (Spinnaker, Full Moon, and Wild Hog) are brewed on Bermuda. The generous lunch buffet is popular with local businesspeople. Dinners are more lavish and hearty, with an emphasis on chicken, seafood, and beef dishes that include amazingly generous (25-oz) portions of prime rib of beef. The restaurant has meat flown in fresh three times a week. Even if it doesn't meet its goal of having "the best meat anywhere outside the U.S.," customers are generally satisfied. The meat is forktender, well flavored, and juicy. The huge baked potatoes are flown in from Idaho. The most popular item is the 8-ounce filet mignon, with the 12-ounce New York strip a close second. The catch of the day generally ranks as a popular third for more health-conscious diners. In the unlikely event you still have room for dessert, we recommend the chocolate brownie with cappuccino ice cream. Although the food at Harley's (see below) has improved, we still prefer the cuisine served here even if some of it still evokes the 50s.

⌒ *Finds* **Where The Locals Eat**

Tired of dining with other tourists? If you have a sense of adventure, head for **Spot Restaurant,** on Burnaby Street (ℂ **441/692-6293**) in Hamilton. Nouvelle cuisine here means food served after the turn of the 20th century. The vittles are basic, unadorned, and delicious if you still like to fill up on those old favorites such as hamburgers, scrambled eggs, bacon, sausages, french fries, pancakes, and the like. Its lunch specials are tasty and filling, and prices are aimed to attract local office workers, so nothing is expensive. Only problem is, no one can convince Spot's owners to serve anything more than breakfast or lunch. It shuts down at night.

In The Fairmont Hamilton Princess, 76 Pitts Bay Rd. ⓒ **441/295-3000.** Reservations recommended for meals. Lunch buffet $22.50; dinner main courses $19–$34. AE, DC, MC, V. Daily 11:45am–2:30pm and 6:30–10pm. Bus: 7 or 8.

Fisherman's Reef SEAFOOD/BERMUDIAN   Above the Hog Penny pub in the heart of Hamilton, Fisherman's Reef is a good choice for local seafood and typical island dishes. Although some locals swear by this place, we still find the seafood dinners slightly better at the Lobster Pot (see below). Fisherman's Reef is predictably nautical, with a separate bar and cocktail lounge; dress is smart casual. You can order wahoo, one of Bermuda's most popular game fish, cut into steaks and topped with banana and bacon strips. Since we've never been fond of wahoo and banana, we usually order Bermuda rockfish; it can be prepared in any of a half-dozen ways. Our favorite is grilled and served with a sauce of Black Seal rum; others prefer it blackened with Cajun spices or Mediterranean style, with herbs and shrimp. In season, Bermuda guinea chicks (that is, small lobsters) are broiled on the half shell, and are they ever good (if only they weren't so expensive!). Ask the waiter about the daily catch—usually snapper, grouper, yellowtail, or shark—which can be pan-fried, broiled, or poached. Although most people come here for fish, the chef also prepares fairly standard meat courses such as pepper-steak flambé.

5 Burnaby Hill. ⓒ **441/292-1609.** Reservations recommended. Lunch main courses $8.75–$23.95; dinner main courses $21.50–$38.50, early-bird dinner (6–7:30pm) $26.95. AE, DC, MC, V. Mon–Fri noon–2pm; daily 6–10pm. Bus: 1, 2, 10, or 11.

Flanagan's Irish Pub & Restaurant INTERNATIONAL   A whiff of shamrocks—even if they've been soaked in beer—is part of the essence of what you'll find at this all-purpose dining and drinking emporium. It occupies a prime position on Front Street, immediately across the street from where cruise ships float at anchor during their Bermuda sojourns. Don't judge the place by what you'll find on the street level, where at least seven big-screen TVs will broadcast up to three different international sporting events at a time, as pinball and automated poker games blare away in strategic corners. Live music appears on an erratic schedule, sometimes as often as five nights a week. Try to get a seat in the upstairs dining room, or on the panoramic veranda. Flanagan's is not known for culinary distinction except in one category. It serves the best fish chowder in Bermuda. This is often a bland bowl in many other places, tasting like boiled fish in milk, but at Flanagan's, the dish has zest and flavor.

That charbroiled eight-ounce Gaelic sirloin that appears on your plate somehow always tastes even more delectable when served with an Irish whiskey sauce. That sauce can also appear with a grilled Angus steak. If you're not a meat-eater, opt for the daily changing menu of fresh fish, which can be grilled to perfection for you.

In the Emporium Building, 69 Front St. Hamilton ⓒ **441/295-8299.** Reservations not necessary. Main courses $13–$25. MC, V. Daily 11:30am–9:30pm. Bar daily 11am–2am. Bus: 7 or 11.

Fresco's Restaurant & Wine Bar ⨍ MEDITERRANEAN   In a building whose vaulted ceiling and thick stone walls date from the early 1900s, this cozy spot feels very much like a European wine cellar. We find dining and drinking wine here less boisterous and more satisfying than the Hog Penny or The Pickled Onion. A trellis-covered courtyard in back holds a handful of tables for alfresco dining. Oenophiles might appreciate the selection of more than 160 different wines from around the world. The dress code is casual and the atmosphere relaxed. The menu changes monthly. Their most celebrated dish—once voted best pork dish in a Caribbean competition—is pork filet mignon, rolled in ginger, with eggplant and star fruit julienne, accompanied by raisin and pineapple polenta, waffle potatoes, and Caribbean salsa. Sea scallops are "framed" with potato and basil dumplings. Whenever possible, local flavors such as papaya, cassava, and loquats are used. One of the best desserts on Bermuda is the chocolate mousse cake, freshly baked and served warm with vanilla ice cream and fresh-mint custard sauce.

Chancery Lane (between Reid and Front sts.). © 441/295-5058. Reservations recommended. Lunch main courses $9.50–$17.50; dinner main courses $17.50–$28. AE, MC, V. Mon–Fri noon–2:30pm; daily 6:30–10:30pm. Bus: 1, 2, 10, or 11.

Harley's MEDITERRANEAN   The food at this popular place used to be merely safe and predictable, but now it exhibits some flair, making this restaurant a worthwhile choice even if you aren't a hotel guest. In warm weather, outdoor tables sit near the swimming pool, creating the effect of a flowering terrace on the Italian Riviera.

Many people who are shopping in Hamilton for the day drop by for lunch, when there's a large selection of salads. Our favorite is the classic Caesar with grilled *goujons* (slices) of grouper. The catch of the day is available grilled, and there are burgers galore, including one served "topless." Pizzas are also featured, and one part of the menu is reserved for kids. The dinner menu is significantly better, with a choice of pastas—the best is grilled salmon fillets on linguine. Many of the main dishes bring back memories of sunny Italy. Beef tenderloin with shrimp and chicken suprême is served with a trio of sauces; tender breasts of chicken come with tomatoes, green peppers, olives, red onions, mushrooms, and fresh herbs. Harley's might be ideal for lunch, but if you want more rib-sticking fare, head for The Colony Pub under the same roof.

In The Fairmont Hamilton Princess, 76 Pitts Bay Rd. © 441/295-3000. Reservations recommended at dinner. Lunch main courses $11–$17.50; dinner main courses $16–$44. AE, DC, MC, V. Tues–Sun 6–10pm. Closed Dec–Mar. Bus: 7 or 8.

La Trattoria ITALIAN   This family-oriented restaurant is tucked away in a narrow alley 2 blocks north of Hamilton's harbor front. There's not a single cutting-edge or glamorous thing about it, and that's not what the loyal regulars are looking for. The decor is straight out of old Naples, with checkered tablecloths in green, red, and white, and hanging Chianti bottles. The attentive if somewhat harried wait staff serves generous portions of rather standard, well-flavored Italian food. You'll find 10 kinds of pizza, and the kitchen is happy to create variations for you. Pastas include lasagna, spaghetti pescatore, and angel hair with shrimp, pesto, and sun-dried tomatoes. Veal can be ordered parmigiana style or as *scaloppini al limone*, and there's a revolving array of fresh fish. If you're very demanding in your Italian dishes, you'll fare better at Little Venice (see below).

Washington Lane (in the middle of the block bordered by Reid, Church, Burnaby, and Queen sts.). © 441/295-1877. Reservations recommended. Main courses $12.75–$24.95. AE, MC, V. Mon–Sat 11:30am–3:30pm; daily 5:30–10:30pm. Bus: 1, 2, 10, or 11.

Little Venice ITALIAN/CONTINENTAL   This is one of the most prominent Italian restaurants on Bermuda, a staple that has been here as long as anyone can remember. The owner, Emilio Barberrio (originally from Capri), is justly proud of his specialties. One is a savory *casseruola di pesce dello chef,* which consists of a medley of local seafood—including lobster, shrimp, mussels, clams, and several kinds of fish—cooked together with white wine, herbs, and tomatoes. Other choices include flavorful fish chowder, spaghetti with seafood,

Kids Family-Friendly Restaurants

Bailey's Ice Cream & Food D'Lites Restaurant (*see p. 136*)   Bailey's is a great place to take the kids for some all-natural ice cream on a hot, sunny day. They also serve sandwiches if you're looking for more than just a snack.

M.R. Onions (*see p. 127*)   M.R. Onions is one of the best family restaurants in the City of Hamilton. Everybody loves the barbecued chicken, ribs, and steak, and the array of burgers can't fail, even with the fussiest kids.

Rosa's Cantina (*see p. 134*)   This house of chili, burritos, fajitas, nachos, tacos, and enchiladas in the City of Hamilton has no equal on the island. The kids get balloons, as well as paper and crayons to keep them busy once they're seated.

Wickets Brasserie & Cricket Club (*see p. 117*)   The children's menus at this popular spot in the Southampton Princess Hotel make this a great place to take the kids. If you arrive before 6:30pm, they can order dinner from the lower-priced lunch menu.

several veal dishes, and an array of pastas, including superb homemade ravioli stuffed with spinach and ricotta. Italian wines are featured, in bottles and (less expensively) in carafes. An abbreviated menu is offered at lunchtime.

Bermudiana Rd. (between Par-la-Ville Rd. and Woodbourne Ave.). © **441/295-3503.** Reservations recommended. Lunch main courses $12.95–$25; dinner main courses $21–$38. AE, DC, MC, V. Mon–Fri 11:45am–2:15pm; daily 6–10pm. Bus: 1, 2, 10, or 11.

Lobster Pot & Boat House Bar ✦ SEAFOOD   For island standards, this traditional favorite has one-upmanship on its neighbors such as M.R. Onions and Hog Penny. Near the Hamilton Princess Hotel, within a 5-minute drive of the heart of Hamilton, this is one of the most consistently popular restaurants on the island, a fixture since 1973. The Lobster Pot's cedar plank walls sport brass and bamboo trim, and such underwater touches as fishnets, branches of coral, and sea fans. There's a bar near the entrance if you want a before-dinner drink, and a dining room behind it. Menu items include both Maine and spiny Caribbean lobster, each prepared four different ways. Fish sandwiches and platters of hogfish, wahoo, tuna, and rockfish are prepared any way you want; we prefer them grilled with amandine, banana, or lemon-butter sauce. The best starter is a cup or bowl of steaming Bermuda fish chowder. It's savory brown and enhanced with cherry peppers and shots of black rum. If you like it, you won't be alone—visitors haul quarts of the stuff (frozen) back to North America.

6 Bermudiana Rd. © **441/292-6898.** Reservations recommended. Lunch main courses $7.95–$17.75; dinner main courses $18.50–$32.50; lobster $26.50–$57.50. AE, MC, V. Mon–Fri 11:30am–3pm; Mon–Sat 6–10:30pm. Bus: 1, 2, 10, or 11.

M. R. Onions Kids AMERICAN/BERMUDIAN   The name of this popular restaurant and bar, a chicken-and-ribs kind of place, is a colloquialism: Bermudians are known as onions, and "M. R." stands for "'em are," or "they are." The restaurant resembles an Edwardian-era bar, with potted palms, leaf-green walls, and brass and oak trim; caricatures of many Bermudians hang on the walls. If you go early, plan to have a drink at the large, rectangular bar that fills most of the front room. During happy hour (daily 5–7pm), it's a favorite rendezvous for local office workers. An addition in the bar is a cybercafe, where you can surf the Web or check e-mail while enjoying a drink.

Both the bar and the dining room serve well-prepared meals that are family favorites with locals and visitors alike. Specialties include the house onion soup and fresh fish—including tuna, wahoo, rockfish, and mahimahi—which can be charbroiled, pan-fried, or served à la amandine or spicy Cajun style. Tasty barbecued chicken, ribs, burgers, and steak (no-fuss meals popular with kids), are also available. Maybe you'll even have enough room left for mud pie, cheesecake, or another creation from the dessert trolley. Meals here are generally satisfying but hardly memorable. There's a no-smoking dining room, much appreciated by families because smoking is allowed in many of Bermuda's restaurants.

Par-la-Ville Rd. ☎ 441/292-5012. Main courses $14–$25; 3-course early-bird dinner (5–6:15pm) $21. AE, DC, MC, V. Daily noon–1am. Bar daily 11:30am–1am. Bus: 1, 2, 10, or 11.

The Porch INTERNATIONAL

Lined with bricks and aged paneling, this warmly decorated restaurant occupies a century-old building. As the restaurant's name implies, it boasts a porch with a sweeping view over Hamilton's harbor; there's also an English-style pub and a wide outdoor terrace for dining in nice weather. (Navigate the stairs carefully as you climb up from Front St., and be even more careful as you come down after having a drink or two.) Food is available throughout, even in the pub-style areas.

The menu offers routine fare, with an emphasis on meat, including prime sirloin steak (10 oz.), prime roast rib of beef with Yorkshire pudding, steak with shrimp, and even wild boar in season (a throwback to Bermuda's early days). Lunch features sandwiches, salads, fresh fish, crab cakes, burgers, and oysters. It's all quite competently prepared and straightforward. This is a nice place to just drop by for a drink and soak up the atmosphere. But don't expect too much.

93 Front St. (between Burnaby and Parliament sts.). ☎ 441/292-4737. Reservations recommended. Lunch main courses $8–$15; dinner main courses $16–$32. AE, MC, V. Mon–Sat 11am–10pm. Bus: 1, 2, 10, or 11.

Port O'Call STEAKS/SEAFOOD

Housed in a cedar- and brass-trimmed room reminiscent of an old-fashioned steamship, this restaurant specializes in fresh local fish, four different preparations of lobster, and steaks. If you're fond of lobster, consider the curried version. Other seafood choices include grilled shrimp and blackened scallops, and Bermuda yellowfin tuna with salsa. Desserts are suitably caloric and include a choice of parfaits. During the off-season, if business is slow, the place might close early, so call ahead to check if you're dining late. The place is more intimate and cozy than Primavera and Red Carpet (see below), and we prefer it for that reason. The food is also slightly better.

87 Front St. ☎ 441/295-5373. Reservations recommended at dinner. Lunch main courses $12–$18; dinner main courses $16–$24. AE, MC, V. Mon–Fri noon–2:30pm; daily 6–11pm.

Primavera ITALIAN

Tired of the traditional steak and seafood served at most Hamilton restaurants? Long a staple on the dining scene, Primavera offers the zesty flavors of Italy, from regions ranging from Rome to Sicily, and even some Sardinian dishes. We won't pretend that this is the best Italian food in Hamilton; many diners prefer Little Venice. But what you get here is retro fare that would have suited the Rat Pack. You might begin with cold or hot antipasto (for example, cold seafood salad or hot baked clams in marinara sauce) and follow with soup (perhaps minestrone) or a salad (probably Caesar). The pasta dishes include tortellini Primavera (the chef's surprise) and black ravioli with lobster. Other options are good chicken cacciatore and sautéed veal with fresh vegetables. Top off your meal with an espresso or a frothy cappuccino. The service is impeccable.

In Hamilton West, 69 Pitts Bay Rd. (between Front St. and The Fairmont Hamilton Princess). ✆ 441/295-2167. Reservations recommended. Lunch main courses $13–$24.70; dinner main courses $28–$50. AE, MC, V. Tues–Fri 11:45am–2:30pm; daily 6:30–10:30pm. Bus: 7 or 8.

Red Carpet Bar & Restaurant ITALIAN/FRENCH/INTERNATIONAL
In a 150-year-old building, Red Carpet serves many Italian dishes despite its English pub–style ambience. This place does a thriving lunch business, thanks to the many offices nearby. After work, the dimly lit bar is a popular place for people to relax with a beer. Lunch offerings include sandwiches, cold platters, and a few hot dishes such as pan-fried fish (including Bermuda tuna and wahoo). Dinners feature a wider array—veal scaloppine, veal Marsala, chicken cacciatore, filet mignon, New York strip sirloin, and a variety of pasta dishes. Both Primavera and Little Venice serve better food, but at higher prices. What you get here is quite good, familiar fare.

In the Armoury Building, 37 Reid St. ✆ 441/292-6195. Reservations recommended. Lunch main courses $14.50–$19; dinner main courses $22–$36. AE, MC, V. Mon–Sat 11:30am–3pm and 6:30–10pm. Bar open until 1am. Bus: 1, 2, 10, or 11.

Tuscany ✎ ITALIAN   When local chefs have a night off, they often dine at this popular local eatery, which serves the best pizzas and the best Italian food of any eatery in Hamilton, including Little Venice (see above). The decor, with beamed ceilings and frescos, evokes the Tuscan countryside. If the weather's right, there's seating on the balcony, with panoramic views of the main street of Hamilton and its harbor. The friendly waiters always seem willing to advise about what's good that evening. Many patrons come here for the delicious pizzas. One good choice is the 4 stagioni (artichoke hearts, asparagus, mozzarella, and tomato). Another specialty is petto di pollo alla Dante, a boneless chicken breast sautéed with tomatoes and sherry and crowned with fried eggplant and

---

⟨*Moments* **Afternoon Tea, Island Style**

Bermuda observes the British tradition of afternoon tea. Many visitors prefer to have tea at their hotels, which provides a good opportunity to meet fellow guests. Others like to visit a variety of hotels for afternoon tea; all of the big resort hotels (including Elbow Beach, The Fairmont Hamilton Princess, Sonesta Beach Resort, and The Fairmont Southampton Princess) offer tea to guests and nonguests. Our favorites are the traditional spreads at the Hamilton Princess and Elbow Beach.

Tea is usually served daily from 3 to 5pm indoors or out, depending on the weather. Dress is more casual than in London; men can wear Bermuda shorts and a shirt with sleeves, and women can wear a simple cotton dress (swimwear, however, is frowned upon unless tea is served right at the pool). It's always a good idea to call ahead and reserve (see chapter 4, "Accommodations," for contact information).

Among restaurants and cafes, the two offering the best traditional afternoon tea are the **Botanic Garden** and **Paradiso Cafe** (reviewed later in this section).

creamy mozzarella. Veal is imported frozen and available almost any way you like it; other tempting selections include the fresh fish of the day and the succulent homemade pastas.

95 Front St. ☏ 441/292-4507. Reservations recommended. Lunch main courses $9.50–$15; dinner main courses $14.75–$26. AE, MC, V. Mon–Fri 11:45am–2:30pm; Mon–Sat 6–10:30pm. Bus: 1, 2, or 10.

INEXPENSIVE

The Beach BRITISH/BERMUDIAN   To escape the routine of dining aboard ship, an international crowd of visitors flocks to this eatery across from the cruise-ship docks. It's one of the most casual and laid-back places in Hamilton. Sports fans watch the giant TV, others enjoy the gaming machines, and others dine at picnic tables. The daily happy hour (4–7pm) features discounted drinks. Pub fare is the order of the day, and most patrons seem to order a big, juicy hamburger. Local fish is available seared in a pan or deep-fried. Sandwiches and tacos round out the bill of fare. At the bar you can sample Bermuda's famous "Dark and Stormy" (black rum and ginger beer). It's a food pit stop—nothing special—but because of its location it attracts a lot of attention.

103 Front St. ☏ 441/292-0219. Main courses $4.95–$10. MC, V. Daily 10am–3am. Bus: 1 or 2.

The Bombay INDIAN   Can't face another meal of grilled fish or steak? The best Indian cuisine on the island might be just the thing to break up Bermuda's routine offerings. This third-floor hideaway serves expertly prepared authentic dishes in a relaxed atmosphere. Visitors from London or New York may be used to better Indian fare; but still, it's a nice change of pace. For lunch, the daily "A Taste of India" buffet includes a variety of dishes, from mulligatawny soup to chicken, beef, lamb, and seafood served with a choice of sauces, in spicy curry, or roasted in the tandoori oven. The Indian chefs will prepare your dishes with the mild, delicate tastes of coastal India if you prefer, but there are more fiery dishes. There are lots of vegetarian options, of course, and even a handful of continental selections. Dress is smart casual.

In the Rego Furniture Building, 75 Reid St. ☏ 441/292-0048. Reservations required. Main courses $13.95–$22; fixed-price lunch $11.95. AE, MC, V. Mon–Fri noon–2:30pm; daily 6–11pm. Bus: 1, 2, 10, or 11.

Botanic Garden (Value) INTERNATIONAL   On the third floor of the most famous department store in Hamilton, this place attracts shoppers who know good value when they see it. It's an informal, self-service spot, ideal for morning coffee or afternoon tea. The pastries, pies, and cakes, especially the banana bread and the gingerbread, are excellent. They also serve an array of sandwiches.

In Trimingham's, 17 Front St. (between Reid and Queen sts.). ☏ 441/295-1183. Reservations not accepted. All items $4–$5. No credit cards. Mon–Sat 9:30am–4:30pm. Bus: 1, 2, 10, or 11.

Chopsticks Restaurant (★) CHINESE/THAI   Sooner or later, that craving for Chinese food rears its head. Although off the beaten track at the eastern end of Hamilton, Chopsticks offers Bermuda's best Chinese and Thai food, including spicy soup, tangy pork ribs, and seafood. The chef specializes in Szechuan, Hunan, Thai, and Cantonese dishes, with an emphasis on fresh vegetables and delicate sauces. We love the excellent jade chicken, with spears of broccoli, mushrooms, and water chestnuts in a mild Peking wine sauce. Peking duck (served only for two) must be ordered 24 hours in advance. The best Thai dish is green curry chicken (chicken breast strips simmered with onions and bamboo shoots and served with fresh basil, coconut milk, and green-curry paste); it can be prepared mild, spicy, or hot. Most of the dishes are the standard ones you'd find in any North American Chinese restaurant, including sweet-and-sour chicken, beef in oyster sauce, and shrimp in lobster sauce. Some dishes, including the duck in red curry, have real flair. Vegetarians will find a haven here.

88 Reid St. © 441/292-0791. Reservations recommended. Lunch main courses $7–$15.95; dinner main courses $7–$25. AE, MC, V. Mon–Fri noon–2:30pm; daily 5–11pm. Bus: 1, 2, 10, or 11.

Coconut Rock INTERNATIONAL/SUSHI   This lively, informal eatery in the center of Hamilton is a drinking and dining destination. German-born Christian Herzog presides over a main restaurant and two popular bars where music videos play. The place is a bit of a discovery and not likely to be overrun. Your best bet for dinner is the fish of the day, most often pan-seared and served in lemon-butter sauce with potatoes and vegetables. Spicy linguine and tiger shrimp in spicy tomato sauce are two of our favorites. Chicken quesadillas are a fast-moving item, as are buffalo chicken wings in honey and hot sauce. Drinks are discounted during the daily happy hour (5–7pm).

The restaurant recently added a sushi bar, Yashi, with one of the widest and best selections in Bermuda, including such exotica as flying fish egg or wahoo.

20 Reid St. © 441/292-1043. Reservations recommended Sat–Sun. Lunch main courses $7.95–$14.95; dinner main courses $9.95–$17.50. AE, MC, V. Mon–Sat 11:30am–2:30pm and 6–10:30pm. Bus: 1, 2, 10, or 11.

Front Street Terrace INTERNATIONAL   On the ground floor of one of Hamilton's largest department stores, this independently managed waterfront bistro opens onto an outdoor patio. It attracts midday shoppers who enjoy healthy salads, sandwiches, soups, and platters. If you're caught in the rain, you can duck onto the cedar-trimmed veranda.

The light cuisine reflects international influences, always with an emphasis on healthy ingredients. Everything, including the rough-textured, six-grain bread, is organic and locally grown. Look for offerings like jerk tuna sandwiches with fresh pineapple-avocado mayonnaise; Thai chicken in a sweet chile-flavored vinaigrette enhanced with fresh cilantro, mint, and Asian greens; and charcoal-grilled vegetable sandwiches served with fresh local goat cheese. A popular salad includes fresh local avocados, tiger prawns, and three-pepper vinaigrette.

In the A. S. Cooper & Sons, Ltd., Building, 59 Front St. © 441/296-5265. Soups, salads, and platters $7.95–$13.95. MC, V. Mon–Sat 9am–4pm. Bus: 1, 2, 10, or 11.

Green Lantern (Value) INTERNATIONAL   This unpretentious restaurant is like an upscale diner. In expensive Hamilton, the place is a good venue at which to fill up, not collect recipes for *Gourmet* magazine. The limited menu changes every day, but you'll always find fresh fish, roasted chicken, and roast beef. It might also feature meat loaf and pork chops; lamb chops and stewed oxtail; or curried chicken and steak. No liquor is served, but you can bring your own bottle. The setting is a century-old house about a mile west of the city limits of Hamilton; the outside is painted—guess what—a pale shade of green.

Serpentine Rd. (at Pitts Bay Rd.). © 441/295-6995. Main courses $10–$15. AE, MC, V. Mon–Tues and Thurs–Sat 9am–9pm; Wed 9am–3pm. Bus: 1, 2, 10, or 11.

The Hickory Stick DELI   Near the rose-colored walls of the Hamilton Princess, The Hickory Stick is the most popular delicatessen and take-out restaurant in the city. It serves 1,000 customers a day, including lots of office workers. Although one section seems like a coffee shop (with scones, doughnuts, and morning coffee), most customers come here for overstuffed sandwiches and take-out meals. Offerings include steaming portions of chicken Parmesan and fish cakes. Even more popular are the salads, sandwiches, and hot dogs, all of which can be wrapped up for a picnic—the staff provides paper napkins and plastic cutlery on request. Advance telephone orders are accepted—a good idea if you don't want to wait.

2 Church St. (at Bermudiana Rd.). © **441/292-1781.** Salads $3.25–$5.50; sandwiches and platters $2.25–$5.75. No credit cards. Mon–Fri 6:30am–4pm. Bus: 1, 2, 10, or 11.

Hog Penny BRITISH/BERMUDIAN   A bit tired these days, Hog Penny remains Bermuda's most famous and enduring pub, serving draft beer and ale to each new generation of mainlanders who head here, probably on the advice of their grandparents. Draft beer and ale are served here, to crowds of visitors and locals. The dark paneled rooms are decorated in the British style, with old fishing and farm tools, bentwood chairs, and antique mirrors. At lunch you can order pub specials (including shepherd's pie) or tuna salad. The kitchen prepares a number of passable curries, including chicken and lamb. Fish and chips and steak-and-kidney pie are the perennial favorites, and they are comparable to what you'd find in a London pub. Dinner is more elaborate; the menu might include a whole lobster, a fresh fish of the day (perhaps Bermuda yellowfin tuna), and excellent Angus beef. The food is better upstairs at the Fisherman's Reef. There's nightly entertainment from 9:30pm to 1am; dress is casual.

5 Burnaby Hill. © **441/292-2534.** Reservations recommended. Lunch main courses $9.50–$15; dinner main courses $10–$25, early-bird dinner (5:30–7:30pm) $23.50. AE, MC, V. Oct–Mar daily noon–3pm and 5:30–10pm; Apr–Sept daily 11:30am–3pm and 5:30–10:30pm. Bus: 1, 2, 10, or 11.

House of India ✶ (Finds) INDIAN   This is one of only two Indian restaurants in Bermuda, and the only one in Hamilton itself. As such, it's viewed as something of a dining oddity in a landscape dominated by more international fare. Within a dining room that's decorated with Indian paintings and woodcarvings, on the northern edge of Hamilton, you'll enjoy a menu that specializes in the slow-cooked, often spicy cuisine of Northern India. Examples include a wide variety of vegetarian, beef, lamb, and chicken dishes, prepared in whatever degree of spiciness you request. Our favorite dishes on the menu are lamb mass and beef roganjosh. A buffet lunch is served daily, including a wide selection of vegetarian dishes, and the chefs point out that all dishes are gluten and wheat free except for breads and pastries.

Park View Plaza, 57 North St. © **441/295-6450.** Reservations not necessary. Main courses $8.75–$12.95. AE, DC, MC, V. Mon–Fri noon–3pm; daily 5–9:45pm. Bus 7 or 8.

Le Figaro Bistro & Bar FRENCH   With its oversize posters and two little dining areas, this bistro attracts visitors and locals in almost equal numbers. The chef comes from Bordeaux, and he brings the flavors of southern France to his kitchen. The setting is *intime,* and the wines are some of the best in Hamilton (the restaurant runs its own wine shop, Bacchus). Dig into hearty cassoulet, rockfish (local grouper) with a coconut crust and a hint of tarragon, or baked oysters with red-pepper pesto. Young duck is stewed in a savory almond and red-wine sauce, and old favorites such as coq au vin (chicken cooked in wine) and a rib-eye steak with *pommes frites* are always on the menu. Save room for the delectable chocolate crème brûlée. Even though Monte Carlo and La Coquille have a better cuisine, this remains a favorite of ours because of its intimate setting and friendly service.

63 Reid St. © **441/296-4991.** Reservations required. Lunch main courses $10–$16; dinner main courses $17–$20. AE, MC, V. Mon–Fri noon–2:30pm; Sat–Sun 6–10:30pm. Bus: 1, 2, 10, or 11.

L'Oriental ASIAN   Thanks to the success of Little Venice, a restaurant on the ground floor of the same building, the owners of this place decided to transform their upper dining room into a pan-Asian restaurant that specializes in the cuisines of the east. The result is a mahogany-and-stone-lined room with bridges, a pagoda, and lots of Oriental art, with a penchant for gracefully mixing cuisines as diverse as those of Malaysia, Thailand, Japan, and China. Within the efficiently organized space, you'll find an oyster, salmon, sushi, and caviar bar; and a teppanyaki table where a team of Japan-trained chefs prepare food on a super-hot grill right in front of you. Since the place prides itself on the variety of its all-Asian cuisine, no one will mind if you "fuse" together a meal deriving from the far corners of the world's biggest continent. One of the most appealing nights here is Tuesday, when an all-Chinese "sampler" menu, with tastings from most of the selections on the menu, is available for $27 per person. The cuisine is reliable and good, without ever rising to the ranks of sublime. This restaurant is part of a growing trend around the world where chefs offer a taste from various countries of Asia under one roof. It's also a good choice for the vegetarian and the health conscious.

Most dishes are at the lower end of the price scale listed below.

32 Bermudiana Rd. (above Little Venice Restaurant). ✆ **441/295-9627**. Reservations recommended. Lunch main courses $11.50–$35.75; dinner main courses $15.75–$35.75. AE, DC, MC, V. Mon–Sat noon–3pm and 6–10pm. Bus 7 and 11.

Monty's INTERNATIONAL   On the western waterfront road leading to the most congested part of Hamilton, this family-style choice is a simple, friendly place to sit down for a meal. The atmosphere is bright, airy, and casual; many guests of the nearby Hamilton Princess head here.

Monty's serves a variety of dishes, with an emphasis on English and classic Bermudian fare. Hot dishes include bangers and mash, meat loaf with mashed potatoes and curried chicken, plus more exotic choices like smoked salmon with mango sauce and pumpernickel bread. There's a selection of hot and cold sandwiches and burgers. This is a great choice for breakfast if you're in the mood to venture out. Stop by on Sunday morning for a traditional Bermudian breakfast of codfish and potatoes. The food—solid, reliable fare—rises above mediocre without ever becoming superlative.

75 Pitts Bay Rd. ✆ **441/295-5759**. Reservations recommended Fri–Sat. Sandwiches and burgers $5–$8; main courses $14–$24. AE, MC, V. Daily 7:30am–2:30pm; Mon–Sat 5:30–10pm. Closed Nov–Mar.

Paradiso Cafe PASTRIES/SANDWICHES/DELI   One of Hamilton's most consistently crowded lunch spots, the Paradiso Cafe serves hundreds of office workers every day. The most popular choices are pastries, sandwiches, and endless cups of tea and coffee, and the platters of the day are full meals in themselves. Depending on what's available at the market, daily specials might include lasagna with a side salad; savory breast of chicken with greens; or a platter of "deep-fried rice" with minced beef or pork.

In the Washington Mall, Reid St. (at Queen St.). ✆ **441/295-3263**. Reservations not accepted. Tea or coffee $1.20; sandwiches $5–6.50; daily specials $6.95. MC, V (for purchases of $25 or more). Mon–Fri 7am–5pm; Sat 8am–5pm. Bus: 1, 2, 10, or 11.

Pasta Basta ITALIAN   This is the larger of two restaurants that serve the same cafeteria-style pasta-and-salad combination. (The other, Pasta Pasta, is in St. George; the slight difference in spelling has caused a lot of discussion.) Its Italian cuisine ranks far below those restaurants already recommended, but so do its prices.

In a summery setting, customers are offered two kinds of salad (tossed and Caesar) and about a dozen varieties of pasta. Served in full or half portions, they include two kinds of lasagna (one is meatless), plus a frequently changing array of pastas topped with a choice of meat, seafood, and vegetarian sauces. The daily special is likely to be shells with sausage and onions in a pink sauce. This restaurant is a great place to fill up on decent food at a reasonable price—don't expect a lot more. *Note:* No wine, beer, or alcohol is served, and local licensing laws do not permit you to bring your own drinks.

1 Elliott St. ℂ **441/295-9785.** Reservations not accepted. Pastas $6 (half portion) or $10 (full portion). No credit cards. Mon–Sat 11:45am–11pm; Sun 5–11pm. Bus: 1, 2, 10, or 11.

Portofino NORTHERN ITALIAN   The warm and inviting decor of this trattoria, complete with hanging lamps, evokes northern Italy. La Trattoria and Little Venice will feed you better, but this place has its devotees.

You'll find well-prepared, reasonably priced specialties, including classic minestrone; three kinds of spaghetti; fresh-made pastas, including lasagna, ravioli, and cannelloni; and 18 varieties of 9-inch pizzas. There are also familiar Italian dishes such as Venetian-style liver, veal parmigiana, chicken cacciatore, and beefsteak pizzaiola. Your best bet is one of the freshly made daily specials. There's a limited selection of Italian wines.

Bermudiana Rd. ℂ **441/292-2375.** Reservations recommended. Main courses $12.95–$26.95; pizzas $11.50–$15.95. AE, MC, V. Mon–Fri 11:30am–3:45pm; daily 6–11:45pm. Bus: 1, 2, 10, or 11.

Rosa's Cantina *(Kids)* TEX-MEX   Head here for your Tex-Mex fix, especially if you're a traveling frugal family who like South of the Border food every week or so. You can fill up here on beef and chicken fajitas, zesty chili, nachos, tacos, enchiladas, and burritos (the largest on the island), accompanied by frozen margaritas to put the fire out. While mariachi music plays in the background, you might begin with hearty black-bean soup, then move on to *carne asada* (mesquite-grilled rib-eye steak)—a chef's specialty. The prices are reasonable, and the best place to sit is on the balcony.

121 Front St. ℂ **441/295-1912.** Reservations required Fri–Sat. Main courses $11.50–$20.95; lunch from $7.95. AE, MC, V. Daily noon–1am. Bus: 1, 2, 10, or 11.

Spring Garden *(Finds)* BAJAN/BERMUDIAN   Battered, convivial, and cheerful, this restaurant duplicated the cuisine of Barbados and the ambience of the southern West Indies. Within a setting that contains a courtyard shaded with palms, and 40-seat dining room that's lined with oil paintings by Barbados-based artists. Victor Alleyne, your host, presides over a bar where activity continues long after the last dinner is served. Beneath a cedar ceiling, or under the open sky, depending on where you sit, you'll enjoy fried flavor-filled dishes that have real Bajan or West Indian flavor. Naturally, peas and rice accompany most dishes. The rotis here are as good as the authentic ones of Trinidad, and salads are made fresh daily, along with well-stuffed sandwiches if you visit for lunch. That specialty of Barbados, pan-fried flying fish, is served here with tartar sauce, and you can also order a savory lamb curry.

You can also order a selection of Bermuda staples such as fish chowder, fish cakes, and a tasty oxtail soup; a great choice for a windy day.

19 Washington Lane. ℂ **441/295-7416.** Reservations recommended. Lunch main courses $8–$15; dinner main courses $9.50–$20. AE, MC, V. Mon–Sat 11:30am–3:30pm; daily 6–10:30pm. Bus 7 or 11.

8 Devonshire Parish

EXPENSIVE

Caliban's *(★★)* BERMUDIAN/INTERNATIONAL   Yes, that is very likely Jack Nicholson dining with his longtime pal, Michael Douglas (one of the resort's owners) at the next table. Vacationing here with his family since 1954, Douglas chipped in $5 million for a much-needed renovation, and that meant launching Caliban's as a top-grade restaurant, one of the finest on the island. After a drink in the bar, decorated with Douglas movie memorabilia, ask for a table overlooking the sea, an alfresco setting popular for those who like moonlight dining. You're literally steps from the water, one of the few restaurants in Bermuda that offers this experience. The chefs create memorable dishes to diners who no longer face the jacket-and-tie requirement. California boy Michael Douglas did away with that.

Lunch is served both indoors and at Caliban's poolside terrace. The lunch menu is more limited than dinner but includes an array of sandwiches, appetizers, soups, and salads, plus full-fledged main courses that range from blackened grouper to beef teriyaki sautéed with red peppers. The main courses at night are often elaborate and generally tasty concoctions that are likely to include a well-prepared baked Atlantic salmon in puff pastry with a Pernod mousse or a zesty chicken tandoori with a mint chutney. Always count on a fresh fish of the day plus a pasta specialty.

In the Ariel Sands Hotel, 34 South Shore Rd., Devonshire. ℂ **441/236-1010**. Reservations required. Lunch main courses $12.50–$21.50; dinner main courses $17.75–$32. AE, DC, MC, V. Daily noon–2:45 pm and 7–9:30pm. Bus: 1.

9 Smith's Parish

MODERATE

North Rock Brewing Company ✸ 𝐹𝑖𝑛𝑑𝑠 INTERNATIONAL   Although beer is brewed by other enterprises in Bermuda, this is the only brewery on the island that serves most, if not all, of its product on the premises. The setting contains a smoky, sometimes rowdy replica of an English pub, complete with ceiling beams and paneling, as well as a tony and casually upscale dining room outfitted, equestrian-style, in tones of burgundy and forest green. Most patrons tend to gravitate to the dining room, but died-in-the-wool locals sometimes opt to spend their entire time, meal and all, in the pub section, where views of copper-sided fermentation vats are visible through plate-glass windows.

If you come here to drink the local brew, that's fine, but we suggest you stick around for the cuisine too This is not the typical pub grub dished up at one of those Front Street drinking emporiums in Hamilton. Dishes here have flair, like the Brewmaster's gingered duck breast resting atop mesclun greens with fresh garden vegetables, to which a lemon-ginger dressing and pine nuts add even more flavor. You can also order pub classics such as steak-and-ale pie or perhaps beef and mushrooms simmered in porter ale. The fish and chips aren't so bad either, and we also like the tender pork tenderloin and the codfish cakes. Unless you order expensive shellfish, most dishes are inexpensively priced.

10 South Rd. ℂ **441/236-6633**. www.bermudashorts.bm/northrock. Reservations not required. Lunch main courses $8.50–$21.50; dinner main courses $14.95–$35. AE, MC, V. Lunch daily 11:30am–3pm; dinner daily 6pm–10pm..

INEXPENSIVE

Specialty Inn INTERNATIONAL   This south-shore restaurant's international menu revolves around Bermudian cuisine with Italian zest. Seating 35 to 40 (mostly locals, not visitors), the inn is known for its good value, generous portions, and fine cooking. Red-bean soup, an ideal starter, reflects the island's Portuguese influence; Bermuda fish chowder is particularly good. The fresh catch of the day might be delectable wahoo. Pasta dishes, including the lasagna, are homemade. Poultry and meat, though frozen, are generally excellent—roast lamb and barbecued chicken are especially tasty.

Many other dishes display influences that run from Chinese and Indian to Mexican, Spanish, and Portuguese.

Collectors Hill. ℂ 441/236-3133. Lunch main courses $8.75–$9.75; dinner main courses $13.75–$16.75. MC, V. Mon–Sat 6am–10pm.

10 Hamilton Parish

VERY EXPENSIVE

Tom Moore's Tavern ⚓ FRENCH/CONTINENTAL Bermuda's oldest restaurant, built in 1652 as a private home, is on Walsingham Bay, near the Crystal Caves. The Irish romantic poet Thomas Moore visited in 1804 and wrote some of his verses here; he referred to a calabash tree that still stands some 200 yards from the tavern. The most famous dining room in Bermuda has gone through many incarnations. Bologna-born Bruno Fiocca and his Venetian partner, Franco Bortoli, opened the present tavern in 1985; it quickly became one of the island's most popular upscale restaurants. With its four fireplaces and darkened cedar walls, this landmark establishment serves classic French and Italian cuisine.

Seafood is a specialty. During the summer, there's usually a tank of Bermuda lobsters outside. Local fish selections are likely to include rockfish and yellowtail, which may be your best bet. One reader wrote that he found the place "very expensive, but worth the price, as the service and atmosphere are both topnotch. The cuisine is not light, however. Extremely well-prepared meals contain very rich sauces." He's right. Nevertheless, we recommend the chef's specialty: quail filled with goose liver, morels, and truffles, then baked in puff pastry. Two other recommendations are sautéed sweetbreads in creamy basil sauce and Latino-style jambalaya. The setting, English silver, German crystal, Luxembourg china, and general ambience contribute to a memorable visit.

Walsingham Lane, Walsingham Bay. ℂ 441/293-8020. Reservations required. Jacket required. Main dishes $24–$37. AE, V. Daily 7–10pm. Closed Jan 5–Feb 1. Bus: 1 or 3.

INEXPENSIVE

Bailey's Ice Cream & Food D'Lites Restaurant Ⓚⁱᵈˢ ICE CREAM/ SANDWICHES/DELI This ice-cream parlor occupies a small cottage across from the Swizzle Inn (see below). For all-natural ice cream, there's no comparable spot in Bermuda—the staff concocts 20 to 25 flavors in the shop's 40-quart ice-cream maker. You can enjoy Bermuda banana, coconut, white-chocolate cherries and chips, or other exotic flavors at one of the outdoor tables. The popular sandwiches are served on fresh-baked bread. Also featured are fresh-fruit ices, frozen yogurt, and bottled juices—perfect on a hot, sunny day.

At Wilkinson Ave. and Blue Hole Hill, Bailey's Bay. ℂ 441/293-8605. Sandwiches $3.75–$4.75; ice cream $2.25 per scoop. No credit cards. Daily 11am–6pm. Closed Dec–Feb. Bus: 1, 3, 10, or 11.

Swizzle Inn BERMUDIAN/BRITISH The oldest pub in Bermuda—some 300 years old—is also the home of the Bermuda rum swizzle. It lies west of the airport, near the Crystal Caves. Thousands of business cards and reams of graffiti cover the walls. The meaty Swizzleburger was voted best in Bermuda; other freshly prepared pub favorites include fish and chips, conch fritters, and shepherd's pie. These dishes are at least a notch above typical Bermudian pub grub.

Popular among both locals and visitors at lunch are the Bailey's Bay fish sandwich and onion rings. The larger, more varied dinner menu appeals to many tastes and diets. Seating is available inside and on the upper and lower patios; upstairs there's also a no-smoking room and a gift shop.

3 Blue Hole Hill, Bailey's Bay. © 441/293-1854. Reservations accepted only for parties of 8 or more. Lunch main courses $6–$16; dinner main courses $9.50–$26. AE, MC, V. June–Sept daily 11am–1am; off-season daily 11am–midnight. Closed Mon Jan–Feb. Bus: 3 or 11.

11 St. George Parish

MODERATE

Black Horse Tavern ✦ INTERNATIONAL/BERMUDIAN   If you should land here, in a section of the island that Bermudians call "the country," you'll dine with the locals, many of whom maintain (with some justification) that this is the best place for "an authentic taste of Bermuda." It looks like a private home, dusty rose with green shutters and a glassed-in porch in the rear that looks over Smith's Sound. Over the years, the tavern has attracted many celebrities; some diners arrive in yachts.

You can begin your meal with curried conch stew, shark hash (made with minced puppy shark), fish chowder, or curried mussels. Other choices include sandwiches, burgers, and platters of fish and chips or chicken and chips. The chef also prepares good sirloin steak. If your luck holds, the only Bermuda Triangle you'll encounter is a drink—pineapple juice, orange juice, black rum, and Bermuda gold liqueur. This place is more of a regular restaurant than the equally famous Dennis's Hideaway (see below).

101 St. David's Rd., St. David's Island. © 441/297-1991. Reservations recommended for parties of 4 or more. Main courses $16–$30. AE, MC, V. Tues–Sat 11am–1am; Sun noon–1am. Bus: 6.

Carriage House STEAKS/SEAFOOD/INTERNATIONAL   In an old waterfront storehouse, the restored Carriage House specializes in beef and seafood. It retains the 18th-century warehouse look with two rows of bare brick arches, spruced up with hanging baskets of greenery. You can dine on the terrace outdoors by the harbor side. The chef specializes in prime rib (priced according to size), which is cut to order and served British style, with a ramekin of creamed horseradish. Other specialties include English lamb chops with rosemary and—our favorite—tasty versions of Bermuda rockfish, black grouper, and snapper. Especially well-prepared dishes are oven-roasted Barbary duck breast and pan-fried steak Diane flambéed at your table with cognac. Ingredients are imported, but chefs somehow manage to conceal that fact. A different soup is offered every day. At lunch, there's a large selection of hamburgers, as well as sandwich platters, Bermuda fish chowder, pastas, soups, and oysters. The dessert choices are always excellent.

Most prices are at the lower end of the price scale below, except for high-priced Bermudian lobster.

22 Water St., Somers Wharf. © 441/297-1730. Reservations recommended. Lunch main courses $7–$18; dinner main courses $24.50–54, 4-course early-bird special (5:30–6:45pm) $23.50; Sun buffet $29.50 per person. AE, DC, MC, V. Daily 11:30am–4:30pm and 5:30–9:30pm; Sun brunch noon–2pm. Bus: 3, 10, or 11.

Dennis's Hideaway ✦ (Moments) BERMUDIAN/SEAFOOD   Dennis Lamb, a burly St. David's islander, is one of the treasures of Bermuda. So is his quaint little restaurant, in the island's easternmost parish. As you approach (by land or sea), you're likely to see Dennis working in his garden in front—he grows cabbage for coleslaw and beets for pickling, among other things. He'll show you

Dining in St. George

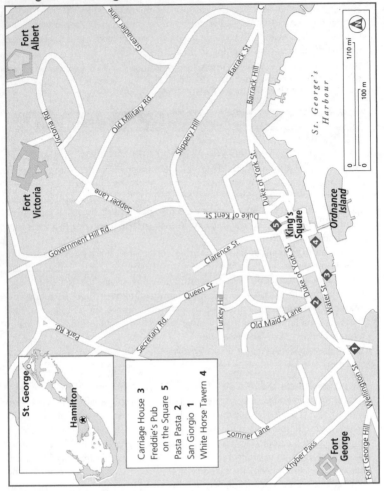

Carriage House **3**
Freddie's Pub
on the Square **5**
Pasta Pasta **2**
San Giorgio **1**
White Horse Tavern **4**

St. George
Hamilton

into his fisher's cottage, situated by one of the island's little coves. Inside, you might feel as if you've left Bermuda and are visiting a pocket-sized country with its own distinctive personality.

Descended from whalers and pilots ("wooden ships and iron men"), Dennis is now retired. His son, "Seaegg," will offer you dishes that have virtually disappeared from Bermuda's restaurants and are normally available only in private homes. For $32.50, you get "the works": an array of dishes, including conch stew, mahimahi, herb-flavored shark hash, shrimp, conch fritters—you name it (but please don't order the turtle, an endangered species). If you don't want to eat so much, ask for the $15.50 fish dinner.

We recommend Dennis's Hideaway only to the adventurous. The offbeat, informal ambience isn't for everyone. Some readers give it high marks and say they've made at least 20 pilgrimages here; others feel that we shouldn't send diners to "this grubby place." You may bring your own wine. Don't dress up.

Cashew City Rd., St. David's Island. ℰ **441/297-0044.** Reservations required. Fixed-price dinners $15.50–$32.50; platters $21.50. No credit cards. Daily 10am–10pm. Bus: 3.

Freddie's Pub on the Square INTERNATIONAL In a restored 18th-century building with a balcony overlooking King's Square, this popular local hangout suits diners on a variety of budgets. You can come here for sandwiches and English pub fare, such as fish and chips or shepherd's pie. The more formal areas serve some very expensive fish dishes, mostly based on the catch of the day. Linen tablecloths and subdued lighting at night enhance the elegant atmosphere. Red snapper is grilled and served with passion-fruit sauce. Wahoo often appears in a coconut curry, and pan-seared tuna has a tangerine flavor. Portions are very large, judging from the Angus beef and rack of lamb. The salads, including Greek, avocado, Caesar, chef's, Mexican, and seafood, are among the best in St. George.

King's Sq. ℰ **441/297-1717.** Reservations recommended. Sandwiches $6–$12; vegetarian dishes $13–$14; meat dishes $19–$29; seafood $19–$43. MC, V. Daily 11am–3am. Bus: 7.

San Giorgio ITALIAN This little restaurant is your best bet for Italian dining in the East End, though not as good as competitors in Hamilton. The building housing the restaurant originated as a sea captain's house 200 years ago, and has been hugely amplified since then. It has the most appealing and panoramic terrace in St. George, with a view of the harbor and of St. David's Island. This is not the most sophisticated Italian cuisine we've ever sampled, but it is reliable, tastes good, and is made with quality products. The antipasto is a bit routine, but there are several savory pastas, including tortellini and creamy lasagna (only if you've already lost the battle of the bulge). The chicken breast was enjoyable, but the bacon wrap won't appeal to certain modern tastes. The freshly made salmon salad looked tempting but lost to freshly broiled wahoo served with a lemon butter sauce.

Water St. (opposite the Post Office) ℰ **441/297-1307.** Reservations recommended. Lunch main courses $8.50–$12; dinner main courses $12.50–$27. Daily 11:30am–3pm and 6:30–10pm. MC, V. Bus: 3,10, or 11.

White Horse Tavern BERMUDIAN The oldest tavern in St. George is the most popular in Bermuda; it's always jammed with visitors. This white building with green shutters has a restaurant and cedar bar with a terrace jutting into St. George's Harbour. In nice weather, guests usually sit on the terrace. The most popular item on the menu is fish and chips, cooked in the manner of St. David's Island and often overdone. Bermuda fish chowder is good, as are pork chops and grilled wahoo (the local catch). At lunch, there are Tavern burgers, fresh salads, and open-faced sandwiches. The food is passable, but not special. Another horsy tavern, the Black Horse Tavern, serves a more authentic Bermudian cuisine.

Finish off with fresh strudel if you have room. Dress is casual, and there's often enjoyable entertainment.

King's Sq. ℰ **441/297-1838.** Reservations accepted only for groups. Lunch main courses $8–$21; dinner main courses $12–$27.50. MC, V. Restaurant daily 11:30am–4pm and 5:30–10pm. Bar daily 11:30am–1am. Bus: 3, 10, or 11.

INEXPENSIVE

Pasta Pasta, York St., St. George (ℰ **441/297-2927**), is the smaller sibling of Pasta Basta (see "City of Hamilton," earlier in this chapter). The menu, prices, and hours are the same at both restaurants. Bus: 8, 10, or 11.

6

Fun in the Surf & Sun

Although people visit Bermuda mainly to relax on its spectacular pink-sand beaches, the island also offers a wealth of activities, both onshore and off. In fact, Bermuda's sports facilities are better than those on most Caribbean and Bahamian islands.

The most popular outdoor pursuits in Bermuda are tennis and golf, but sailing ranks high, too. You'll find a fair number of tennis courts and renowned golf courses around the island. If you hesitate to pick up a racket or golf club because you've neglected your game, fear not: Your

Bermudian partner, on the court or on the links, would deem it quite improper to remark that your play was anything but superb. If a word of friendly criticism is ever offered, be assured that it will be as gentle as the island's ocean breezes.

Bermuda's waters are the clearest in the western Atlantic. Its reefs; shipwrecks (many in such shallow water that they're even accessible to snorkelers); variety of marine life and coral formations; and underwater grottoes make Bermuda ideal for scuba diving and snorkeling.

1 Beaches

Bermuda is one of the world's leading beach resorts. It boasts miles of pink shoreline, broken only now and then by cliffs that form sheltered coves. Many stretches have shallow, sandy bottoms for some distance out, making them safe for children and nonswimmers. Some beaches (usually the larger ones) have lifeguards; others do not. The Parks Division of the Department for Agriculture and Fisheries supervises public facilities. Hotels and private clubs often have their own beaches and facilities. Even if you're not registered at a hotel or resort, you can often use their beach and facilities if you become a customer by having lunch there.

You'll find dozens of spots for sunbathing, swimming, and beachcombing; here's a list of the island's most famous sands, arranged clockwise beginning with the south-shore beaches closest to the City of Hamilton.

ELBOW BEACH

One of the most consistently popular beaches in Bermuda, Paget Parish's Elbow Beach incorporates almost a mile of (occasionally interrupted) pale-pink sand. Private homes and resort hotels dot the edges. Because protective coral reefs surround it, Elbow Beach is one of the safest on the island—and it's the family favorite. This is also the beach of choice for college students on spring break.

The Bermuda government provides lifeguards as a public service. The **Elbow Beach Hotel** (© **441/236-3535**) offers a variety of facilities and amenities free to guests, but off-limits to others. They include sun chairs, cabanas, changing rooms, showers, rest rooms, and beach towels distributed three times a day by beach attendants who are trained in water safety and lifeguard techniques. The hotel also rents paddleboats and sea kayaks (around $20 per hr. for one kayak,

$25 per hr. for two), and snorkeling equipment ($10 per hr.). Take bus no. 2 or 7 from Hamilton.

ASTWOOD COVE

This Warwick Parish public beach has no problem with overcrowding during most of the year—it's in a remote location, at the bottom of a steep, winding road that intersects with South Shore Road. Many single travelers and couples head here to escape the families that tend to overrun beaches like Elbow in the high season. We like this beach for many reasons, one of them being that its cliffs are home to longtail bird nests. Astwood Beach has public rest rooms but not many other facilities. An added advantage is nearby Astwood Park, a favorite picnic and hiking area. If you like your beaches small and secluded, head here. Take bus no. 2 or 7 from Southampton.

WARWICK LONG BAY

Like Astwood Cove, this is one of the best places for people who want solitude and are trying to escape the family crowds. Unlike the sheltered coves of nearby Chaplin and Horseshoe bays (see below), this popular beach features a half-mile stretch of sand, the longest on the island. It allows for either social interaction or plenty of space to yourself. Against a backdrop of scrubland and low grasses, the beach lies on the southern side of South Shore Park, in Warwick Parish. Despite the frequent winds, the waves are surprisingly small thanks to an off-shore reef. Jutting above the water less than 200 feet from the shore is a jagged coral island that, because of its contoured shape, appears to be floating above the water's foam. There are rest rooms at the beach's western end, plus lots of parking, but no other facilities. There are no lifeguards because the undertow is not very strong.

JOBSON'S COVE

This Warwick Parish beach has the feel of a secret hideaway, thanks to pink sands, gentle waves, and calm waters. Where the horseshoe-shaped bay opens to the ocean, it's only 30 feet wide. Adjacent to the much larger and more popular Warwick Long Bay, it's excellent for snorkeling—the water is about 6 feet deep for a long way out into the bay. There are no buildings along the water, adding to the feeling of seclusion and peace. There are no facilities here, but it's close enough to Warwick Long Bay to walk over and use their restrooms if necessary.

STONEHOLE BAY

Near Jobson's Cove in Warwick Parish, Stonehole Bay is more open and less sheltered, with a sandy shoreline that's studded with big rocks. It's almost never crowded, and wading is safe even though strong waves sometimes make the waters cloudy (so they're less than ideal for snorkeling). There are no facilities at Stonehole Bay.

CHAPLIN BAY

Straddling the boundary between Warwick and Southampton parishes, this small but secluded beach disappears almost completely during storms and exceptionally high tides. Geologists come here to admire the open-air coral barrier that partially separates one half of the beach from the other. Chaplin Bay, like its more famous neighbor, Horseshoe Bay (see below), lies at the southern extremity of South Shore Park. From Chaplin, you can walk over to use the facilities and equipment at Horseshoe, but you'll enjoy more solitude here than at more active Horseshoe Bay. Take bus no. 7 from Hamilton.

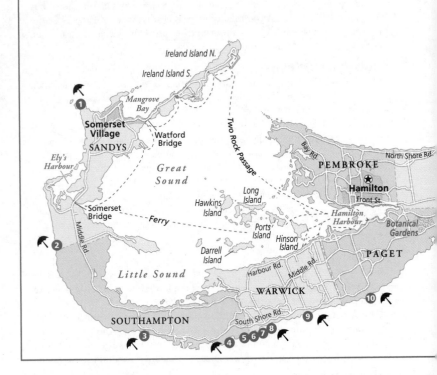

ATLANTIC OCEAN

Ireland Island N.

Ireland Island S.

Mangrove Bay

Somerset Village

Watford Bridge

SANDYS

Ely's Harbour

Great Sound

Two Rock Passage

Bay Rd

North Shore Rd.

PEMBROKE

★ **Hamilton**
Front St.

Long Island

Hawkins Island

Somerset Bridge

Ferry

Ports' Island

Hamilton Harbour

Hinson Island

Botanical Gardens

PAGET

Middle Rd

Darrell Island

Little Sound

Harbour Rd.

Middle Rd.

WARWICK

South Shore Rd.

SOUTHAMPTON

HORSESHOE BAY

With its long, curved strip of pink sand, Horseshoe Bay, on South Shore Road in Southampton Parish, is one of Bermuda's most famous beaches. That means it's likely to be crowded, especially if cruise ships are in port. Although families flock here, Horseshoe Bay isn't the safest beach on Bermuda. Don't be fooled by the seemingly smooth surface; there can be dangerous undercurrents. If you're using the beach after a storm, be especially careful that you don't encounter a Portuguese man-of-war—they often wash up here in greater numbers than elsewhere on the island.

One advantage this beach has over others is the **Horseshoe Bay Beach Cafe** (② **441/238-2651**), which offers changing rooms, toilets, beach-gear rentals, and showers. It also serves snacks and sandwiches from 9am to 5pm daily. A lifeguard is on duty from May to September. *Insider's tip:* When you tire of the crowds at Horseshoe Bay, take one of the little trails that wind through the park nearby; they'll lead you to secluded cove beaches that afford more privacy. Our

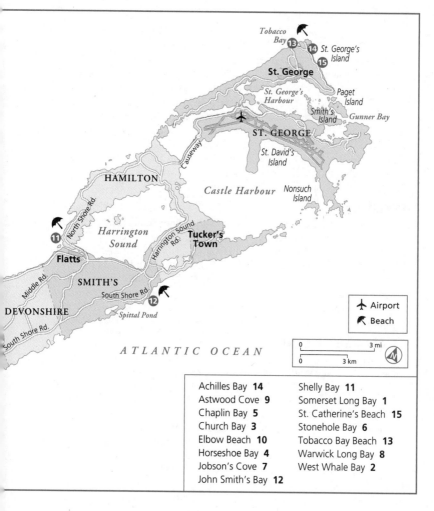

Achilles Bay **14**	Shelly Bay **11**
Astwood Cove **9**	Somerset Long Bay **1**
Chaplin Bay **5**	St. Catherine's Beach **15**
Church Bay **3**	Stonehole Bay **6**
Elbow Beach **10**	Tobacco Bay Beach **13**
Horseshoe Bay **4**	Warwick Long Bay **8**
Jobson's Cove **7**	West Whale Bay **2**
John Smith's Bay **12**	

favorites are Port Royal Cove to the west, and Peel Rock Cove and Wafer Rocks Beach to the east. You might also sneak over to Chaplin Bay to the east (see above). Take bus no. 7 from Hamilton.

CHURCH BAY

This beach off West Side Road lies along Bermuda's southwestern edge, at the point in Southampton Parish where the island hooks off to the northeast. The waves pound the shore mercilessly, but rows of offshore reefs shelter Church Bay. Marine life abounds in the relatively calm waters, much to the delight of snorkelers. If you're just planning to lounge in the sun, this is a great place: The beach offers unusually deep pink sands. There are toilets at the top of the hill near the parking area, but don't expect much in the way of facilities (unless a concession has opened by the time you visit). Rent your snorkeling equipment before you get here. Take bus no. 2 or 7 from Hamilton.

SOMERSET LONG BAY

When offshore storms stir up the waters northwest of Bermuda, the water here is unsafe for swimming. Because its bottom isn't always sandy or of a consistent depth, many people find Somerset Long Bay better suited to beachcombing or long walks than to swimming. Nevertheless, many single travelers favor this beach when they're looking for seclusion. The undeveloped parkland of Sandys Parish shelters it from the rest of the island, and the beach's crescent shape and length—about a quarter mile—make it unusual by Bermudian standards. It has rest rooms and changing facilities. We think this is one of the best places on Bermuda to watch the sunset. A plus is the beach's proximity to the Bermuda Audubon Society Nature Reserve, where you can go for long walks and enjoy moments of solitude—except on weekends, when family picnics abound. Take bus no. 7 from Hamilton, or take Cambridge Road in Sandys Parish.

SHELLY BAY

This beach of abundant pink sand is suitable for both families and those seeking solitude. Because it's not well known, it's unlikely to be crowded, and its calm, shallow basin makes it safe for swimming. Off North Shore Road in Hamilton Parish, Shelly Bay lies in a cove whose encircling peninsula partially shelters it from mid-Atlantic waves. There are trees to sit under when the beach gets too hot, and the beach house rents snorkeling equipment, lounge chairs, beach towels, and other items; there are also public rest rooms. Buses from Hamilton heading east along the north shore stop here.

ST. GEORGE'S ISLAND

This island makes up St. George Parish, the easternmost parish on Bermuda. It's the site of the island's oldest community and the airport, plus lots of low-lying, sun-blasted scrublands. A single bridge (the St. George Causeway) connects this island to the other, more congested islands of the archipelago. St. George's Island's beaches include Achilles Bay, Tobacco Bay, and St. Catherine's Beach (formerly known as the Club Med beach), all of which are sandy, with clean bottoms. The water on the south shore is a bit rougher than the north shore's.

One of the loveliest beaches on St. George's Island is, unfortunately, open only to members of the private Mid-Ocean Golf Club. At **Natural Arches Beach,** near Tucker Town, wave and wind erosion have worn away the limestone to a weird series of jagged rocks. Swimmers sunbathe near striking rock formations, a few of which have formed arches.

TOBACCO BAY

Lovely **Tobacco Bay** is an East End family favorite. It's the most popular beach on St. George's Island, especially among those who come for the day to visit the historic town of St. George. With its broad sands, Tobacco Bay resembles a south-shore beach. Its pale pink sand lies within a sheltering coral-sided cove just a short walk west of Fort St. Catherine and St. Catherine's Beach. The major disadvantage here is that the beach is likely to be overrun with cruise-ship passengers; when they're in port, you may want to seek more secluded beaches such as St. Catherine's. You can get a suntan here and even go for a swim, but don't venture out too far; the currents are dangerously strong.

Look for the **Tobacco Bay Beach House,** Naval Tanks Hill, St. George, which has toilets, changing rooms, showers, and a snack bar. At beachfront kiosks you can rent flotation devices and snorkeling gear by the hour from May to September; stands also sell cold sodas and sandwiches (tuna, grilled cheese and the like, hamburgers, hot dogs, and french fries). Take bus no. 10 or 11 from Hamilton.

JOHN SMITH'S BAY

This is the only public beach in Smith's Parish. It's more popular with residents of Bermuda's eastern end than with visitors, who often don't know about it. It's ideal for those seeking solitude. Long, flat, wide, and rich with pale pink sand, this beach has a lifeguard from May to September. Some shallow areas are ideal for snorkeling. There are toilet and changing facilities. Take bus no. 1 from Hamilton.

2 Snorkeling

Bermuda is known for the gin-clear purity of its waters and for its vast array of coral reefs. If you're ready to explore, all you need is a snorkel, mask, and fins—if you can swim, you can snorkel. A handful of companies can help you; otherwise, you can hit the water on your own.

The best places to go snorkeling are public beaches (see "Beaches," above). Many hotels that are right on the beach will lend or rent you fins, masks, and snorkels, and will advise you of the best sites in your area. You almost never have to travel far.

Die-hard snorkelers, some of whom visit Bermuda every year, prefer **Church Bay** above all other snorkeling spots on Bermuda. It lies on the south shore, west of the Fairmont Southampton Princess Golf Club and Gibbs Hill Lighthouse. The little cove, which seems to be waiting for a movie camera, is carved out of coral cliffs. It's well protected and filled with snug little nooks. Another advantage

---

Moments Walking Underwater

Helmet diving enjoys great popularity in Bermuda. Underwater walkers—clad in helmets equipped with air hoses connected to the surface—stroll along the sandy bottom in water to depths of 10 to 12 feet.

Anybody can take part in this adventure, which has been featured in *Life* magazine. Undersea walks among the coral reefs are safe for anyone from age 5 to 85, even nonswimmers. You can walk underwater wearing your contact lenses or glasses, and you won't even get your hair wet. A guide places a helmet on your shoulders as you climb down the ladder of the boat to begin your walk. An experienced guide conducts the tours. It's as simple was walking through a garden. On your helmet dive, you can feed dozens of rainbow-hued fish, which take food right from your hands. You can also see sponges breathing and coral feeding.

You can arrange your walk with Bermuda's original helmet-diving company by contacting **Bermuda Bell Diving,** 5 North Shore Rd. (P.O. Box FL 281), Flatts FL BX, Bermuda (© **441/292-4434**). A 50-foot boat, *Carioca,* leaves Flatts Village daily at 10am and noon. The underwater wonderland walk costs $50 per adult or $40 for children 5 to 12. Children under 5 aren't allowed. Take bus no. 10 or 11.

⌒Moments A Murky Look at Bermuda's Last Frontier

The Ocean Discovery Centre at the new Bermuda Underwater Exploration Institute, East Broadway (© 441/292-7219), has opened to give visitors an adventure underwater. The highlight of a visit is a simulated dive 12,000 feet to the bottom of the Atlantic. Author Peter Benchley's videotaped commentary adds to the fun of the underwater exploration in and around Bermuda's reefs. You'll learn about newly discovered ocean animals that live in the murky depths during what is called "an in-depth investigation of earth's final frontier." Displays include large murals of sea creatures, artifacts rescued from long-sunken vessels off the coast, and even a scale model of a ship that went to the deep centuries ago. On-site facilities include gift shops, a theater showing films, and La Coquille, a French bistro that specializes, of course, in seafood. Admission is $9.75 for adults, $5 for children; hours are daily 9am to 5pm.

---

is that the reefs are fairly close to land. However, the seas can be rough (as is true anywhere in Bermuda), so we always advise caution.

At the eastern end of the south shore, **John Smith's Bay,** east of Spittal Pond Nature Reserve and Watch Hill Park, is another top spot, especially if your hotel is nearby. Even more convenient, especially for snorkelers staying at St. George or at a hotel near the airport, is **Tobacco Bay,** north of St. George's Golf Club. Another good small snorkeling spot is **West Whale Bay;** it lies along the south shore at the west end of Southampton, west of the Port Royal Golf Course.

Although snorkeling is a year-round pursuit, it's best from May to October. Snorkelers usually wear wet suits in winter, when the water temperature dips into the 60s. The waters of the Atlantic, which can be tempestuous at any time of the year, can be especially rough in winter. Winter snorkelers should head for the more sheltered waters of **Castle Harbour** and **Harrington Sound,** both on the East End, where you'll find bizarre coral formations, underwater caves, grottoes, and schools of brilliantly hued fish.

Some of the best snorkeling sites are accessible only by boat; you can swim to others, but it's usually a long way. If you want to head out on your own, we suggest renting a small boat (see "Sailing," under "More Fun in the Water," below), some of which have glass bottoms. If you rent a boat, the rental company will advise you on where to go and not to go. Countless wrecked boats lie on the many reefs that surround Bermuda. If you're not familiar with Bermuda's waters, you should stay in the sounds, harbors, and bays, especially in Castle Harbour and Harrington Sound. If you want to visit the reefs, it's better to take one of the snorkeling cruises recommended below. The use of snorkeling equipment is included in the prices listed.

Also see "Scuba Diving," below.

Bermuda Water Sports Friendly captain Paul Wakefield offers a glass-bottom snorkel cruise aboard a 60-foot motorized catamaran. The design allows the boat to anchor in very shallow waters, which is ideal for novices or unsure swimmers. The cost—around $40 for a 3½-hour cruise—includes free use of snorkeling equipment and the expertise of a crew that really knows the marine life of Bermuda's offshore reefs. There's a cash bar and a shower on board.

St. George's Island. © 441/293-2640. Booking mid-Apr to Oct daily 9am–9pm. Bus: 10 or 11.

Bermuda Water Tours Ltd. Capt. Butch offers two options. The shorter cruise, 2 hours on a glass-bottom boat, costs $30 and departs daily at 10am. The 3-hour glass-bottom-boat cruise includes time for snorkeling; it costs $45 and departs daily at 1:15pm.

Tours leave from the docks near Hamilton's Ferry Terminal. © **441/236-1500.** Booking 24 hrs. Bus: 1, 2, 10, or 11.

Salt Kettle Yacht Charters Salt Kettle offers private sailing charters on a 55 foot sloop, the luxury yacht *Bright Star.* The outfitter books charters on its 35-foot motorized *Magic Carpet* for sightseeing or snorkeling among the wrecks and reefs. Charters for 8 to 18 people cost $420 for 3 hours, $520 for 4 hours, and $740 for 6 hours.

Salt Kettle, Paget Parish. © **441/236-4863.** Booking 24 hrs. Ferry from Hamilton every 30 min.

3 Scuba Diving

Diving in Bermuda is great for novices, who can learn the fundamentals and go diving in 20 to 25 feet of water on the same day as their first lesson. In general, Bermuda's reefs are still healthy despite talk about dwindling fish and dying coral formations. On occasion, in addition to the rainbow-hued schools of fish, you may even find yourself swimming with a barracuda.

Although scuba fanatics dive all year, the best diving months are May to October. The sea is the most tranquil at that time, and the water temperature is moderate—it averages 62°F in the spring and fall, 83°F in summer.

Weather permitting, scuba schools function daily. Fully licensed scuba instructors oversee all dives. Most dives are conducted from a 40-foot boat, and outfitters cover a wide range of dive sites. Night dives and certifications are also available.

All dive shops display a map of wreck sites that you can visit—there are nearly 40 in all, the oldest of which dates to the 17th century. Although locals believe there may be some 300 wrecks, the mapped sites are the best known and in the best condition. Dive depths at these sites run 25 to 85 feet. Inexperienced divers may want to stick to the wreck sites off the western coast, which tend to be in shallower waters—about 32 feet or less. These shallow wreck sites are popular with snorkelers as well.

Many hotels have their own water-sports equipment. If yours doesn't, the outfitters below rent equipment.

Note: Spearfishing is not allowed within 1 mile of any shore, and spear guns are not permitted in Bermuda.

Blue Water Divers & Watersports Ltd. Bermuda's oldest and largest full-service scuba-diving operation offers introductory lessons and half-day dives for $95. Daily one- and two-tank dive trips cost $50 and $75, respectively. Snorkeling trips are $40 per half day. Full certification courses are available through PADI, NAUI, and SSI. All equipment is provided, and reservations are required. In 2002, the outfitter added something new in the form of underwater scooters called DPVs or "diver propulsion vehicles." This exciting new vehicle takes adventurers through underwater caves and canyons, perhaps by a shipwreck from long ago.

Robinson's Marina, Southampton. © **441/234-1034.** Daily 9am–5pm. Bus: 6 or 7.

Daily Dives This outfitter is a year-round operation, specializing in wreck diving. It arranges daily dives at 8:30am and 1:30pm. The "Discover Scuba" course costs $95 for 3½ hours. The popular reef wreck dive at various depths costs $75 for 3 hours. A two-tank dive may appeal to experienced divers who want to see wrecks and reefs; it lasts 4½ hours and costs $75. Night dives, for experienced divers only, run $60 for 2 to 3 hours. Snorkeling trips can be arranged, and underwater cameras are available for rent to scuba divers and snorkelers for $32.

Darrells Wharf, Harbour Rd., Paget Parish. ✆ **441/236-6339.**

Fantasea Diving This outfitter is known for its daily two-tank wreck and reef dives costing $70, although you can also go out on a one-tank dive for $50. A resort course lesson plus dive is $91. It's also possible to go along just to snorkel off the boat, costing $38. A one-tank night dive, increasing in popularity, costs $60. The company has two fully equipped, custom-built fiberglass dive boats with the latest approved safety gear. This is a NAUI- and PADI-affiliated dive center. Prices do not include equipment rentals.

At the Sonesta Beach Resort, South Shore Rd., Southampton. ✆ **441/238-1833.** Call a day in advance. Daily 8:30am–6pm. Closed 2 weeks in Feb. or Mar. Bus: 7.

Nautilus Diving Ltd. This is one of the island's leading dive operators. It offers a popular "Discover Scuba" resort course ($99 for 3 hr.) that begins daily at 1:30pm. All dives are from a 40-foot boat. The one-tank dive ($60) goes to reef or wreck sites. A two-tank dive, including a view of a shipwreck and the exploration of a reef in 25 to 30 feet of water, costs $80 (equipment not included). This is a PADI, five-star center.

At The Fairmont Southampton Princess, 101 South Shore Rd., Southampton Parish; and The Fairmont Hamilton Princess, 76 Pitts Bay Rd., Pembroke Parish. ✆ **441/238-2332** or 441/295-9485. Daily 8am–6pm.

4 More Fun in the Water

FISHING

Bermuda is one of the world's finest destinations for anglers, especially in light-tackle fishing. Blue marlin catches have increased dramatically in recent years, and Bermuda can add bill fishing to its already enviable reputation. Fishing is a year-round sport, but it's best from May to November. No license is required.

You can obtain fishing information from the International Game Fish Association's representatives for Bermuda: **Keith Winter** at **441/292-7131** or **John Barnes** at **441/234-2070.** They can only be reached at home in the evening.

DEEP-SEA FISHING

Wahoo, amberjack, blue marlin, white marlin, dolphin, tuna, and other varieties of fish call Bermuda's warm waters home. A number of island outfitters offer the equipment to help you fish for them; this is our favorite:

Bermuda Sportsfishing The David De Silva family runs Bermuda Sportsfishing, which has been in business for many years. They charge $650 for a half day of fishing and $900 to $1,200 for a full day, depending on the size of the boat. Boats range from 35 to 46 feet.

Creek View House, 8 Tulo Lane, Pembroke Parish HM 02, Bermuda. ☎ 441/295-2370. Daily 7am–10pm. Bus: 1, 2, 10, or 11.

REEF FISHING

Three major reef banks lie off Bermuda, and they're likely to yield such catches as greater amberjack, almaco jack, great barracuda, little tunny, Bermuda chub, gray snapper, yellowtail snapper, and assorted bottom fish. The closest one

---

Tips **Anglers Aweigh: How to Make Your Big Catch
a Winning One**

The **Bermuda Game Fishing Tournament** is open to any angler who takes
the time and trouble to fill out the tournament application when he or
she catches a really big fish. No special license is required, but your catch
must be weighed and three witnesses must sign an affidavit attesting to
its weight. Special prizes are awarded each year for top catches of 17
species of game fish. For more information on registering the ones that
didn't get away, contact the **Bermuda Department of Tourism,** Global
House, 43 Church St., Hamilton HM 12, Bermuda (① **441/292-0023**).

---

begins about a half mile offshore and stretches for nearly 5 miles. The Chal-
lenger Bank is about 14 miles offshore, and Argus Bank is about 30 miles distant. The farther out you go, the more likely you are to turn up larger fish.

Several companies offer half- or full-day charters. Arrangements can also be
made through Bermuda Sportsfishing (see "Deep-Sea Fishing," above).

SHORE FISHING

Shore fishing turns up such catches as bonefish, palometa (pompano), gray
snapper, and great barracuda. Locals and most visitors prefer shore fishing at
Spring Benny's Bay or West Whale Bay; Great Sound and St. George's Harbour
are other promising grounds. The activities director at your hotel can help make
fishing arrangements for you.

PARASAILING

Bermuda Island Parasail Company This outfitter features harness-style
parasail rides that last 7 to 8 minutes. Adults pay $50; children under 12, $35.
Tandem rides go for $80. Dry takeoff and landing are on the *Nordic 28;* you'll
parasail above Hamilton Harbour.

Ordnance Island, St. George. ① **441/232-2871**. Apr–Oct daily 9am–5pm (7pm in summer).

St. George's Parasail Water Sports Ltd.   Parasailers soar above St. George's
Harbour after taking off from the *Krant Craft* deck. Rides are single or tandem
and cost $50 per person for adults, $35 for children under 12. Rides last approximately 8 to 10 minutes.

Somers Wharf, St. George. ① **441/297-1542**. Apr–Oct Mon–Fri 9am–6pm, Sat 11am–5pm.

Skyrider Bermuda Ltd.   Skyrider takes a maximum of eight passengers into
the Great Sound and north-shore area for two-person chair parasail rides. The
8- to 10-minute ride costs $45 for adults, $32 for children under 12. Boat passengers who do not parasail pay $45.

Royal Naval Dockyard, Sandys Parish. ① **441/234-3019**. Apr–Oct Tues–Sun 10am–5pm.

SAILING

Bermuda is one of the world's sailing capitals. Sail-yourself boats are available to
rent for 2, 4 (half day), and 8 (full day) hours. A number of places charter yachts
with licensed skippers.

Bermuda Caribbean Yacht Charter   The owner of the 35-foot ketch *Selina
King,* Hal White, operates from April to November and offers keen insight on

the islands. He charges $350 for a half day (10am–1pm or 1:30–4:30pm) or $600 for a full day for six passengers. Each extra person pays $20.

2A Light House Rd., Southampton Parish. ☎ **441/238-8578.** Daily 9am–5pm. Bus: 7 or 8.

Blue Hole Water Sports   This outfitter rents Windsurfers or Sunfish for $25 for the first hour, $10 for each additional hour. Sun Cats are available for $35 per hour. A wide range of other equipment is on hand, including single and double kayaks.

Grotto Bay Beach Hotel, 11 Blue Hole Hill, Hamilton Parish. ☎ **441/293-2915.** Daily 8:30am–5:30pm. Bus: 1, 3, 10, or 11.

Somerset Bridge Watersports   Somerset Bridge is the best outlet for renting Boston whalers for islandhopping on your own. A 13-foot Boston whaler (25 or 30 hp) carries four and costs $65 for 2 hours, $100 for 4 hours, and $165 for 8 hours. Somerset provides lots of extras, such as canopies, special maps, a ladder, a viewing box, and a fish and coral ID card. "Jet Ski Adventures" cost $90 for one, $115 for two, and $135 for three people. The craft reach speeds of up to 50 mph. There may be a fee for gas ($10–$20).

Somerset Bridge, Ely's Harbour, Sandys Parish. ☎ **441/234-0914.** Daily 8am–sunset.

Pompano Beach Watersports Centre   This is one of the island's best outfitters, mainly because of its variety of modern boats. Windsurfers, which hold one novice or experienced passenger, rent for $12 per hour or $36 for 4 hours. One or two people can rent a Sunfish sailboat or a Dolphin paddleboat. Single-person kayaks go for $10 for 1 hour, $30 for 4 hours. Two-person Sun Cats, which travel 6 mph and look like motorized lawn chairs, go for $35 per hour or $25 per half hour.

36 Pompano Beach Rd., Southampton Parish. ☎ **441/234-0222.** May to late Oct daily 10am–6pm.

WATER-SKIING

You can water-ski in the protected waters of Hamilton Harbour, Great Sound, Castle Harbour, Mangrove Bay, Spanish Point, Ferry Reach, Ely's Harbour, Riddells Bay, and Harrington Sound. May to September, when the waters are usually calm, is the best time for water-skiing. Bermuda law requires that a licensed skipper take water-skiers out. Only a few boat operators handle this sport, and charges fluctuate with fuel costs. Rates include the boat, skis, safety belts, and usually an instructor. Hotels and guesthouses can assist with arrangements.

Bermuda Waterski Centre   Up to five people can water-ski from a specially designed Ski Nautique. Lessons are also available. The charge for a party of any size (not per person) is $40 for a 15-minute session, $70 for a 30-minute session, and $120 for a 60-minute session.

Robinson's Marina, Somerset Bridge, Sandys Parish. & 441/234-3354. May–Sept daily 8am–7:30pm. Bus: 6 or 7.

---

5 Where to Play Some of the World's Best Golf

Since the island's first course was laid out in 1922, golf has been one of Bermuda's most popular sports. You can play year-round, but spring, fall, and early winter offer the best seaside conditions. You must arrange tee times at any of the island's eight courses in advance through your guesthouse or hotel. Women's and men's clubs (right- and left-handed) are available at each course, and most leading stores in Bermuda sell golf balls. Generally speaking, children

CENTRAL AMERICA   MIDDLE AMERICA

AT&T Direct® Service

The easy way to call home from anywhere.

Global
connection
with the AT&T
Network

AT&T
direct
service

or the easy way to call home, take the attached wallet guide.

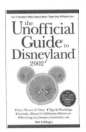
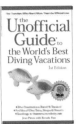
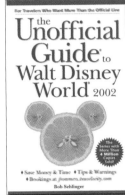

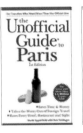
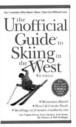
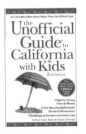
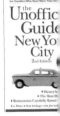

are not welcome on golf courses; definitely check in advance if you have any underage duffers in your party.

The **Tucker's Point Club** is one of the most scenic courses on the island; the **Port Royal** course, designed by Robert Trent Jones, is a challenge. Two famous courses—the **Mid Ocean Club** at Tucker's Town and the **Riddells Bay Golf and Country Club**—are private, and require introduction by a member before you can play. Certain luxury hotels can sometimes secure playing privileges at the Riddells Bay course. One of the most photographed courses on Bermuda is the **Southampton Princess Golf Club,** where rolling hills and flowering shrubs add to the players' enjoyment.

The golf courses listed below that are part of hotel complexes permit nonguests to use their facilities. All of these golf courses have pros and offer lessons.

Top players participate in tournaments throughout the year. For information, contact the **Bermuda Golf Association,** P.O. Box HM 433, Hamilton HM BX, Bermuda (© **441/238-1367**).

Belmont Golf & Country Club   Scotsman Emmett Devereux designed this course in 1923, and its layout has long been a challenge to golfers. The golfing magazines write of its par-5 11th hole, with a severe dogleg left and blind tee shot. It's sometimes difficult to finish uphill at number 18. Crystal caves under the turf sometimes cause the ball to roll unpredictably. In spite of these disadvantages, golf pros recommend the Belmont for beginners; the first hole is said to be "confidence building." It's estimated that with a 9 or 10 handicap, golfers will shoot in the 70s at Belmont—but there are no guarantees. Most of the course is inland; unlike many golf courses in Bermuda, this one provides few views of the Atlantic.

Greens fees (which include golf carts) are $86 Monday to Friday, $91 weekends. A full set of clubs rents for $28. The dress code requires shirts with collars. Between Harbour and Middle rds., Warwick Parish. © **441/236-6400.** Mon–Fri 8am–5pm, Sat–Sun 7am–5pm. Holes: 18. Par: 70. Length: 5,777 yds. Ferry from Hamilton.

Ocean View Golf Course   In the 1950s, this was a club for African Bermudians; later, as other clubs started to admit black players, the course fell into disrepair. Its reputation for spotty maintenance lives on despite a $2 million renovation that vastly improved the course; it's nicer than many people think it is. In the center of Bermuda in Devonshire Parish, the course offers panoramic views of the ocean from many of its elevated tees. Many golfers consider the terrain unpredictable; that, combined with rambling hills, makes the course more challenging than it appears. A few holes have as many as six tees. Winds from the Great Sound can have a greater effect on your score than you might think. The green on the 177-yard, par-3 5th hole has been cut into the coral hillside; because it's draped with semitropical vines, golfers sometimes have the eerie feeling that they're hitting the ball into a cave.

On weekdays, this course tends to be the least crowded on Bermuda. Greens fees are $38 weekdays, rising to $40 on weekends, with carts costing $10. Golf shoes are mandatory and can be rented for $8. Dress code: shirts with collars; no jeans or "short shorts."

2 Barkers Hill Rd., Devonshire Parish. © **441/295-9092.** Daily 7:30am–6:30pm. Holes: 9. Par: 35. Length: 2,940 yds. Bus: 2.

Port Royal Golf Course   Famed golf architect Robert Trent Jones designed this government-owned and -operated course, which lies along the ocean. Jack

Nicklaus might be found at the famous 16th hole, a favorite for photo layouts in golf magazines. The 15th and 16th holes ring the craggy cliffs around Whale Bay; sometimes winds from the Atlantic taunt the golf balls hit from these tees. The 7th and 8th holes are a dogleg par-5 and a windy par-3, respectively.

Port Royal is so popular that some avid golfers reserve starting times a year in advance. Greens fees for 18 holes are $82 Monday to Friday, $92 on weekends. There are no caddies. A full set of clubs rents for $25, and handcarts rent for $9. Gas-powered carts go for $20. The clubhouse, which overlooks the ocean and the 9th and 18th greens, contains a bar and a restaurant that serves breakfast, lunch, and dinner. Dress code: shirts with collars.

Middle Rd., Southampton Parish. ✆ 441/234-0974. Daily 7:30am–6:30pm. Holes: 18. Par: 71. Length: 6,565 yds. Bus: 7 or 8.

Fairmont Southampton Princess Golf Club   On the grounds of one of the most luxurious hotels on Bermuda, this course occupies not only the loftiest but also one of the most scenic settings on the island. Elevated tees, strategically

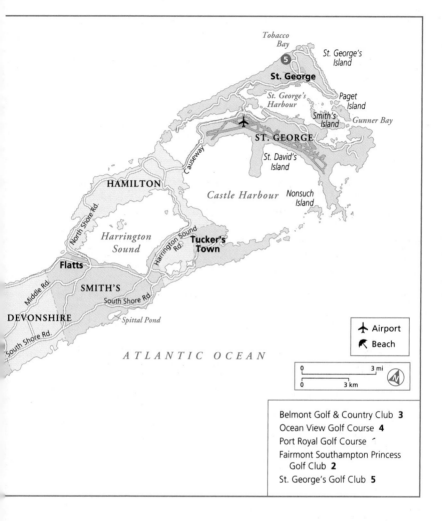

✈	Airport
⚑	Beach

Belmont Golf & Country Club **3**
Ocean View Golf Course **4**
Port Royal Golf Course **˄**
Fairmont Southampton Princess
  Golf Club **2**
St. George's Golf Club **5**

placed bunkers, and plenty of water hazards make it a challenge; golfers have been known to use every club in their bags when the wind blows in from the Atlantic. Against the backdrop of the Gibbs Hill Lighthouse, the 16th hole sits in a cup ringed by flowering bushes. The vertical drop on the 1st and 2nd holes is almost 200 feet. Even experienced golfers like to "break in" on this course before taking on some of Bermuda's more challenging ones. This well-irrigated course often is green when some others suffer a summer brownout.

Greens fees are $59 for 18 holes for hotel guests, $65 for visitors. There are no caddies. Club rental is $25. Dress code: shirts with collars; no bathing suits or cutoffs.

101 South Shore Rd., Southampton Parish. ☏ **441/239-6952**. Daily 7am–sunset. Holes: 18. Par: 54. Length: 2,684 yds. Bus: 7 or 8.

St. George's Golf Club Redesigned by Robert Trent Jones, this is the newest of the Bermuda government's courses. On a headland at the northeastern tip of the island, it's within walking distance of St. George. Links run along the hillsides, providing panoramic vistas of the ocean; the winds off the water will significantly affect your game. On some par-3s, players need everything from a 9 iron to a driver to reach the green. The greens are the smallest on the island; some appear to be no more than 24 feet across. The abundant salt air makes them slick.

This course isn't usually crowded at midweek. Greens fees for 18 holes are $49. There are no caddies. A full set of clubs rents for $20; gas golf carts go for $20 per person, handcarts for $7. Dress code: Bermuda-length shorts or slacks with a collared shirt; no jeans.

1 Park Rd., St. George Parish. (C) 441/297-8067. Apr–Oct Mon–Fri 7:45am–6pm; off-season Mon–Fri 7:45am–5:30pm. Holes: 18. Par: 62. Length: 4,043 yds. Bus: 6, 8, 10, or 11.

6 Other Outdoor Pursuits: Biking, Horseback Riding & Tennis

BIKING

With a year-round average temperature of 70°F, Bermuda is often ideal for bicycling. Not only is biking a great way to have fun and stay in shape, but it allows you to take a hands-on approach to your sightseeing. Although many tourism brochures extol the glories of bicycling on Bermuda, the roads are not suitable for beginners. Think carefully and ask around when you're deciding where you or your children can ride safely and comfortably.

Most roadways are well paved and maintained. Although the island's speed limit is 20 mph for all vehicles, exercise caution when riding a bike or scooter. The roads are narrow and winding, and car traffic, especially during the day, tends to be heavy. Most drivers are considerate of cyclists, but a car may approach without warning, because the government discourages unnecessary horn honking. You might even be overtaken by fellow cyclists—bicycle racing is one of the most popular local sports.

Much of the island's terrain consists of flat stretches, although the hills provide what the locals call "challenges." Some climbs are steep, especially on roads that run north and south. South Shore Road through Southampton and Warwick parishes often leaves bikers huffing and puffing.

RENTING A BIKE

Push bikes (or pedal bikes), the term Bermudians use to distinguish bicycles from mopeds, are a popular form of transportation. You can rent a bicycle by the hour, by the day, or for your entire stay. For information about cycle and scooter rentals, see "Getting Around," in chapter 3, "Getting to Know Bermuda." All of the recommended shops also rent bicycles. Many hotels have bicycles for guests' use, with or without a fee. Rentals generally cost $20 for the first day, plus $5 for each additional day. Three- and ten-speed bikes are usually available. It's always a good idea to call as far in advance as possible, because demand is great, especially from April to October.

WHERE TO BIKE ON BERMUDA

Only the hardiest cyclists set out to traverse the 21-mile length of Bermuda in 1 day. For most people, it's far better to focus on smaller sections at different times. So, decide what interests you parish by parish, and proceed from there. To save time, you can take your bike aboard various ferries (it's free), then begin cycling.

A good choice for beginning riders is the **Bermuda Railway Trail** (see below). Some of the most interesting cycling trails are in **Devonshire and Smith's parishes.** The hills throughout these areas guarantee that you'll get your exercise

---

Finds   Exploring Bermuda's Natural Wonderlands

The National Trust in Bermuda has wisely protected the island's nature reserves. If you play by the rules—that is, don't disturb animal life or take plant life for a souvenir—you can explore many of these natural wonderlands. If you enjoy nature trails, they're one of the most rewarding reasons to visit Bermuda.

The best and largest sanctuary is **Spittal Pond Nature Reserve** in Smith's Parish. Birders visit the reserve—especially from September to April—to see herons, ducks, flamingos, terns, and many migratory fowl (which can't be seen after Mar). This 60-acre untamed seaside park is always open to the public with no admission charge. **The Department of Parks** (© 441/236-4201) offers free guided tours. Tours are offered primarily from November to May; call for schedules and additional information.

The island abounds with other places of natural wonder. Craggy formations shaped over the centuries out of limestone and coral dot the beaches along the southern coast, with towering cliffs forming a backdrop. The best of these is **Natural Arches,** one of the most photographed sights in Bermuda. Two limestone arches, which took nature centuries to carve, rise 35 feet above the beach. Natural Arches is signposted almost at the end of South Shore Road, directing you to Castle Harbour Beach.

---

for the day, and the beautiful landscapes make your effort worthwhile. **Spittal Pond,** a wildlife sanctuary with bike paths running along seaside cliffs, is one of the most rewarding destinations. Stop by a cycle shop for a trail map and some advice. Nearly all bike shops owners know Bermuda intimately and will mark up a map for you or give you any special guidance you need.

If you're a real demon on a bike, you can go farther west for the challenge of pumping up to **Gibbs Hill Lighthouse,** the oldest cast-iron lighthouse in the world. The panoramic view from the foot of the lighthouse is well worth the effort.

If you'd like to combine a picnic with your bicycle outing, head for **Sandys Parish.** First cross Somerset Bridge, the smallest drawbridge in the world, then pedal along Somerset Road to Fort Scaur Park. There you can relax and admire the view of Ely's Harbour while enjoying your picnic.

THE BERMUDA RAILWAY TRAIL   Another interesting bicycle option is the **Bermuda Railway Trail** (see p. 190 in chapter 8, "Island Strolls," for more information), which is restricted to bicyclists and pedestrians. The Railway Trail consists of seven sections, each with its own character. You can decide how much of the trail you'd like to cover in 1 day, and which sections to focus on. Pick up a copy of *Bermuda Railway Trail Guide,* available at the Bermuda Department of Tourism in Hamilton or the Visitors Service Bureaus in Hamilton and St. George, to help you plan your route.

HORSEBACK RIDING

Spicelands Riding Centre   This stable offers trail rides for $50 per person hourly. The regularly scheduled 1-hour jaunts begin at 7am, 9am, and 10:30am

Moments **For Birders in Pursuit of the Fork-Tailed Flycatcher**

Bermuda has a group of bird-watching enthusiasts, but not many organized tours. Visiting bird watchers can arrange tours with local enthusiasts, who can greatly increase the chance of seeing some rare birds. (Bermuda is home to some 40 species of eastern warblers alone.) The island's vast array of feathered friends includes everything from the heron to the fork-tailed flycatcher, and even the rare cahow, a gray-and-white petrel.

Visiting birders should pick up a copy of David Wingate's *Check List and Guide to the Birds of Bermuda* or Eric Amos's *A Guide to the Birds of Bermuda,* both available at local bookstores. You might also want to contact **David Wingate** (© **441/297-2623**), a conservation officer for the Bermuda government, or **Eric Amos** (© **441/297-2354**), a bird painter. They occasionally, but not always, give advice over the phone about the island's best retreats, walkways, and hideaways.

You can also contact the **Bermuda Audubon Society,** P.O. Box HM 1328, Hamilton HM FX, Bermuda (© **441/297-2623**), for information about organized field trips that might be scheduled while you're on Bermuda.

The trail begins in Sandys Parish, where the Gilbert Nature Reserve and the Heydon Trust Estate provide contrasting views of rural Bermuda. The first part of the trail ends at Somerset Bridge.

The second section begins as you cross into Southampton Parish, where you'll get a sense of 19th-century Bermudian life. In Southampton, you'll find much of Bermuda's 500 acres of arable land, as well as examples of traditional manor houses.

As it enters Warwick Parish, the trail skirts Little Sound, then passes through an allspice forest. Toward the center of the island, traditional old houses start to dot the West End's woodlands and fields. Some houses still have domed water tanks and old stone butteries.

The trail then rises above Paget Marsh, a National Trust Nature Reserve, which includes Bermuda's oldest palmetto forest and a wide variety of bird life. The tour of Paget Parish ends with a ride through a 450-foot-long railway tunnel, partially covered with the thick roots of a rubber tree.

Picking up beyond the City of Hamilton, the trail leads to Palmetto House, built in the shape of a cross and virtually unchanged since the 1700s.

After traversing a cricket pitch (field) while it takes you from Devonshire into Hamilton Parish, the trail then edges the wild coastline along Bailey's Bay.

The final section of the trail is in St. George Parish, where the windswept coast is rocky and rugged. The mariner's landmark of Sugarloaf Hill offers a panoramic seascape and views of the historic seafaring town of St. George.

daily year-round. On spring, summer, and fall weekends, there are also rides at 3 and 5:30pm. Book at least 1 day ahead, calling between 9am and 5pm.

Middle Rd., Warwick Parish. ✆ 441/238-8212. Bus: 8.

TENNIS

Nearly all the big hotels, and many of the smaller ones, have courts, most of which can be lit for night play. Pack your tennis clothing and sneakers, because a tennis outfit (which no longer needs to be white) may be required.

Each of the facilities listed below has a tennis pro on duty, and lessons can be arranged. All rent racquets and sell balls.

Elbow Beach Hotel   The Elbow Beach Hotel has five LayKold courts (one for lessons only). Hotel guests play free. Lessons cost $30 for 30 minutes, $60 for 1 hour. Racquets can be rented for $5, and balls are $6 per can of three.

60 South Shore Rd., Paget Parish. ✆ 441/236-3535. Call for bookings daily 9am–5pm. Bus: 1, 2, or 7.

The Fairmont Southampton Princess   This resort has Bermuda's largest tennis court layout, with 11 Plexipave courts, of which three are lit for night play. Hotel guests pay $12 per hour, nonguests $14 per hour. Racquets rent for $6 per hour, balls cost $6 per can, and court lighting at night, lasting until 10:30pm, is $4.

101 South Shore Rd., Southampton Parish. ✆ 441/238-8000. Daily 8am–7pm (until 6pm in winter). Bus: 7 or 8.

Government Tennis Stadium   There are three clay and five Plexicushion courts here. Charges to play are $8 per adult, $4 per junior. Playing at night on one of the three lit courts costs $8 extra. Tennis attire is mandatory. Racquets rent for $5 per day; balls cost $6 per can.

Cedar Ave., Pembroke Parish. ✆ 441/292-0105 to reserve a court or arrange lessons. Mon–Fri 8am–10pm, Sat–Sun 8am–7pm. Bus: 1, 2, 10, or 11.

Grotto Bay Beach Club   This resort across from the airport has some of the best tennis courts on the island. The 21-acre property offers four courts, two of which are well lit for night games. Hotel guests pay $10 for daytime play, $12 for night play; nonguests pay $12 and $15, respectively. The hotel also rents rackets ($6) and tennis balls ($6) at the on-site pro shop.

11 Blue Hole Hill, Hamilton. ✆ 441/293-8333. Daily 24 hours. Bus: 1, 3, 10, or 11.

7 Spectator Sports

In this tradition-bound British colony, the most popular spectator sports are cricket, soccer, field hockey, and the not-terribly-genteel game of rugby. As you might expect, boating, yachting, and sailing are also popular. The Bermuda Department of Tourism can provide dates and venues for upcoming events; see "Visitor Information," in chapter 2, "Planning Your Trip to Bermuda," for contact information before you go, and "Orienting Yourself: The Lay of the Land," in chapter 3, "Getting to Know Bermuda," for information once you've arrived. Also see the "Bermuda Calendar of Events," in chapter 2, "Planning Your Trip to Bermuda."

CRICKET

Far more Bermudians than you might suspect have memorized this terribly British sport's arcane rules. If you arrive in midsummer (the game's high season), you'll probably see several regional teams practicing on cricket fields throughout the island. Each match includes enough pageantry to remind participants of the game's imperial antecedents and enough conviviality (picnics, socializing, and chitchat among the spectators) to give you a real feel for Bermuda.

The **Cup Match Cricket Festival** is Bermuda's most passionately watched cricket event, with hundreds of viewers turning out to cheer on family members and friends. Conducted during late July or early August, it pairs Bermuda-based teams against one another in ways that read like a geography lesson to the island itself. The event usually occurs at the headquarters of two of the island's approximately 30 cricket teams, either the **St. George's Cricket Club,** Willington Slip Road (© **441/297-0374**), or the **Somerset Cricket Club,** Broome Street off Somerset Road (© **441/234-0327**). Buy your tickets at the gate on the day of each event, and expect to pay between $12 and $15 per ticket for entrance to a long-standing Bermuda tradition. For more information, contact the **Bermuda Tourist Office** (© **441/292-0023**).

FIELD HOCKEY

One of the great women's competitive sports is field hockey, played with curved wooden mallets. Each team—usually clad in knee socks and shorts or kilts—tries to drive a small white ball into the opposing team's net. Several teams compete against one another on Sunday afternoons between October and April at the **National Sports Club,** Middle Road, Devonshire Parish (© **441/ 236-6994**). Admission is usually free.

GOLF TOURNAMENTS

Bermuda offers some of the finest golfing terrain in the world. Part of this is because of the climate, which supports lush driving ranges and putting greens. In addition, the ever-present golfers play at surprisingly high levels. Golf tournaments are held throughout the year, culminating in the annual, much-publicized **Bermuda Open** at the Port Royal Golf Course in early October. Amateurs and professionals are welcome to vie for one of the most sought-after golfing prizes in the world. For information or an application, contact the secretary of the Bermuda Golf Association (© **441/238-1367;** fax 441/238-0983).

HORSE RACING & EQUESTRIAN COMPETITIONS

Contact the **National Equestrian Centre,** Vesey Street, Devonshire Parish (© **441/234-0485**), for information about upcoming events. From September to Easter, harness races take place about twice a month.

A major equestrian event is in October: the FEI/Samsung Dressage Competition and Show-Jumping. Details are available from the **Bermuda Equestrian Federation,** P.O. Box DV 583, Devonshire DV BX, Bermuda (© and fax **441/ 234-0485**). If you can't reach the federation on the phone (which is quite likely), ask for information at the tourist office, or check the local newspaper.

RUGBY

A blend of American-style football and European soccer, this rough-and-tumble game has many Bermudian fans; the island has several hotly competitive teams. Rugby players—completely devoid of protective padding—seem to revel in their violent sport. The Easter Rugby Classic attracts teams from throughout the British Commonwealth. It's the final event in the island's rugby season, which runs from September to April. The usual venue for rugby is the **National Sports Club,** Middle Road, Devonshire Parish (© **441/236-6994**).

SOCCER

Bermudians view soccer as an important part of elementary education and actively encourage children and teenagers to participate. In early April, teams from countries around the Atlantic and Caribbean compete in three age divisions for the Diadora Youth Soccer Cup. Games are held on various fields throughout the island. More accessible to spectators at other times are the many high school games held regularly throughout the year.

YACHTING

Bermuda capitalizes on its geographical position in the mid-Atlantic to lure the yachting crowd. The racing season runs from March to November, with most races scheduled on weekends in the relatively calm waters of Bermuda's Great Sound. The best land vantage points include Spanish Point, the islands northeast of Somerset, and Hamilton Harbour—but shifting sightlines can make it confusing to watch races from land. Even better views are available from the decks of privately owned boats that anchor near the edge of the racecourse. Although the carefully choreographed regattas might be confusing to newcomers, the sight of a fleet of racing craft with spinnakers and pennants aloft is always exciting.

In late June, Bermuda is the final destination in two of the most important annual yacht races: the **Annapolis–Bermuda Race** and the even more prestigious **Newport–Bermuda Race.** Both provide enough visual distraction and maritime pageantry to keep you enthralled. Participating yachts range from 30 to 100 feet in length, and their skippers are said to be among the most dedicated in the world.

Around Halloween, the autumn winds propel dozens of less exotic racing craft through the waters of the Great Sound. They compete in a series of one-on-one playoffs for the **King Edward VII Gold Cup International Match Racing Tournament.**

The island's yachting events are by no means limited to international competitions. Bermuda's sheltered bays and windswept open seas provide year-round enticement for anyone who has ever wanted to experience the thrill of a snapping jib and taut mainsail. See "Sailing," under "More Fun in the Water," above, for details on yacht charters.

7

Seeing the Sights

Even though a large number of people live on this small island, you should never feel crowded. There are no billboards or neon signs, and relatively few cars to spoil the rolling countryside. Most houses seem to fit quite naturally into the landscape.

Bermuda consists of nine parishes (or counties). From west to east, they are: Sandys (pronounced "sands"), Southampton, Warwick, Paget (which has the greatest concentration of hotels), Pembroke (home to the City of Hamilton), Devonshire, Smith's, Hamilton (not to be confused with the City of Hamilton), and St. George, which includes the U.S. naval air base and the little island of St. David's. In the early days, these districts, which encompass about 21 square miles, were called "tribes." By the beginning of the 18th century, the term *Tribe Road* referred to the boundaries between parishes. Pembroke, which encloses the capital city of Hamilton, is the largest parish in population; St. George has the largest land area.

Because of its small size, it's easy to get to know the island parish by parish. There's much to see, whether you travel by bike, ferry, bus, or taxi. You'll need plenty of time, though, because the pace is slow. Cars and other motorized vehicles, such as mopeds, must observe the maximum speed of 15 mph in Hamilton and St. George, 20 mph in the countryside. The speed limits are rigidly enforced, and there are severe penalties for violations.

If you're visiting for the first time, you'll want to follow the tourist route, basically the equivalent of visiting New York and seeing the Statue of Liberty and the Empire State Building: the Aquarium, Devil's Hole, and cruise-boat outings. For visitors on a second, third, or fourth visit to Bermuda, a different experience unfolds. Once you've done all the "must-sees," you'll want to walk around and make discoveries on your own. The best parishes for walking are Somerset, St. George, and Hamilton.

But don't fill your days with too much structured sightseeing. You'll want time to lounge on the beach and play in the water or hit the links, and to enjoy moments like sitting by the harbor in the late afternoon, enjoying the views as the yachts glide by. Absorbing Bermuda's beauty at your own pace, and stopping to chat with the occasional islander, is really the point.

In this chapter, we'll go on a do-it-yourself tour, taking in Bermuda parish by parish. Also consider taking one or more of the walking tours that we describe in chapter 8, "Island Strolls."

1 What to See If You Don't Have Much Time: The Island's Highlights

THE TOP ATTRACTIONS

Although Bermuda is small, you really can't see much of it in a day or two. If you have more time, you may want to explore it methodically, parish by parish.

> **Tips   The Fun of Getting Lost**
>
> Many guidebooks contend that you can't get lost in Bermuda. Don't
> believe them! Along the narrow, winding roads, originally designed for
> the horse and carriage, you can go astray—several times—especially if
> you're looking for an obscure guesthouse on some long-forgotten lane.
> But don't worry, because you won't stay lost for long. Bermuda is so nar-
> row that if you keep going east or west, you'll eventually come to a main
> road. At its broadest point, Bermuda is only about 2 miles wide. The prin-
> cipal arteries are the North Shore Road, the Middle Road, and the South
> Shore Road, so you'll usually have at least some sense of what part of the
> island you're in.

That's what we'll do in this chapter—visit each parish's attractions in detail, from
west to east. If your time is limited, however, you may want to consider heading
straight for the following highlights. For details, see the appropriate parish section in this chapter.

- A walking tour of historic St. George town (see chapter 8, "Island Strolls").
- A walking tour of the City of Hamilton, Bermuda's largest city and the
  seat of its government. (See chapter 8, "Island Strolls"; if you want to com-
  bine shopping and sightseeing, also check out chapter 9, "Shopping.")
- A fascinating ode to Bermuda's nautical heritage housed in a 19th-century
  fortress: the Bermuda Maritime Museum, at the Royal Naval Dockyard on
  Ireland Island in Sandys Parish.
- The Bermuda Aquarium, Natural History Museum & Zoo, a wonderful
  complex along North Shore Road across Flatts Bridge in Hamilton Parish.
- A guided tour of spectacular Crystal Caves, including crystal-clear Cahow
  Lake, in Hamilton Parish.
- The 18th-century mansion known as Verdmont in Smith's Parish. It stands
  on property once owned by the man who left Bermuda to found South
  Carolina.
- Fort Hamilton, a massive Victorian fortification overlooking the City of
  Hamilton and its harbor. (See Walking Tour 1, "The City of Hamilton,"
  in chapter 8, "Island Strolls.")
- The Botanical Gardens, a Shangri-La in the mid-Atlantic, on South Shore
  Road in Paget Parish.
- Gibbs Hill Lighthouse in Southampton Parish, the oldest cast-iron light-
  house in the world.
- Southampton Parish's Horseshoe Bay Beach, the most photographed of the
  island's pink sandy beaches. (See "Beaches," in chapter 6, "Fun in the Surf
  & Sun.")
- Paget Parish's Elbow Beach, Bermuda's top stretch of sand for fun in the
  surf and sun.

HIGHLIGHTS FOR ARCHITECTURE LOVERS

All of Bermuda interests architecture aficionados. Mark Twain wrote of the color
of Bermuda houses and roofs: "It is exactly the white of the icing of a cake, and
has the same emphasized and scarcely perceptible polish. The white of marble is
modest and retiring compared with it . . . clean-cut fanciful chimneys—too pure

and white for this world—that will charm one's gaze by the hour." For more details and lore, see the Appendix.

THE TOWN OF ST. GEORGE

The oldest and most historic settlement on the island is likely to hold the greatest fascination for architecture buffs. Also see chapter 8, "Island Strolls," for a walking tour.

The **Old State House,** constructed in 1620, is the oldest stone house on Bermuda. The governor at the time, Nathaniel Butler, believed he was building the house in an Italianate style. He ordered the workmen to use a combination of turtle oil and lime as mortar. That established a style for other buildings in Bermuda. You can view the inside of the house on Wednesdays only, from 10am to 4pm. Admission is free.

Many architects have wanted to finish the **Unfinished Cathedral,** reached using Blockade Alley. Construction began in 1874, but a schism developed in the church, and there was no money to continue the project. To this day, it remains unfinished.

The **Old Rectory,** now a private residence, was built by a former pirate in 1705. Located on Broad Alley, it's distinguished by its Dutch doors, chimneys, shutters, and what's called a "welcoming arms" staircase. It's open for visitors November to March only, daily from noon to 5pm. Admission is free.

From an architectural point of view, one of the most intriguing structures in St. George is **St. Peter's Church,** on Duke of York Street. This is the oldest Anglican Church in the Western Hemisphere, dating from 1620. It was constructed to replace an even older structure (from 1612) that had been poorly built from posts and palmetto leaves. A storm destroyed that church in 1712. The present St. Peter's was rebuilt and enlarged in 1713. In 1833, the church gained galleries on each side. The section around the triple-tiered pulpit is believed to be the oldest part of the structure, dating from the 1600s. The first governor of the island, Richard Moore, ordered construction of the dark red Bermuda cedar altar in 1615. It's the oldest surviving piece of woodwork from the colonial period.

Tucker House, on Water Street, was built of native limestone. The house is furnished in an interesting manner, mostly with pieces from the mid-1700s and early 1800s. It's open Monday to Saturday from 10am to 4pm. Admission is $3 adults, $2 children.

SMITH'S PARISH

Another notable architectural monument is **Verdmont,** on Verdmont Lane. Dating from around 1710, it was once owned by a wealthy ship owner, and by the founder of the colony of South Carolina. Other owners included an American Loyalist, John Green, who fled from Philadelphia to Bermuda at the end of the Revolutionary War. Built to resemble an English manor house, Verdmont has a striking double roof and a quartet of large chimneys. Each room has a fireplace. The style of the sash windows was once fashionable in certain English manor houses.

2 Organized Tours

You can more or less explore Bermuda on your own. If you prefer help from island-born and -bred residents, it's available.

OFFSHORE TOURS

Bermuda Island Cruises   This outfitter offers the best sojourns at sea. You can book over the phone or through various hotel tour desks.

> ## *Moments* Frommer's Favorite Bermuda Experiences
>
> - **Strolling Bermuda's Pink Sands.** The pink-sand beaches are reason enough to come to the island. Find your favorite cove (perhaps Whale Bay, Astwood Cove, or Jobson's Cove) and stroll aimlessly at dawn, at twilight, or whenever your fancy dictates.
> - **Cycling.** On a rented bicycle, or maybe a moped built for two, explore Bermuda from end to end. Start in St. George in the East End and go all the way to the Royal Naval Dockyard in the West End, or vice versa. You can do this in 1 day or stretch it out.
> - **Following the Bermuda Railway Trail.** As you follow this intermittent trail from one end of the island to the other, you'll take in panoramic seascapes, see exotic flora and fauna, hear the soothing sounds of the island's bird life, and often have long stretches of trail completely to yourself.
> - **Touring by Horse and Buggy.** No one has ever improved on this old-fashioned method of sightseeing and shopping along Hamilton's Front Street. Better yet, go on a 2-hour shopping tour of Somerset Village in the West End.
> - **Viewing Bermuda from Gibbs Hill Lighthouse.** Climb the 185 steps of the oldest cast-iron lighthouse in the world for one of the greatest views of the Atlantic Ocean. Springtime visitors may be lucky enough to see migrating whales beyond the shore reefs.

Two-hour glass-bottom–boat tours cover Bermuda's famous reefs and shipwrecks. The cruises, which include commentary by a knowledgeable guide, leave Monday to Saturday at 10am and 1:30pm from Hamilton Harbour. The cost is $30 for adults, $15 for children 6 to 12.

The "Don't Stop the Carnival" evening cruise at Hawkins Island includes a barbecue dinner, music from a "Tropical Heat" band, a "Hot Spice Limbo" show, and an open bar. The cost is $75 per adult, $41.50 for children 7 to 12, free for children under 7. A parent must accompany children under 18. The cruise runs from 7 to 10:30pm on Tuesday, Wednesday, Friday, and Saturday.

The Island Band Cruise leaves Hamilton at 2pm and returns at 5pm. It includes complimentary swizzles and costs $45 per person. The Wednesday luncheon cruise, from Hamilton to the dockyard and to St. George, costs $65. It departs at 9:30am and returns at 3:30pm.

East Broadway Marina, Pembroke Parish. © 441/292-8652.

Bermuda Water Tours Ltd. This company offers 2- and 3½-hour trips for $30 and $45, respectively. Most include a visit to the sea gardens, where you can see the wonders of coral reefs and fish through the boat's glass bottom. Also available are a variety of water trips, ranging from 2-hour sea-garden tours to snorkeling.

P.O. Box 1572, Hamilton. © 441/236-1500.

ENVIRONMENTAL TOURS

The nonprofit **Bermuda Biological Station for Research** has collected the world's most comprehensive data on the oceanographic absorption of human-released carbon dioxide. It has tracked carbon dioxide levels for more than 40

Attractions Around the Island

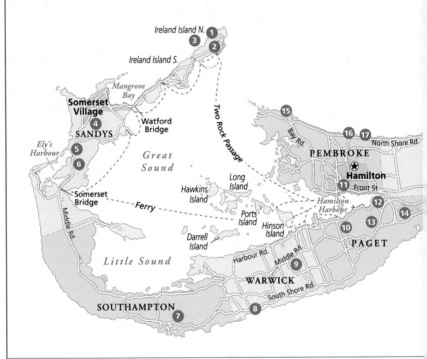

ATLANTIC OCEAN

Ireland Island N.
Ireland Island S.
Mangrove Bay
Somerset Village
Watford Bridge
SANDYS
Ely's Harbour
Two Rock Passage
Great Sound
Bay Rd
North Shore Rd
PEMBROKE
Hamilton
Front St.
Somerset Bridge
Ferry
Hawkins Island
Long Island
Ports Island
Hinson Island
Hamilton Harbour
Middle Rd
Darrell Island
PAGET
Little Sound
Harbour Rd.
Middle Rd
WARWICK
South Shore Rd.
SOUTHAMPTON

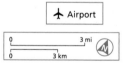

Airport

| 0 | | 3 mi |
| 0 | 3 km | |

years over a 13-mile area southeast of Bermuda. The National Science Foundation awarded the station a $500,000 grant to study climate change, the greenhouse effect, and the carbon cycle. The station has also compiled an extensive record on acid rain in the North American atmosphere.

You can learn firsthand what the station's scientists are studying by taking a free 90-minute guided tour of the grounds and laboratory in St. George. Guides explain what scientific studies are being conducted in Bermuda and how they relate to the overall world environment. They also discuss the island's natural areas, including the coral reefs, which are protected by strict conservation laws, and how humans have produced changes in the fragile ecological environment.

Trained volunteers and scientists who are carrying out the study projects conduct the special educational tours, offered at 10am on Wednesday. Visitors should assemble before 10am in the Biological Station's Hanson Hall. For more information, contact the **Bermuda Biological Station for Research,** 17 Biological Lane, Ferry Reach, St. George (© **441/297-1880**).

3 Sandys Parish

Sandys Parish is one of the island's real beauty spots. If you're looking for a place to just wander about and get lost on a summer day, this lovely parish is well worth your time. Fort Scaur and the Royal Naval Dockyard on Ireland Island are the major attractions; if you're pressed for time, skip the Gilbert Nature Reserve and St. James' Anglican Church.

To explore this tip of the fishhook of Bermuda, it's best to take a ferry (the fare is $4); the trip from Hamilton to Watford Bridge takes 45 minutes. You can take your bike free; there's a $3.50 charge for scooters and mopeds. Ferries also stop at Cavello Bay, Somerset, and the Royal Naval Dockyard. The **Visitors Service Bureau** is at the Royal Naval Dockyard (© **441/234-3824**), across from the ferry terminal. From May to October, hours are Monday to Friday and Sunday from 9am to 5pm (closed Sat); off-season hours are Monday to Friday from 9:30am to 2pm and Sunday from 11am to 3pm.

Scaur Hill Fort Park ⨀ On the highest hill in Somerset, Fort Scaur was part of a ring of fortifications constructed in the 19th century, during a period of troubled relations between Britain and the United States. Intended as a last-ditch defense for the Royal Naval Dockyard, the fort was skillfully constructed, taking advantage of the land contours to camouflage its presence from detection at sea. The fort has subterranean passages and a dry moat that stretches across the land from Ely's Harbour to Great Sound.

Open to visitors since 1957, Fort Scaur has become one of Somerset's most popular tourist attractions. The fort has panoramic views of Ely's Harbour and Great Sound; using the free telescope, you'll see such faraway points as St. David's Lighthouse and Fort St. Catherine. The fort sits on 22 acres of parkland filled with interesting trails, picnic areas, a rocky shoreline for fishing, and a public dock. Picnic tables, benches, and rest rooms are available.

Ely's Harbour, Somerset Rd. © **441/236-5902**. Free admission. Daily 9am–6pm. Closed Dec 25, Jan 15. Bus: 7 or 8 from Hamilton.

Gilbert Nature Reserve In the center of the island lies the Gilbert Nature Reserve, 5 acres of unspoiled woodland. It bears the name of the family that owned the property from the early 18th century until 1973, when the Bermuda National Trust acquired it (in conjunction with the Bermuda Audubon Society).

Somerset Rd. © **441/236-6483**. Free admission. Daily sunrise–sunset. Bus: 7 or 8 from Hamilton.

Kids Especially for Kids

Bermuda is a great destination for the entire family. Most resorts offer children's activities and special family packages. Most of the larger properties also give Mom and Dad an opportunity to spend some time alone by offering baby-sitting services for minimal fees.

Even more important, Bermuda offers many activities that will keep the kids going all day long. They include sailing, waterskiing, snorkeling, and glass-bottom–boat trips from April to October; tennis; visits to museums and caves; and a wide array of walking tours. Here are some of Bermuda's top sights and activities for kids:

Bermuda Aquarium, Natural History Museum & Zoo (see p. 176)   This complex offers kids a wonderful introduction to the undersea world. Hand-held cassette tapes let you listen to a history of marine life while visiting live exhibits of Bermuda's native fish.

Bermuda Maritime Museum (see p. 168)   Everyone in the family takes equal delight in seeing the exhibits of Bermuda's nautical history in this authentic Victorian fortress museum.

Bermuda Railway Trail (see p. 178)   This nature walk, with strolls overlooking the seashore and along quiet tree-lined alleyways, is suitable for the entire family. You can pick up the 21-mile trail at many points and explore as many sections as you like, according to your stamina and interests.

Devil's Hole Aquarium (see p. 177)   This aquarium near Harrington Sound, founded in 1834, was the first established attraction on Bermuda. Kids toss baited lines (without hooks) to feed fish and turtles in this natural marine environment.

Crystal Caves (see p. 176)   Two boys chasing a runaway ball in 1907 discovered an enormous cavern surrounded by an underground lake. Easily navigable walkways take parents and kids down into the caverns in Hamilton Parish.

Undersea Walk (see. p. 145)   Your kids can explore the ocean floor on their own—all they need is an underwater helmet and a little guidance. Following a pre-dive educational lecture aboard the ship, kids of all ages can walk along the ocean floor for face-to-face encounters with friendly sea creatures.

St. James' Anglican Church   This is one of the most beautiful churches on Bermuda. It was constructed on the site of a structure that was destroyed by a hurricane in 1780. The present church was built 9 years later. A unique feature is the altar, which faces west instead of the customary east. The north and south aisles were added in 1836, the entrance gate in 1872, and the spire and chancel in 1880. The church was struck by lightning in 1939 and restored shortly thereafter.

90 Somerset Rd. ✆ 441/234-0834. Free admission. Daily 8am–5pm. Bus: 7 or 8 from Hamilton.

IRELAND ISLAND & THE ROYAL NAVAL DOCKYARD

The Royal Naval Dockyard ✶✶   The Dockyard, with its Bermuda Maritime Museum, is the number-one tourist attraction on the island. Even if you plan to spend all your precious Bermuda time on the pink sandy beaches, try to schedule at least a half-day to check it out.

The Royal Naval Dockyard has been transformed into a park, with Victorian street lighting and a Terrace Pavilion and bandstand for concerts. When the Bermudian government bought this dockyard, which had been on British Admiralty land, in 1953, it marked the end of British naval might in the western Atlantic. A multimillion-dollar cruise-ship dock has been built and a tourist village has emerged; today, vendors push carts filled with food, dry goods, and local crafts. There's a full-service marina with floating docks, a clubhouse, and showers. The area also houses the Bermuda Maritime Museum, the Neptune Theatre, the Crafts Market, and the Bermuda Arts Centre.

Ferries from Hamilton stop at Ireland Island, at the western end of Bermuda, once each hour 7am–6pm. The fare is $4 each way. Buses (no. 7 or 8) leave Hamilton for the Royal Naval Dockyard Mon–Sat every 15 min. from 6:45am–11:45pm. The trip takes 1 hr. and costs $4 for adults, $1 for children 5–15; free for children under 5. *Note:* Drivers accept this bus fare in coins only.

Bermuda Arts Centre Works by local artists are the focus in this gallery, with exhibits changing about every 6 weeks. An eclectic range of original art and prints is for sale. Local artists in residence include a cedar sculptor, a watercolorist, and a silversmith and jewelry maker.

4 Freeport Rd. ℂ **441/234-2809**. Free admission. Daily 10am–5pm.

Bermuda Craft Market This is the place to watch local artists at work and to buy their wares, which make ideal souvenirs. Established in 1987, it offers items made from Bermuda cedar, candles, clothing, dolls, fabrics, hand-painted goods, jewelry, metal and gem sculpture, needlework, quilts, shell art, glass panels, and woven-cane goods, among other things.

In the Cooperage Building, 4 Freeport Rd. ℂ **441/234-3208**. Free admission. Mon–Sat 9:30am–6pm; Sun 11am–6pm.

Bermuda Maritime Museum ⟨⟨ In a 19th-century fortress built by convict labor, this museum exhibits artifacts, models, and maps pertaining to Bermuda's nautical heritage. The fortress's massive buildings of fitted stone, with their vaulted ceilings of English brick, are worth a visit on their own. So are the 30-foot defensive ramparts; the underground tunnels, gun ports, and magazines; and the water gate and pond for entering by boat from the sea. Exhibits in six large halls illustrate the island's long, intimate connection with the sea—from Spanish exploration to 20th-century ocean liners; from racing dinghies to practical fishing boats; from shipbuilding and privateering to naval exploits.

The museum's most famous exhibit is in the 1837 Shifting House, which opened in 1979. You can see such artifacts as gold bars, pottery, jewelry, silver coins, and other items recovered from 16th- and 17th-century shipwrecks. The collection includes some earthenware and pewter that belonged to the English settlers on their way to Jamestown aboard the *Sea Venture,* which was wrecked in 1609. Most visitors come here to gaze at the Tucker Treasure. A well-known

The World's Smallest Drawbridge

After leaving Fort Scaur, you can continue over the much-photographed 17th-century **Somerset Bridge,** the world's smallest drawbridge. When it's open for marine traffic, the space between the spans is a mere 22 inches at road level—just large enough for the mast of a sailboat to pass through.

(*Moments* **Stepping Back into the Ice Age**

Bermuda has one of the highest concentrations of limestone caves in the world. Most began forming during the Pleistocene Ice Age. As early as 1623, the adventurer Capt. John Smith complained that he had encountered "vary strange, darke, cumbersome caves."

In Bermuda, nature's patient, relentless underground sculpting has left behind a dream world for even the casual spelunker. Deep in the majestic silence of the earth's interior, you can roam in caverns of great stalactites and stalagmites of Gothic grandeur, delicacy, and beauty. This awesome underground has been the inspiration for creative achievements as diverse as Shakespeare's *The Tempest* and Henson Associates' "Fraggle Rock" Muppets.

You can visit Crystal Caves on guided tours; the cave complex is along Harrington Sound Road in Hamilton Parish (see p. 176 for more information).

---

local diver, Teddy Tucker, made a significant find in 1955 when he discovered the wreck of the *San Antonio*, a Spanish vessel that had gone down off the coast of Bermuda in a violent storm in 1621. One of the great treasures of this find, the Pectoral Cross, was stolen in 1975 just before Queen Elizabeth II officially opened the museum. The priceless original cross was replaced by a fake. To this day, the original cross has not been recovered, and its mysterious disappearance is still the subject of much discussion.

As you enter the Parade Ground at the entrance to the museum, you'll notice a 10-foot-high figure of King Neptune. This comes from HMS *Irresistible*, recovered when the ship was broken up in 1891; it has been duplicated in Indiana limestone. The Queen's Exhibition Hall houses general maritime exhibits, including displays on navigation, whaling, and cable and wireless communications. A "Bermuda in Five Hours" exhibit focuses on Pan American's early "flying boats." The building itself was constructed in 1850 for the purpose of storing 4,860 barrels of gunpowder.

The Forster Cooper Building (1852) illustrates the history of the Royal Navy in Bermuda, including the Bromby Bottle Collection. Princess Margaret opened the exhibit in 1984. The Boatloft houses part of the museum's boat collections, including the century-old fitted dinghy *Victory,* the 17-foot *Spirit of Bermuda,* and the *Rambler,* the only surviving Bermuda pilot gig. On the upper floor, the original dockyard clock, which is still working, chimes the hours and the quarter-hours.

Royal Naval Dockyard. (*C* **441/234-1418**. Admission $9 adults, $6 seniors and students, $2 children 5–18, family (2 adults and up to 5 children) $15; free 4 and under. Daily 9:30am–5pm. Closed Dec 25.

4 Southampton Parish

All visitors pass through Southampton for the beaches, if for no other reason. Even if you're not staying here, it's worth a journey to see the view from Gibbs Hill Lighthouse—there's no finer panorama in all of Bermuda.

Gibbs Hill Lighthouse (* Southampton's main attraction is this lighthouse, built in 1846. It's the oldest cast-iron lighthouse in the world. Although there's a 185-step climb to the top, the panoramic view of Bermuda and its shoreline from the balcony make the exertion worthwhile. The lighthouse keeper will explain the workings of the machinery. If you visit in the spring, you may spot migrating whales beyond the south-shore reefs.

Gibbs Hill, Lighthouse Rd. (between South Shore and Middle rds.). © 441/238-0524. Admission $2.50; free for children under 5. Daily 9am–5pm. Bus: 7 or 8 from Hamilton.

5 Warwick Parish

This parish has few sightseeing attractions, but it is a place of natural beauty. Visitors come here mostly for the sandy beach, **Warwick Long Bay,** on South Shore Road; it's one of the finest on Bermuda (see "Beaches," in chapter 6, "Fun in the Surf & Sand," for details). Nearby, you can visit **Christ Church,** across from the Belmont Hotel on Middle Road. Built in 1719, it's one of the oldest Scottish Presbyterian churches in the New World.

Warwick is also the site of some of the best golf and horseback riding in Bermuda; see chapter 6, "Fun in the Surf & Sand," for specifics.

6 Paget Parish

On every visit to Bermuda, we schedule a long stopover at the Botanical Gardens. They are worth the trip, even if you're staying in the East End. Once here, Waterville, one of the oldest houses in Bermuda, merits a look. You could cap your visit with a walk through unspoiled Paget Marsh, although you might skip it if you've already seen Spittal Pond (see "Smith's Parish," below).

The Birdsey Studio   Jo Birdsey Lindberg, daughter of the island's best-known artist, Alfred Birdsey (1912–96), sells original artwork, watercolors, and oils. An experienced painter, she continues a family tradition by producing and showing her work here, in a garden setting. Her impressionistic style appears in compositions ranging from landscapes of Bermuda to architectural and nautical themes. Prices range from $50 to $700. Also available are note cards reproduced from paintings by Alfred Birdsey. Studio hours are Monday to Friday 10:30am to 1pm March to July and September to November, and by appointment.

5 Stowe Hill. © 441/236-6658, or 441/236-5845 in the evening. Bus: 8 from Hamilton.

Botanical Gardens ⊛   This 36-acre landscaped park, maintained by the Department of Natural Resources, is one of Bermuda's major attractions. Hundreds of clearly identified flowers, shrubs, and trees line the pathways. Attractions include collections of hibiscus and subtropical fruit, an aviary, banyan trees, and even a garden for the blind. It's best to take one of the 90-minute walking tours, which depart at 10:30am on Tuesday, Wednesday, and Friday from the visitor center. The cafe sells sandwiches and salads (soup and chili in winter).

Point Finger Rd. (at South Shore Rd.). © 441/236-5291. Free admission. Daily sunrise–sunset. Bus: 1, 2, 7, or 8. By bike or moped, turn left off Middle Rd. onto Tee St.; at Berry Hill Rd., go right; about ½ mile farther on the left is the signposted turnoff to the gardens; take a right fork to the parking lot on the left.

Paget Marsh   This nature reserve comprises 25 acres of unspoiled native woods and marshland, with vegetation and bird life of ecological interest. Because it's a fully protected area with few trails, prospective visitors should make special arrangements and obtain a map from the Bermuda National Trust. A boardwalk installed in 1999 allows you to view the marsh better.

Middle Rd. © 441/236-6483. Free admission. Mon–Fri 9am–5pm by special arrangement. Bus: 8 from Hamilton.

Waterville   Built before 1735, this is one of the oldest houses on Bermuda; it was home to seven generations of the prominent Trimingham family. From the house's cellar storage rooms in 1842, James Harvey Trimingham started the business that was to become Trimingham Brothers—now one of Bermuda's finest Front Street department stores. Major renovations were undertaken in 1811, and the house has been restored in that period's style. The two main rooms hold period furnishings, mainly Trimingham family heirlooms specifically bequeathed for use in the house. Waterville is the headquarters of the Bermuda National Trust, and houses its offices and reception rooms. It's just west of the Trimingham roundabout, near the City of Hamilton.

5 The Lane (Harbour Rd.), at Pomander Rd. ℂ **441/236-6483**. Free admission. Mon–Fri 9am–5pm. Bus: 7 or 8 from Hamilton.

7 Pembroke Parish & the City of Hamilton

The ideal way to see the City of Hamilton and its parish, Pembroke, for the first time is to sail in through Hamilton Harbour, past the offshore cays.

In 1852, the cornerstone was laid for the Hamilton Hotel, Bermuda's first hotel, completed in 1863. It survived until a fire destroyed it 1955. When the Hamilton Princess opened in 1887, it overshadowed the Hamilton and became the island's hotel of choice. Its colorful history includes being taken over by Allied agents during World War II.

If Queen Victoria's daughter Princess Louise were to visit Bermuda today, she would probably stay at **Government House,** on North Shore Road and Langton Hill. Because this is the residence of the governor of the island, it's not open to the public. This Victorian home has housed many notable guests, including Queen Elizabeth II and Prince Philip, Prince Charles, Sir Winston Churchill, and President John F. Kennedy. In 1973, Gov. Sir Richard Sharples, his aide, Capt. Hugh Sayers, and the governor's dog were assassinated while they were walking on the grounds. The tragedy led to a state of emergency in Bermuda.

While touring Pembroke Parish, visitors often stop at **Black Watch Well,** at the junction of North Shore Road and Black Watch Pass. Excavated by a detachment of the Black Watch Regiment, the well was dug in 1894, when Bermudians were suffering through a long drought.

Another choice spot to visit is **Admiralty House Park,** off North Shore Road at Spanish Point Road. In the 1800s, this scenic area formed the estate of John of Dunscombe, who later became lieutenant governor of Newfoundland. After he sold the property to the British military in 1816, a house was erected here to offer accommodations for the commanding British admiralty, who worked at the naval base at the dockyard. Over the years the house was rebuilt several times. In the 1850s, it gained a series of subterranean tunnels, plus a number of galleries and caves carved into the cliffs above the sea. By 1951, the Royal Navy withdrew, and most of the house was torn down—except for a ballroom, which survives. Today, you can explore the park-like grounds; the sheltered beach at Clarence Cove is good for swimming.

THE CITY OF HAMILTON ⭐⭐⭐

The capital of Bermuda was once known as the "show window of the British Empire." Both Mark Twain and Eugene O'Neill, who lived in places that opened onto Hamilton Harbour, cited its beauty.

Named for a former governor, Henry Hamilton, Hamilton was incorporated as a town in 1793. Because of its central location and its large, protected harbor,

---

> (*Tips* **From the Land and from the Sea**
>
> Hamilton should be seen not only from land, but also from the water; try to make time for a boat tour of the harbor and its coral reefs. If you're visiting from another parish, the ferry will let you off at the west end of Front Street, which is ideal if you'd like to drop by the Visitors Service Bureau and pick up a map. It's near the Ferry Terminal. The staff also provides information and helpful brochures; hours are 9am to 4:45pm Monday to Saturday.

---

it replaced St. George as the island's capital in 1815. Hamilton encompasses only 182 acres of land, so most visitors explore it on foot.

Long before it became known as "the showcase of the Atlantic," Hamilton was a modest outlet for the export of Bermuda cedar and fresh vegetables. Today, it's the hub of the island's economy.

The City of Hamilton is more popular for its shops and restaurants than for its attractions. Hamilton boasts the largest number of restaurants and bars on Bermuda, especially on and near Front Street. The restaurants charge a wide range of prices, and there are many English-style watering holes if you'd like to go on a pub-crawl. And religion isn't neglected—there are also 12 churches within the city limits, one or two of which merit a visit.

If you'd like to go sightseeing, take our walking tour (see chapter 8, "Island Strolls") for an overall view. The only sights worth in-depth visits are Fort Hamilton (seen on the walking tour), the Bermuda Historical Society Museum, and the Bermuda National Gallery. You can safely skip the rest if you're pressed for time.

A stroll along **Front Street** ⟨⟩ will take you by some of Hamilton's most elegant stores, but you'll want to branch off into the little alleyways to check the shops and boutiques. If you get tired of walking or shopping (or both), you can go down to the docks and take one of the boats or catamarans waiting to show you the treasures of Little Sound and Great Sound.

Ferries back to Paget, Warwick, and Sandys parishes leave daily between 6:50am and 11:20pm. On Saturday and Sunday, there are fewer departures.

On certain days you may be able to see locals buying fresh fish—the part of the catch that isn't earmarked for restaurants—right from the fishers at the **Front Street docks.** Rockfish is the most abundant, and you'll also see snapper, grouper, and many other species.

Opposite the Visitors Service Bureau stands the much-photographed **"Birdcage,"** where you used to be able to see a police officer directing traffic. Such a sight is rare now. For many years, visitors wondered if the traffic director was for real or placed there for tourist photographs.

Nearby is Albouy's Point, site of the Royal Bermuda Yacht Club, founded in 1844. The point, named after a 17th-century professor of "physick," is a public park overlooking Hamilton Harbour.

To reach the sights listed below, take bus number 1, 2, 10, or 11.

Bermuda Historical Society Museum   After leaving the harbor, proceed up Queen Street to the public library and the Bermuda Historical Society Museum. The museum has a collection of old cedar furniture, antique silver, early Bermuda coins (hog money), and ceramics imported by early sea captains. You'll see the sea chest and navigating lodestone of Sir George Somers, whose flagship, the *Sea Venture,* became stranded on Bermuda's reefs in 1609. You'll also find portraits of Sir George and Lady Somers, and models of *Patience, Deliverance,* and the ill-fated *Sea Venture.*

The museum is in Par-la-Ville Park on Queen Street. It was designed by William Bennett Perot, Hamilton's first postmaster (from 1818–62), who was somewhat eccentric. As he delivered mail around town, he is said to have placed letters in the crown of his top hat in order to preserve his dignity.

13 Queen St., Par-la-Ville Park. 🌀 **441/295-2487.** Free admission. Mon–Sat 9:30am–3:30pm.

Bermuda National Gallery   Located in the east wing of City Hall, the Bermuda National Gallery is the home of the Masterworks Foundation Bermudiana Collection, with works by such artists as Georgia O'Keeffe, Winslow Homer, Charles Demuth, Albert Gleizes, Ogden Pleissner, and Jack Bush. The Masterworks Foundation was established in 1987 to return to the island works of art that depict Bermuda, and to exhibit them. The gallery is also home to the Hereward T. Watlington Collection, which includes 15th- to 19th-century paintings by such masters as Reynolds, Gainsborough, and de Hooch. The gallery also displays smaller paintings and watercolors collected by the Bermuda Archives and National Trust.

Bermuda's humid climate and damaging sunlight make proper climate control and lighting essential. To create an appropriate gallery, the Bermuda Fine Art Trust was developed and incorporated by an Act of Parliament in 1982. In 1988, the Hon. Hereward T. Watlington bequeathed his collection of European paintings to the people of Bermuda on the condition that they be housed in a European-standard climate-controlled environment. The Corporation of Hamilton offered the use of the East Exhibition Room of City Hall and made a financial contribution toward the construction of a proper facility.

City Hall, 17 Church St. 🌀 **441/295-9428.** Admission $3 adults; free for children under 16. Mon–Sat 10am–4pm. Tours Mon, Tues, Thurs, and Fri at 1pm.

Cathedral of the Most Holy Trinity (Bermuda Cathedral)   This is the mother church of the Anglican diocese in Bermuda. It became a cathedral in 1894 and was formally consecrated in 1911. The building features a reredos (or ornamental partition), stained-glass windows, and ornate carvings. If you have the stamina, climb the 157 steps to the top of the tower for a panoramic view of Hamilton and the harbor.

Church St. 🌀 **441/292-4033.** Free admission to cathedral; admission to the cathedral tower $3 adults, $2 seniors and children. Cathedral daily 8am–5pm and for Sun services; tower Mon–Fri 10am–3pm.

Hamilton City Hall & Arts Centre   The City Hall, also home of the Bermuda Society of Arts, is an imposing white structure with a giant weather vane and wind clock to tell maritime-minded Bermudians which way the wind is blowing. Completed in 1960, the building is the seat of Hamilton's municipal government. The theater on the first floor books stage, music, and dance productions throughout the year, and is the main site of the Bermuda Festival. The Bermuda National Gallery (see above) is also here.

Since 1956, the Bermuda Society of Arts has encouraged and provided a forum for contemporary artists, sculptors, and photographers. Its gallery, with ever-changing exhibitions, displays the work of local and visiting artists. This society is a separate entity from the newer Bermuda National Gallery.

17 Church St. 🌀 **441/292-1234.** Free admission. City Hall: Mon–Fri 9am–5pm. Bermuda Society of Arts: Mon–Sat 10am–4pm.

Perot Post Office   Bermuda's first stamp was printed in this landmark building. Beloved by collectors from all over the world, the stamps—signed by William Bennett Perot, Bermuda's first postmaster—are priceless. It's said that Perot and his friend Heyl, who ran an apothecary, conceived the first postage stamp to protect the post office from cheaters. People used to stop off at the post office and leave letters, but not enough pennies to send them. The postage stamps were printed in black or carmine.

Philatelists can purchase contemporary Bermuda stamps here. For its 375th anniversary, Bermuda issued a series of stamps honoring its discovery in 1609. One stamp portrays the admiral of the fleet, Sir George Somers, along with Sir Thomas Gates, the captain of the *Sea Venture*. Another depicts the settlement of Jamestown, Virginia, which was on the verge of extinction when Sir George and the survivors of the Bermuda shipwreck finally arrived with supplies late in 1610. A third shows the *Sea Venture* stranded on the coral reefs of Bermuda. Yet another shows the entire fleet, originally bound for Jamestown, leaving Plymouth, England, on June 2, 1609.

Queen St., at the entrance to Par-la-Ville Park. © **441/292-9052** or 441/295-5151, ext. 1192. Free admission. Mon–Fri 9am–5pm.

Sessions House   This Italian Renaissance–style structure was originally built in 1819. Its clock tower, added in 1887, commemorates the Golden Jubilee of Queen Victoria. The House of Assembly meets on the second floor from November to May, and visitors are permitted in the gallery. Call ahead to learn when meetings are scheduled. On the lower level, the chief justice presides over the Supreme Court.

21 Parliament St. © **441/292-7408**. Free admission. Mon–Fri 9am–12:30pm and 2–5pm.

8 Devonshire Parish

If you're passing through Devonshire, consider a stop at the following attractions.

Old Devonshire Parish Church   The Old Devonshire Parish Church is believed to have been built on this site in 1624, although the present foundation dates from 1716. An explosion virtually destroyed the church on Easter in 1970, but it was reconstructed. Today, the tiny structure looks more like a vicarage than a church. Some of the church's contents survived the blast, including its silver from 1590, which may be the oldest on the island. The church, designed by Sir George Grove and built of limestone, has an early English-style high-pitched roof. The Old Devonshire Parish Church stands northwest of the "new" Devonshire Parish Church, which dates from 1846.

Middle Rd. © 441/236-3671. Free admission. Daily 9am–5:30pm. Bus: 2.

Palm Grove   This private estate, 2½ miles east of Hamilton, is one of the delights of Devonshire Parish. It's famous for its pond with a relief map of Bermuda in the middle. Each parish is an immaculately manicured grassy division. The site, which has well-landscaped flower gardens, opens onto a view of the sea.

38 South Shore Rd. No phone. Free admission. Mon–Thurs 8:30am–5pm. Bus: 1.

9 Smith's Parish

Even if you're staying in remote Sandys Parish, the 18th-century mansion of Verdmont is worth a detour, as the good folks at Michelin say. If you're in the area, Spittal Pond Nature Reserve also merits some attention.

Spittal Pond Nature Reserve   Follow steep Knapton Hill Road west to South Shore Road, turning at the sign for Spittal Pond, Bermuda's largest wildlife sanctuary. The most important of the National Trust's open spaces, it occupies 60 acres and attracts about 25 species of waterfowl, which can be seen from November to May. Visitors are asked to stay on the scenic trails and footpaths provided. Bird-watchers especially like to visit in January, when as many as 500 species can be observed wintering on or near the pond.

South Shore Rd. © 441/236-6483. Free admission. Daily sunrise–sunset. Bus: 1 or 3.

Verdmont 🎯   This 18th-century mansion is of special significance to Americans who are interested in colonial and Revolutionary War history. It stands on property that was owned in the 17th century by William Sayle, who left Bermuda to found South Carolina and then become its first governor. The house was built before 1710 by John Dickinson, a prosperous ship owner who was also speaker of the House of Assembly in Bermuda from 1707 to 1710. Verdmont passed to Mr. Dickinson's granddaughter, Elizabeth, who married the Hon. Thomas Smith, collector of Customs. Their oldest daughter, Mary, married Judge John Green, a Loyalist who came to Bermuda in 1765 from Philadelphia. During and after the American Revolution, Green was judge of the Vice-Admiralty Court and had the final say on prizes brought in by privateers. Many American ship owners lost their vessels because of his decisions. The house, which the National Trust now administers, contains many

---

⟨Moments The Search for Solace

In overcrowded Bermuda, the search for solace and tranquillity grows harder and harder. But one of our staff recently stumbled upon the 43-acre **Heydon Trust,** Somerset Rd. (© **441/234-1831**), in Smith's Parish, open daily dawn to dusk. This setting, which is also a sanctuary for migratory birds, is Bermuda the way it used to be. The grounds are filled with flower gardens, citrus orchards, walkways, and even a tiny chapel dating from 1620, where Monday to Saturday services are held at 7am and 3pm in Gregorian chant. Park benches are found throughout the preserve where you can sit and contemplate nature or your navel.

antiques, china, and portraits, along with the finest cedar stair balustrade on Bermuda.

6 Verdmont Lane, Collectors Hill. © **441/236-7369**. Admission $3 adults, $2 children 6–18; free for children under 6. Tues–Sat 10am–4pm. Bus: 1 from Hamilton or St. George.

10 Hamilton Parish

Even if you have limited sightseeing time, try to budget at least a half-day for Hamilton Parish. It has some of the most intriguing attractions on the island, notably the Bermuda Aquarium, Natural History Museum & Zoo, plus Crystal Caves and Leamington Caves. If you have time for only one set of caves, we recommend Crystal Caves. However, if you've seen some of the great caves of America or Europe (or even beyond), you may find Bermuda's caves less thrilling. While you're in the neighborhood, and if you have time, you might also want to check out the Bermuda Perfumery.

Bermuda Aquarium, Natural History Museum & Zoo ⚐   This complex is home to a large collection of tropical marine fish, turtles, harbor seals, and other forms of sea life. In the museum you'll see exhibits on the geological development of Bermuda, deep-sea exploration, and humpback whales. The zoo is home to Galapagos tortoises, alligators, and monkeys, along with a collection of birds, including parrots and flamingos.

The North Rock Exhibit, in a 140,000-gallon tank, allows visitors to experience a coral reef washed by ocean surge. The tank houses a living coral reef, as well as reef and pelagic fish species. It's the first living coral exhibit on this scale in the world, made possible by the Bermuda Aquarium, Natural History Museum & Zoo's success in the science of coral husbandry.

There's parking for cycles and cars across the street from the aquarium.

North Shore Rd., Flatts Village. © **441/293-2727**. Admission $10 adults, $5 seniors and children 5–12; free for children under 5. Daily 9am–5pm. Closed Dec 25. Bus: 10 or 11 from Hamilton or St. George. From Hamilton, follow Middle Rd. or North Shore Rd. east to Flatts Village; from St. George, cross the causeway and follow North Shore Rd. or Harrington Sound Rd. west to Flatts Village.

Bermuda Perfumery   The perfumery makes Lili Perfumes. On guided tours, visitors can see the perfume-making process, including the old method of extracting scents from native flowers. Among the fragrances produced are passionflower, Bermuda Easter lily, and oleander jasmine. A small botanical garden with a seating area and walkways provides an attractive resting place. You can also visit the orchid house, which contains more than 500 varieties of orchids. The nature trail passes through a large area planted with tropical flowers, shrubs, and trees. The perfumery also has a gift shop.

212 North Shore Rd., Bailey's Bay. © **441/293-0627**. Free admission. Apr–Oct Mon–Sat 9am–5pm, Sun 10am–4pm; Nov–Mar Mon–Sat 9am–4:30pm. Closed Sun in winter. Bus: 1 or 3.

Crystal Caves ⚐   This network of subterranean lakes, caves, and caverns consists of translucent formations of stalagmites and stalactites; the setting includes the crystal-clear Cahow Lake. A sloping path and a few steps lead to the Crystal Caves, which were discovered in 1907; at the bottom, about 120 feet below the surface, is a floating causeway. It follows the winding cavern, where hidden lights illuminate the interior. All tours through Crystal Caves are guided. Using the lighting system, the guides make silhouettes and are fond of pointing out the similarity to the skyline of Manhattan. If you suffer from claustrophobia, you might find this space too tight.

8 Crystal Caves Rd., off Wilkinson Ave., Bailey's Bay. ⓒ **441/293-0640**. Admission $8 adults, $5 children 5–11; free for children under 5. Daily 9:30am–4:30pm. Bus: 1 or 3.

Devil's Hole Aquarium   The sea feeds the pool of this former cave through a half-mile of subterranean passages. A natural aquarium open to the public since 1834, it's stocked with some 400 individual fish, including moray eels, sharks, giant groupers, and massive green turtles. Visitors can tempt the pond's inhabitants with baited (but hookless) lines.

92 Harrington Sound Rd. ⓒ **441/293-2072**. Admission $10; free for children 4 and under. Daily 9:30am–4:30pm. Bus: 1 or 3.

11 St. George Parish

A great way to explore this historic town is by following the "Historic St. George Town" walking tour in chapter 8.

THE TOWN OF ST. GEORGE ✶✶✶

King's Square, also called Market Square and King's Parade, is the center of life in St. George. It holds the colorful **White Horse Tavern,** where you may want to stop for a drink after your tour of the town.

The street names in St. George evoke its history. Petticoat Lane (sometimes called Silk Alley) reputedly got its name when two recently emancipated slaves paraded up and down the lane rustling their colorful new silk petticoats. Barber's Lane is also named for a former slave. It honors Joseph Hayne Rainey, a freedman from the Carolinas who fled to Bermuda aboard a blockade-runner during the Civil War and became a barber. After the war he returned to the United States and was elected to Congress, becoming the first black member of the House of Representatives during Reconstruction.

The St. George branch of the **Visitors Service Bureau** is on King's Square (ⓒ **441/297-1642**); it's open Monday to Saturday from 9am to 5pm. Here you can get a map and other information before setting out to explore. The bureau is opposite the Town Hall.

⟮ **Fun Fact** **That'll Teach You!**

Right on King's Square you'll see a pillory and stock. Honeymooners like to be photographed in them today, but in earlier times they were used in deadly earnest. Victims were placed in the pillory for a certain number of hours—sometimes with one ear nailed to the post! Criminals were burned on the hand or branded, fined in tobacco, nailed to the post, or declared "infamous." Often, they had their ears cut off or were forced to "stand in a sheet on the church porch."

The list of offenses for which Bermudians were punished in the early 1600s offers a glimpse into the life of the time. Along with such "usual" crimes as treason, robbery, arson, murder, and "scandal," punishable offenses included concealing finds of ambergris, exporting cedarwood, railing against the governor's authority, hiding tobacco, being "notorious cursers and swearers," leading an "uncivil life and calling her neighbor an old Bawd and the like," neglecting to receive Holy Communion, acting in a stage play of any kind, and playing at unlawful games such as dice, cards, and ninepins.

(Moments   **Special Places Where You Can Be Alone**

Bermuda is both popular and small—but that doesn't mean that you can't escape the crowds and find peace and serenity in a lovely spot, hopefully with someone you love.

Sandys Parish   Visitors don't seem to spend a lot of time here, but for wandering about, getting lost, and finding enchanting little vistas, Sandys is without equal on Bermuda. Where Daniel's Head Road meets Cambridge Road, paths will take you to Somerset Long Bay Park, where you can swim. After that, take one of the unmarked trails to the Bermuda Audubon Society Nature Reserve, a gem of nature. Families come here on weekends, but the place is often deserted on weekdays; on occasion, we've had it all to ourselves. When the white-eyed vireos and the bluebirds call to you from fiddlewood trees, you'll really feel close to nature.

Southampton Parish   In this windswept, tourist-trodden parish, you'd think there was no place to find solitude. Not so! Signposted from Middle Road, a trail goes a half mile down to the entrance to Seymour's Pond Nature Reserve. Under the management of the Bermuda Audubon Society, this 2½-acre site attracts the occasional birder as well as romantic couples looking for a little privacy. Just past the pond, you'll spot pepper trees and old cedars that escaped the blight; you might encounter bluebirds and an egret or two as well. After traversing Cross Church Road, you'll come upon the old Bermuda Railway Trail, where in summer you can see fennel growing wild. In the distance are panoramic views of shipwreck-clogged Black Bay and Five Star Island.

Warwick Parish   With its beautiful pink-sand beaches, seaside parklands, natural attractions, and winding country lanes, this is one of the most charming parishes for exploring and escaping the crowds. Even many longtime local residents haven't seen some of Warwick's beauty spots. The place to head is Warwick Pond, a sanctuary for several rare

If you're really rushed for time, don't worry that you're missing out if you skip interior visits to the sights listed below. The entire town of St. George, with its quaint streets and old buildings, is the attraction, not one particular monument. If you have time to visit only one attraction's interior, make it St. Peter's Church. Otherwise, just wander around, do a little shopping, and soak in the atmosphere.

To reach these attractions, take bus number 1, 3, 8, 10, or 11 from Hamilton.

The Bermuda National Trust Museum   This was once the Globe Hotel, headquarters of Maj. Norman Walker, the Confederate representative in Bermuda. Today, it houses relics from the island's involvement in the American Civil War—from a Bermudian perspective. St. George was the port from which ships carrying arms and munitions ran the Union blockade. A replica of the Great Seal of the Confederacy is fitted to a Victorian press so that visitors can emboss copies as souvenirs. There's also a video presentation, *Bermuda: Centre of the Atlantic,* tracing the island's early history.

At the Globe Hotel, King's Sq. ℂ **441/297-1423.** Admission $4 adults, $2 children 7–18; free for children under 7. Mon–Sat 10am–4pm. Closed Dec 25.

species of birds. Administered by the Bermuda National Trust, it's open daily from sunrise to sunset. You can reach it by following the Bermuda Railway Trail until you come to Tribe Road No. 3; climb this road for a few hundred yards before it dips down a hill to the pond. You might spot the occasional birder in search of a kiskadee blue heron or a cardinal. The pond, fed by a subterranean channel from the sea, reminds us of Thoreau's Walden Pond.

St. David's Island   Part of St. George Parish, St. David's is Bermuda "the way is was." Virtually unknown to the average visitor, it awaits your discovery. This is real down-home Bermuda—it's said that some St. David's islanders have never even visited "mainland" Bermuda. You can begin your walk at Great Head Park in the eastern part of St. David's, southeast of the cricket fields. At the end of the parking lot, follow the trail into a wooded area filled with cherry trees and palmettos. After about 250 yards, bear right at the fork. Eventually you'll spot St. David's Lighthouse, an octagonal red-and-white tower in the distance to the southwest. The trail forks left until you come to a ruined garrison with a panoramic sea view; it's one of the remotest, loveliest spots on the island—and, chances are, you'll have it all to yourself.

Devonshire Parish   This parish is off the beaten track but home to some lovely spots—if you're adventurous enough to seek them out. Old Devonshire Church on Middle Road is a landmark; almost directly across the road lies Devonshire Marsh, a natural water basin still in an untamed state. You'll also find two nature reserves, Firefly and Freer Cox Memorial, here on some 10 acres of marshland. The Bermuda Audubon Society has set aside this protected area as a bird sanctuary for many endangered wild species; you can also see some of the most unusual Bermudian plants, including orchids. The marsh is always open to the public.

Bridge House Gallery   This long-established gallery displays antiques and collectibles, old Bermudian items, original paintings, and Bermuda-made crafts. It contains a studio belonging to Jill Amos Raine, a well-known Bermuda watercolor artist. The house, constructed in the 1690s, was home to several of the colony's governors. Its most colorful owner was Bridger Goodrich, a Loyalist from Virginia, whose privateers once blockaded Chesapeake Bay. So devoted was he to the king that he also sabotaged Bahamian vessels trading with the American colonies. The building is named Bridge House because a bridge used to stand over a muddy creek (since filled in).

1 Bridge St. ✆ 441/297-8211. Free admission. Mon–Fri 10am–5pm, Sat 10am–4pm; mid-Jan to mid-Feb Wed and Sat 11am–4pm.

Deliverance   Across from St. George's town square and over a bridge is Ordnance Island, where visitors can see a full-scale replica of *Deliverance*. The shipwrecked survivors of the *Sea Venture* built the pinnace (small sailing ship) in 1610 to carry them on to Virginia. A tape recording guides visitors through the ship. Alongside *Deliverance* is the ducking stool, a replica of the horrible

---

Fun Fact The Spice of Life

In old Bermuda, peppercorns were sometimes a form of payment. In the late 18th century, for example, two small islands off King's Square were sold for a peppercorn apiece. In 1782, Henry Tucker bought Ducking Stool Island, and in 1785, Nathaniel Butterfield bought Gallows Island. Several years later, Simon Fraser purchased both for 100 peppercorns and made them into one island, today's Ordnance Island.

---

contraption used in 17th-century witch trials; it's demonstrated on Wednesday and Thursday at noon.

Adventures Enterprises owns *Deliverance* and runs sightseeing and snorkeling adventures aboard its boat *ARGO*. Bermuda's only high-speed tour boat, *ARGO* takes passengers along the barrier reef, the south-shore beaches, the historic forts, and the billionaires' mansions at Tucker's Town. *ARGO* was custom built to allow access to the most beautiful parts of the island where larger vessels can't gain entrance. Call for details, which change seasonally.

Ordnance Island. ☎ **441/297-1459**. Admission $3 adults, $1 children under 12. Apr–Oct daily 10am–6pm; Nov–Mar call for hours.

Old Rectory Built by a reformed pirate in 1705, this charming old cottage was later home to Parson Richardson, who was nicknamed "the Little Bishop." Now a private home, it's administered by the Bermuda National Trust.

At the head of Broad Alley, behind St. Peter's Church. ☎ **441/236-6483**. Free admission; donations appreciated. Nov–Mar Wed noon–5pm.

Old State House Behind the Town Hall is Bermuda's oldest stone building, constructed with turtle oil and lime mortar in 1620. Unless there's a special event, the landmark building doesn't offer much to see—you might settle for a look at the exterior, then press on with your sightseeing. The Old State House, where meetings of the legislative council once took place, was eventually turned over to the Freemasons of St. George's. The government asked the annual rent of one peppercorn and insisted on the right to hold meetings here upon demand. The Masonic Lodge members, in a ceremony filled with pageantry, still turn over one peppercorn in rent to the Bermuda government every April.

For those who have never witnessed the 45-minute spectacle of the annual **rent payment,** it begins around 11am with the gathering of the Bermuda Regiment on King's Square. Then the premier, mayor, and other dignitaries arrive, amid the bellowing introductions of the town crier. As soon as all the principals have taken their places, a 17-gun salute is fired as the governor and his wife make a grand entrance in their open horse-drawn landau. His Excellency inspects a military guard of honor while the Bermuda Regiment Band plays. The stage is now set for the presentation of the peppercorn, which sits on a silver plate atop a velvet cushion. Payment is made in a grand and formal manner, after which the Old State House is immediately used for a meeting of Her Majesty's Council.

Princess St. ☎ **441/297-1206**. Free admission. Wed 10am–4pm or by appointment.

St. George's Historical Society Museum In a home built around 1700, this museum contains an original 18th-century Bermuda kitchen, complete with utensils from that period. Other exhibits include a 300-year-old Bible, a letter from George Washington, and Native American ax heads. Some early set-tlers on St. David's Island were Native Americans, mainly Pequot.

3 Featherbed Alley. © 441/297-0423. Admission $5 adults, $2 children under 12. Mon–Fri 10am–4pm.

St. Peter's Church ☞   From King's Square, head east to Duke of York Street, where you'll find St. Peter's Church, believed to be the oldest Anglican place of worship in the Western Hemisphere. Colonists built the original church in 1612 almost entirely of cedar, with a palmetto-leaf thatch roof. A hurricane in 1712 destroyed it almost completely. Some of the interior, including the original altar from 1615 (still used daily), was salvaged, and the church was rebuilt in 1713. It has been restored many times since, providing excellent examples of the archi-tectural styles of the 17th to the 20th centuries. The tower was added in 1814. On display in the vestry is a silver communion service given to the church by King William III in 1697. Before the Old State House was built, the colony held public meetings in the church. The first assize convened here in 1616, and the first meeting of Parliament was held in 1620. The church holds Sunday and weekday services.

Some of the tombstones in the Graveyard of St. Peter's (entrance opposite Broad Alley) are more than 3 centuries old; many tombs mark the graves of slaves. Here you'll find the grave of Midshipman Richard Dale, an American who was the last victim of the War of 1812. The churchyard also holds the tombs of Gov. Sir Richard Sharples and his aide, Capt. Hugh Sayers, who were assassinated while strolling on the grounds of Government House in 1973.

Duke of York St. © 441/297-8359. Free admission; donations appreciated. Daily 10am–4:30pm and for Sun services; guide available Mon–Sat.

Somers Garden   The heart of Sir George Somers was buried here in 1610; a stone column perpetuates the memory of Bermuda's founder. The garden was opened in 1920 by the Prince of Wales (later King Edward VIII, and then the Duke of Windsor).

Duke of York St. © 441/297-1532. Free admission. Daily 9am–5pm.

Town Hall   Officers of the Corporation of St. George's, headed by a mayor, meet in the Town Hall, located near the Visitors Service Bureau. There are three aldermen and five common councilors. The Town Hall holds a collection of Bermuda cedar furnishings, along with photographs of previous mayors.

7 King's Sq. © 441/297-1532. Free admission. Mon–Sat 10am–4pm.

Tucker House Museum   This was the home of the well-known Tucker fam-ily of England, Bermuda, and Virginia. It displays a notable collection of Bermudian furniture, portraits, and silver. Also in the Tucker House is the Joseph Rainey Memorial Room, where the African-American refugee (men-tioned above) of the Civil War practiced barbering. A new exhibit on the ground floor traces the archaeological history of the site.

5 Water St. © 441/297-0545. Admission $3 adults, $2 children 6–18; free for children under 6. Mon–Sat 10am–4pm.

Unfinished Cathedral   After leaving Somers Garden, head up the steps to the North Gate, which opens onto Blockade Alley. The structure here is known as the "folly of St. George's." The cathedral, begun in 1874, was intended to replace St. Peter's. But the planners ran into money problems, then a schism developed. As if that weren't enough, a storm swept over the island, causing considerable damage to the structure. Result: the Unfinished Cathedral.

Blockade Alley.

HISTORIC FORTS THAT NEVER SAW MUCH ACTION

From its earliest days, St. George has been fortified. Although it never saw much military action, reminders of that history are interesting to explore. Take Circular Drive to reach the forts, on the outskirts of town. As forts go, these two are of relatively minor interest (unless, of course, you're a fort buff—in that case, be our guest). If you have time for only one fort on Bermuda, Fort Hamilton on Happy Valley Road is the most intriguing. See Walking Tour 1, "The City of Hamilton," in chapter 8, "Island Strolls," for details.

Along the coast is Building Bay, where the shipwrecked victims of the *Sea Venture* built their vessel, the *Deliverance,* in 1610.

Fort St. Catherine ⋒   Towering above the beach where the shipwrecked crew of the *Sea Venture* came ashore in 1609 is Fort St. Catherine, completed in 1614 and named for the patron saint of wheelwrights and carpenters. The fortifications have been upgraded over the years. The last major reconstruction took place from 1865 to 1878, so the fort's appearance today is largely the result of work done in the 19th century.

In the museum, visitors first see a series of dioramas, "Highlights in Bermuda's History." Figures depict various activities that took place in the magazine of the fort, restored and refurnished as it was in the 1880s. Large Victorian muzzle-loading cannons can be seen on their original carriages. In the keep, which served as living quarters, you can see information on local and overseas regiments that served in Bermuda. Also here are a fine small-arms exhibit, a cooking-area display, and an exhibit of replicas of England's crown jewels. There's a short audiovisual show on St. George's defense systems and the forts of St. George.

15 Coot Pond Rd. ℭ 441/297-1920. Admission $5 adults, $2 children under 12. Daily 10am–4pm. Closed Dec 25.

Gates Fort   Gates Fort was built in 1609 by Sir Thomas Gates, one of the original band of settlers from the *Sea Venture.* Gates was governor-designate for the colony of Virginia.

Cut Rd. No phone. Free admission. Daily 10am–4:30pm.

8

Island Strolls

You can cover much of Bermuda, especially the harbor city of Hamilton and the historic town of St. George, on foot. Indeed, if you had the time, you could walk or bike through all of the parishes and visit the major attractions. But most visitors would rather devote their vacation time to less taxing pursuits, such as relaxing on the beach or playing a leisurely game of golf. If you're interested in seeing the island's sights, however, do consider taking at least one walking tour.

WALKING TOUR 1   THE CITY OF HAMILTON

Start:	The Visitors Service Bureau/Ferry Terminal.
Finish:	Fort Hamilton.
Time:	2½ hours.
Best Time:	Any sunny day.
Worst Time:	When cruise ships are anchored in Hamilton Harbour.

Begin your tour along the harbor front at the:

❶ Visitors Service Bureau/Ferry Terminal

Pick up some free maps and brochures of the island here.

From the bureau, you'll emerge onto Front Street, Hamilton's main street and principal shopping area. Before 1946, there were no cars here. Today, the busy traffic includes small automobiles (driven only by Bermuda residents), buses, mopeds, and bicycles. You'll also see horse-drawn carriages, which are the most romantic (and the most expensive) way to see Hamilton.

At the docks behind the Ferry Terminal you can find the ferries to Warwick and Paget parishes; for details on their attractions, see chapter 7, "Seeing the Sights." You can also take a ferry across Great Sound to the West End and Somerset.

Walk south from the Ferry Terminal toward the water, taking a short side street between the Visitors Service Bureau and the large Bank of Bermuda. You'll come to:

❷ Albouy's Point

This is a small, grassy park with benches and trees that opens onto a panoramic vista of the boat- and ship-filled harbor. Nearby is the Royal Bermuda Yacht Club, an elite rendezvous for the Bermudian and American yachting set—including the rich and famous—since the 1930s. To use the word *royal* in its name, the club obtained special permission from Prince Albert, Queen Victoria's consort. The club sponsors the widely televised Newport–Bermuda Race.

After taking in the view, walk directly north, crossing Point Pleasant Road, to the:

❸ Bank of Bermuda

You can visit the bank Monday to Friday from 9:30am to 3pm. On its mezzanine is Bermuda's most extensive

---

Tips   **Planning Pointer**

You might want to take a ferry ride around the inner harbor before or after your walking tour. You can get an overview of Hamilton before concentrating on specific landmarks or monuments, or gain new perspective on what you've just seen.

---

coin collection—there's at least one sample of every coin minted in the United Kingdom since the reign of King James I in the early 17th century. Many Spanish coins used in colonial days are on display. You'll also see the most famous Bermudian currency, the first coins minted on the island, called "hog money." In use since the early 1600s, the hog coin is stamped on one side with the ill-fated *Sea Venture* and on the other side with a wild hog, the main source of food (except fish) for the early settlers. Look for an 1887 £5 piece depicting Queen Victoria; its appearance led to a protest throughout the British Empire, when critics claimed that the queen's small crown made her look foolish.

Upon leaving the bank, head east along Front Street to the intersection with Queen Street. This is the site of the:
④ "Birdcage"

This is the most photographed sight in Bermuda. Here you can sometimes find a police officer directing traffic; if the "bobby" is a man, he's likely to be wearing regulation Bermuda shorts. The traffic box was named after its designer, Michael "Dickey" Bird. It stands at Heyl's Corner, which was named for an American southerner, J. B. Heyl, who operated a nearby apothecary in the 1800s.

Continue north along Queen Street until you reach:
⑤ Par-la-Ville Park

This was once a private garden attached to the townhouse of William B. Perot, Bermuda's first postmaster. Perot, who designed the gardens in the 19th century, collected rare and exotic plants from all over the globe, including an Indian rubber tree, which was seeded in 1847. Mark Twain wrote that he found the tree "disappointing" in that it didn't bear rubber overshoes and hot-water bottles.

Also opening onto Queen Street at the entrance to the park is the:
⑥ Bermuda Historical Society Museum

The museum, at 13 Queen St., is also the Bermuda Library. It's filled with curiosities, including cedar furniture, collections of antique silver and china, hog money, Confederate money, a 1775 letter from George Washington, and other artifacts. The library has many rare books, including a 1624 edition of John Smith's *General Historie of Virginia, New England and the Somers Isles.* If you'd like to rest and catch up on your reading, you'll also find a selection of current local and British newspapers and periodicals here.

Across the street is the:
⑦ Perot Post Office

William Perot ran this post office from 1818 to 1862. It's said that he'd collect the mail from the clipper ships, then put it under his top hat in order to maintain his dignity. As he proceeded through town, he'd greet his friends and acquaintances by tipping his hat, thereby delivering their mail at the same time. He started printing stamps in 1848. A Perot stamp is extremely valuable today—only 11 are known to exist; Queen Elizabeth II owns several. The last time a Perot stamp came on the market, in 1986, it fetched $135,000.

Walking Tour: The City of Hamilton

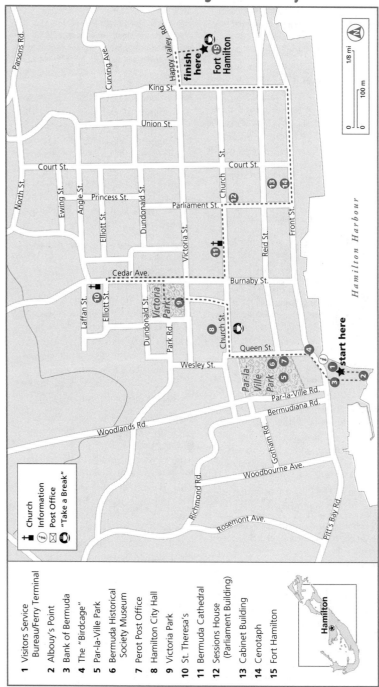

Legend:
- ✚ Church
- ⓘ Information
- ⊠ Post Office
- ☕ "Take a Break"

1. Visitors Service Bureau/Ferry Terminal
2. Albouy's Point
3. Bank of Bermuda
4. The "Birdcage"
5. Par-la-Ville Park
6. Bermuda Historical Society Museum
7. Perot Post Office
8. Hamilton City Hall
9. Victoria Park
10. St. Theresa's
11. Bermuda Cathedral
12. Sessions House (Parliament Building)
13. Cabinet Building
14. Cenotaph
15. Fort Hamilton

Continue to the top of Queen Street, then turn right onto Church Street to reach:

⑧ Hamilton City Hall

Located on 17 Church St., the city hall dates from 1960 and is crowned by a white tower. The bronze weather vane on top is a replica of the *Sea Venture*. Portraits of the queen and paintings of former island leaders adorn the main lobby. The Bermuda Society of Arts holds frequent exhibitions in this hall. The Benbow collection of stamps is also on display.

TAKE A BREAK
The **Paradiso Cafe**, on the ground floor of the Washington Mall, a shopping and office complex on Reid Street (© 441/295-3263), serves the most irresistible pastries in town. You can also order ice cream, tartlets, quiches, croissant sandwiches, espresso, and cappuccino. (For a review, see chapter 5, "Dining.")

In back of Hamilton City Hall, opening onto Victoria Street, lies:

⑨ Victoria Park

Office workers frequent this cool, refreshing oasis on their lunch breaks. It features a sunken garden, ornamental shrubbery, and a Victorian bandstand. The 4-acre park was laid out in honor of Queen Victoria's Golden Jubilee in 1887. Outdoor concerts are held here in summer.

Cedar Avenue is the eastern boundary of Victoria Park. If you follow it north for 2 blocks, you'll reach:

⑩ St. Theresa's

This Roman Catholic cathedral is open daily from 8am to 7pm and for Sunday services. Its architecture was inspired by the Spanish Mission style. Dating from 1927, it's one of a half-dozen Roman Catholic churches in Bermuda; its treasure is a gold-and-silver chalice—a gift from Pope Paul VI when he visited the island in 1968.

After seeing the cathedral, retrace your steps south along Cedar Avenue until you reach Victoria Street. Cedar Avenue now becomes Burnaby Street; continue south to Church Street and turn left. A short walk along this street (on your left) will bring you to:

⑪ Bermuda Cathedral

Also known as the Cathedral of the Most Holy Trinity, this is the seat of the Anglican Church of Bermuda, and it towers over the city skyline. Its style is neo-Gothic, characterized by stained-glass windows and soaring arches. The lectern and pulpit duplicate those of St. Giles in Edinburgh, Scotland.

Leave the cathedral and continue east along Church Street to the:

⑫ Sessions House (Parliament Building)

Located on Parliament Street, between Reid and Church streets, the Sessions House is open to the public Monday to Friday from 9am to 12:30pm and 2 to 5pm. The speaker wears a full wig and a flowing black robe. The Parliament of Bermuda is the third oldest in the world, after Iceland's and England's.

Continue south along Parliament Street to Front Street, and turn left toward the:

⑬ Cabinet Building

The official opening of Parliament takes place here in late October or early November. Wearing a plumed hat and full regalia, the governor makes his "Throne Speech." If you visit on a Wednesday, you can see the Bermuda Senate in action. The building is located between Court and Parliament streets, and is open Monday to Friday from 9am to 5pm.

In front of the Cabinet Building is the:

⑭ Cenotaph

The Cenotaph is a memorial to Bermuda's dead in World War I (1914–18) and World War II (1939–45). In 1920, the Prince of Wales laid the cornerstone. (In 1936, as King Edward VIII, he abdicated to marry an American divorcée, Wallis Simpson; during World War II, as the Duke of Windsor, he served as governor of the Bahamas.) The landmark is a replica of the Cenotaph in London.

Continue east along Front Street until you reach King Street, then turn left and head north until you come to Happy Valley Road. Go right on this road until you see the entrance (on your right) to:

⓯ Fort Hamilton
This imposing old fortress lies on the eastern outskirts of town. The Duke of Wellington ordered its construction to protect Hamilton Harbour. Filled with underground passageways and complete with a moat and 18-ton

guns, the fort was outdated before it was even completed, and it never fired a shot. It does, however, offer panoramic views of the city and the harbor; it's worth a trip just for the view. In summer, try to be here at noon, when the kilted Bermuda Isles Pipe Band performs a skirling ceremony on the green, accompanied by dancers and drummers.

WINDING DOWN
Enjoy old-fashioned tea at the **Fort Hamilton Tea Shoppe** (no phone), where you can also order light refreshments.

WALKING TOUR 2   HISTORIC ST. GEORGE TOWN

Start:	King's Square.
Finish:	Somers Wharf.
Time:	2 hours, not counting the time you spend inside the buildings.
Best Time:	Any sunny day except Sunday, when many destinations are closed.
Worst Time:	When a cruise ship is anchored in the harbor.

At the eastern end of the island, St. George was the second English town established in the New World (after Jamestown, Virginia). For the history buff, it holds more interest than Hamilton.

We'll begin the tour at:
❶ King's Square
Also known as Market Square and King's Parade, the square is the very center of St. George. Only about 200 years old, it's not as historic as St. George itself. This was formerly a marshy part of the harbor—at least when the shipwrecked passengers and crew of the *Sea Venture* first saw it. At the water's edge stands a branch of the Visitors Service Bureau, where you can pick up additional information on the area. On the square you'll notice a replica of a pillory and stocks. The devices were used to punish criminals—and, in many cases, the innocent. You could be severely punished here for such "crimes" as casting a spell over your neighbor's turkeys.

From the square, head south across the small bridge to:
❷ Ordnance Island
The British army once stored gunpowder and cannons on this island, which juts into St. George's Harbour. Today, the island houses the *Deliverance,* a replica of the vessel that carried the shipwrecked *Sea Venture* passengers on to Virginia. Alongside the vessel is a ducking stool, a contraption used in 17th-century witch trials.

Retrace your steps across the bridge to King's Square. On the waterside stands the:
❸ White Horse Tavern
This restaurant juts out into St. George's Harbour. Consider the tavern as a possible spot for lunch later (for a review, see chapter 5, "Dining"). For now, we'll focus on its history: It

Walking Tour: Historic St. George Town

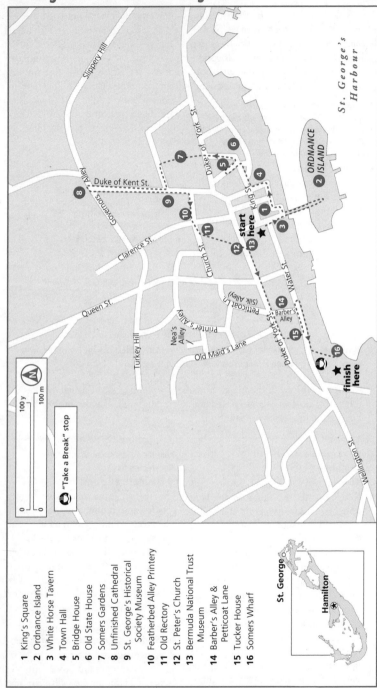

St. George's Harbour

Slippery Hill

Duke of York St.

Duke of Kent St.

Governors Alley

Clarence St.

King St.

ORDNANCE ISLAND

start here

Queen St.

Church St.

Water St.

Turkey Hill

Nea's Alley

Printer's Alley

Old Maid's Lane

Petticoat Ln. (Silk Alley)

Duke of York St.

Barber's Alley

finish here

Wellington St.

0 ___ 100 y
0 ___ 100 m

🖐 "Take a Break" stop

1 King's Square
2 Ordnance Island
3 White Horse Tavern
4 Town Hall
5 Bridge House
6 Old State House
7 Somers Gardens
8 Unfinished Cathedral
9 St. George's Historical
    Society Museum
10 Featherbed Alley Printery
11 Old Rectory
12 St. Peter's Church
13 Bermuda National Trust
    Museum
14 Barber's Alley &
    Petticoat Lane
15 Tucker House
16 Somers Wharf

St. George

Hamilton

was once the home of John Davenport, who came to Bermuda in 1815 to open a dry-goods store. Davenport was a bit of a miser; upon his death, some £75,000 in gold and silver was discovered stashed away in his cellar.

Across the square stands the:

❹ Town Hall

Located near the Visitors Service Bureau, this is the meeting place of the corporation governing St. George. It has antique cedar furnishings and a collection of photographs of previous lord mayors. *Bermuda Journey,* a multimedia audiovisual presentation, is shown here several times a day.

From King's Square, head east along King Street, cutting north (left) on Bridge Street. You'll come to the:

❺ Bridge House

Constructed in the 1690s, this was once the home of several governors of Bermuda. Located at 1 Bridge St., it's furnished with 18th- and 19th-century antiques, and houses an art gallery and souvenir shop.

Return to King Street and continue east to the:

❻ Old State House

The State House opens onto Princess Street, at the top of King Street. This is the oldest stone building in Bermuda, dating from 1620, and was once the home of the Bermuda Parliament. It's the site of the ancient Peppercorn Ceremony, in which the Old State House pays the government "rent" of one peppercorn annually. See chapter 7, "Seeing the Sights," for details on this grand ceremony.

Continue your stroll down Princess Street until you come to Duke of York Street and the entrance to:

❼ Somers Garden

The heart of Sir George Somers, the admiral of the *Sea Venture,* is buried here. The gardens, opened in 1920 by the Prince of Wales, contain palms and other tropical plants.

Walk through Somers Gardens and up the steps to the North Gate onto Blockade Alley. Climb the hill to the structure known as "the folly of St. George's," the:

❽ Unfinished Cathedral

This cathedral was intended to replace St. Peter's Church (see stop number 12 on this tour). Work began on the church in 1874, but eventually ended; the church was beset by financial difficulties and a schism in the Anglican congregation.

After viewing the ruins, turn left onto Duke of Kent Street, which leads down to the:

❾ St. George's Historical Society Museum

Located at Featherbed Alley and Duke of Kent Street, the museum building is an example of 18th-century architecture. It contains a collection of Bermudian historical artifacts and cedar furniture.

Around the corner on Featherbed Alley is the:

❿ Featherbed Alley Printery

Here you can see a working replica of the type of printing press invented by Johannes Gutenberg in Germany in the 1450s.

Go up Featherbed Alley and straight onto Church Street. At the junction with Broad Lane, look to your right to see the:

⓫ Old Rectory

The Old Rectory is located at the head of Broad Alley, behind St. Peter's Church. Now a private home but administered by the National Trust, it was built in 1705 by a reformed pirate. You can go inside only on Wednesdays from noon to 5pm.

After seeing the Old Rectory, go through the church's back yard, opposite Broad Alley, to reach:

⓬ St. Peter's Church

The church's main entrance is on Duke of York Street. This is believed to be the oldest Anglican place of worship in the Western Hemisphere. In the churchyard, you'll see many headstones, some 300 years old. The

Rattle & Shake: The Bermuda Railway Trail

One of the most unusual sightseeing adventures in Bermuda is follow-ing the Bermuda Railway Trail (or parts thereof), which stretches for 21 miles along the old railroad right-of-way across three of the intercon-nected islands that make up Bermuda. Construction of this rail line may have been one of the most costly ever on a per-mile basis. Opened in 1931, the Bermuda Railway ceased operations in 1948. Once the island's main mode of transportation, the train eventually gave way to the automobile.

Before setting out on this trek, arm yourself with a copy of the *Bermuda Railway Trail Guide*, which is available at the Bermuda Department of Tourism in Hamilton and the Visitors Service Bureaus in Hamilton and St. George. You're now ready to hit the trail of the old train system that was affectionately called "Rattle and Shake." You can explore the trail on horseback, bicycle, or foot.

Although the line covered 21 miles from St. George in the east to Somerset in the west, a 3-mile stretch has been lost to roads in and around the capital city of Hamilton. For the most part, however, the trail winds along an automobile-free route, permitting some views of Bermuda not seen by the public since the end of World War II.

In the West End, the trail begins near the Watford Bridge, but there are many convenient access points. In the East End, it's most conven-ient to pick up the trail on North Shore Road.

Along the way, you'll see some rare Bermuda cedar, which nearly vanished as a result of the blight that struck the island in the early 1940s. There's also much greenery and semitropical vegetation, such as the poinsettia, oleander, and hibiscus. You can also see and visit Fort Scaur, the 1870s fortress in Sandys Parish. The tour of Sandys Parish, above, follows the detailed section of the route that includes Fort Scaur.

If you only have time to see a small part of the trail, we recommend you take in something of the 5-acre Gilbert Nature Reserve. The most scenic view begins at Somerset Bridge; head west from there.

---

assassinated governor, Sir Richard Sharples, was buried here. The present church was built in 1713, with a tower added in 1814.

Across the street is the:

⑬ Bermuda National Trust Museum

When it was the Globe Hotel, this was the headquarters of Maj. Norman Walker, the Confederate representa-tive in Bermuda. It was once a hotbed of blockade running.

Go west along Duke of York Street to:

⑭ Barber's Alley & Petticoat Lane

Barber's Alley honors Joseph Hayne Rainey. A former slave from South Carolina, Rainey fled to Bermuda with his French wife at the outbreak of the Civil War. He became a barber in St. George and eventually returned to South Carolina, where in 1870 he was elected to the U.S. House of Repre-sentatives—the first African American to serve in Congress.

Nearby is Petticoat Lane, also known as Silk Alley. The name dates from the 1834 emancipation, when two former slave women who'd always wanted silk petticoats like their former mistresses finally got some—and paraded up and down the lane to show off their new finery.

Continue west until you reach:

⑮ Tucker House

Opening onto Water Street, this was the former home of a prominent Bermudian family, whose members included an island governor, a treasurer of the United States, and a captain in the Confederate Navy. The building houses an excellent collection of antiques, including silver, portraits, and cedar furniture. One room is

devoted to memorabilia of Joseph Hayne Rainey.

TAKE A BREAK
Diagonally across from the Tucker House is the **Carriage House**, 22 Water St., Somers Wharf (© **441/297-1730**), a former waterfront storehouse and an excellent place for lunch. You can sample the famous Bermuda fish chowder here. Sandwich platters, soups, salads, and juicy burgers are also available. (For a review, see chapter 5, "Dining.")

End your tour across the street at:

⑯ Somers Wharf

This multimillion-dollar waterfront restoration project contains shops, restaurants, and taverns.

WALKING TOUR 3 | SANDYS PARISH

Start:	Somerset Bridge.
Finish:	Somerset Long Bay Park.
Time:	7 hours.
Best Time:	Any sunny day.
Worst Time:	When the weather's bad.

Sandys (pronounced "sands"), the far western parish of Bermuda, consists of Somerset Island (the largest and southernmost), Watford, Boaz, and Ireland islands. When Bermudians cross into Somerset on Somerset Bridge, they say they are "up the country."

Craggy coastlines, beaches, nature reserves, fisher's coves, old fortifications, winding lanes, and sleepy villages characterize this area. All of Sandys' major attractions lie along the main road from Somerset Bridge to the Royal Naval Dockyard, which is at the end of Ireland Island.

Although we describe this as a walking tour, you may want to rent a bicycle or moped to help you cover the longer stretches.

From the center of Hamilton, you can take a ferry to Somerset. Check the schedule: Some boats take only 30 minutes, others up to an hour. The longer trip affords a more leisurely opportunity to enjoy the waters of Great Sound. You can bring your cycle or moped aboard the ferry. You can also see the West End by bus (for details, see "Getting Around," in chapter 3, "Getting to Know Bermuda").

To begin the tour, take the ferry from Hamilton to:

❶ Somerset Bridge

This bridge links Somerset Island with the rest of Bermuda. It was among the

first three bridges constructed on Bermuda in the 1600s, and it's said to be the smallest drawbridge in the world—its opening is just wide

Walking Tour: Sandys Parish

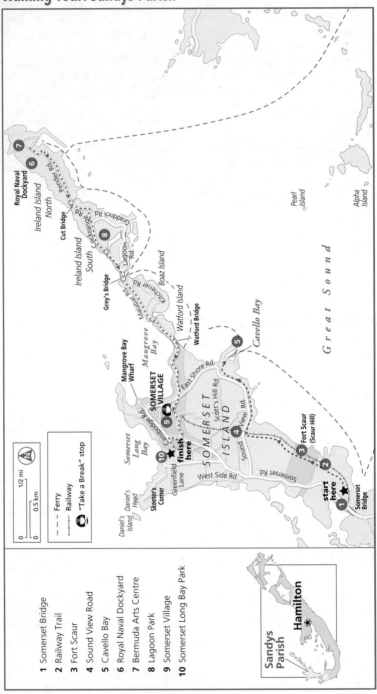

Legend:

- - - Ferry
-+-+- Railway
🚶 "Take a Break" stop

1 Somerset Bridge
2 Railway Trail
3 Fort Scaur
4 Sound View Road
5 Cavello Bay
6 Royal Naval Dockyard
7 Bermuda Arts Centre
8 Lagoon Park
9 Somerset Village
10 Somerset Long Bay Park

Royal Naval Dockyard
Ireland Island North
Pender Rd.
Cut Bridge
Ireland Island South
Craddock Rd.
Lagoon Rd.
Boaz Island
Grey's Bridge
Kitchener Rd.
Malabar Rd.
Watford Island
Watford Bridge
Mangrove Bay Wharf
Mangrove Bay
SOMERSET VILLAGE
East Shore Rd.
Cavello Bay
Cambridge Rd.
Scott's Hill Rd.
SOMERSET ISLAND
Somerset Long Bay
Sound View Rd.
Fort Scaur (Scaur Hill)
finish here
Skeeter's Corner
Greenfield Lane
West Side Rd.
Sound Rd.
Somerset Rd.
start here
Somerset Bridge

Daniel's Island
Daniel's Head

Pearl Island
Alpha Island

Great Sound

Sandys Parish
Hamilton

enough to accommodate a sailboat mast. Near the bridge you can see the old Somerset Post Office and an 18th-century cottage known as Crossways.

Next, walk up Somerset Road about 75 yards to the entrance to the:

❷ Railway Trail

Open only to pedestrians and bikers, the trail follows the path of old "Rattle and Shake," the Bermuda Railway line that once ran the length of the island. This section of the trail—between Somerset Bridge and Sound View Road—is one of its most attractive (good to know if you don't want to walk the whole trail—although some hearty visitors do just that). Parts of the trail open onto the coast, affording panoramic vistas of the Great Sound.

TAKE A BREAK The trail goes across the parkland of Fort Scaur (see below), with its large moat. If you're here around noontime, you might want to consider this as a picnic spot. If you can spend all day in Somerset (which we highly recommend), you might also want to take time out for a swim before returning to your walking or cycling.

Follow the signposts to:

❸ Fort Scaur

In the 1870s, the British feared an attack from the United States, so they built this fort on the highest hill in Somerset to protect Her Majesty's Royal Naval Dockyard. It sits on 22 acres of land and opens onto Somerset Road; the huge dry moat cuts right across Somerset Island. You can wander at leisure around this fort, which proved unnecessary because the invasion never materialized. If you stand on the ramparts, you'll be rewarded with a marvelous view of Great Sound. Through a telescope, you can see such distant sights as St. David's

Lighthouse and Fort St. Catherine in the East End of Bermuda. If you follow the eastern moat all the way down to the Great Sound shore, you'll find ideal places for swimming and fishing.

After exploring the surrounding Scaur Hill Fort Park, resume your walk along the railway track and continue north for more than a mile, then turn right onto:

❹ Sound View Road

Take a stroll along this sleepy residential street, which has some of the finest cottages in Bermuda.

Continue around a wide arc, passing Tranquillity Hill and Gwelly and Saltsea lanes. When you come to Scott's Hill Road, take a right and go about 85 yards to East Shore Road. At the first junction, take a little road, Cavello Lane, which branches off to the right; it will take you to:

❺ Cavello Bay

The sheltered cove is a stopping point for the Hamilton ferry. Wait for the next ferry and take it (with your cycle or moped) to Watford Bridge or directly to the:

❻ Royal Naval Dockyard

There's so much to see here, you could spend an entire afternoon. The dockyard is a sprawling complex encompassing 6 acres of Ireland Island. The major attraction is the **Bermuda Maritime Museum,** opened by Queen Elizabeth II in 1975. There's an exhibit of Bermuda's old boats, documenting the island's rich maritime history. You can cross a moat to explore the keep and the 30-foot-high defensive ramparts.

Across the street from the Maritime Museum is the Old Cooperage Building, site of the Neptune Cinema. Adjacent to the cinema is the Craft Market, which sells interesting items. Next door is the:

❼ Bermuda Arts Centre

Princess Margaret opened the Centre in 1984. Showcasing the visual arts and crafts of the island, this nonprofit organization has a volunteer staff.

From the dockyard, it's a long walk to Somerset Village, but many people who have walked or cycled the distance considered it one of the highlights of their Bermuda trip. You'll find some of the best beaches here, so if you get tired along the way, take time out for a refreshing dip in the ocean.

Leave through the dockyard's south entrance and walk down Pender Road about a half-mile. Cross Cockburn's Cut Bridge and go straight along Cockrange Road, which will take you to:

8 Lagoon Park

Enter the park as you cross over the Cut Bridge onto Ireland Island South. Walking trails crisscross the park, which has a lagoon populated with ducks and other wild fowl. There are places for picnicking in the park, which is free and open to the public.

To continue, cross Grey's Bridge to Boaz Island, and walk or cycle along Malabar Road. On your right you'll see the calm waters of Mangrove Bay. You'll eventually arrive at:

9 Somerset Village

Somerset is one of the most charming villages on Bermuda. Only one road goes through the village. Most of the stores are just branches of larger stores in Hamilton.

 TAKE A BREAK
Somerset Country Squire Tavern, 10 Mangrove Bay Rd. (℡ **441/234-0105**), is an English-style pub that serves sandwiches, burgers, and such pub grub as steak-and-kidney pie and bangers and mash (sausages and mashed potatoes). The kitchen is also noted for its desserts. (For a review, see chapter 5, "Dining.")

Follow Cambridge Road west to:

10 Somerset Long Bay Park

Families like this park because of its good beach and shallow waters opening onto Long Bay. You can also picnic here. The Bermuda Audubon Society operates the nature reserve, and the pond attracts migrating birds in both spring and autumn. They include the Louisiana heron, the snowy egret, and the purple gallinule.

9

Shopping

Retailers on less prosperous islands attribute Bermuda's continuing popularity not only to the superb climate, but also to many years of skillful marketing. Indeed, no one has ever accused Bermudians of not knowing how to sell their island—or their rich inventories of goods.

Bermuda, once widely hailed as a "showcase of the British Empire," is still that, at least in its variety of goods. The retail scene draws upon its British antecedents: Shopkeepers are generally both polite and discreet, merchandise unusual and well made. In addition, most retailers take full advantage of location. Shops usually occupy charming cottages or historically important buildings, making shopping more fun. Even visitors who intend to do no more than window-shop are likely to break down and make a purchase or two.

In most cases, shopping on Bermuda is about quality, not bargains. The low prices of yesterday have gone with the wind. Shops face huge import tariffs, plus employer-related taxes; costs have had a ripple effect in the retail industry, leading to what some view as outrageously high prices. Once you're on Bermuda, it rarely pays to comparison-shop. Prices are rather uniform: The price of a watch in a branch store in St. George is likely to be exactly the same as in the main shop in Hamilton.

BERMUDA'S BEST BUYS

Most of Bermuda's best shops are along Front Street in Hamilton, where shopping is relaxed and casual. Among the choicest items are imports from Great Britain and Ireland, such as Shetland and cashmere sweaters, Harris tweed jackets, Scottish woolen goods and tartan kilts, and even fine china and crystal. Many items cost appreciably less than in their country of origin.

Because of a special "colony"-like arrangement with Great Britain, certain British goods can be cheaper in Bermuda than in the United States, thanks to lower import tariffs. Some frequent visitors stock up on porcelain, crystal, silverware, jewelry, timepieces, and perfume, perhaps anticipating a wedding gift several months in advance. The island abounds with merchandisers of fine tableware, including Royal Copenhagen, Wedgwood, and Royal Crown Derby. Crystal is also plentiful, with many of the finest manufacturers in Europe and North America providing wide selections of merchandise. For a fee, items can be shipped, usually in well-wrapped packages that minimize breakage.

Liquor is also a good buy in Bermuda. U.S. citizens are allowed to bring back only 1 liter duty-free, but even adding U.S. tax and duty, you can save 35 to 50% on liquor purchases, depending on the brand. Liqueurs offer the largest savings.

The island's wealth of antiques and collectibles is extraordinary. Antique lovers appreciate Bermuda's fusion of British aesthetic and mid-Atlantic charm. The island has a wealth of antique engravings and 19th-century furniture. Its modern artwork and handmade pottery and crafts might become elegant heirlooms. And anyone interested in carrying home a piece of Bermuda's nautical heritage is likely to find oversized ship's propellers, captain's bells, brass nameplates, scale models of sailing ships, or maybe even an old-fashioned ship's steering wheel from a salvaged shipwreck.

Other good buys are "Bermudiana"— products made on Bermuda or manufactured elsewhere exclusively for local stores. They include cedarwood gifts, carriage bells, coins commemorating the 375th anniversary of the island's settlement, flower plates by Spode, pewter tankards, hand-crafted gold jewelry, traditional-line handbags with cedar or mahogany handles, miniature cottages in ceramic or limestone, shark's teeth polished and mounted in 14-karat gold, decorative kitchen items, Bermuda shorts (of course), silk scarves, and watches with a map of Bermuda on their faces.

Although some items might be less expensive than they are stateside, be aware that this isn't always the case. In fact, many, many items are overpriced. You should be familiar with prices on comparable goods back home before committing yourself to serious purchases.

1 The Shopping Scene

WHERE TO GO

THE CITY OF HAMILTON

The best and widest range of shopping choices is in Hamilton (see "In the City of Hamilton," below). Most shops are on Front Street, but you should explore the back streets as well, especially if you're an adventurous shopper.

The Emporium on Front Street, a restored building constructed around an atrium, houses a number of shops, including jewelry stores. Windsor Place on Queen Street is another Bermuda-style shopping mall.

HISTORIC ST. GEORGE

The "second city" of St. George also has many shops, stores, and boutiques, including branches of famous Front Street stores. King's Square, the center of St. George, is home to many shops; the other major centers are Somers Wharf and Water Street.

In recent years this historic port has emerged as a big-time competitor to Hamilton. It's easier to walk around St. George, and more interesting architecturally than Hamilton, so more and more customers are doing their shopping here. Of course, St. George doesn't have as vast an array of merchandise as Hamilton, so the serious shopper might want to explore both cities.

SANDYS PARISH

Don't overlook the shopping possibilities of the West End. Somerset Village in Sandys Parish has many shops (though quite a few are just branches of Hamilton

---

(*Tips* **The Eternal Search for Bargains**

To find real bargains, you must shop harder and longer than before; you'll usually find them in the off-season (autumn and winter), when, with no uniformity, stores often reduce prices to make way for goods for the new season. But sales come and go year-round—there's no particular season. Keep an eye out for "sale" signs no matter when you're in Bermuda.

---

stores). Of even greater interest may be the Royal Naval Dockyard area on Ireland Island. You can visit the Craft Market, Island Pottery, and the Bermuda Arts Centre at Dockyard, where you'll see local artisans at work.

WHAT YOU SHOULD KNOW
STORE HOURS
Stores in Hamilton, St. George, and Somerset are generally open Monday to Saturday 9am to 5:30pm. When large liners are in port, stores sometimes stay open later, and are sometimes open on Sundays.

FINDING AN ADDRESS
Some Front Street stores post numbers on their buildings; others don't. Sometimes the number posted or used is the "historic" number of the building, which has nothing to do with the modern number. You can always ask for directions, and most Bermudians are willing to help. Outside Hamilton, don't expect to find numbers on buildings at all—or even street names in some cases.

SALES TAX & DUTY
There's no sales tax in Bermuda, but it's not a duty-free island. Depending on which country you're returning to, you may have to pay duty. See "Entry Requirements & Customs," in chapter 2, "Planning Your Trip to Bermuda," for details.

Note: Like various other countries and territories, including several in the Caribbean, Bermuda is covered by the U.S. law regarding "Generalized System of Preferences" status. That means that if at least 35% of an item has been crafted in Bermuda, you can bring it back duty-free, regardless of how much you spent. If you've gone beyond your $400 allotment, make a separate list of goods made in Bermuda. That will make it easier for the customs officials and, ultimately, for you.

2 In the City of Hamilton
DEPARTMENT STORES
H. A. & E. Smith, Ltd.   This store has sold top-quality merchandise since 1889, at substantial savings over U.S. prices. Smith's comprehensive stock includes sweaters for men and women (in cotton, cashmere, lamb's wool, and Shetland), British cosmetics, and a collection from the top French parfumeurs. Smith's is noted for its selection of handbags, gloves, a very limited array of Liberty fabrics by the yard, and children's clothing. It also carries such merchandise as Fendi handbags from Italy, Burberry's rainwear from London, and Rosenthal china. A subsidiary, "The Treasure Chest," across the street from the main store, carries a full line of French perfumes and gifts, plus souvenirs. 35 Front St. ✆ 441/295-2288.

Marks & Spencer   This branch of the famous British chain (sometimes oddly called "St. Michael") carries the same reliable merchandise as its sibling stores in the British Isles. You'll find men's, women's, and children's fashions in everything from resort wear to sleepwear, including lingerie. There are also well-tailored dresses and suits, dress shirts, blazers, and British-tailored trousers, as well as swimwear, toiletries, and English sweets and biscuits. 7 Reid St. ✆ 441/295-0031.

Trimingham's   Since 1842, Trimingham's has been Bermuda's largest department store, offering a full range of fine merchandise and featuring the largest selection of duty-free items on the island. You'll find Bermuda's best selection of cosmetics and perfumes, including exclusives from Estée Lauder and Clinique. Waterford, Lenox, Portmeirion, and other fine china and crystal are for sale at rates up to 30% off U.S. prices. Fine jewelry is often a good buy here. The store also stocks a wide range of Bermuda shorts, cashmere sweaters, and polo shirts. 2 Front St. ℂ 441/295-2615.

GOODS A TO Z
ANTIQUES

Heritage House   This outlet sells nautical prints, English antiques, old maps, modern porcelain, and the largest collection of fine art on the island. Many new gift items have been recently added, including one of the best collections of costume jewelry in town. Look for the large collection of "Halcyon Days" pillboxes. 2 Front St. W. ℂ 441/295-2615.

Pegasus   Pegasus carries a wide range of antique prints, engravings, and magazine illustrations. Owner Robert Lee and his wife, Barbara, scour the print shops of the British Isles to stock this unusual store. This is the best selection on Bermuda: The inventory is varied, with old maps of many regions of the world and more than 1,000 literary, sporting, medical, and legal caricatures from *Vanity Fair*. Most prints date from the late 1700s to the late 1800s and are carefully grouped according to subject. The authenticity of whatever you buy is guaranteed in writing.

The Lees also offer ceramic house signs made at a small pottery in England. Each is unique—the buyer chooses the design, and the "house" and the house name or a number and street are hand-painted to specifications.

The shop also carries a wide range of English greeting cards, many with botanical designs. Maps, lithographs, and engravings are duty-free and will not affect your take-home quota. 63 Pitts Bay Rd. (at Front St. W.), across from The Fairmont Hamilton Princess. ℂ 441/295-2900.

ART

Bermuda Society of Arts   Loosely associated with the Bermudian government, this store devoted to the exhibition of works by Bermuda-based artists is one of the focal points of the island's arts scene. In the West Wing of Hamilton's City Hall (the island's Fine Arts Museum occupies the East Wing), it's the permanent home of the oldest arts society on Bermuda. The association of respected artists and art patrons received a formal seal of approval from Bermuda's Parliament in 1956. The site contains two separate exhibition areas, where the artwork changes every 2 to 3 weeks. Themes range from the moderately avant-garde to the conservative, and every show includes dozens of examples of Bermudian landscapes, seascapes, or architectural renderings, any of which would make worthwhile souvenirs of your stay on the island. All merchandise can be packed for airplane transport. W. Wing of City Hall, 17 Church St. ℂ 441/292-3824.

Carole Holding Studios   Carole Holding is well known and well respected for her skill in what might be Bermuda's most-loved art form: watercolor painting. Many of Ms. Holding's works depict the peace and serenity of Bermuda's homes and gardens. A few of her works are commissioned by individuals; more frequently, however, the subjects of her paintings come from her own imagination. Although other gift shops around the island carry Ms. Holding's works, most of them are in one of her shops. Her main store is now in Hamilton (the St. George shop has been closed). She has another store at the Royal Naval Dockyard on Ireland Island. 81 Front St., Hamilton. ℂ 441/296-3431.

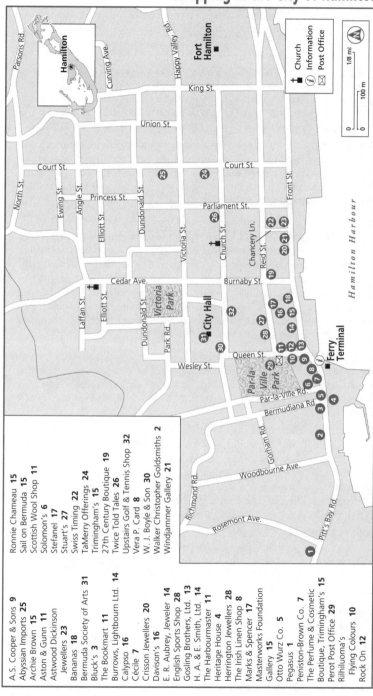

A.S. Cooper & Sons 9
Abyssian Imports 25
Archie Brown 15
Aston & Gunn 11
Astwood Dickinson
  Jewellers 23
Bananas 18
Bermuda Society of Arts 31
Bluck's 3
The Bookmart 11
Burrows, Lightbourn Ltd. 14
Calypso 16
Cécile 7
Crisson Jewellers 20
Davison's 16
E. R. Aubrey, Jeweler 14
English Sports Shop 28
Gosling Brothers, Ltd. 13
H. A. & E. Smith, Ltd. 14
The Harbourmaster 11
Heritage House 4
Herrington Jewellers 28
The Irish Linen Shop 8
Marks & Spencer 17
Masterworks Foundation
  Gallery 15
Otto Wurz Co. 5
Pegasus 1
Peniston-Brown Co. 7
The Perfume & Cosmetic
  Boutique, Trimingham's 15
Perot Post Office 29
Rihiluoma's
  Flying Colours 10
Rock On 12

Ronnie Chameau 15
Sail on Bermuda 15
Scottish Wool Shop 11
Solomon's 6
Stefanel 17
Stuart's 27
Swiss Timing 22
TaMerry Offerings 24
Trimingham's 15
27th Century Boutique 19
Twice Told Tales 26
Upstairs Golf & Tennis Shop 32
Vera P. Card 8
W. J. Boyle & Son 30
Walker Christopher Goldsmiths 2
Windjammer Gallery 21

Masterworks Foundation Gallery   Established in 1987 by a group of international philanthropists, this foundation showcases paintings by renowned European, Bermudian, and North American artists. It serves to some extent as the island's most visible arts center. The foundation sponsors frequent art exhibitions, which have included works by Georgia O'Keeffe (who painted in Bermuda during the early 1930s), seascapes by Winslow Homer, and watercolors by Ogden Pleissner. The foundation also arranges guided art and architectural tours around the island and coordinates other artistic endeavors and exhibitions throughout the year. Bermuda House Lane, 97 Front St. ✆ 441/295-5580.

Windjammer Gallery   In a coral cottage, this gallery exhibits paintings and bronze sculptures by local and international artists; it also carries an extensive selection of cards, prints, and limited editions. Adjacent to the gallery is the last private garden in the city, used for the display of sculpture and exhibitions. Reid and King sts. ✆ 441/292-7861.

ARTS & CRAFTS

Ronnie Chameau   Noted local artist Ronnie Chameau, known throughout the island for her charming handmade dolls, crafts doll-shaped ornaments from such natural ingredients as banana leaves, hazelnuts, and grapefruit leaves, gathered from her own and her friends' gardens. Each ornament has a unique personality and comes individually boxed and gift-wrapped. The small dolls are reasonably priced. Ms. Chameau also makes dolls wearing authentic 19th-century costumes, as well as wooden doorstops designed to look like Bermuda cottages. At Trimingham's, 37 Front St. ✆ 441/295-1183.

BEACHWEAR & SUNGLASSES

Bananas   This outlet offers colorful, good-quality Bermuda signature items. You'll find T-shirts, jackets, beach bags, and beach umbrellas that will let your friends know where you've been. Front St. W. (opposite the Bank of Bermuda). ✆ 441/295-8241.

Calypso   Calypso carries casual, fun fashions (including unusual garments from around the world) and the most comprehensive selection of swimwear on Bermuda. The shop also features Italian leather goods, espadrilles, hats, bags, pareos, Italian ceramics, and whimsical gift items. It's the exclusive island retailer of Louis Vuitton luggage and accessories. There are branches at The Fairmont Southampton Princess, The Fairmont Hamilton Princess, the Sonesta Beach Hotel, the Coral Beach Club, and the dockyard. 23–24 Front St. ✆ 441/295-2112.

Sail on Bermuda   The locals shop at this store, which carries a unique collection of casual wear, bathing suits, and gifts. A recent poll of shoppers named Sail on Bermuda's T-shirts the best on Bermuda. A small addition, called "Shades of Bermuda," has the finest collection of sunglasses on the island. Old Cellar, Front St. ✆ 441/295-0808.

BOOKS

The Bookmart   This is the biggest bookstore on Bermuda. It specializes in bestsellers—mainly from the U.S. market—and carries works by British authors as well. One section is devoted to books about the island. There's also a well-stocked section for the kiddies. Phoenix Centre, 3 Reid St. ✆ 441/295-3838.

CHINA & GLASSWARE

Also see Trimingham's under "Department Stores, above.

A. S. Cooper & Sons   Bermuda's oldest and largest china and glassware store—family-owned since 1897—offers a broad range of fine bone china, earthenware, and jewelry. Among the famous names represented are Minton, Royal Doulton, Belleek, Aynsley, Wedgwood, and Royal Copenhagen. The Crystal Room displays Orrefors, Waterford, Royal Brierley, and Kosta Boda, among others. The Collector's Gallery is known for its limited editions of Bing & Gröndahl, Royal Doulton, and Lladró. The perfume department offers selections from the world's greatest perfumeries. 59 Front St. ☎ **441/295-3961.**

Bluck's   Established in 1844, Bluck's is well known for carrying some of the finest names in china and crystal, including Royal Worcester, Spode, Aynsley, Royal Doulton, and Herend porcelain from Hungary. The choice in crystal is equally impressive: Kosta Boda, Waterford, Baccarat, Daum, and Lalique (exclusive with Bluck's). Upstairs is the Antiques Room, filled with fine English furniture, antique Bermuda maps, and an array of old English silver. Bluck's has branch shops on Water Street in St. George and in The Fairmont Southampton Princess. 4 Front St. ☎ **441/295-5367.**

FASHION

Also see "Shoes," "Sportswear," and "Woolens," below.

Aston & Gunn   This shop sells career-oriented clothing for men (imported from Germany and Holland), with a small women's department, as well. In addition to the usual collection of shirts, ties, jackets, and suits, Aston & Gunn is the exclusive island distributor of Calvin Klein underwear. 2 Reid St. ☎ **441/295-4866.**

Cécile   Well-stocked Cécile is a center for high fashion on Bermuda. Management claims that visiting one of Cécile's shops (the others are in England) is like calling upon the fashion capitals of the world—you'll find everything from German high fashion to Gottex swimwear. Its sweater and accessory boutique is also outstanding. 15 Front St. W. (near the Visitors Service Bureau and the Ferry Terminal). ☎ **441/295-1311.**

Stefanel   This is the island's only outlet for the clothing of Carlo Stefanel, a well-known Italian designer. Stocking merchandise for both men and women, the store sells tropical-weight men's suits (in cotton and linen) and handmade skirts (some of them knit) with contrasting jackets for women. There's a stylish array of accessories and a line of clothing for infants and children. 12 Reid St. ☎ **441/295-5698.**

27th Century Boutique   Long known as a stylish, trendsetting shop, this boutique carries designer clothing, silver costume jewelry, and accessories. The European clothing is styled for women ages 13 and up—on our recent visit, a 16-year-old and a grandmother bought the same shirt. The clothing is rather conservative and in good taste. The store also has a nice collection of shoes, for both men and women, from Canada and London. 4 Burnaby St. (between Front and Church sts.). ☎ **441/292-2628.**

GIFTS

Riihiluoma's Flying Colours   This is everybody's favorite catchall emporium for inexpensive, impulse-purchase souvenirs and T-shirts with perky slogans. You'll also find paperweights; beach cover-ups; sarongs like actress Dorothy Lamour used to wear; key chains shaped like the island of Bermuda; and arts and crafts. The establishment's hard-to-spell name comes from the Finnish-born family that established it in 1937 and still manages it today. 5 Queen St. ℭ **441/ 295-0890.**

Vera P. Card   Vera P. Card is known for its "gifts from around the world," including the island's largest collection of Lladró and Hummel figurines. Famous-name watches include Nivada, Borel, and Rodania. The dinnerware collection features such brands as Rosenthal, and the crystal department offers a wide assortment of Czech and Bohemian crystal, giftware, and chandeliers. Look for the "Bermuda Collection" of 14-karat gold jewelry. Other branches are at 7 Water St. in St. George and at the Sonesta Beach Resort. 11 Front St. ℭ **441/ 295-1729.**

JEWELRY

Astwood Dickinson Jewellers   Here you'll find a treasure trove of famous-name watches, including Patek Philippe, Cartier, Tiffany, Tag Heuer, Tissot, Omega, and Swiss Army, plus designer jewelry, all at prices generally below U.S. retail. From the original Bermuda collection, you can select an 18-karat gold memento of the island. The jewelers are also the agents for Colombian Emeralds International. There are branches in the Walker Arcade and in the H. A. & E. Smith, Ltd. department store. 83–85 Front St. ℭ **441/292-5805.**

Crisson Jewellers   Crisson is the exclusive Bermuda agent for Rolex, Ebel, Seiko, Cyma, and Gucci watches, and for other well-known makers. It also carries an extensive selection of fine jewelry and gems. Branches are on Queen Street and in several of the major hotels, including the Elbow Beach Hotel, the Sonesta Beach Resort, and the Fairmont Princess hotels. 55 and 71 Front St. ℭ **441/ 295-2351.**

E. R. Aubrey, Jeweler   This shop carries an extensive collection of gold chains, rings with precious and semiprecious stones, and charms, including the Bermuda longtail. 19 Front St. W. (opposite the Ferry Terminal). ℭ **441/295-3826.**

Herrington Jewellers   This leading jewelry store offers a good selection of gold and silver items. It's the authorized dealer for Citizen watches, sells Timex watches, and carries a vast selection of 14-karat gold chains and rings set with precious and semiprecious stones. 1 Washington Mall. ℭ **441/292-6527.**

Solomon's   Many jewelry stores hawk their glittering wares to the cruise-going public, but some aficionados of the shopping scene consider this one of the most appealing. Don't expect a supermarket-style emporium with vast inventories: Solomon's is small, select, and ever so polite, with a range of valuable stones mostly set in 18-karat gold (and, to a lesser degree, in platinum). 17 Front St. (opposite the cruise-ship terminal). ℭ **441/292-4742.**

Swiss Timing   All the best names in Swiss watchmaking are found here, including Maurice Lacroix, Michel Herbelin, and Favre Leuba, along with a selection of semi-precious jewelry, gold chains, and bracelets. Walker's Arcade Chancery Lane. ℭ **441/295-1376.**

Walker Christopher Goldsmiths   For the last decade or so, the *Bermudian* magazine has cited this goldsmith for selling the finest jewelry on the island. The shop showcases everything from classic diamond bands to strands of South Sea pearls to modern hand-hammered chokers. The store also carriers a collection of rare coins—gold doubloons and silver "pieces of eight" salvaged from sunken galleons, as well as Greek and Roman coins which can be mounted and worn as

(Finds Counterculture Shopping

If you view yourself as part of the counterculture, and much of Bermuda is a bit prim for you, we have a few unusual stores to suggest. Try dropping in at **Twice Told Tales,** 34 Parliament St. (✆ **441/296-1995**), in Hamilton, where kindred spirits gather at one of the few tables for coffee and conversation. We can't think of a better name for this store, which is a secondhand bookshop.

Here's a chance to meet the locals—**Rock On,** 23 Queen St. (✆ **441/295-3468**), in Hamilton, provides a full range of herb teas, nutritional supplements, and books and magazines devoted to health issues.

TaMerry Offerings, 43 Court St. (✆ **441/292-7389**) in Hamilton, means "Happy Land" in ancient Egyptian. At this unusual store you'll find all sorts of clothing and products made from hemp, including soap, shower gel, body lotions, bags, shoes, shirts, and dresses. There's also selection of books on African culture and an array of moderately priced jewelry.

Ethiopia provides the stock to fill **Abyssian Imports,** 79 Court St. (✆ **441/292-3208**) in Hamilton. African garments, incense, silver, leather bags, oils, and carvings from the continent's west coast are sold.

---

pendants, earrings, and cufflinks. Even Egyptian artifacts have been transformed into wearable art. Customers who have their own design in mind can work with a master jeweler to craft a one-of-a-kind piece. The workshop onsite also produces Bermuda-inspired gold jewelry and sterling silver Christmas ornaments. 9 Front St. ✆ **441/295-1466**.

LEATHER GOODS

The Harbourmaster   This is your best bet for luggage and leather goods. The good value items are from Colombia—often sold at prices 30% lower than in the United States. There are more expensive leather goods from Italy (such as handbags), an extensive collection of wallets, and nylon and canvas tote bags. The shop also stocks travel accessories, including luggage carts. The branch at the corner of Reid and Queen streets (✆ **441/295-4210**) carries essentially the same merchandise. Washington Mall. ✆ **441/295-5333**.

LINENS

The Irish Linen Shop   At Heyl's Corner, near the "Birdcage" police officer post, this shop stocks pure linen tablecloths from Ireland and a large variety of other merchandise from Europe—everything from quilted place mats to men's shirts in French cotton from Souleiado of Provence. The owners go to Europe twice a year and bring back exceptional items such as Madeira hand embroidery and Belgian lace. You can often save as much as 50% over American prices. 31 Front St. (at Queen St.). ✆ **441/295-4089**.

LIQUOR & LIQUEURS

Burrows, Lightbourn Ltd.   This store has been in business since 1808. The maximum you can take from Bermuda is 1 liter of spirits. Orders must be placed 24 hours before your departure, except on Sunday, when 48 hours' advance purchase is required. The store will deliver your packages to the airport or to your

---

Tips Shoppers Beware

Many of our readers carry only the Discover Card. But be warned in advance that the popular U.S. card isn't accepted in Bermuda. One reader, John Fisher, writes that, "Many of the items we had looked forward to purchasing in Bermuda we had to pass up." It seems that Discover is owned by Sears, and Bermuda won't allow Sears to open stores on the island, so Sears won't allow its card to be accepted anywhere in Bermuda. MasterCard and Visa are accepted by most stores.

---

ship. There are two locations in Hamilton and one each in St. George, Flatts Village, Paget, Somerset, and the Royal Naval Dockyard. 57 Front St. ✆ 441/295-0176.

Gosling Brothers, Ltd.   This large competitor of Burrows, Lightbourn has been selling liquor on Bermuda since 1806. You can buy Gosling's Black Seal dark rum—perhaps one bottle to sample on the island and another as an "in-bond" purchase to take home. The bottle you drink on the island is likely to cost 50% more than the "in-bond" bottle. If you want to buy liquor to take home under your duty-free allowance, you can arrange to have it sent to the airport. There's another location, the Black Seal Shop (under the same ownership despite having a different name), at 69 Front St. Front and Queen sts. ✆ 441/295-1123.

PERFUMES
Peniston-Brown Co.   This shop carries almost all of the world's most popular perfumes. Its "fragrance specialists" will be happy to teach you something about the art of choosing and wearing perfume. 23 Front St. W. (opposite the Ferry Terminal). ✆ 441/295-0570.

The Perfume and Cosmetic Boutique, Trimingham's   On the ground floor of Bermuda's largest department store is the island's most comprehensive emporium of prestigious fragrance and cosmetics lines—available duty-free. The beauty-care exclusives include Estée Lauder, Elizabeth Arden, Chanel, and Christian Dior. Famous-name fragrance exclusives include Boucheron, Tiffany, and Issey Miyake. 37 Front St. ✆ 441/295-1183.

PHOTOGRAPHIC EQUIPMENT
Stuart's   This is Bermuda's leading outlet for photographic and electronic equipment. Name brand cameras include Nikon and Pentax. Also sold are tapes, film, tape recorders, and other supplies. Reid St. ✆ 441/295-5496.

SHOES
W. J. Boyle & Son   In business since 1884, this shop offers footwear for men, women, and children. With the best collection in town, it specializes in brand-name footwear from England, Spain, Brazil, and the United States (including Clarks of England and Enzo Angiolini). Queen and Church sts. ✆ 441/295-1887.

SILVER
Otto Wurz Co.   Otto Wurz is at the western end of Front Street, past the Ferry Terminal and the Bank of Bermuda. It specializes in articles made of silver, including jewelry, charms, and bracelets. One section of the store is devoted to gift items, such as pewter ware, cute wooden signs, and glassware, which the

store can engrave. 2 Vallis Building, 3–5 Front St. (between Par-la-Ville and Bermudiana rds.). ✆ **441/295-1247.**

SPORTSWEAR

Davison's   Sportswear with a Bermudian flair is the specialty at this emporium. Along with virtually anything you'd need to wear for almost any sport on Bermuda—or to the country club at home—it carries accessories and sporting equipment. The store features bags by Vera Bradley. Also available are culinary gift packages including such items as Bermuda fish or clam chowder, fish-based sauces, and island herbs. Other locations are at the Clocktower in the Royal Naval Dockyard, on Water Street in St. George, and at The Fairmont Southampton Princess. 27 and 73 Front St. ✆ **441/292-2083.**

Upstairs Golf & Tennis Shop   Everything you'll need for the tennis courts or the golf links is available in this amply stocked store. For golfers, there's merchandise by Ping, Callaway, Titleist, and Lynx. Tennis enthusiasts will recognize products by Dunlop, Slazenger, and many others. There's also men's and women's rainwear from Scotland, which is suitable for Bermuda's wet winters. 26 Church St. ✆ **441/295-5161.**

STAMPS

Perot Post Office   Philatelists from all over the world visit this office to buy postage stamps from Bermuda. Highly prized by collectors, they often feature historic figures and the island's flora and fauna. A stamp showing the *Sea Venture* stranded on coral reefs is one of the most coveted. Open Monday to Friday 9am to 5pm. Queen St., at the entrance to Par-la-Ville Park. ✆ **441/292-9052** or 441/295-5151, ext. 1192. Mon–Fri 9am–5pm.

WOOLENS

Archie Brown   In business for more than half a century, this shop features sweaters for men and women in cashmere, cotton, lamb's wool, and Shetland; it also carries matching skirts. Colors range from neutral to vibrant. 55 Front St. ✆ **441/295-2928.**

English Sports Shop   This shop, established in 1918, is one of the island's leading retailers of quality classic and British woolen goods for men, women, and children. 49 Front St. ✆ **441/295-2672.**

Scottish Wool Shop   This shop carries a wide range of tartans for men, women, and children, all imported from Great Britain. Many woolen and cotton goods are made especially for this shop. The stock includes women's accessories; children's toys; and Shetland, cashmere, lamb's wool, and cotton sweaters. Special orders can be placed for more than 500 tartan items. 7 Queen St. ✆ **441/295-0967.**

Branching Out

You'll often find branches of Hamilton stores at major resorts. The prices—even when there's a sale—are the same as those charged by the parent stores in Hamilton. Although the selection is more limited, resort boutiques remain open on Sunday when most stores in the City of Hamilton are shuttered.

3 Around the Island

As you leave Hamilton and tour the island, you may want to continue looking for typical Bermudian items at the shops listed below.

For other shopping suggestions, consider the **Bermuda Craft Market** (see "Sandys Parish," in chapter 7, "Seeing the Sights") and the **Birdsey Studio** in Paget Parish (see "Paget Parish," in chapter 7, "Seeing the Sights").

SANDYS PARISH
IRELAND ISLAND

Bermuda Arts Centre at Dockyard   In one of the stone-sided warehouses originally built by the British during their military tenure in Bermuda, this art gallery specializes in paintings, sculptures, and crafts, mostly by Bermudian artisans. Not to be confused with the nearby Bermuda Crafts Centre, with which it is not associated, it's sponsored by a local foundation and strives for more than a purely commercial approach to art. Canvases range in price from $50 to around $5,000; less expensive craft items are also for sale. Some staff members are well versed in the nuances of the art, while newcomers can be much less sophisticated. Museum Row, 4 Freeport Rd., Royal Naval Dockyard. ✆ 441/234-2809.

Kathleen Kemsley Bell   At her studio in Paget Parish, Kathleen Kemsley Bell creates papier-mâché dolls with historically accurate, hand-stitched costumes. Each is an original work of art. Mrs. Bell has sold top-of-the-line dolls, known for their expressive faces, to collectors in Europe and North America. Prices begin at $275 and can go much higher. Mrs. Bell will work on commission; for this purpose, she can visit a buyer at any hotel. 7 Seabright Lane. ✆ 441/236-3366.

SOUTHAMPTON PARISH

Desmond Fountain Sculpture Gallery   Bermuda's most prominent sculptor, Desmond Fountain, has created some of the island's most visible public art. In recent years much of his work has been commissioned for upscale private homes and gardens around the world. On the mezzanine of The Fairmont Southampton Princess, 101 South Shore Rd. ✆ 441/238-8840.

Rising Sun Shop   This eclectic outlet, the only real "country store" left on Bermuda, lies half a mile west of the Waterlot Inn. The owner, Anne Powell, has assembled a little bit of everything. We always like to stop in just in case we'll see something we can't live without. In addition to one of Bermuda's warmest welcomes, it offers a frequently changing inventory. You'll find everything from weather vanes to old hobbyhorses, saddlery to wine coolers. Middle Rd., Southampton. ✆ 441/238-2154.

Finds Searching for That Little Treasure

In Southhampton Parish, **Deja-Vu Flea Market** (✆ 441/238-8525; 40 Middle Road) has recently started to attract a lot of attention from shoppers looking for offbeat and secondhand items. You never know what's been resting in those Bermudian attics all these years. On this island of seagoing men, many unusual finds were brought back from around the world. As you rummage around, you could find anything from Tibetan rubbings to a complete dinner set used by the Carringtons on the TV soap *Dynasty.*

Branching Out

The best place to begin shopping is at the new **Somers Wharf & Branch Stores** along Water Street, a coterie of shops that include all the big names from Hamilton's such as A.S. Coopers, Trimingham's and the Crown Colony Shop. Of course, the merchandise of the parent stores in Hamilton is better stocked, but Somers Wharf makes shopping a pleasure because all the island's "name" shops are clustered together, making comparison shopping much easier.

HAMILTON PARISH

Bermuda Glass-Blowing Studio and Showroom   Bermuda's only glass-blowing studio employs both locally trained Bermudians and Europeans. Although some of the studio's glass pieces have been commissioned, most are inspired by cutting-edge developments in the art-glass world. Pieces on display cost $5 to $1,000. The minimum commission accepted is usually more than $500. 16 Blue Hole Hill. ✆ **441/293-2234.**

ST. GEORGE PARISH

Bermuda Gombey Trader   To New York sophisticates who always dress in black, this place will seem corny. But it has its fans in those who like to shop for Gombey rag dolls, handcrafted straw hats, handmade baskets and bags, or even local jam and marmalades. 13 York St., St. George. ✆ **441/297-0399.**

The Book Cellar   Built in the 18th century, this small but choice bookshop lies below Tucker House, a National Trust property. It caters to both visitors and locals, including a lot of "yachties" who stop by to pick up reading material for their time at sea. A lot of people come here for the Cellar's line of books on Bermuda. There's also a wide array of fiction and nonfiction by British and American writers. Parents might be interested in picking up one of the children's books published in Britain—many are quite different from similar editions in America. Water St., St. George. ✆ **441/297-0448.**

Bridge House Gallery   In one of the parish's oldest buildings—a two-story 18th-century building that was home to two of the island's governors and is now maintained by Bermuda's National Trust—this may be the best-stocked empo-rium on the island's East End. It carries a wide selection of antique and modern Bermudiana, including old lace, Christmas ornaments, imported English porce-lain, antique maps, old bottles, postcards, and unique mementos of Bermuda's unusual geography and history. One corner of the building is the studio and sales outlet of local artist Jill Amos Raine (see chapter 7, "Seeing the Sights"). 1 Bridge St., St. George. ✆ **441/297-8211.**

Cow Polly   Named after a rather unpleasant-looking fish that abounds in Bermuda's waters, this upscale gift shop prides itself on its collection of unusual objects imported from virtually everywhere. The theme is aquatic designs, often inspired by fish and underwater mythology. Items for sale include hand-painted shirts, jackets, costume jewelry, and unusual neckties. 16 Water St., Somers Wharf, St. George. ✆ **441/297-1514.**

Frangipani   This is a world of fun, color, and "dressy casual" fashion for women. You'll find a large selection of comfortable cottons, bright silks, and soft rayons. The store is known for its unusual merchandise, including exclusive

> ### *Tips* Last-Minute Purchases
>
> The international airport in Bermuda has recently launched duty-free shops for those last-minute purchases. One shop is found in the international departures lounge, and the other lies near the U.S. departures lounge. U.S. citizens clear customs before flying back to the States. For that specialty purchase, you should still shop around the island. But now you can buy routine duty-free purchases such as perfume, cigarettes, and liquor right before getting on the plane. That sure beats the old system of buying such goods a day or so in advance and having them delivered to the airport.

island designs. There's also a fine collection of swimwear and unusual accessories. 16 Water St., Somers Wharf, St. George. © **441/297-1514.**

Guerlain   This shop has one of the best local selections of fragrances for women and men, including all the big names from Chanel to Gucci; from Fendi to Drakkar. You'll definitely leave this store with an international scent. Water St., St. George. © **441/297-1525.**

Taylors   Go here for the finest selection of kilts, skirts, and other tartans from Scotland, even if you can't play the pipes. 30 Water St., St. George. © **441/297-1626.**

X-Pressions   This is a petite little shop devoted to the island pottery of Bermuda. It lies near St. Peter's Church, the oldest Anglican church in use in the Western hemisphere. 26 York St., St. George. © **441/297-1173.**

10

Bermuda After Dark

As we mentioned already, nightlife is not one of the compelling reasons to go to Bermuda, although there is some after-dark action, mainly in the summer. If you visit during the winter, we trust you'll be content to nurse a drink in a pub.

In the summer, activity seems to float from hotel to hotel, which makes it hard to predict which pub or nightspot will have the best steel-drum or calypso band at any given time. Many pubs feature singalongs at the piano bar, a popular form of entertainment in Bermuda. Most of the big hotels offer shows after dinner, with combos filling in between shows for couples who like to dance.

The island's visitor centers and most hotels distribute free copies of such publications as *Preview Bermuda, Bermuda Weekly,* and *This Week in Bermuda,* which list the latest scheduled activities and events. There's also a calendar of events in the *Bermudian,* sold at most newsstands.

You can also tune in to the local TV station, which constantly broadcasts information for visitors, including details on cultural events and nightlife offerings around the island. Radio station 1160 AM (VSB) broadcasts news of Bermuda cultural and entertainment events from 7am to noon daily.

1 The Club & Music Scene

PAGET PARISH
After Hours The idea of an after-hours club in sleepy Bermuda, where many guests turn in at 9pm, seems incongruous. But there is such a place. Local night owls flock here for good burgers and good times, downing food and drink until they're turned away. The club is very popular with the locals, especially those who don't have to get up at 7am to report to work. The kitchen also turns out well-stuffed sandwiches and curries for those late-night munchies. Open Monday to Thursday 7pm to 2am, Friday to Sunday 7pm to 5am. 117 South Rd. (past the intersection with Middle Rd.). ℂ 441/236-8563.

SOUTHAMPTON PARISH
Henry VIII This restaurant (see chapter 5, "Dining," for a review) is also a good bet for music and comedy. Piano music and singing are often featured, and comedians often join in. Performances begin at 9pm and last until the restaurant closes at 1am. The stage is visible from the pub and from one of the restaurant's three dining areas. South Shore Rd., Southampton Parish. ℂ 441/238-1977. No cover. Bus: 7 or 8.

PEMBROKE PARISH (CITY OF HAMILTON)
Club 40 This upscale spot features music from the '70s and '80s, along with Latin and top 40 selections. Live music is also featured. The dress code forbids jeans or sneakers—smart casual is the way to go. Open daily 9pm to 3am. 119 Front St. ℂ 441/292-9340. Cover $10 after 11pm. Bus: 1, 2, 10, or 11.

Coconut Rock   With a name more evocative of the Caribbean than Bermuda, this restaurant has two of the most active bars in town. It draws locals and visitors (in equal numbers) with background music and videos of the hottest acts in the U.K. and America, including the inevitable Ricky Martin. On slow nights, only one bar is open; on Friday, the second, the Bourgon Lounge, becomes a venue for jazz. Every other week there's jazz and poetry on "Flow Sundays," when musicians and poets in the audience get 15-minute "spots." Happy hour is daily from 5 to 7pm. Open daily 11am to 1am. Williams House, 20 Reid St. ℂ 441/292-1043. No cover. Bus: 7 or 8.

The Oasis Nightlife & The Rock Room   One of Bermuda's leading clubs, the Oasis is on the third floor of a stylish commercial building in the center of Hamilton. It has been renovated in New York warehouse style, and there's lots of special-effects lighting. TV monitors throughout provide background video effects; the extensive music repertoire includes the latest Top 40 dance music. Top North American club bands complement local bands playing rock and blues in the Rock Room. Drink prices range from $5.50 to $7. Open daily 10:30pm to 3:30am. In the Emporium Building, 69 Front St. ℂ 441/292-4978. Cover $10 daily May–Sept; $10 off-season Fri–Sat only. Bus: 3, 7, or 11.

The Spinny Wheel   If you'd like to escape from the tourist hordes and enjoy a pint with the locals, head to this longtime favorite, a virtual institution since opening in 1970. Named for the Fifth Dimension (remember them?) song, it's a relaxing place that has an outdoor pool area with a bar. There's live music downstairs. An upstairs section for disco dancing draws a young crowd. Happy hour is 6 to 9pm Monday to Friday. Open daily noon to 3am. 33 Court St. ℂ 441/292-7799. No cover. Bus: 7 or 8.

DEVONSHIRE PARISH

Clay House Inn   Although calypso and steel-band music originated on islands south of Bermuda, this nightclub offers up those musical forms with panache. You're likely to see a folkloric celebration of island dances, with vocal and instrumental music; it's a carefully contrived package of Caribbean-style nostalgia. Shows are Wednesday and Thursday year-round; doors open at 9:45pm, and the entertainment lasts until right after midnight. Friday and Saturday the club features reggae music from 11pm to 3am. 77 North Shore Rd. ℂ 441/292-3193 for reservations. Cover $22.50 per person (includes 2 drinks). Bus: 10 or 11.

2 The Bar Scene

SANDYS PARISH

Frog & Onion   Converted from an 18th-century cooperage, or barrel-making factory, this British-style pub is in the Royal Naval Dockyard (see chapter 5, "Dining," for a restaurant review). It serves bar snacks throughout the afternoon and evening. Operated by a "frog" (a Frenchman) and an "onion" (a Bermudian), the pub is open daily noon to 1am. The Cooperage, Royal Naval Dockyard, Ireland Island. ℂ 441/234-2900. No cover. Bus: 7 or 8.

PEMBROKE PARISH (CITY OF HAMILTON)

Casey's   There's nothing flashy about this long, narrow room, which seems to be a favorite with locals. The owner, Wesley Robinson, knows many of his patrons, and is an expert at mixing the house specialty, a "Dark and Stormy" (black rum with splashes of ginger beer). Look for yellowed photographs of old Bermuda and a carefully preserved, wall-mounted marlin caught by the owner in 1982. Friday nights here are the most popular on the island, and the joint overflows. There's no live music or food (although no one will mind if you bring your lunch from any of the take-out places nearby). Go here only if you like to wander far off -the beaten tourist trail and want a look at the more ethnic side of Bermuda. Open Monday to Saturday from 10am to 10pm. 25 Queen St. (between Reid and Church sts.). No phone. No cover. Bus: 1, 2, 10, or 11.

Docksider   This sports bar on Hamilton's main drag is lively until the early hours. At a long cedar bar, you'll see some of the most avid sports fans on Bermuda. There are 15 TVs. One section is a wine bar, which is more intimate; another section is a pool bar. You can also order pub grub, such as fish-and-chips or shepherd's pie. Happy hour is daily from 5 to 7pm. Open daily 1:30am to 1am (until 2am on Fri and Sat). 121 Front St. © 441/296-3333. No cover. Bus: 1, 2, 10, or 11.

Flanagan's   On the second floor of a landmark building, this restaurant-pub is the domain of Irishman Thomas Gallagher, who extends a *cead mile failte,* or "100,000 welcomes." This club has some of the town's best music—reggae, rock, soca, and what is often called "party music." There are two bars that feature exotic drinks. Happy hour is daily from 5 to 7pm. In the sports bar you can watch European soccer matches; there are eight other 27-inch screens. Open daily 10am to 1pm. Emporium Building, 69 Front St. © 441/295-8299. No Cover. Bus: 7 or 8.

Hubie's Bar   Islanders come here to listen to jazz with an interesting mix of people of various backgrounds and ages. There's jazz on Friday from 7 to 10pm—go early, because the club fills quickly. On other nights there's jukebox music. Open Monday to Saturday 10am to 10pm. Angle St. © 441/293-9287. No cover. Bus: 7 or 8.

The Pickled Onion   For years, Ye Old Cock & Feather was one of Bermuda's landmark pubs. In 1997, it glaringly changed its image (as well as its name), and the once fairly staid pub became a stop on the after-dark circuit. Funky fabrics cover the booths and tables where patrons listen to music that ranges from blues to oldies of the past 50 years. Live music starts at 10pm. Happy hour is Monday to Saturday from 5 to 7pm. Open daily 11:30am to around midnight. 53 Front St. © 441/295-2263. Bus: 7 or 8.

Robin Hood Pub & Restaurant   The merry women and men of Bermuda flock here for a variety of entertainment options. It serves fine pub fare, including some of Bermuda's best pizzas. It's also the island's number-one sports bar, with video coverage of various U.S. and British league competitions. From April to October, a deejay plays reggae on Monday nights. On other nights you can enjoy everything from live entertainment to quizzes. Friday and Saturday are jukebox nights devoted to reggae or rock. Sometimes prizes are awarded to the patron who can drink a pint of ale fastest. Open Monday to Saturday 11am to 1am, Sunday noon to 1am. 25 Richmond Rd. © 441/295-3314. Bus: 1 or 2.

SMITH'S PARISH

North Rock Brewing Company   If you want to find us in Bermuda, chances are we'll be at this watering hole, Bermuda's first brewpub. The draft beer is brewed on the premises right before your eyes. Pub seating envelops the glass-enclosed brewery where you can see such brew as Old Colony Bitters and

Somers Ale being brewed. Some of the mugs are 22 ounces. These brews are only for local consumption and not sold elsewhere. You'll find a selection of fresh ales on any given day, including "Whale of a Wheat" and "North Rock Porter." The outdoor roadside patio adds a British flavor. See previous restaurant recommendation in chapter 5, "Dining," for more details. The pub is open daily from 11am to 11pm year-round. 10 South Rd. Tel. **441/236-6633**. No Cover. Bus: 1.

HAMILTON PARISH

Swizzle Inn   The home of the Bermuda rum swizzle, this bar and restaurant lies west of the airport, near the Crystal Caves and the Bermuda Perfumery. You can order a Swizzleburger and fish-and-chips throughout the day (see chapter 5, "Dining," for a restaurant review). In the old days, you might've run into Ted Kennedy here; now his wife steers him to more sedate places. The tradition is to tack your business card to anyplace you can find a spot, even the ceiling. The jukebox plays both soft and hard rock. Open daily 11am to 1am; closed Monday in January and February. 3 Blue Hole Hill, Bailey's Bay. © **441/293-1854**. No cover. Bus: 3 or 11.

SOUTHAMPTON PARISH

Longtail Lounge & Café   Set on the lobby of the also-recommended hotel, this place functions as a simple garden-style restaurant during the lunch hour, and as a pulsating bar and lounge every evening after sundown. From one of its deep-cushioned armchairs, you'll have a sweeping view of the beach through big windows, as you enjoy live entertainment, usually a pianist or calypso trio, every night from 9:30am till closing. The house specialty drink, priced at $7.25, is a Dark and Stormy, made from local Black Seal rum mixed with ginger beer. Lunch is served daily from noon to 3pm (no dinner), with platters costing $10 to $15. Bar and snack service is daily from 11:30am to 12:45am. In the Sonesta Beach Resort South Shore Rd. Tel. **441/238-8122**. Bus: 7.

ST. GEORGE PARISH

The little port of St. George and adjoining St. David's Island are a pubber's haven. The best place for suds is one of the restaurants previously recommended. Our favorite is **Black Horse Tavern** (see p. 137), a perfect spot for a congenial evening in good company. It lies on St. David's Island immediately adjoining St. George and is worth the trek over there. If you get hungry, you can always order a plate of shark hash to go with your beer. Back in St. George itself, **Freddie's Pub on the Square** (see p. 139) is always a lot of fun. Its selection of draft beers is among the best on the island. The oldest pub in St. George, **White Horse Tavern** (see p. 139), remains an enduring favorite. It's often jammed most evenings with a mixture of locals and visitors. We especially like the location of this one, as it stands at water's edge overlooking the harbor. Don't expect speedy service in any of these joints.

3 The Performing Arts

You can order tickets for Bermuda's major cultural events through the **Box Office at the Visitors Service Bureau** in Hamilton (© **441/292-8572**) with your MasterCard, Visa, or American Express card.

Students and senior citizens are sometimes eligible for discounts to various entertainment events. Note that for performances of the Bermuda Philharmonic Society (see below), discount tickets aren't usually available.

The Big Event: The Bermuda Festival

Bermuda's major cultural event is the Bermuda Festival, staged every January and February. Outstanding international classical, jazz, and pop artists perform, and major theatrical and dance companies from around the globe stage productions. During the festival, performances take place every night except Sunday. Ticket prices start at $30. Some festival tickets are reserved until 48 hours before curtain time for visitors. Tickets can also be ordered online at www.bermudafestival.com. Most performances are at City Hall Theatre, City Hall, Church Street, Hamilton. For more information and reservations, contact the **Bermuda Festival**, P.O. Box HM 297, Hamilton HM AX, Bermuda (© **441/295-1291;** fax 441/295-7403).

CLASSICAL MUSIC

The **Bermuda Philharmonic Society,** conducted by Graham Garton, presents four regular concerts during the season. Special outdoor **"Classical Pops" concerts** are presented on the first weekend in June in St. George and at the Royal Naval Dockyard. Concerts usually feature the Bermuda Philharmonic orchestra, the choir, and guest soloists. You can get tickets and concert schedules from the **Harbourmaster,** Washington Mall (© **441/295-5333).** Tickets generally cost $18 to $20; seniors and students are often granted discounts, depending on the performance.

GOMBEY DANCING

Ask at the tourist office or call the box office (see above) to see whether the gombey dancers will be performing during your stay. This is the island's single most important cultural expression of African heritage; once part of the slave culture, the tradition dates from the mid-1700s. The local dance troupe of talented men and women often performs at one of the big hotels (and on occasion aboard cruise ships for passengers) in winter. On all holidays, you'll see the gombeys dancing through the streets of Hamilton in their colorful costumes.

BALLET

The Bermuda Civic Ballet presents classical ballets at various venues. On occasion a major European or American guest artist appears with the troupe. The National Dance Theater of Bermuda also stages performances, both classical and modern, around the island. Ask at the tourist office or call the box office (see above) to check the troupes' schedules during your visit; prices vary with the performance.

MUSICAL THEATER

An all-volunteer organization based in Hamilton, the **Gilbert & Sullivan Society** of Bermuda, P.O. Box HM 3098, Hamilton HM NX (© **441/ 295-3218),** is known for producing at least one large-scale musical per year. These days, only about 20% of the repertoire is based on the works of Gilbert and Sullivan; it now includes such musicals as *Evita* and Sondheim's *A Little Night Music,* among others. The society performs at Hamilton's City Hall, on Church Street. Be warned that this is a volunteer organization; the sole production runs for 2 weeks at most, usually in October. Tickets cost $30. Society members sometimes contribute their talents to the Bermuda Festival (see the box above).

Bermuda is the only place outside of Cambridge where Harvard University's **Hasty Pudding Theatricals** are staged. Performances have been presented in Bermuda during College Weeks (in Mar and Apr) since the 1960s. They're staged at the City Hall Theatre on Church Street in Hamilton; call the box office at the Visitors Service Bureau (see above) for tickets, which cost about $25 each.

Appendix:
Bermuda in Depth

Welcome to an island of no pollution, no billboards, no graffiti, no litter, no rental cars, no unemployment (well, almost), no tolerance for drugs, no illiteracy (well, almost), and no nude or topless beaches. In a changing world, especially as epitomized by islands in the Caribbean, Bermuda remains . . . well, Bermuda.

If there's a sore point among Bermudians today, it's their extreme desire to separate themselves from the islands of the Caribbean, and particularly from The Bahamas. They often send angry letters insisting that Bermuda is not in the Caribbean to publishers of maps, reference sources, and travel guides. As one irate Bermudian put it, "You don't claim that Washington, D.C., is part of Dallas, Texas. They're the same distance apart that Bermuda is from the Caribbean."

Bermuda wants to distance itself from the islands of the Caribbean, many of which are plagued by economic, socioeconomic, and racial problems, including abject poverty. Bermuda does not tolerate unsavory businesses, money launderers, and tax evaders. Bermuda promotes not just tourism, but its stellar reputation in banking and multinational business.

At the beginning of the millennium, international business was positioning itself to overtake tourism as a primary source of revenue. With China's takeover of Hong Kong, Bermuda has persuaded some of the biggest names in world business to create official domiciles on the island. The trend began in the 1970s, when some Hong Kong businesspeople formed low-profile shipping, trading, and investment companies in Bermuda—companies that became, in essence, corporate cash cows. That trend continues to significantly affect Bermuda's economy for the better.

When Britain surrendered Hong Kong to China in 1997, Bermuda became the largest British colony. A local businessman watched the televised ceremonies in which Britain handed over control, and gleefully remarked, "All we can say is: Thank you very much, Hong Kong, because here come the insurance companies and pension funds." By the end of the 20th century, nearly half of the companies listed on the Hong Kong Stock Exchange—and even some of the Chinese government's own holding companies—had established a legal presence in Bermuda.

Amazingly, tiny Bermuda has emerged as the biggest and most prosperous of all the colonies, the bulk of which are now in the Caribbean. Britain prefers to call Bermuda and its other possessions "dependent territories," not colonies. (Technically, the sun still doesn't set over the diminished British Empire—Britain still reigns over everything from the Falkland Islands to Gibraltar, from Diego Garcia Island in the Indian Ocean to the Pitcairn Islands in the South Pacific.)

And as aggressively as Bermuda is pursuing business, it's also more aware than ever of its fragile environment. There aren't too many Al Gores on the scene, but attention is being paid. Bermuda's population density is the third highest in the world, after Hong Kong and Monaco. Because the number of annual visitors is

10 times higher than the population, Bermuda has had to take strong initiatives to protect its environment and natural resources. Environmental protection laws take the form of stiff antilitter laws, annual garbage clean-up campaigns, automobile restrictions, cedar replanting (a blight in the '40s and '50s wiped out the native trees), lead-free gasoline, a strict fishing policy, and other measures.

Along the shaky road to self-government, Bermuda had some ugly racial conflicts. Riots in 1968 gave way to the assassination of the British governor in 1973. But that was a long time ago; today, Bermuda has the most harmonious race relations in this part of the world, far better than those in the United States, the Caribbean, or The Bahamas. There's still a long way to go, but Bermudians of African descent have assumed important political, administrative, and managerial posts in every aspect of the local economy. Bermuda hasn't quite reached the point where the color of your skin is unimportant, but it has made more significant advancement toward that goal than its neighbors to the south.

By 2000, Bermuda's average household income rose to a healthy $68,500—contrast that to some of the less fortunate islands in the south, many of which don't even have budgets to compile such statistics. On the downside, home prices in Bermuda are at least three times the median cost of a house in the United States or Canada. Compared to Puerto Rico, Jamaica, and certainly Haiti, no one is really poor in Bermuda.

As a tourist destination, Bermuda has impeccable credentials. It was a resort long before Florida, Hawaii, Mexico, and many other places. Over the years, it has successfully exploited its position in the northwest Atlantic between North America and Europe. It is even working to throw off its image as a staid resort, hoping to project a lively, more with-it atmosphere (although it has a long way to go in that department). The United States remains its largest market—about 86% of visitors are Americans—but in recent years more and more visitors from Europe, the Far East, and the Near East have been seen dining, drinking, and shopping in Hamilton.

1 The Natural World: An Environmental Guide to Bermuda

Lying 570 miles east-southeast of Cape Hatteras, North Carolina, Bermuda is actually a group of some 300 islands, islets, and coral rocks clustered in a fishhook-shaped chain about 22 miles long and 2 miles wide at its broadest point. The archipelago forms a landmass of about 21 square miles that's formally known as "The Bermudas."

Only 20 or so of the islands are inhabited. The largest one, called the "mainland," is Great Bermuda; about 14 miles long, it's linked to the other nearby major islands by a series of bridges and causeways. The capital, Hamilton, is on the mainland.

The other islands include Somerset, Watford, Boaz, and Ireland in the west, and St. George's and St. David's in the east. This chain of islands encloses the archipelago's major bodies of water, which include Castle Harbour, St. George's Harbour, Harrington Sound, and Great Sound. Most of the other smaller islands, or islets, lie within these bodies of water.

Bermuda is far north of the Tropic of Cancer, which cuts through the Bahamian archipelago. Bermuda is based on the upper parts of an extinct volcano, which may date from 100 million years ago. Through the millennia, wind and water brought limestone deposits and formed the islands far from any continental landmass; today, the closest is the coast of the Carolinas. Bermuda is about 775 miles southeast of New York City, some 1,030 miles northeast of Miami, and nearly 3,450 miles from London. It has a balmy climate year-round, with sunshine prevailing almost every day. The chief source of Bermuda's mild weather is the Gulf Stream, a broad belt of warm water formed by equatorial currents. The stream's northern reaches separate the Bermuda islands from North America and, with the prevailing northeast winds, temper the wintry blasts that sweep across the Atlantic from west and north. The islands of Bermuda are divided, for administrative purposes, into parishes. (See "Orienting Yourself: The Lay of the Land," in chapter 3, "Getting to Know Bermuda.")

MORE THAN ONIONS: THE ISLAND'S FLORA

Bermuda's temperate climate, abundant sunshine, fertile soil, and adequate moisture account for some of the most verdant gardens in the Atlantic. Some of the best of these, such as the Botanical Gardens in Paget Parish, are open to the public. Bermudian gardeners pride themselves on the mixture of temperate-zone and subtropical plants that thrive on the island, despite the salty air.

Bermuda is blessed with copious and varied flora. Examples include the indigenous sea grape, which flourishes along the island's sandy coasts (it prefers sand and saltwater to more arable soil), and the cassava plant, whose roots resemble the tubers of sweet potatoes. When ground into flour and soaked to remove a mild poison, the roots are the main ingredient for Bermuda's traditional Christmas pies. Also growing wild and abundant are prickly pears, aromatic fennel, yucca, and the Spanish bayonet, a spiked-leaf plant that bears a single white flower in season.

To the early settlers, Bermuda's only native palm, the palmetto, proved particularly useful; its leaves were used to thatch roofs. When crushed and fermented, the leaves produced a strong alcoholic drink called bibby, whose effects the early Puritans condemned. Its leaves were also fashioned into women's hats during a brief period in the 1600s, when they represented the height of fashion in London.

The banana, one of Bermuda's most dependable sources of fresh fruit, was introduced to the island in the early 1600s. It is believed that Bermudian bananas were the first to be brought back to London from the New World. They created an immediate sensation, leading to the cultivation of bananas in many other British colonies.

The plant that contributed most to Bermuda's renown was the Bermuda onion (*Allium cepa*). Imported from England in 1616, it was later grown from seed brought from the Spanish and Portuguese islands of Tenerife and Madeira. The Bermuda onion became so famous along the East Coast of the United States that Bermudians themselves became known as "onions." During the 1930s, Bermuda's flourishing export trade in onions declined because of high tariffs, increased competition from similar species grown in Texas and elsewhere, and the limited arable land on the island.

Today, you'll see oleander, hibiscus, royal poinciana, poinsettia, bougainvillea, and dozens of other flowering shrubs and vines decorating Bermuda's gently rolling land. Of the island's dozen or so species of morning glory, three are indigenous; they tend to grow rampant and overwhelm everything else in a garden.

CLOSE ENCOUNTERS WITH THE LOCAL FAUNA
AMPHIBIANS

Because of the almost total lack of natural freshwater ponds and lakes, Bermuda's amphibians have adapted to seawater or slightly brackish water.

Amphibians include the tree frog (*Eleutherodactylus johnstonei* and *Eleutherodactylus gossei*), whose nighttime chirping newcomers sometimes mistake for the song of birds. Small and camouflaged by the leafy matter of the forest floor, the tree frog appears between April and November.

More visible are Bermuda's giant toads, or road toads (*Bufo marinus*), which sometimes reach the size of an adult human's palm. Imported from Guyana in the 1870s in the hope of controlling the island's cockroach population, giant toads search out the nighttime warmth of the asphalt roads—and are often crushed by cars in the process. They are especially prevalent after a soaking rain. The road toads are not venomous and, contrary to legend, do not cause warts.

Island reptiles include colonies of harmless lizards, often seen sunning themselves on rocks until approaching humans or predators scare them away. The best-known species is the Bermuda rock lizard (*Eumeces longirostris*), also known as a skink. It's said to have been the only non-marine, non-flying vertebrate on Bermuda before the arrival of European colonists. Imported reptiles include the Somerset lizard (*Anolis roquet*), whose black eye patches give it the look of a bashful bandit, and the Jamaican anole (*Anolis grahami*), a kind of chameleon.

BIRD LIFE

Partly because of its ample food sources, Bermuda has a large bird population; many species nest on the island during their annual migrations. Most of the birds arrive during the cooler winter months, usually between Christmas and Easter. Serious birders have recorded almost 40 different species of eastern warblers, which peacefully coexist with species of martins, doves, egrets, South American terns, herons, fork-tailed flycatchers, and even some species from as far away as the Arctic Circle.

Two of the most visible imported species are the cardinal, introduced during the 1700s, and the kiskadee. Imported from Trinidad in 1957 to control lizards and flies, the kiskadee has instead wreaked havoc on the island's commercial fruit crops.

The once-abundant eastern bluebird has been greatly reduced in number since the depletion of the cedar trees, its preferred habitat. Another bird native to Bermuda is the gray-and-white petrel, known locally as a cahow, which burrows for most of the year in the sands of the isolated eastern islands. The rest of the year it feeds at sea, floating for hours in the warm waters of the Gulf Stream. One of the most rarely sighted birds in the world—it was once regarded as extinct—the petrel is now protected by the Bermudian government.

Also native to Bermuda is the cliff-dwelling tropic bird, which you can recognize by the elongated plumage of its white tail. Resembling a swallow, the island's harbinger of spring appears annually in March.

Although the gardens and golf courses of many of the island's hotels attract dozens of birds, some of the finest bird-watching sites are maintained by the Bermuda Audubon Society or the National Trust. Isolated sites known for sheltering thousands of native and migrating birds include Paget Marsh, just south of Hamilton; the Walsingham Trust in Hamilton Parish; and Spittal Pond in Smith's Parish.

SEA LIFE

In the deep waters off the shores of Bermuda, photographers have recorded some of the finest game fish in the world, including blackfin tuna, marlin, swordfish, wahoo, dolphin, sailfish, and barracuda. Also prevalent are bonefish and pompano, both of which prefer sun-flooded shallow waters closer to shore. Any beachcomber is likely to come across hundreds of oval-shaped chitons (*Chiton tuberculatus*), a mollusk that adheres tenaciously to rocks in tidal flats; locally, it is known as "suck-rock."

Beware of the Portuguese man-of-war (*Physalia physalis*), a floating colony of jellyfish whose stinging tentacles sometimes reach 50 feet in length. Give this dangerous and venomous marine creature a wide berth: Severe stings may require hospitalization. When it washes up on Bermuda beaches, usually between March and July, the man-of-war can sting even when it appears to be dead.

The most prevalent marine animal in Bermuda is responsible for the formation of the island's greatest tourist attraction, its miles of pale-pink sand. Much of the sand consists of broken shells, pieces of coral, and the calcium carbonate remains of other marine invertebrates. The pinkest pieces are shards of crushed shell from a single-celled animal called foraminifer. Its vivid pink skeleton is pierced with holes, through which the animal extends its rootlike feet (*pseudopodia*), which cling to the underside of the island's reefs during the animal's brief life, before its skeleton is washed ashore.

2 Life in the Onion Patch

GETTING TO KNOW THE "ONIONS"

Even though Bermuda isn't in the onion business the way it used to be, a born and bred islander is still called an "Onion." The term dates from the early 20th century, when the export of Bermuda onions and Easter lilies to the U.S. mainland were the island's major sources of income.

The "Onions"—a term that still carries a badge of pride—have their own lifestyle and even their own vocabulary. For example, "Aunt Haggie's children" are frustrating, stupid people; "married by 10 parsons" is a reference to a woman with huge breasts; "backin' up" means gay. You don't vomit in Bermuda, you "Go Europe." "Cockroach killers" (a term you may also hear in the American Southwest) are pointy-toed shoes. Although you'll rarely see it on local menus, the bream fish is called a "shit-bubbler."

Residents of more troubled islands to the south often look with envy upon the "Onions," who have a much higher standard of living than Caribbean islanders do; they also pay no personal income tax and suffer from only a 7% unemployment rate. The literacy rate is high: An estimated 99% of females age 15 and older can read and write, as can 98% of all Bermudian males.

Fun Fact Bermuda Shorts: Not Too Far Above the Knee

Most Bermudians consider the winter months too cold for Bermuda shorts; but by May, just about every businessman along Front Street has traded in his trousers for a pair. Bermuda shorts weren't initially Bermudian; they originated with the British army in India. Later, when British troops were stationed in Bermuda, they were issued the shorts as part of the military's tropical kit gear.

By the 1920s and 1930s, the shorts had become quite fashionable, although they were not considered acceptable at dinner parties or at church. Now suitable attire for businessmen, the shorts are worn with a blazer, collared shirt, tie, and knee socks. They shouldn't be more than 3 inches above the knee, and must have a 3-inch hem.

Today's 61,000 residents are mostly of African, British, and Portuguese descent. Bermuda's population density, one of the highest in the world, is about 3,210 per square mile. The population is about 61% black, 39% white. Many minority groups are represented, the largest and most established being the Portuguese; most, however, are islanders from the Caribbean or The Bahamas. Some Bermudians can even trace their ancestry back to the island's first settlers, and some to successful privateers and slaves.

Britain's influence in Bermuda is obvious in predominantly English accents, police who wear helmets like those of London bobbies, and cars that drive on the left. Schools are run along the lines of the British system and provide a high standard of preparatory education. Children 5 to 16 years of age must attend school. The Bermuda College, which offers academic and technical studies, boasts a renowned hotel and catering program.

WHO'S MINDING THE STORE?

In essence, Bermuda is a self-governing dependency of Britain, which protects its security and stability. The governor, appointed by the Queen, represents Her Majesty in the areas of external affairs, defense, and internal security.

By choosing to remain a British dependency, Bermuda rejected the trail that many former colonies in the Caribbean (including Antigua) blazed by declaring their independence. Although they remain under the protection of the British, Bermudians manage their own day-to-day affairs. And ever since the people of Bermuda were granted the right to govern themselves in 1968, they have done so admirably well.

Bermuda has a 12-member cabinet headed by a premier. The elected legislature, referred to as the Legislative Council, consists of a 40-member House of Assembly and an 11-member Senate. Bermuda's oldest political party is the Progressive Labour Party, formed in 1963. In 1964, the United Bermuda Party was established; it was in power until it was topped by Labour in 1998.

Bermuda's legal system is founded on common law. Judicial responsibility falls to the Supreme Court, headed by a chief justice in a powdered wig and a robe. English law is the fundamental guide, and in court, English customs prevail.

The island consists of nine parishes, each managed by an advisory council. The capital, Hamilton, is in Pembroke Parish. (For details on the individual parishes, see "Orienting Yourself: The Lay of the Land," in chapter 3, Getting to Know Bermuda.")

TOURIST DOLLARS & NO INCOME TAX

Bermuda's political stability has proved beneficial to the economy, which relies heavily on tourism and foreign investment.

For much of the island's early history, the major industry was shipbuilding, made possible by the abundant cedar forests. In the second half of the 19th century, when wooden ships gave way to steel ones, the island turned to tourism. Today, it's the country's leading industry, with annual revenues estimated at $450 million. Approximately 550,000 visitors come to Bermuda each year; an estimated 86% arrive from the United States, 4% from Britain, and 7% from Canada. Bermuda enjoys a 42% repeat-visitor rate.

Because Bermuda has enacted favorable economic measures, more than 6,000 international companies are registered there. The companies engage mostly in investment holding, insurance, commercial trading, consulting services, and shipping—but fewer than 275 companies are actually on the island. The reason for this curious situation? Bermuda has no corporate or income tax.

The island's leading exports are pharmaceuticals, concentrates (primarily black rum and sherry peppers), essences, and beverages. Leading imports include foodstuffs, alcoholic beverages, clothing, furniture, fuel, electrical appliances, and motor vehicles. Bermuda's major trading partners are the United States, Great Britain, Canada, the Netherlands, and the Caribbean states.

3 History 101

THE EARLY YEARS

The discovery of The Bermudas is attributed to the Spanish—probably the navigator Juan Bermúdez—sometime before 1511, for in that year a map published in the *Legatio Babylonica* included "La Bermuda" among the Atlantic islands. A little over a century later, the English staked a claim to Bermuda and began colonization.

In 1609, the flagship of Admiral Sir George Somers, the **Sea Venture,** was wrecked on Bermuda's reefs while en route to the colony at Jamestown, Virginia. The dauntless crew built two pinnaces (small sailing ships) and headed on to the American colony, but three sailors hid out and remained on the island. They were Bermuda's first European settlers. Just 3 years later, the Bermuda islands were included in the charter of the Virginia Company, and 60 colonists were sent there from England; St. George Town was founded soon after.

Bermuda's status as a colony dates from 1620, when the first parliament convened. Bermuda's is the oldest parliament in continuous existence in the British Commonwealth. In 1684, Bermuda became a British Crown Colony under King Charles II. Sir Robert Robinson was appointed the colony's first governor.

Slavery became a part of life in Bermuda shortly after the official settlement. Although the majority of slaves came from Africa, a few were Native Americans. Later, Scots imprisoned for fighting against Cromwell were sent to the islands, followed in 1651 by Irish

Dateline

- ca. 1511 Juan Bermúdez discovers Bermuda while sailing aboard the Spanish ship *La Garza.*
- 1609 The British ship *Sea Venture* is wrecked on the reefs of Bermuda; all on board make it to shore safely and the settlement of Bermuda begins.
- 1612 The Virginia Company dispatches the *Plough* to Bermuda with 60 colonists on board. Richard Moore is appointed governor of Bermuda.
- 1620 The first Bermuda parliament session is held in St. Peter's Church, St. George.
- 1684 The British Crown takes over the Bermuda Company's charter. Sir Robert Robinson is appointed the Crown's first governor of Bermuda.
- 1775 Gunpowder is stolen in St. George and shipped to the American colonies for use against the British.
- 1861 Bermuda becomes involved in the American Civil War when it runs supplies to the South to undermine the Union's blockade.
- 1919–33 Bermudians profit from Prohibition in the United States by engaging in rumrunning.
- 1940–45 Bermuda plays an important role in World War II counterespionage for the Allies.
- 1946 The automobile is introduced on Bermuda.
- 1957 Great Britain withdraws militarily after 2 centuries of rule.
- 1963 Voter registration is open to all citizens.
- 1968 Bermudians are granted a new constitution that, while protecting them under the umbrella of the British Commonwealth, allows them to govern themselves.

continues

slaves. The fate of these bondservants, however, was not as cruel as that of plantation slaves in America and the West Indies. The British Emancipation Act of 1834 freed all slaves.

RELATIONS WITH AMERICA

Bermuda established close links with the American colonies. The islanders set up a thriving mercantile trade on the Eastern Seaboard, especially with southern ports. The major commodity sold by Bermuda's merchant ships was salt from Turks Island.

During the American Revolution, the rebellious colonies cut off trade with Loyalist Bermuda, despite the network of family connections and close friendships that bound them. The cutoff in trade proved a great hardship for the islanders, who, having chosen seafaring over farming, depended heavily on America for their food. Many of them, now deprived of profitable trade routes, turned to privateering, piracy, and "wrecking" (salvaging goods from wrecked or foundered ships).

- **1973** The governor, Sir Richard Sharples, and an aide are assassinated.
- **1979** Bermudians celebrate as their own Gina Swainson wins the Miss World contest.
- **1987** Hurricane Emily causes millions of dollars' worth of damage; some 70 people are injured.
- **1990** Prime Minister Margaret Thatcher confers with President George Bush in Bermuda.
- **1991** Prime Minister John Major meets with President Bush in Bermuda.
- **1995** Bermudians vote to maintain traditional ties with Britain.
- **1997** Pamela Gordon, 41, becomes the island's first female prime minister.
- **1998** The Labour Party sweeps into power with another woman prime minister.
- **2000** It's announced that 75% of U.S. Fortune 500 companies make Bermuda their home port.

Britain's loss of its important American colonial ports led to a naval buildup in Bermuda. Ships and troops sailed from Bermuda in 1814 to burn Washington, D.C. and the White House during the War of 1812.

Bermuda got a new lease on economic life during the American Civil War. The island was sympathetic to the Confederacy. With approval of the British government, Bermuda ran the blockade that the Union had placed on exports, especially of cotton, by the Southern states. St. George's Harbour was a principal Atlantic base for the lucrative business of smuggling manufactured goods into Confederate ports and bringing out cargoes of cotton and turpentine.

When the Confederacy fell, so did Bermuda's economy. Seeing no immediate source of income from trading with the Eastern states, the islanders turned their attention to agriculture and found that the colony's fertile soil and salubrious climate produced excellent vegetables. Portuguese immigrants arrived to farm the land, and soon celery, potatoes, tomatoes, and especially onions were being shipped to the New York market. So brisk was the onion trade that Hamilton became known as "Onion Town."

During Prohibition, Bermudians again profited from developments in the United States—they engaged in the lucrative business of rumrunning. The distance from the island to the East Coast was too great for quick crossings in small booze-laden boats, as could be done from The Bahamas and Cuba. Nevertheless, Bermuda accounted for a good part of the alcoholic beverages transported illegally to the United States before the repeal of Prohibition in 1933.

A HOTBED OF ESPIONAGE

Bermuda played a key role in World War II counterespionage for the Allies. The story of the "secret war" with Nazi Germany is told dramatically in William Stevenson's *A Man Called Intrepid.*

Beneath the Hamilton Princess Hotel, a carefully trained staff worked to decode radio signals to and from German submarines and other vessels operating in the Atlantic, close to the United States and the islands offshore. Unknown to the Germans, the British, early in the war, had broken the Nazi code through use of a captured German coding machine called "Enigma." The British also intercepted and examined mail between Europe and the United States.

Bermuda served as a refueling stop for airplanes flying between the two continents. While pilots were being entertained at the Yacht Club, the mail would be taken off the carriers and examined by experts. An innocent-looking series of letters from Lisbon, for example, often contained messages written in invisible ink. The letters were part of a vast German spy network. The British became skilled at opening sealed envelopes, examining their written contents, and carefully resealing them.

The surreptitious letter-readers were called "trappers." Many of them were young women without any previous experience in counterespionage work, yet some performed very well. As Stevenson wrote, it was soon discovered that "by some quirk in the law of averages, the girls who shone in this work had well-turned ankles." A medical officer involved with the project even reported it as "fairly certain that a girl with unshapely legs would make a bad trapper." So, amazingly, the word went out that women seeking recruitment as trappers would have to display their gams.

During the course of their work, the trappers discovered one of the methods by which the Germans were transmitting secret messages: They would shrink a whole page of regularly typed text to the size of a tiny dot, then conceal the dot under an innocuous-looking punctuation mark! The staff likened these messages with their secret-bearing dots to plum duff, a popular English dessert, for these "punctuation dots [were] scattered through a letter like raisins in the suet puddings." The term "duff method" came to be applied to the manner in which the Germans were sending military and other messages through the mail.

When the United States entered the war, FBI agents joined the British in their intelligence operations in Bermuda.

BERMUDA COMES INTO ITS OWN

In 1953, British prime minister Winston Churchill chose Bermuda, which he had visited during the war, as the site for a conference with U.S. president Dwight D. Eisenhower and the French premier. Several such high-level gatherings have followed in the decades since; the most recent one, between British prime minister John Major and U.S. president George Bush, took place in 1991.

Bermuda's increasing prominence led to changes in its relations with Great Britain and the United States, as well as significant developments on the island itself. In 1957, after nearly 2 centuries of occupation, Britain withdrew its military forces, having decided to grant self-government to its oldest colony. Under the Lend-Lease Agreement signed in 1941, the United States continues to maintain a naval air station at Kindley Field, in St. George Parish. The agreement is due to expire in 2040. Nearby, on Cooper's Island, the U.S. National Aeronautics and Space Administration operates a space-tracking system.

As Bermudians assumed greater control over their own affairs, they began to adopt significant social changes, but at a pace that did not satisfy some critics. Although racial segregation in hotels and restaurants ceased in 1959, schools were not integrated until 1971. Women received the right to vote in 1944, but the law still restricted suffrage only to property holders. That restriction was rescinded in 1963, when voter registration was opened to all citizens.

On the rocky road to self-government, Bermuda was not without its share of problems. Serious rioting broke out in 1968, and British troops were called back to restore order. Then, in 1973, Sir Richard Sharples, the governor, was assassinated; in 1977, those believed to have been the assassins were executed.

Those events, which occurred at a time when several of the islands in the region and in the Caribbean were experiencing domestic difficulties, proved to be the exception rather than the rule. In the years since, the social and political climate in Bermuda has been markedly calm—all the better for the island's economic well-being, because it encourages the industries on which Bermuda depends, including tourism.

In 1972, the Bermuda dollar gained its independence from the pound sterling; it's now pegged through gold to the U.S. dollar on an equal dollar-for-dollar basis.

During the 1990s, the political status of their island again became a hot topic among Bermudians. Some people feel it would be advantageous to achieve complete independence from Britain, whereas others believe it's in Bermuda's best interest to maintain its ties to the Crown. In 1995, the majority of voters in an independent referendum rejected a proposal to sever ties with Great Britain, preferring to maintain the current status.

In 1997, the governing party of Bermuda chose the daughter of a well-known civil rights leader as its prime minister. Pamela Gordon, former environment minister, was named to the post at the age of 41, the youngest leader in the island nation's 400-year history and the first woman to be prime minister. David Saul, the reigning prime minister, resigned in favor of a younger and more popular leader. In her first months in office, Ms. Gordon, a relative political newcomer, pledged to bridge differences between Bermuda's majority black population and its white business elite.

In that stated goal, at least based on election returns, she did not succeed. In November 1998, the Progressive Labour Party, supported by many of Bermuda's blacks, ended 30 years of conservative rule by sweeping to its first victory in general elections. Although Ms. Gordon is black, as was most of her cabinet, many locals saw her party as "part of the white establishment."

The Labour Party's leader, Jennifer Smith, became the new prime minister, claiming Bermuda's residents had met their "date with destiny." The Labour Party has moved more from the left to the center in recent years, and Ms. Smith has sought to reassure the island's white-led business community that it will be "business as usual" with her in power. The Labour Party made the economy an issue in the campaign, even though Bermuda residents enjoy one of the highest standards of living in the world.

At the millennium, Bermuda faces many problems, including what many see as a declining way of life. There are environmental concerns—notably overfishing and damage to its precious reefs. Traffic jams are now common in spite of the ban against visitors renting automobiles. Affordable housing becomes scarcer year by year. Nonetheless, the more unfortunate islands to the south still envy Bermuda's standard of living.

Hotel news dominated Bermuda's headlines in 1999. Fairmont, the famed hotel chain, took over the venerable Princess Hotels in Hamilton and Southampton.

As more and more cruise lines launch megaliners, Bermuda is concerned that its tight harbors will not handle the traffic. Massive efforts are under way to prepare for the constantly changing conditions in the cruise industry in the new millennium.

Although Bermuda and tourism seemed linked like a horse and carriage, business with the Bermuda shorts wearers dominated the focus at the turn of the new century when it was announced that 75% of U.S. Fortune 500 companies have made Bermuda their home base.

At the beginning of the millennium, Bermuda is also looking to honor its past as the island nation prepares to commemorate the 500th anniversary of Bermuda's first sighting by Spanish explorer Juan Bermúdez in 1503.

For its quincentennial celebrations, Bermuda is planning an activity-filled agenda with all sorts of events.

Index

See also Accommodations and Restaurant indexes, below.

FROMMER'S® COMPLETE TRAVEL GUIDES

Alaska
Amsterdam
Argentina & Chile
Arizona
Atlanta
Australia
Austria
Bahamas
Barcelona, Madrid & Seville
Beijing
Belgium, Holland &
  Luxembourg
Bermuda
Boston
British Columbia & the
  Canadian Rockies
Budapest & the Best of Hungary
California
Canada
Cancún, Cozumel & the
  Yucatán
Cape Cod, Nantucket &
  Martha's Vineyard
Caribbean
Caribbean Cruises & Ports
  of Call
Caribbean Ports of Call
Carolinas & Georgia
Chicago
China
Colorado
Costa Rica
Denmark
Denver, Boulder & Colorado
  Springs
England
Europe

European Cruises & Ports of Call
Florida
France
Germany
Greece
Greek Islands
Hawaii
Hong Kong
Honolulu, Waikiki & Oahu
Ireland
Israel
Italy
Jamaica
Japan
Las Vegas
London
Los Angeles
Maryland & Delaware
Maui
Mexico
Montana & Wyoming
Montréal & Québec City
Munich & the Bavarian Alps
Nashville & Memphis
Nepal
New England
New Mexico
New Orleans
New York City
New Zealand
Nova Scotia, New Brunswick &
  Prince Edward Island
Oregon
Paris
Philadelphia & the Amish
  Country
Portugal

Prague & the Best of the Czech
  Republic
Provence & the Riviera
Puerto Rico
Rome
San Antonio & Austin
San Diego
San Francisco
Santa Fe, Taos & Albuquerque
Scandinavia
Scotland
Seattle & Portland
Shanghai
Singapore & Malaysia
South Africa
Southeast Asia
South Florida
South Pacific
Spain
Sweden
Switzerland
Texas
Thailand
Tokyo
Toronto
Tuscany & Umbria
USA
Utah
Vancouver & Victoria
Vermont, New Hampshire
  & Maine
Vienna & the Danube Valley
Virgin Islands
Virginia
Walt Disney World & Orlando
Washington, D.C.
Washington State

FROMMER'S® DOLLAR-A-DAY GUIDES

Australia from $50 a Day
California from $70 a Day
Caribbean from $70 a Day
England from $70 a Day
Europe from $70 a Day

Florida from $70 a Day
Hawaii from $70 a Day
Ireland from $60 a Day
Italy from $70 a Day
London from $85 a Day

New York from $80 a Day
Paris from $80 a Day
San Francisco from $60 a Day
Washington, D.C.,
  from $70 a Day

FROMMER'S® PORTABLE GUIDES

Acapulco, Ixtapa &
  Zihuatanejo
Alaska Cruises & Ports
  of Call
Amsterdam
Australia's Great Barrier Reef
Bahamas
Baja & Los Cabos
Berlin
Boston
California Wine Country
Charleston & Savannah
Chicago

Dublin
Hawaii: The Big Island
Hong Kong
Houston
Las Vegas
London
Los Angeles
Maine Coast
Maui
Miami
New Orleans
New York City
Paris

Phoenix & Scottsdale
Portland
Puerto Rico
Puerto Vallarta, Manzanillo &
  Guadalajara
San Diego
San Francisco
Seattle
Sydney
Tampa & St. Petersburg
Vancouver
Venice
Washington, D.C.

FROMMER'S® NATIONAL PARK GUIDES

Family Vacations in the
  National Parks
Grand Canyon

National Parks of the American
  West
Rocky Mountain
Yellowstone & Grand Teton

Yosemite & Sequoia/
  Kings Canyon
Zion & Bryce Canyon

FROMMER'S® MEMORABLE WALKS

Chicago	New York	San Francisco
London	Paris	Washington, D.C.

FROMMER'S® GREAT OUTDOOR GUIDES

Arizona & New Mexico	Northern California	Southern New England
New England	Southern California & Baja	Vermont & New Hampshire

FROMMER'S® BORN TO SHOP GUIDES

Born to Shop: France	Born to Shop: Italy	Born to Shop: New York
Born to Shop: Hong Kong,	Born to Shop: London	Born to Shop: Paris
Shanghai & Beijing		

FROMMER'S® IRREVERENT GUIDES

Amsterdam	Los Angeles	Seattle & Portland
Boston	Manhattan	Vancouver
Chicago	New Orleans	Walt Disney World
Las Vegas	Paris	Washington, D.C.
London	San Francisco	

FROMMER'S® BEST-LOVED DRIVING TOURS

America	France	New England
Britain	Germany	Scotland
California	Ireland	Spain
Florida	Italy	Western Europe

THE UNOFFICIAL GUIDES®

Bed & Breakfasts in California	Golf Vacations in the	New Orleans
Bed & Breakfasts in	Eastern U.S.	New York City
New England	The Great Smoky &	Paris
Bed & Breakfasts in the	Blue Ridge Mountains	San Francisco
Northwest	Inside Disney	Skiing in the West
Bed & Breakfasts in Southeast	Hawaii	Southeast with Kids
Beyond Disney	Las Vegas	Walt Disney World
Branson, Missouri	London	Walt Disney World for
California with Kids	Mid-Atlantic with Kids	Grown-ups
Chicago	Mini Las Vegas	Walt Disney World for Kids
Cruises	Mini-Mickey	Washington, D.C.
Disneyland	New England with Kids	World's Best Diving Vacations
Florida with Kids		

SPECIAL-INTEREST TITLES

Frommer's Britain's Best Bed & Breakfasts and Country Inns	Hanging Out in Europe
Frommer's France's Best Bed & Breakfasts and Country Inns	Hanging Out in France
	Hanging Out in Ireland
	Hanging Out in Italy
Frommer's Italy's Best Bed & Breakfasts and Country Inns	Hanging Out in Spain
	Israel Past & Present
Frommer's Caribbean Hideaways	Frommer's The Moon
Frommer's Adventure Guide to Australia & New Zealand	Frommer's New York City with Kids
	The New York Times' Guide to Unforgettable Weekends
Frommer's Adventure Guide to Central America	Places Rated Almanac
Frommer's Adventure Guide to India & Pakistan	Retirement Places Rated
Frommer's Adventure Guide to South America	Frommer's Road Atlas Britain
Frommer's Adventure Guide to Southeast Asia	Frommer's Road Atlas Europe
Frommer's Adventure Guide to Southern Africa	Frommer's Washington, D.C., with Kids
Frommer's Gay & Lesbian Europe	Frommer's What the Airlines Never Tell You
Frommer's Exploring America by RV	
Hanging Out in England	

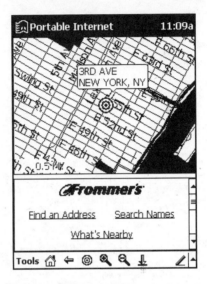

Let Us Hear From You!

Dear Frommer's Reader,

You are our greatest resource in keeping our guides relevant, timely, and lively. We'd love to hear from you about your travel experiences—good or bad. Want to recommend a great restaurant or a hotel off the beaten path—or register a complaint? Any thoughts on how to improve the guide itself?

Please use this page to share your thoughts with me and mail it to the address below. Or if you like, send a FAX or e-mail me at frommersfeedback@hungryminds.com. And so that we can thank you—and keep you up on the latest developments in travel—we invite you to sign up for a free daily Frommer's e-mail travel update. Just write your e-mail address on the back of this page. Also, if you'd like to take a moment to answer a few questions about yourself to help us improve our guides, please complete the following quick survey. (We'll keep that information confidential.)

Thanks for your insights.

Yours sincerely,

Michael Spring

Michael Spring, *Publisher*

Name (Optional) _____

Address_____

_____

City_____ State_____ ZIP _____

Name of Frommer's Travel Guide _____

Comments_____

_____

_____

_____

_____

_____

_____

_____

_____

Please tell us a little about yourself so that we can serve you and the Frommer's community better. We will keep this information confidential.

Age: ( )18-24; ( )25-39; ( )40-49; ( )50-55; ( )Over 55

Income: ( )Under $25,000; ( )$25,000-$50,000; ( )$50,000-$100,000; ( )Over $100,000

I am: ( )Single, never married; ( )Married, with children; ( )Married, without children; ( )Divorced; ( )Widowed

Number of people in my household: ( )1; ( )2; ( )3; ( )4; ( )5 or more

Number of people in my household under 18: ( )1; ( )2; ( )3; ( )4; ( )5 or more

I am ( )a student; ( )employed full-time; ( )employed part-time; ( )not employed at this time; ( )retired; ( )other

I took ( )0; ( )1; ( )2; ( )3; ( )4 or more leisure trips in the past 12 months

My last vacation was ( )a weekend; ( )1 week; ( )2 weeks; ( )3 or more weeks

My last vacation was to ( )the U.S.; ( )Canada; ( )Mexico; ( )Europe; ( )Asia; ( )South America; ( )Central America; ( )The Caribbean; ( )Africa; ( )Middle East; ( )Australia/New Zealand

( )I would; ( )would not buy a Frommer's Travel Guide for business travel

I access the Internet ( )at home; ( )at work; ( )both; ( )I do not use the Internet

I used the Internet to do research for my last trip. ( )Yes; ( )No

I used the Internet to book accommodations or air travel on my last trip. ( )Yes; ( )No

My favorite travel site is ( )frommers.com; ( )travelocity.com; ( )expedia.com;

other_____

I use Frommer's Travel Guides ( )always; ( )sometimes; ( )seldom

I usually buy ( )1; ( )2; ( )more than 2 guides when I travel

Other guides I use include _____

What's the most important thing we could do to improve Frommer's Travel Guides?

_____

_____

_____

_____

Yes, please send me a daily e-mail travel update. My e-mail address is

_____

Mail to: Michael Spring, Publisher and Vice President, Frommer's Travel Guides
909 Third Ave., New York, NY 10022   FAX: 212.884.5432